The Graceful Guru

The Graceful Guru

Hindu Female Gurus in India
and the United States

EDITED BY KAREN PECHILIS

OXFORD
UNIVERSITY PRESS

2004

OXFORD
UNIVERSITY PRESS

Oxford   New York
Auckland   Bangkok   Buenos Aires   Cape Town   Chennai
Dar es Salaam   Delhi   Hong Kong   Istanbul   Karachi   Kolkata
Kuala Lumpur   Madrid   Melbourne   Mexico City   Mumbai   Nairobi
São Paulo   Shanghai   Taipei   Tokyo   Toronto

Copyright © 2004 by Oxford University Press, Inc.

Published by Oxford University Press, Inc.
198 Madison Avenue, New York, New York 10016

www.oup.com

Oxford is a registered trademark of Oxford University Press

Library of Congress Cataloging-in-Publication Data
The graceful guru : Hindu female gurus in India and the United States /
Edited by Karen Pechilis.
p. cm.
ISBN 0-19-514537-2; ISBN 0-19-514538-0 (pbk.)
1. Hindu women saints.   2. Gurus—India—Biography.   I. Pechilis, Karen.
BL1171 .W44 2004
294.5'61'082—dc21   2003011221

9 8 7 6 5 4 3 2 1
Printed in the United States of America
on acid-free paper

Preface

This book stems from a project I began in 1998, as a new direction of a study that I had undertaken for an affiliate project of the Harvard University Pluralism Project. For that initial study, I worked with Drew University colleagues Wesley Ariarajah, Dorothy Austin, and Christopher Taylor, plus graduate students, on mapping historical religions new to the New Jersey context. When word spread on the Drew campus that I was involved in mapping Hinduism, several women with various connections to Drew mentioned that I might include Siddha Yoga in my study, with its United States headquarters at the Shree Muktananda Ashram in South Fallsburg, New York; they had all been to the ashram, and some were devotees. While the geographical limits of my affiliate project precluded its inclusion, I was intrigued by their suggestion. I began to view the study of Siddha Yoga and its current guru as a new, yet related, direction of my work in understanding the presence of historical religions from other cultures in the United States context.

I felt encouraged in expanding my study by the ethos of the Pluralism Project, especially by the inclusive vision of Diana L. Eck, the founder and director of the Pluralism Project. Diana's supportive enthusiasm for all those who undertake affiliate projects is a wellspring of inspiration, which was quite evident at one of the Pluralism Project receptions held during an annual meeting of the American Academy of Religion (AAR). At that event, I looked around the crowded room and saw a diverse group of people, composed of students and teachers from various backgrounds and from various regions of the United States, animatedly and happily discussing their research on religion in the United States with one another, and I thought: "Diana has truly brought out the best in everyone."

At the AAR annual meeting in Orlando, Florida in 1998, I proposed the possibility of a conference panel on female gurus in the United States plus a subsequent published volume to close colleagues, including Selva Raj, Rebecca Manring, and Carol Anderson. I was fascinated to learn that they had already been engaged in studying specific female gurus. Encouraged by the correspondence of our research interests, I proposed a panel on Hindu female gurus in the United States to the Religion in South Asia Section of the AAR for the next year's annual meeting. That proposal was successful: at the annual AAR meeting in Boston in 1999, we presented the panel, "Female Gurus: Indian Paradigms and Contemporary Leaders in the U.S.," with Diana Eck presiding, papers by Rebecca Manring, Carol Anderson, Selva Raj, and myself, and Kathleen Erndl as respondent, before an audience of more than seventy-five people on the morning of the last day of the conference. Many people from the audience made very helpful comments at that time, and other scholars who were researching female gurus in India and the United States stepped forward to share their research and be included in this volume.

I am indeed grateful to the contributors to this volume for their stimulating discussion and research on the topic of Hindu female gurus. As a group with a common focus, we were able to explore and contextualize the many details of individual gurus. Each article in this volume is a distinctive narrative, and yet each engages the other articles through patterns in Hinduism, biography, gender, and spiritual leadership.

I would like to thank Cynthia Read of Oxford University Press for her interest in this project, and OUP Associate Editor Theodore Calderara and Production Editor Christi Stanforth for their work in bringing the manuscript to publication. I thank Margaret Case for her careful copyediting of the manuscript. Two anonymous reviewers for the press also deserve my thanks for their helpful critical comments on the manuscript.

I would also like to thank individuals who shared their insights on female gurus and religion in the United States, among other relevant topics, with me during the course of this study: Diana Eck, Dorothy Austin, Bill Stroker, Mary Ann Stroker, Sara Henry-Corrington, Robert Corrington, Mary Cole, Wesley Ariarajah, Christopher Taylor, Mala Kadar, Julie Pechilis, Jonathan Z. Smith, Vishwa Adluri, Joanne Waghorne, Archana Venkatesan, Layne Little, Serinity Young, Divakar Masilamani, Mary Masilamani, and Yudith Greenberg. I would also like to thank my students, who helped me as academic research assistants during the course of this research: Lauren Griffith, Melinda Haley, Diana Sette, and Alissa Colby. I am also ever thankful to my parents, and my sister and brother and their families, for their enthusiastic and supportive interest in my studies.

Contents

Contributors

CAROL S. ANDERSON is an Associate Professor in the Department of Religion and in the Women's Studies Program at Kalamazoo College. In the field of the history of religions, her research focuses on South Asian Buddhism, with an occasional foray into Hinduism. She is the author of *Pain and Its Ending: The Four Noble Truths in the Theravada Canon* (Curzon Press, 1999) and is engaged in ongoing projects in Sri Lanka. She further specializes in theoretical approaches to the study of feminism and religion and is completing a manuscript entitled "Teaching Courses on Women and Religion" for the American Academy of Religion Teaching Series (Oxford University Press).

LORILIAI BIERNACKI teaches in the Department of Religious Studies at the University of Colorado–Boulder. Her dissertation, "Bridging the Subject's Abyss: A 10th Century Tantric Hermeneutic" (University of Pennsylvania), is a translation and analysis of a text by the Kashmiri Shaivite Abhinavagupta. She is currently working on a book on representations of the feminine in medieval Tantra.

CATHERINE CORNILLE teaches at Boston College and at the Weston Jesuit School of Theology. She has published books and articles on the questions of gender, inculturation, and interreligious dialogue, including *The Guru in Indian Catholicism: Ambiguity or Opportunity of Inculturation* (Peeters, 1991) and *Many Mansions? Multiple Religious Belonging and Christian Identity* (Orbis, 2002).

KATHLEEN M. ERNDL is Associate Professor of Religion at Florida State University. She is the author of *Victory to the Mother: The*

Hindu Goddess of Northwest India in Myth, Ritual, and Symbol (1993) and coeditor of *Is the Goddess a Feminist? The Politics of South Asian Goddesses* (2001), along with a number of articles on Hindu goddesses and the role of women in Hinduism. She is currently writing a book entitled *The Play of the Mother: Goddess Possession, Women, and Power in Kangra Hinduism.*

LISA LASSELL HALLSTROM has studied Hindu spirituality through personal practice and through doctoral studies at Harvard Divinity School and Harvard University. She has taught Religion and Asian Studies at Bard, Mt. Holyoke, and Smith Colleges and at the University of New Mexico. She has recently published a book, *Mother of Bliss: Ānandamayī Mā (1896–1982)*, with Oxford University Press (1999).

REBECCA J. MANRING earned her Ph.D. in Asian Languages and Literature (Sanskrit, Hindi, Bengali) from the University of Washington in 1995. She is currently Assistant Professor of India Studies and Religious Studies at Indiana University, Bloomington. Research interests include early hagiography of the Gaudiya Vaishnava tradition and the many varieties of tantra in Bengal. Her book, entitled *Reconstructing Tradition: Advaita Ācārya and Gauḍīya Vaiṣṇavism at the Cusp of the Twentieth Century*, will be published by Columbia University Press in 2004.

JUNE MCDANIEL is Professor of Religious Studies at the College of Charleston in Charleston, S.C. Her MTS was from Emory University, with work on visionary experience in religion and psychology, and her Ph.D. was from the University of Chicago, in history of religions. Her area of study is religious experience and mysticism, with a special focus on Bengali devotional religion. She has spent almost two years in India studying and interviewing ecstatics and is interested in the impact of religious experience on both individuals and cultural traditions. She is the author of *The Madness of the Saints: Ecstatic Religion in Bengal* (University of Chicago Press, 1989), *Making Virtuous Daughters and Wives: An Introduction to Women's Brata Rituals in Bengali Folk Religion* (SUNY Press, 2003), and *Offering Flowers, Feeding Skulls: Popular Goddess Worship in West Bengal* (Oxford University Press, forthcoming 2004).

VASUDHA NARAYANAN is a Professor in the Department of Religion at the University of Florida and a former president of the American Academy of Religion (2001–2002). She did her graduate work at Harvard University and the University of Bombay. Dr. Narayanan has written and edited five books and is the author of over eighty articles and encyclopedia entries. Forthcoming publications include *The Hindu Tradition/s: An Introduction* (Prentice Hall) and *The Hindu Traditions in the United States: Temple Space, Domestic Space, and Cyber Space* (Columbia University Press). She is the recipient of several grants, including the John Simon Guggenheim fellowship (1991) and a National Endowment for the Humanities fellowship for 1998–99. Dr. Narayanan's current work focuses on Hindu traditions in Cambodia.

KAREN PECHILIS is Associate Professor of Religious Studies at Drew University and has recently been appointed the NEH Distinguished Teaching Professor and Director of the Humanities at Drew. She received her doctorate in the history of religions from the University of Chicago, specializing in the history of religion in south India. She has pursued research in Tamilnadu, south India, under grants from the American Institute of Indian Studies, the Fulbright Program, and the Asian Cultural Council. She has written articles on pilgrimage, Shaiva Siddhanta philosophy, and the canon of *Tevaram*, as well as encyclopedia articles on women in religion. Her first book, *The Embodiment of Bhakti*, was published by Oxford University Press (1999).

SELVA J. RAJ is Stanley S. Kresge Associate Professor and Chair of Religious Studies at Albion College and president of the Midwest American Academy of Religion. He is also a past president of the Society for Hindu-Christian Studies. At Albion, he teaches courses on Indian religions and comparative religions. A graduate of the University of Chicago, his research interests are in the area of popular Catholicism in India, and he has written several articles on this subject. He is a coeditor of two volumes: *Popular Christianity in India: Riting Between the Lines* (State University of New York Press, 2002), with Corinne Dempsey, and *Dealing with Deities: The Ritual Vow in South Asia*, with William Harman (State University of New York Press, forthcoming). Currently, he is working on a monograph, "The Dialogue of Rituals in Tamil Catholicism," and an edited volume with Corinne Dempsey entitled "Ritual Levity, Ritual Play in South Asian Religions."

The Graceful Guru

Introduction: Hindu Female Gurus in Historical and Philosophical Context

Karen Pechilis

With thousands of followers, leadership of translocal organizations, and power that is constituted by both authority and spirituality, Hindu female gurus have a noticeable and meaningful presence in religious life today. For many people, the topic of Hindu female gurus is intrinsically interesting, especially as it relates to women's religious leadership, globalization, spirituality, and cultural contact between India and the West. For these same reasons, the topic is also of interest to scholars, who have recently begun to publish detailed analyses of Hindu female gurus, especially from the twentieth century. In this volume, all of the contributors are specialists in the study of Hinduism who have been studying Hindu female gurus for several years. The focus of the volume is on one category of leadership within Hinduism, and a diversity of women in this leadership role is represented. These factors distinguish the approach of this volume from recent books on women in new religions, in which a wide variety of traditions—Western, Asian, African, and so on—and modes of women's participation in them are covered.[1] This volume is also distinguished from book-length studies of a single female guru.[2] In addition, the academically critical stance of the articles sets this volume apart from studies that profile female gurus in an adulatory tone.[3]

The public visibility of current Hindu female gurus, through Web sites, world tours, ashrams and devotional groups across the globe, and devotional publications and videos is a significant development in a tradition that historically defined the public role of gurus as exclusive to men. There is historical evidence of women gurus in the esoteric traditions of tantra, and there are traditional stories of women who acted as gurus to their husbands, but these examples locate women's guruhood in private domains.[4] Women have held public religious positions in Hindu tradition: women saints are well represented in scholarly studies, and recent studies have illuminated female practitioners of Vedic rituals, philosophers, and religious reformers.[5] The variety of roles for women in Hindu tradition is influential in the emergence of women as gurus.

In terms of their status as public gurus, the female gurus of today are participating in a very established category of Hindu religious leader; however, their assumption of this leadership role also stands in contrast to that same established category. As gurus, they complicate the facile equivalence between women and tradition promoted by some nationalists and fundamentalists of yesterday and today. Katheryn Hansen identifies and refutes this equivalence: " 'Traditional' in reference to women is widely employed to translate 'normative'. It is my aim to show that non-normative as well as normative models of gendered conduct have 'traditions.' . . . These paradigms are continuously being redefined as the representation of woman is contested anew in each historical period."[6]

The title of this volume, *The Graceful Guru*, signals the participation of women in the modalities of continuity and change in Hindu tradition. "Grace" has both aesthetic and theological connotations. Aesthetically, it is a feminized term that is used to evaluate a woman's perceived embodiment of, or distance from, an ideal standard of beauty. This feminization of the term is perhaps linked to the Greek mythology of the Three Graces; the Greek term is *charis*, and it is also notable that a primary mode of women's religious leadership in history is through charismatic, or noninstitutional, avenues. Theologically, the term carries the connotation that one embodies the favor of the divine. This volume explores how Hindu female gurus respond to social expectations of femininity and how they are understood to embody the divine; how these two modes intersect in the personae of the gurus; and how their leadership is constituted by the negotiation of the two in distinctive ways.

"Guru" is a category of religious leadership in many traditions of Indian origin, including Buddhism, Jainism, and Sikhism. In Hindu tradition, there are several characteristics that preeminently define a guru. The first is that a guru is understood to experience the real continuously. Most often, the real is defined as *brahman*, which, among many possible meanings, denotes the subtle, sacred essence that pervades the universe. Hindu philosophical tradition tends to characterize ordinary consciousness as pervaded by duality; in contrast, the experience of *brahman* is a pure, unmediated unity.

The experience of the real is expressed in diverse ways in biographical stories of gurus, although it is always represented as contrasting with ordinary experience. For example, the contemporary female guru Anandi Ma is said to have experienced such a high concentration of energy that "she wasn't functional at all on our level, so [her guru] had to work with her, bringing down the energy constantly so that gradually it would be more in her control."[7] As a young woman, the internationally famous female guru Anandamayi Ma, then known as Nirmala, was able to experience various modes of consciousness from her grounding in the experience of the real, which she described as follows: "What I am I have always been, even from my infancy. . . . Nevertheless, different stages of *sadhana* [spiritual practice] manifested through this body. Wisdom was revealed in a piecemeal fashion, integral knowledge was broken into parts." Linda Johnsen, who has authored a book on female gurus, comments: "Nirmala—born experiencing the unity of all creation—found it astonishing to experience the world in bits and pieces, as the rest of us do."[8] Another example is June McDaniel's discussion of "full fusion" as Jayashri Ma's self-description of her spiritual state, in this volume. I further discuss the nature of the real, or *brahman*, in Hindu tradition in the section of this introduction entitled "The Nature of the Self."

The guru's access to the real is at least in part understood by tradition in terms of initiation. Many of the female gurus, such as Gauri Ma, Jayashri Ma, Meera Ma, and Gurumayi, participate in the classical guru tradition by taking instruction and initiation from a male guru. Other female gurus challenge the traditional male guru lineage (*parampara*) mode by taking initiation from a woman, or by being self-initiated. For example, one contemporary female guru, Anasuya Devi, took initiation from an older female guru.[9] The gurus Anandamayi Ma, Ammachi, and Karunamayi Ma are understood to be self-initiated.

Initiation is not only a credential in the female guru's past; it also forms a link with her present and future disciples. The guru is able to inspire the experience of the real in others, for the purposes of spiritual advancement, total self-realization, or evolution as a human being—there are many ways in which tradition describes the necessity and the effects of such an experience. The gurus are interactive teachers. As with the experience of the real, the female gurus represent a diversity of initiation and teaching methods. For example, the contemporary female guru Swami Chidvilasananda was intitiated by her guru, Swami Muktananda, in a formal ceremony; following her guru, she initiates devotees en masse through the bestowal of shakti (spiritual power) at formal intensive meditation sessions, and her teachings are verbally rendered at formal lectures and events as well as through her prolific publications. In contrast, the contemporary female guru Ammachi was self-enlightened; she initiates devotees en masse demonstratively and individually, by physically hugging each one and whispering a mantra in his or her ear, and her teachings are primarily verbally rendered at gatherings, although there are some books of her teachings available.

Female gurus thus participate in an established, traditional category of Hindu religious leadership: "Essentially, the role of the female *guru* is not different from that of a [male] *guru*." Their feminine gender does challenge the traditional association of guruhood with the masculine gender, however, as reflected in the Sanskrit terminology. Unlike other terms for religious adepts which, like the guru, are in the ascetic mode, including *brahmachari*, which has the feminine form, *brahmacharini*, *yogi*, which has the feminine form, *yogini*, and *sadhu*, which has the feminine form *sadhvi*, there is no feminine form of *guru*: "[the expression 'female guru'] does not correspond to any Indian term. The simple reason for this is that the *guru's* role having been traditionally a masculine one, the word *guru* does not accept a feminine form. The closest Sanskrit term to our 'female *guru*' is *gurumata* but, as anyone acquainted with the classical religious literature of India knows, this means the wife of the *guru*. . . . The *gurumata* was no doubt a highly respected person but never one entitled to impart any kind of philosophical instruction."[10]

Is there a feminine way of being a guru, as there may be feminine ways of leadership and feminine ways of participating in religious organizations?[11] Elizabeth Puttick challenges us to divide contemporary female gurus along feminist lines. In her thematic approach to the study of women in religions new to North America, she identifies bhakti (devotional participation) as a feminine mode, and associates the female gurus Ammachi, Anandamayi Ma, and Mother Meera with this mode; in contrast, she views the female gurus Nirmala Devi and Gurumayi as "explicitly anti-feminist" leaders of patriarchal traditions that promote sexist teachings.[12]

On one level, Puttick's comment seeks to classify female gurus on the basis of their behavior. As the quotation from Catherine Clémentin-Ojha, as well as my earlier discussion of the major traits of a guru, demonstrate, as a general rule female gurus follow established, male behavioral modes for guruhood, even if they did not take initiation from a male guru. In the ideal category of the guru, the female gurus have the following major characteristics in common with each other, and with male gurus. First, they are understood to experience and to embody the real, and are thus understood to be divine or perfectly spiritually self-realized; second, the message of the guru is the divinity of the inner self, and the necessity of her or his devotees' own self-realization, to which the guru guides the devotee; third, the guru is an ascetic, and is thus assumed to be pure in body and in spirit, especially in the sense of purity of motive through lack of self-interest.

It is important to understand that female gurus self-consciously associate themselves with received tradition because of the compelling belief that traditional methods are considered efficacious, and that their continuity in the present day carries with it all of the spiritual power accumulated over time. In self-consciously linking themselves to tradition, the female Hindu gurus do not have to be understood as patriarchal, for, as historian of religions Rita M. Gross argues, there are multiple models for practicing feminism and religion. What is required is a nuanced approach to tradition and innovation in women's religious leadership. Female spiritual leaders who work within their tradition can be radical, as Gross acknowledges in her discussion of feminist theologian Carol P. Christ's terminology of reformers and revolutionaries in reference to explicitly feminist leaders in religion:

> [Although there has been criticism of the terms "reformer" and "revolutionary,"] the distinction named by that terminology is real and basic, and the critical difference between the two positions is disagreement over how feminist vision is best served. The degree to which feminists retain personal links and loyalties with traditional religions, rather than how "radical" they are, is the dividing factor.

In fact, some reformists are exceedingly radical in the changes they want to make in their traditions, but they maintain dialogue with their tradition and recognize kinship with it. Revolutionaries, though they sever links with the conventional religions, can be quite conservative in the way in which they identify with the rejected ancient traditions.[13]

The female gurus discussed in this volume "maintain dialogue with their tradition and recognize kinship with it," but they are also innovative within that context, by their distinctive contributions to tradition and by distinguishing themselves from each other. For example, Sita Devi was recorded and remembered as a guru by members of an orthodox, established Hindu guru lineage (Gaudiya Vaishnavism); Gauri Ma established spiritual and social work centers for women; Anandamayi Ma was self-initiated; Jayashri Ma is independently employed in the working world alongside her religious activities; Mother Meera has no ashram; Shree Maa has self-consciously attempted to synthesize her Bengali tantric heritage with the Christian background of many of her followers; Ammachi was born into a low caste, yet she physically embraces all devotees; Ma Jaya Sati Bhagavati is from a Jewish background; Karunamayi Ma performed spiritual austerities alone in the forest for fourteen years; and Gurumayi has intitiated new teaching methods, including the yearly message. In these and many other ways, the female gurus in this volume locate themselves within tradition, yet they interpret tradition in their own ways.

The most radical challenge of the female gurus is not directed toward the received guru tradition but rather the received social expectations. Their asceticism is in keeping with the guru ideal, but it challenges the Hindu social norms of womanhood, which are marriage and bearing children. In the case of female gurus, there are multiple models of asceticism. Several of the female gurus are or were married: Sita Devi's husband passed away before she became a guru; Anandamayi Ma was married but her marriage was not consumated, and her husband was a disciple; Meera Ma is married but her husband does not play a role in her mission; and Ma Jaya Sati Bhagavati was married and has three children, but withdrew from her family prior to becoming a guru. Some of the female gurus were never married, though their desire to remain unmarried caused conflict in their families; these include Gauri Ma and Ammachi. In the case of some of the female gurus who were never married, the issue does not seem to have created conflict in their families; these include Jayashri Ma, Karunamayi Ma, Gurumayi, and Shree Maa. In all cases, their status as guru is in large part constituted by their present asceticism; thus, if a guru was or is married, this relationship is subordinated to her status as guru.

In subordinating or avoiding marriage, female gurus deemphasize their sexuality. "Mysticism is *not* morality," argues Jeffrey Kripal, urging "that we not lock mystical experience away in some airtight categorical safe (like 'purity' or 'perfection')," and yet morality is constitutive of authority over others, through trust and loyalty.[14] Biographies of female gurus do stress that they are pure and perfect, ontological claims that are made in the context of social pressures that define and malign women on the basis of their sexuality, either real or imagined. Further, the purity and perfection signaled by asceticism permit women to have a public religious status; for example, Anandamayi Ma went from purdah to appearing before thousands with her head and face uncovered, framed by her long unbound hair.[15] An assumption of purity had to accompany such a gesture, in order that it not be viewed as shameful. The purity of the female gurus is constituted by and expressed through their nature as perfected embodiments of the divine as well as their performance of personal morality. Both of these elements contrast with the inherited ritual purity of caste. None of the twentieth-century female gurus emphasize—or in many cases, even mention—caste in their self-descriptions or in their teachings. This omission of caste identity is more a function of the female gurus' mode of purity than it is a modification of Hindu tradition for a Western audience.

Through their asceticism, the female gurus reject key aspects of socially defined womanhood. This has implications for another dimension of Puttick's comment, which speaks to the nature or essence of the female gurus. What is feminine about the female gurus? Is bhakti feminine, as Puttick suggests? Although bhakti (devotional participation) can be a prominent mode of a female guru—for example, bhakti for her guru Muktananda is prominent in the teachings and demeanor of Gurumayi—the more relevant concept for understanding female gurus is shakti.[16]

Shakti is a classical term in Hinduism meaning spiritual power. It is explicitly associated with the feminine in classical texts; for example, the philosophy of Samkhya, in which the feminine principle *shakti* (energy) swirls the masculine principle *purusha* (stasis) into action, thereby initiating creation. Shakti is also understood in Hindu tradition as a description of the spiritual and moral power inherent in women and in goddesses.[17] Many of the female gurus are explicitly associated with feminine imagery; ironically, this association also supports the paradigm of renunciation and the rejection of socially defined womanhood. For example, all but two of the female gurus profiled in this volume use the appellation Ma (Mother) in their titles. As Madhu Khanna notes, citing June McDaniel: "In *Śākta* circles, all women–be they young maidens or mature women–are addressed as *Mā* or *Devī* or *Vīrā*. This title protects women from being looked on in sexual terms. As it is rightly pointed out, 'To call a woman "mother" is a classic way for an Indian male to deflect a woman's hint at marriage or a courtesan's proposition.' "[18] The deflection, of course, works in both ways. In related examples, Sita Devi's male followers "became" female in order to become her students, whereas Gauri Ma and Anandamayi Ma established institutions exclusively for women to engage in spiritual practices, especially renunciation, thus providing women with a legitimate alternative to the culturally mandated roles of wife and mother.

All of the female gurus are associated with the Goddess through the concept of shakti, for they, like the Goddess, are paramount embodiments of shakti. In Hindu theory and practice, the Goddess comes to life in a variety of ways. For example, the Goddess transforms a stone, bronze, or painted image with her presence during ritual worship (puja), so that worshipers may express their honor and devotion to her. Or, to take another example, the Goddess appears to people who meditate on her; they construct a mental image of her in order to train the mind to realize the fundamentally shared identity between the divine nature of the self and the divinity of the Goddess. In addition to these more formal, ritualized modes, the Goddess may spontaneously appear to devotees, and even possess them, transforming them into active and often ecstatic instruments of her divine will.[19]

Female gurus are understood by Hindu tradition and by their followers alike to be manifestations of the Goddess; that is, as perfect embodiments of shakti. Biographies of the gurus will often stress both their special nature at birth and their spiritual practice toward self-realization. Some gurus may distance themselves from such understanding of their identity; in this case, they stress their bhakti for their own guru. As gurus, they distinctively blend the formality and authority of classical tradition with the spontaneity of interactive encounter. Further, many of the female gurus profiled in this volume are understood to embody the essence of specific goddesses, either through their self-interpretation or the interpretation of their followers. For example, Sita Devi is identified with Lakshmi; Jayashri Ma is identified with Adya Shakti Kali; Meera Ma is identified with Adiparashakti; Ma Jaya Sati Bhagavati is identified as the "daughter of the black mother Kali"; Karunamayi Ma is identified with Saraswati, Bala Tripurasundari, Lalita (Parvati), and Lakshmi; Ammachi is identified with Devi. In addition, Ammachi and Jayashri Ma engage in performances in which they become the Goddess (devibhava).

Female Hindu gurus are thus distinguished from female Hindu saints through the distinction between shakti and bhakti; through the gurus' identification with the Goddess; and through the gurus' explicit connection to teaching and to students, involving initiation and philosophical instruction. I shall further discuss the emergence of the female guru in Hinduism with respect to these relationships, to bhakti and tantra theology, and to the ongoing social conflict in the "Wives, Saints, and the Goddess" and "Early Female Hindu Gurus" sections of this introduction, but I emphasize here that the special nature of Hindu female gurus as embodiments of the divine has implications for feminist interpretations of them. As journalist Linda Johnsen notes, there may be a gap between Hindu tradition and Western feminism in understanding the significance of the female gurus: "Power, self affirmation, and celebration of earth energy are not the goal: conscious immersion in a reality that precedes earth and ego is more to the point. Because of this divergence of emphasis the teachings of India's women of spirit are to some degree out of sync with the present evocation of Goddess energy in the West."[20] Largely, this fault line exists between the two traditions of Hinduism and Western feminism. Is there a way of making feminist sense of the female gurus that acknowledges values in both of these traditions? A complicating factor, as Johnsen's comment suggests, is that traditional Hindu teachings promote abandoning dualistic thought (such as, I and you, male and female) in favor of experiencing unqualified divine unity. For example, in her book-length study of Anandamayi Ma, Lisa Hallstrom discusses both the guru's and her disciples' ambivalence toward viewing Ma as a woman, in favor of viewing her as Ultimate Reality.[21] Thus, at the most profound level, these Hindu teachings reject gender considerations. The focus of the teachings of Hindu female gurus is not specifically expressed as "empowering women," although many women devotees participating in their spiritual paths do experience them as empowerment.[22]

This ultimate teaching of Hindu female gurus contributes the premise that female is universal to a feminist understanding of women's religious leadership. The guru is both divine and universal, as with the Goddess, and she is an embodied, religiously devoted woman, as with the saints. The female guru is both, and in that capacity the demonstration that female is universal belongs most appropriately to her. As Western feminists have discussed, the operative formula in patriarchal societies is to view male as universal, while female is limited. Hindu female gurus challenge this paradigm. The nature, presence, and teaching of the Hindu female gurus is universal. As gurus, they distinctively blend the formality and authority of classical tradition with the spontaneity of interactive encounter, harmonizing personal experience and the ultimate. Although the actual status of guru is attained only by a few, the guru instantiates the goal for many.

This volume highlights the translocal aspect of the female gurus' universality, especially their presence in the West, primarily in the United States. That Hindu female gurus frequently visit, or reside, in the United States is a post-1965 development, occurring in the context of the abolition of immigration quotas; in the context of profound social criticism through the antiwar, civil rights, and feminist movements; and in the context of popular interest in Asian religious traditions, especially meditation. As I discuss in the section of this introduction on "Female Hindu Gurus in the Twentieth Century," current female Hindu gurus are a "third wave" of gurus in the West, globalizing, harmonizing, and naturalizing Hindu-inspired tradition. The case studies of the female gurus in the individual chapters are arranged chronologically up to the contemporary gurus, who are then presented in terms of their degree of establishment in the United States. In the case of Mother Meera, her international reputation and popularity are established in the United States; she has visited the United States but resides in Germany. Ammachi and Karunamayi reside in India but are well known in the United States. The final chapter, on Siddha Yoga with its highly developed network of centers and ashrams, discusses what is in a real sense the "Establishment" of traditions headed by a female guru.

Toward enabling the reader to recognize, understand, and appreciate the nuanced relationship between tradition and innovation in the nature and leadership of female gurus, I devote the remainder of this introduction to providing philosophical and historical information that contextualizes the female gurus profiled in this volume, in a discussion that is primarily addressed to nonspecialists. My selective discussion identifies influential factors involved in the emergence and public recognition of Hindu female gurus, including philosophical theories of a unity beyond duality, the validation of personal experience, women's consistent participation in the development of Hinduism through a variety of exemplary roles, the rise of the Goddess as a universal teacher, and the mass popularity of twentieth century male gurus and their initiation of female devotees, who then became gurus in their own right.

The Nature of the Self

Namaskar is a traditional greeting in India, said while facing another and bowing with palms pressed together. It is understood to mean, "I salute the divinity within you." This greeting is emblematic of a worldview that sees a profound commonality in the midst of diversity, and one that understands that fundamental commonality to be a sharing in the divine essence that is foundational for life. In this theory, the true nature of humankind is divine, yet this does not mean either that everyone is equal in social terms or that people in general are deified; instead, the direct experience of the divine source is a category of honor that is bestowed only upon special religious adepts, including gurus.

In Hindu tradition, the earliest explicit and sustained discussion of the nature of the self as divine (rendered as "Self" in many translations) is in the Upanishads, a genre of oral texts—the name of the genre is understood to mean "to sit beside," and indeed the texts have a dialogic structure—that were composed during the period from the seventh century b.c.e. to the beginning of the Common Era.[23] Hindu tradition views the Upanishads as part of the revealed (*shruti*) canon of oral and written texts, and minimizes the distinction between them and the earlier hymns of the Vedas. For example, the Upanishads are known as Vedanta or "the culmination of the Vedas," in the sense of expounding truths already contained in the Vedic hymns. One translator boasts that the Upanishads represent the first time in history that the knower became the focus for the inquiry of knowledge.[24] Another translator singles out the Upanishads as preeminently authoritative in Hinduism: "Even though theoretically the whole of the vedic corpus is accepted as revealed truth, in reality it is the Upaniṣads that have continued to influence the life and thought of the various religious traditions that we have come to call Hindu. Upaniṣads are the vedic scriptures *par excellence* of Hinduism."[25]

The texts themselves use the term *upanishad* in the sense of "hidden teaching." The oral nature of the texts gives the impression of a face-to-face encounter between a teacher and a student; in this intimate transmission of knowledge, the hidden or esoteric nature of the knowledge is preserved through its passage only to qualified hearers. In general, the qualified hearers would be male brahmans, members of the traditional priestly caste. However, in the *Brihadaranyaka Upanishad*, which is one of the two oldest Upanishads (the other being the *Chandogya Upanishad*), this sacred knowledge is imparted to two brahman women. Both of the women, one of whom is named Gargi Vacaknavi and the other Maitreyi, challenge the *Brihadaranyaka Upanishad*'s central character, a learned man named Yajnavalkya, though they do so in

different ways, for Gargi is a learned woman and thus his colleague, whereas
Maitreyi is his wife. That the two women, colleague and wife, share in sacred
knowledge may suggest that in Vedic times women were partners to men both
in terms of religious practice and marriage, and that they had access to education.[26] Indeed, there were women seers associated with the earlier Vedic
hymns, including Ghosa, Apala, and Lopamudra.[27]

The context of Gargi's challenge to Yajnavalkya is a formal philosophical
debate staged by a king, who offered prize money to the brahman who could
demonstrate the greatest knowledge of *brahman*. At first, a teacher named
Yajnavalkya assumes that he is the best and tries to claim the prize. Other
brahman scholars, including Gargi, the one woman scholar, rise to challenge
him. In the first of their two meetings as represented in the text, Gargi questions Yajnavalkya. The text makes it clear that Gargi truly presses the sage, she
describes herself as like "a fierce warrior . . . stringing his unstrung bow and
taking two deadly arrows in his hand, would rise to challenge an enemy." In
front of a group of male brahman scholars, she elicits from Yajnavalkya the
answer that *brahman* ("the imperishable") is the foundation of all things: "This
is the imperishable, Gargi, which sees but can't be seen; which hears but can't
be heard; which thinks but can't be thought of; which perceives but can't be
perceived. Besides this imperishable, there is no one that sees, no one that
hears, no one that thinks, and no one that perceives. On this very imperishable,
Gargi, space is woven back and forth."[28]

Yajnavalkya's answer is that *brahman*, or the "imperishable," is the real;
the source and the vivifyer of all, yet beyond human conceptualization. Gargi
publicly indicates that his answer is correct: " 'Distinguished Brahmins!' said
Gargi. 'You should consider yourself lucky if you escape from this man by
merely paying him your respects. None of you will ever defeat him in a theological debate.' "[29] Her status as a learned person in the public domain (in the
rarified sense of a group of learned brahmans) has implications for the understanding of guru as teacher. Yajnavalkya is the most learned of the group,
which would make him the guru; yet it is precisely through Gargi's challenging
questions (as well as those of other scholars) that his status is established.
Moreover, Gargi is also represented to be in the position of evaluating his
answers, as she does when she commends him to the others. Who is the
teacher in this case? Ellison Banks Findly argues that Gargi challenges Yajnavalkya through "regressive questioning," which violates the guru model operative in the Upanishads:

> Instead of meditating upon the scriptures of ancient tradition or af-
> firming the new tradition by consulting a forest teacher, Gārgī does
> the obvious thing: she asks a series of straightforward questions us-
> ing the relationships she observes in the world. . . . If taken to their
> extreme, then, Gārgī's questions would violate the sanctity of *guru*-
> knowledge as currently formulated by Upaniṣadic society—secret
> widsom not personally discovered from one's own experience, but

understood and accepted (with personal insight, to be sure) as given by the master.[30]

Findly intriguingly asks, "what better way to introduce slightly off-beat elements than through the character of a woman?"[31] Gargi contributes a novel approach in the domain of the public discussion of philosophy by emphasizing the role of personal experience in the context of learning, as opposed to rote repetition of received tradition. Although her methodology challenged the understanding of guru in her time, in fact her understanding came to dominate subsequent understanding of the guru path, which came to be viewed and is understood today to combine both received teaching and personal experience.

The relationship between *brahman* as the universal essence and as the inner self is explored in Yajnavalkya's discussion with his wife, Maitreyi.[32] As the scene opens, Yajnavalkya is preparing to leave his home for a life of renunciation, in which he will more deeply contemplate spiritual matters in a context unburdened by householder responsibilities. He has two wives, but he chooses to address Maitreyi, for "of the two, Maitreyi was a woman who took part in theological discussions, while Katyayani's understanding was limited to womanly matters."[33] When he tells Maitreyi that he wishes to settle his estate with both of his wives, she immediately asks him whether material wealth will make her immortal. Yajnavalkya of course answers that one cannot expect immortality through wealth; one can only expect to live as a wealthy person. " 'What is the point in getting something that will not make me immortal?' retorts Maitreyi. 'Tell me instead, sir, all that you know.' "[34]

He explains that it is only through the inner self that one can make a connection with others: "One holds a husband dear, you see, not out of love for the husband; rather, it is out of love for oneself (*atman*) that one holds a husband dear. One holds a wife dear not out of love for the wife; rather, it is out of love for oneself that one holds a wife dear." Thus one must contemplate the nature of the inner self as a window unto ultimate reality: "You see, Maitreyi—it is one's self (*atman*) which one should see and hear, and on which one should reflect and concentrate. For by seeing and hearing one's self, and by reflecting and concentrating on one's self, one gains the knowledge of this whole world."[35]

The advantage of understanding this deep-structure commonality of all things as *brahman* is twofold. In the first place, one will be able to discern the true nature of the world and its relationship to reality. In the second place, this knowledge (again, in the sense of higher knowledge beyond the duality of knower and known) of *brahman* will propel one beyond the ordinary human condition—including the cycle of birth and rebirth, which Indian traditions presuppose as a fundamental condition of humankind—toward an unmediated experience of identity with ultimate reality. Yajnavalkya illustrates this experience, using one of the most famous images in the Upanishads: "It is like this. When a chunk of salt is thrown in water, it dissolves into that very water, and it cannot be picked up in any way. Yet, from whichever place one may take a sip, the salt is there! In the same way this Immense Being has no limit or boundary and is a single mass of perception. It arises out of and together with these beings and disappears after them—so I say, after death there is no awareness."[36] Traditionally, this liberation (*moksha*) from the human condition through identification with *brahman* is understood to be salvation.

Like Gargi, Maitreyi challenges Yajnavalkya to tell her the "hidden teaching"—to articulate the nature of *brahman*. In both cases, the women know to ask the right questions; Gargi, from the perspective of being learned in classical tradition, and Maitreyi, from the perspective of being "theologically minded," as well as her suspicion that an opportunity is about to be missed. Neither woman is content to let Yajnavalkya walk off without sharing his knowledge, whether he is departing with material wealth (in the case of the prize money) or without it (in the case of his worldly possessions). In the domestic realm, Yajnavalkya's two wives accept his guidance; Katyayani, who is "limited to womanly matters," seemingly accepts her husband's departure and his provisions for her mutely, while Maitreyi, who "took part in theological discussions," challenges her husband but then accepts his teaching (she is not represented as following him into the forest). In contrast to Gargi, who assumes a gurulike status, for Maitreyi Yajnavalkya is her husband and her teacher, or guru.

The three models of women in the *Brihadaranyaka Upanishad* capture tensions in the linking of women to sacred knowledge during Vedic times. On one hand, women were not precluded from having an affinity for sacred knowledge (Maitreyi) or solid education in it (Gargi). On the other hand, the text explicitly contrasts "womanly matters" with sacred knowledge; thus, Katyayani, whose concerns are "limited" to such matters, is mentioned only in passing as one of the two recipients of Yajnavalkya's worldly possessions when he departs for spiritual contemplation in the forest.

Although granting women access to sacred knowledge in varying degrees, the Upanishads in some sense prefigure the marginalization of women in later periods: "Gradually, however, the position of women declined and by the time of the Dharmaśāstras [treatises on dharma or duty], in the early centuries B.C.E., women were looked upon as equal to men of the lowest caste as far as formal education was concerned."[37] A philosophical rationalization of the seeming paradox between the spiritual axiom that all people are essentially the same (*atman*) and the social fact of numerous distinctions made on the basis of gender, caste, and duty, was provided by the revered philosopher Shankara in the late eighth century. Shankara founded the school of Advaita Vedanta, which designated the theory of nondualism as the "culmination of the Vedas"; he understood the unity of *brahman* to be the key teaching of the Vedas and especially the Upanishads. Within his sophisticated philosophy, a key principle is that *brahman* alone is real, while everything else—especially individualized forms—are illusion, or maya. Although these forms are not real (that is, they are not permanent and thus not of ultimate value), however, they do exist, and thus impose themselves as a condition of existence for all save those few who have experienced the unity of *brahman*.[38]

Worldly distinctions of gender and caste were therefore simultaneously justified as markers of spiritual inferiority in the social realm and undercut as illusions in the brahman male-dominated domain of higher philosophical education. For example, since *maya* is a feminine noun in Sanskrit, it could be understood as an emblem of women's essential nature. In the Advaita Vedanta system, maya is ambiguous: it is the power (shakti) of *brahman* by which the world of forms comes into existence, and it empowers both ignorance (*avidya*) and knowledge (*vidya*). Ignorance is equivalent to not realizing that ultimate reality is the unqualified unity of *brahman*; it is the delusion of taking the world of forms as reality. Yet maya is also knowledge, not only because it is a power of *brahman* but also because it produces an illusion that can be known and critiqued. Reviewing the *Brihadaranyaka Upanishad* through this philosophy, Katyayani is a symbol of spiritual ignorance, Gargi is a symbol of spiritual knowlege, and Maitreyi is a combination of the two, like maya.

Wives, Saints, and the Goddess

Diverse Hindu texts from the sixth century through the medieval period, including stories of wives who are gurus, devotional poetry authored by women, and treatises on the Goddess, challenged the classifications of women in the Upanishads and their marginalization with respect to sacred knowledge in subsequent shastras and philosophy.[39] This period was an important era in the development of paradigms of women's religious leadership, with the religious perspectives of tantra and bhakti being particularly important in promoting authoritative images of women adepts and goddesses. Generally speaking, bhakti contributed the poetry and hagiography of women who were and are recognized as saints, whereas tantra contributed an ideal of the feminine as divine. In this very selective discussion, I seek to highlight main themes in the historical emergence of the Hindu female guru.

Bhakti and tantra texts are especially concerned with the relationship between wifehood as a social duty for women and the compatability or incompatability of sacred knowledge with that duty. Two medieval texts, one framed by bhakti and the other framed by tantra, present stories of women who were gurus to their husbands; thus, the women teachers are safely located within domestic marriage relationships. Although their stories are publicly told in the texts, their activities as gurus are imagined to take place in the private, domestic realm. In both cases, the wives are queens who are knowledgable of the higher wisdom according to Vedanta (the unity of *brahman*). The queens are praised as gurus by their husbands, reversing the story of Maitreyi, and their teachings are efficacious; through them, their husbands are assured of being able to rule justly during this lifetime, and of salvation at the conclusion of this lifetime. In contrast, the biographies and poetry of women bhakti and tantra saints portray them as being in conflict with worldly duty, foresaking marriage to a mortal man in favor of the spiritual quest and dedication to God. The women saints left the domestic realm and authored poems that can be viewed as teachings. However, they are remembered as saints, not gurus, perhaps because teaching is an inherently social act; yet the saintly paradigm for women tends to emphasize a rupture with the social world.[40]

An unambiguously public feminine guru, who has the ability to teach any and all seekers, is represented in medieval texts by the great Goddess. I turn at the end of this section to consider the promotion of the great Goddess as a teacher in the important tantric text, the *Devi Gita*.

Both the *Yoga Vasishtha* and the *Tripura Rahasya* present nonbrahman women (they are queens, and thus from the warrior or kshatriya caste) who teach their husbands spiritual principles compatible with Advaita Vedanta.[41] Arguably, the unconventional elements of these stories, including the women as gurus and their nonbrahman status, signal the alternative perspectives of the texts, for they both frame the Advaita Vedanta teachings by different, and distinctive, religious perspectives; the *Yoga Vasishtha* is framed by bhakti, and the *Tripura Rahasya* by tantra.[42] In both cases, the texts explicitly challenge the idea that married women are cut off from spiritual knowledge; both female protagonists are represented as gaining spiritual knowledge through the personal experience of self-realization, which echoes the character of Gargi from the *Brihadaranyaka Upanishad*, and then they teach their husbands, in the process relegating the idea that married women are cut off from spiritual knowledge to the realm of illusion.

The *Yoga Vasishtha* presents the story of a married royal couple, King Shikhidhvaja and Queen Chudala.[43] In this story, marriage itself is a symbol of the Advaita Vedanta teaching on unity: "Śikhidhvaja and Cūḍālā were so greatly devoted to each other that they were one jīva [individual aspect of *brahman*] in two bodies." In a poignant corrollary, two married people who are truly in love are understood to encounter each other and be married even in successive lives, as were Shikhidhvaja and Chudala.[44] This king and queen do everything together, including studying spiritual texts, from which "[t]hey came to the conclusion that self-knowledge alone can enable one to overcome sorrow."[45]

However, the queen alone continues her contemplation and proceeds deeper into self-discovery, achieving an awareness of pure consciousness (*brahman*) beyond the illusions of duality and ego. "Day by day the queen grew more and more introverted, rejoicing more and more in the bliss of the self. She was utterly free from craving and attachment. Without abandoning anything and without seeking anything, she was natural in her behavior and spontaneous in her actions. All her doubts were at rest. She had crossed the ocean of becoming. She rested in an incomparable state of peace."[46] King Shikhidhvaja recognizes Chudala's state of radiance and peace, and he asks her to explain to him how she has attained that state. Her response, given that she is in a different state of consciousness, is rather opaque: "I remain rooted in that which is the truth, not in the appearance. Hence I am radiant. I have abandoned all these, and I have resorted to something other than these, which is both real and unreal. Hence I am radiant."[47] Unfortunately, the king does not understand that her words are signifiers of a higher consciousness, so he paternalistically dismisses her teaching: "You are childish and ignorant, my dear, and surely you are prattling!"[48]

The king sets off into the forest to pursue the attainment of higher knowledge in the way he deems appropriate, which is to become an ascetic. Knowing that his methodology is flawed, the queen remains at the palace and conducts the affairs of state, although she surreptitiously checks on him from time to time with powers she has achieved through her self-awareness, including divine vision and the ability to fly through the air. After the king practices vegetarianism, mantra repetition, and meditation for eighteen years—in contrast to the queen's immediate results by focusing directly on the teaching and personal experience—the queen divinely sees that his mind is finally "ripe" to achieve self-awareness, and she goes to him, though in disguise. "Afraid that Śikhidhvaha might once again spurn her teaching, considering that she was an ignorant girl, Cūḍālā transformed herself into a young brāmaṇa [brahman] ascetic and descended right in front of her husband."[49]

Disguised as the young male brahman ascetic, Chudala teaches her husband the truth through many discourses, parables, and patient response to his questions. When it appears that he has achieved the higher consciousness, the "brahman" decides to test the equilibrium of his mind; interestingly, the tests primarily involve situations that will inspire lust and jealousy. For example, the "brahman" discloses that he has had a curse placed upon him, so that he becomes a woman during the night only; would the king mind marrying him so that he could be fulfilled as a woman by living as a wife at night? This does not bother the king, and he marries "her" and then consummates the marriage. The "brahman" devises another test: he creates an elaborate pleasure-garden, complete with a beautiful bed and a handsome young man. Then, the king's "wife" makes love to the young man when she knows that the king is surreptitiously watching. When confronted, the "wife" hurriedly makes excuses for herself, by denigrating the nature of women: "They are wavering in their loyalty. They are eight times as passionate as men. They are weak and so cannot resist lust in the presence of a desirable person. Hence, please forgive me and do not be angry." The king does not dispute this characterization, but his response indicates that he is free from anger: "It is appropriate that I should henceforth treat you as a good friend and not as my wife." This is the right answer, "Cūḍālā was delighted with the king's attitude which conclusively proved that he had gone beyond lust and anger."[50]

Chudala immediately reveals to him that she had created illusionary forms, including the "brahman," in order to teach him. In terms of Advaita Vedanta teachings, this story is an example of how maya (illusion) can be a power (shakti) that brings one to the consciousness of *brahman*. In this story, the illusions are patriarchal, including the supposed ignorance of women and the seeming necessity of a brahman male to teach the king. At the conclusion of the story, the king recognizes the true nature of illusions, and he praises his queen as the greatest among wives, for she has led him to liberation. When Chudala challenges him to describe his state, however, he recognizes the limits of language—which he had failed to notice when she spoke earlier from the enlightened state—and transforms the praise of his wife into the praise of his guru: "What I am that I am—it is difficult to put into words! You are my guru, my dear: I salute you. By your grace, my beloved, I have crossed this ocean of samsāra [birth and rebirth]; I shall not once again fall into error."[51]

The *Tripura Rahasya* also presents a story of a princess who teaches her husband awareness of the divine self. The tale of Princess Hemalekha and Prince Hemachuda is introduced in the context of a teaching on the importance of associating with wise people; as a means to realization of the truth, such association is known as *satsang*. The prince's association with Hemalekha is an illustration of this lesson, for he becomes enlightened by her. Hemachuda meets Hemalekha at a forest hermitage, whereupon he is immediately attracted to her and marries her with her foster father's permission. During the course of married life at the palace, Hemachuda notices that his princess does not seem to take pleasure in anything, especially his advances.[52] Hemalekha reveals to him that she is pondering an important question: "It is not that I do not love you, only that I am trying to find what the greatest joy in life is which will never become distasteful. I am always searching for it, but have not attained it yet."[53]

She claims that though she has been looking for it for quite some time, she has "not reached any definite decision, as is a woman's way," and requests his help. Amplifying her self-deprecating manner, her husband remarks that "women are indeed silly," and then asserts that the answer should be obvious to her, just as it is known to any living creature—including a crawling insect: "That which is pleasing is clearly good and that which is not so, is bad." At first, Princess Hemalekha appears to adopt his perspective, as she accepts him as a teacher: "True that women are silly and cannot judge rightly. Therefore I should be taught by you, the right discerner." However, she proceeds by radically deconstructing his answer:

> The same object yields pleasure or pain according to circumstances.
> Where is then the finality in your statement? Take fire for example.
> Its results vary according to seasons, the places and its own size or
> intensity. It is agreeable in cold seasons and disagreeable in hot sea-
> sons. Pleasure and pain are, therefore, functions of seasons; simi-
> larly of latitudes and altitudes. Again, fire is good for people of cer-
> tain constitutions only and not for others. Still again, pleasure and
> pain depend on circumstances.[54]

Through a related discussion of beauty, the princess makes the point that pleasure is in the mind's eye; she teaches that the mind must be steered from such partiality toward pure consciousness. She illustrates this point further through a series of parables, in which she teaches about the bondage of the inconsistent mind in contrast to the liberating bliss of pure consciousness; the importance of having faith in the words of a worthy person; the necessity of contemplating the Absolute Being, who is the Goddess Parameshwari (Tripura); and the role of God's grace in maturing a soul so that it is "ripe" for enlightenment.[55]

After these teachings, the prince is convinced that he can experience the bliss of the divine self, though only if he sits in meditation with his eyes closed. Again, the princess deconstructs his perspective: "Your small measure of wisdom is as good as no wisdom, because it is not unconditional, but remains conditioned by closing or opening your eyes. Perfection cannot depend on activity or the reverse, on effort or no effort."[56] On hearing these words, the prince at last reaches a state of equanimity, and becomes a *jivanmukta* (one who reaches liberation while still alive in the material body), who actively rules the kingdom through promoting this higher wisdom. The further dissemination of the teachings is represented in the text as following gender lines: The prince teaches his father, brother, and ministers; and Princess Hemalekha teaches her mother-in-law.[57] Ultimately, everyone in the kingdom—including mothers, servants, professors, children, older people, artisans, ministers and harlots—acts in an enlightened manner befitting true realization of the divine self, rather than from selfish motive.[58] Thus, from Princess Hemalekha's original act of teaching—being a guru to—Prince Hemachuda, the entire kingdom becomes enlightened, a giant *satsang*.

Both Chudala and Hemalekha are represented as behind-the-scenes partners to their husbands who quietly yet dramatically change for the better the lives of many people. Paradoxically, the texts publicize the private role of these women as wives to royal men, but the message to be taken from the texts remains a private, though influential, role for women. This private role contrasts with the very public role of female saints of India, who authored poems that have been preserved and who were the subject of hagiographies in medieval times; today their works and stories are widely known in India, and these female saints have become a main field of academic inquiry into women in classical Hinduism.[59] Generally, these female saints are associated with bhakti, a religious path that promotes active participation in the worship of God. The poetry of the female saints, as well as traditional accounts, represent them as devotees of the male gods Vishnu and Shiva. Historically, women whose voices were raised in praise of male gods were the ones who were themselves elevated by tradition as exemplars.

In contrast to the female gurus presented in the *Yoga Vasishtha* and the *Tripura Rahasya*, medieval female saints were not represented as partners to their husbands. The female gurus were *sahadharmini*, "an intellectual companion to her husband in issues of the mind, who still exercised a good deal of independent judgement."[60] In contrast, the ethos that formed the context for the poetry and biographies of the female saints was one of *parivrata*, in which a wife's duty was primarily to bear and raise sons for economic, social, and ritual reasons.[61]

The feminine challenge of this ethos involved alternative strategies. Unlike Advaita Vedanta, which is dismissive of duality, bhakti and tantra tend to explore this pervasive modality of human consciousness through sophisticated philosophies on the dynamic interplay among aspects of human life and thought. The worldview is that of a unity, but one that is in motion. Bhakti explores the tension between higher consciousness and action in the world, as well as the oscillation of human emotion in sensing both identity with and separation from God, of which a corollary is the imagination of God as both formless and with form.[62] As recently described by Ram Dass, "The essence of the Bhakti path is to use dualism to go beyond dualism by way of the heart."[63] Tantra is a religious path that has been influential in both Hinduism and Buddhism; thus, it has many permutations and vicissitudes. In Hinduism, tantra has been characterized by a contemporary scholar as "interpenetrating":

> Tantra perceives reality as an interpenetrating set of physical, verbal, mental, psychological, and spiritual elements and forces. These elements and forces, manifesting on both macrocosmic and microcosmic levels, constitute through their interidentification the one absolute reality that is both the nondual Brahman of Advaita and the supreme God or Goddess of the theists . . . [Tantric] practices include various meditative visualizations aimed at purifying the body and transforming it into the divine body of God or the Goddess, special forms of yoga, most notably the Kuṇḍalinī Yoga, and special forms of worship that emphasize the interpenetrating unity of worshiper, worshiped, and the worship service itself.[64]

It is this perceived and practiced identity between the particular and the whole—for example, between the Goddess and *brahman*—that enabled the feminine aspect to be elevated to a supreme status in tantric spirituality.

Tantra contributed a feminine spiritual principle to sacred knowledge; one of the prominent schools of tantra, called Shakta, emphasized worship of the Goddess.[65] Bhakti contributed a feminine approach to the divine (usually a male God), through the poetry of women saints. In emphasizing the feminine, tantra and bhakti self-consciously involved an interplay of dualistic and nondualistic theories of the sacred. As a corollary, both of these paths valorized embodiment as an approach to the sacred and thus regrounded traditions of renunciation, making it justifiable for women to dedicate their lives to spiritual pursuit.[66] Their approaches were a controversial critique of social expectations for women, expressed in a tendency toward secrecy in the case of tantra and in explicit rejection of women's social roles in the case of bhakti. Through these paths, women were able to express their own views of the nature of spirituality, and, on the basis of their expressions, to achieve recognition as religious adepts.

Lalla Ded, also known as Lal Ded, Lalli, and Lalleshwari, was a brahman woman born in Kashmir who probably lived from 1320 to 1391 c.e.[67] She is claimed by both Hindus and Muslims as a religious exemplar; within Hinduism, she is most often considered to be a voice within Shaiva tantra.[68] Characteristics of her poetry, which is in the form of four-line stanzas called *vakh*, that encourage the identification of her perspective with Shaiva tantra include her frequent reference to God as Shiva, her praise of the guru (sources tell us her guru was named Siddha Mol) and the persistent image in her poetry that her religious quest is for the unity, and reality, of the divine self within.[69] Using the contrast between cold and heat as a metaphor, two of her poems illustrate this experience of divine unity:

101

Just as intense cold
freezes water into ice,
so the water of Consciousness
contracts into three different forms:
the individual, the world, and God.
But when the sun of Consciousness shines,
once again everything,
both movable and immovable,
melts into the one Supreme Principle.
Lalli herself dissolved like that
into Consciousness.

102

I entered the blazing furnace
of the practice of yoga.
Like ice, I melted
in that fire of love.
My inner impurities burned away,
leaving pure gold.

When the sun of knowledge rose,
the dew of ignorance disappeared.
When I realized my oneness
with the name of God,
my "I"-ness was obliterated
and Lalli found peace.[70]

These two poems of Lalla Ded are representative in that they describe the experience of unity, especially the melting of the self into the universal consciousness, and the concomitant releasing of the mind from the dualistic thinking with which conventional society operates. In Lalla's heightened state of awareness, there are no distinctions between subject and object, between self and other, and between female and male. When she speaks of Shiva in other poems, she does not describe his masculine persona, which is celebrated in mythology and iconography; instead, she speaks of God as a reality to be experienced. This reality is none other than the unity of the self with the subtle divine.

Mirabai, whose historicity is complicated by the lack of "a corpus of poetry that can convincingly be associated with an historical person," is believed to have lived in the sixteenth century in Rajasthan.[71] Although she means many things to many people, she is definitively claimed by the north Indian Hindu tradition of bhakti saints, as evidenced by her inclusion in Nabhadas's anthology, the *Bhaktamal* (Garland of *Bhaktas*), composed around 1600 C.E. Her hagiography was later greatly elaborated upon by an influential commentator of the *Bhaktamal*, Priyadas, in 1712 C.E. In most of the poems attributed to

Mirabai, it is clear that the poetic voice is that of a woman longing for her Lord. Significantly, although Mirabai is the sole woman poet included in this north Indian bhakti canon, she is not alone in assuming a female poetic voice, for the male poets Kabir and Surdas do so, as well. "They understood a woman's gift for feeling to be a *bhakti* virtue and willingly stripped themselves of the status that went with their male rank to learn what true feeling meant. . . . The image of the tenacious woman whose strength is learned in love and suffering was the one that seemed most relevant to the religious needs of male figures in the *bhakti* world."[72] Through bhakti, the female poetic voice became a legitimized religious expression, as in the following poems from Mirabai:

153
Go to where my loved one lives,
    go where he lives and tell him
        if he says so, I'll color my sari red;
        if he says so, I'll wear the godly yellow garb;
        if he says so, I'll drape the part in my hair with pearls;
        if he says so, I'll let my hair grow wild.
Mira's Lord is the clever Mountain Lifter;
    listen to the praises of that king.

117
Oh, the yogi—
    my friend, that clever one
    whose mind is on Siva and the Snake,
    that all-knowing yogi—tell him this:

"I'm not staying here, not staying where
    the land's grown strange without you, my dear,
But coming home, coming to where your place is;
    take me, guard me with your guardian mercy,
        please.
I'll take up your yogic garb—
    your prayer beads,
        earrings,
        begging-bowl skull,
            tattered yogic cloth—
                I'll take them all
and search through the world as a yogi does
    with you—yogi and yogini, side by side.[73]

In these poems, Mirabai brings together the seemingly contrasting images of a married woman in society (the red sari, pearls in the hair) and a woman ascetic who has left society (the yellow robes, the unkempt hair). In poem 153, these images are juxtaposed to suggest the inclusive spectrum of possibilities that she will undertake for her Lord at his bidding. In poem 117, they are brought together to imagine two inseparable male and female ascetics wandering the earth. In combining these images, Mirabai's poetry is distinguished from the poetry of her male contemporaries. For her, the rich symbolism of gender roles is not a canvas on which to apply the experience of bhakti as a trope; rather, she insists that women's participation in bhakti stems from a spiritual discipline within, which challenges social categories by juxtaposing categories ordinarily deemed opposites.[74] This paradigm of intense love and desire for spiritual union with a male God is shared by other female bhakti poets, notably Mahadeviyakka and Andal of south India.

The hagiographies of Lalla Ded and Mirabai have in common stories of the hostility expressed toward them as they sought to realize their spiritual aspirations—especially from their in-laws, for they were both married. They overcame various harassments through a combination of their own spiritual dedication and divine occurrances. A prominent pattern in stories of the lives of Hindu classical saints is that the mind is problematized in stories of male saints, while the body is problematized in stories of female saints. This is a patriarchal formulation that conveys the social concern for the bodily purity of women, which is grounded in caste ideology.[75] Eventually, Lalla Ded extricated herself from society and became a wandering ascetic who eschewed even clothing. Mirabai left her in-laws' home and attempted to study with a famous theologian at Vrindavan. At first he refused, but then he relented when she pointed out that all of the world is female before God. Mirabai is also represented in the hagiography as staying in Vrindavan for some time, "as the focus of a large circle of devotees who gathered around her in song."[76]

Mirabai's association with followers, and indeed the public acceptance of these women saints, which made possible the survival of their works (although this is problematic in the case of Mirabai) and generated stories about them, connect these women to religious communities. The problem is in defining their influence within those communities, for it is intrinsic to the nature of a saint that the figure overlaps with the ordinary social world, yet stands quite apart from it; this is why saints cannot be uncritically considered as models for the rest of us. It seems all too human that both Lalla Ded and Mirabai are represented as female embodiments of serious spiritual discipline, yet they experienced hardship and lack of control over their own lives in their realization of that discipline due to social norms. It seems all too set apart from human experience that Mirabai drank unscathed an offering to Krishna that had been poisoned by her in-laws, and that Lalla Ded wandered around Kashmir without wearing any clothes. The women saints present poems and stories that we can admire and learn from, but they themselves are not remembered as teachers; although their works are in approachable regional languages (rather than Sanskrit), they lack a dialogic, instructional quality, and the saints' relationship to the social world is arguably too controversial to place them in the inherently social role of teacher.[77]

In the medieval period, there is an ultimate feminine guru represented in a classical text: the Goddess. It is she, not a wife or a saint, who assumes the public role of teacher and is capable of teaching all of humankind, which is the perspective advanced in the *Devi Gita*, composed during the thirteenth to fifteenth centuries. The text belongs to one of the dominant streams in Hindu tantra, Shakta, or worship of the Goddess. This path views shakti as more than an ancillary power of *brahman*: shakti is the Goddess, and the Goddess is *brahman*. The *Devi Gita* is the culmination of earlier stories of the Goddess found in the puranic mythological stories and in early tantric texts, precisely because the *Devi Gita* raises the Goddess to the level of Supreme Ruler.[78] In the *Devi Gita*, supreme cosmic power is unambigously female: she is a beautiful goddess, her power is the feminine shakti, and she is not linked to a male god, being most frequently referred to as Mother.[79] In the text, she first appears as a blazing light, symbolizing *brahman*, then transforms into a womanly figure, who is the Supreme Ruler (Bhuvaneshvari):

> It blazed like ten million suns, yet soothed like ten million moons. Flashing like ten million streaks of lightening tinged with red, that supreme lustrous power shone forth unencompassed above, across, and in the middle. Without beginning or end, it had no body, no hands, no other limbs. Nor did it have a woman's form, a man's form, nor the two combined.
>
> The dazzling brilliance blinded the eyes of the gods, O King. When again their vision returned, the gods beheld that light appearing now in the form of a woman, charming and delightful. She was exceedingly beautiful of limb, a maiden in the freshness of youth.[80]

The Goddess is independent yet benevolent in the *Devi Gita*, in contrast to the portrayal of goddesses in mythological stories, where they tend to be consorts of male gods, while the rare independent goddesses tend to be ferocious. Thus, in the mythology, the benevolence of goddesses is directly linked to the presence of a god. Not so in the *Devi Gita*, where the Goddess is envisioned as "the embodiment of compassion," a gracious and knowledgable teacher, and the ultimate goal of religious contemplation. Himalaya, the mountain king, speaks to the Goddess: "As you have already granted me one favor through your loving compassion, would you please describe for me your true nature as explained in all the Upanisads. And further describe the paths of both yoga and knowledge combined with devotion, as approved by scripture. Explain these, Supreme Ruler, so that I may become one with you.[81] And indeed the Goddess does teach him about all subjects, including knowlege of creation, of the divine self, of illusion (maya) and pure consciousness, the yoga of knowledge, the yoga of devotion, the practice of kundalini yoga, and methods of worshiping the Goddess, including internal and external, Vedic and tantric. Bhuvaneshvari is the Supreme Ruler, and the supreme guru.

Importantly, the *Devi Gita* posits an equivalence between the categories of mother and guru, thus recasting the dominant image of women's duty: "As a mother feels no lack of compassion whether indulging or chastening her child, just so the World-Mother feels when overseeing our virtues and vices. A son transgresses the limits of proper conduct at every step: Who in the world forgives him except his mother? Therefore go for refuge to the supreme Mother without delay, with sincere hearts. She will accomplish what you want."[82] Here, "mother" is both an intimate, familial figure, and a universal one who guides any and all seekers in the world. Private and public realms merge in the *Devi Gita*'s image of mother as guru.

This recasting of the category of mother raises the issue of whether women were involved in the text as creators, compilers, or audience. It is unclear whether women had anything to do with the creation and compilation of the *Devi Gita*; the identity of the author(s) is occluded, perhaps because the text purports to be the teachings of the Goddess herself.[83] Also problematic is whether the text is directed to women. Translator C. Mackenzie Brown addresses the issue of whether women are included in the Goddess's teachings, exhortations, and soteriological benefits. Although evidence that suggests women are generally excluded from them is sprinkled throughout the text, Brown states that it is the inclusive nature of devotion (bhakti) that led him to understand the text to be directed to women as well as to men, and to translate it using gender-inclusive language. He says that the author of the *Devi Gita*'s use of androcentric language "seems largely undercut by his much greater emphasis on the necessity for true devotion to the Goddess on the part of the recipient. Nowhere does the author of the *Devī Gītā* suggest that such devotion is restricted to males only."[84]

What is unambiguous in the text is that all of humankind is essentially female. The *Devi Gita* asserts this axiom in two ways. On one level, the Goddess is *brahman*; thus, humankind's true inner essence, the divine self, is the Goddess. On another level, the *Devi Gita* explicitly connects the Goddess to the concept of kundalini from yoga theory. The theory of kundalini yoga is known from other texts, on which the *Devi Gita* draws in presenting the Goddess's teaching on the subject.[85] Basic concepts in this theory of yoga include the understanding that humankind possesses a "subtle body" alongside the material body. This subtle body is homologized to cosmic entities (such as Mount Meru, rivers, the sun, and the moon) and their corresponding cosmic energies. The power center is the kundalini, imagined to be coiled like a serpent at the base of the spine. Uncoiling this shakti energy through disciplined activities, including controlled breathing, correct posture, and meditation, is the goal, for it is only through the release of the kundalini that humankind can reach its full potential in sharing the fundmental essence of the universe. With its emphasis on the Goddess as the Supreme Ruler, the *Devi Gita* can make a further connection not possible in other texts: The kundalini is the essence of the Goddess.[86] The Goddess is the source, and the force, of life; everyone has the feminine within, and must embrace it, then release it, in order to achieve liberation. The feminine is universal, through the female bhakti poetic voice, and through the Goddess.

Early Hindu Female Gurus

Guru is a relational, third-person term; it is a title by which one person acknowledges the wisdom of another. Within this general framework, there are two prominent ways of understanding the guru. As the term *guru* suggests, the guru is "weighty"—one who is invested with the capacity to give philo-sophical instruction to others, which leads to their salvation. In this more formal sense of the term, the guru is the path. On the popular level, the term *guru* is understood to denote one who is a "dispeller of darkness"; this sense of *guru* involves someone pointing out the way. For example, the guru could dispense an important piece of advice, or lead another to the truth. In this latter sense, for example, the Jain guru who leads the hero and heroine to Madurai in the Tamil *Cilappatikaram* epic is a guru; similarly, the sister of the Tamil Shiva-bhakti saint, Appar, who led him back to Shaivism from Jainism, is a guru in this sense. The stories of Chudala and Hemalekha are also examples of female gurus acting on a personal, familial level. In the popular sense, the title *guru* can be bestowed on anyone, by anyone, in the context of personal meaning.

On the more formal level, the guru is a representative of a specific religious tradition, has a publicly recognized status, and has a universal authority to teach. The status of the guru as a transmitter of salvific teachings permits the formal sense of the term *guru* to encompass both the informal sense of the term, which tends to privilege personal assessment, and the category of saint, which tends to signify a virtuoso devotional achievement. As Lisa Hallstrom notes, "It seems that almost all Hindu gurus are considered saints, but that not all saints are considered gurus."[87]

Was it an option for Hindu women to become gurus in the formal sense of the term prior to the sixteenth century? From the *Yoga Vasishtha* and the *Tripura Rahasya*, we saw that women were represented as gurus in the private realm of family; specifically, they acted as gurus to their husbands. In contrast, the stories of the tantra and bhakti saints celebrated the women as public exemplars—but this involved severe tension with their families, since an in-dividual woman known publicly was perceived to threaten the authority and status of her husband and parents. Esoteric tantric traditions seem to have celebrated women gurus prior to the sixteenth century.[88] Only the Goddess, who was independent of a male God, however, is uncontroversially represented as a public, universal teacher.

These medieval texts provided images of female religious adepts that served to establish women's capacity for leadership; further, they defined a set of characteristics and issues specific to women religious leaders, especially the relationship of religious commitment to women's wifely duty or dharma. These images and issues coalesced in the emergence of publicly recognized female gurus in the sixteenth through nineteenth centuries. These early female gurus had both public roles and public recognition; yet their stories preserve a sense of conflict between women's pursuit of the religious path and her duties as wife. This volume includes a case study of Sita Devi, a sixteenth-century Vaish-nava woman who is represented in seventeenth- and nineteenth-century hag-iographies as a guru in a defined lineage. The hagiography of Sita Devi con-cerns both her wifely dharma and her role as teacher to disciples. Sita Devi balanced the two modes: She was a dutiful wife while her husband was alive, then reluctantly accepted the solicitation of sectarian members to be their guru after his death.[89] As we shall see, stories of three subsequent female gurus from the seventeenth to nineteenth centuries revisit the tension between public and private, as well as the tension between exemplary spirituality and marriage. These historical tensions resonate with modern feminist analysis; while it is problematic to view historical religious women as feminists, it is very possible to suggest that their struggles contribute to modern feminist consciousness.

The story of Bahinabai (1628–1700) directly explores the conflict between devotion and dharma that permeates the poetry and biographies of female bhakti saints; the context of this conflict in the story of Bahinabai, however, is her devotion to a guru. We know about Bahinabai from her autobiographical verses as well as her verses that, rather like the Goddess's teachings in the *Devi Gita*, expound religious themes, including the *satguru* (true guru), bhakti, repentance, sainthood, morality, God's names, the nature of a "true brahman," the sacred place of Pandharpur, the bhakta Pundalik, and wifely duties.[90]

The first chapter of Bahinabai's autobiography locates her in a guru *parampara*, or unbroken lineage of gurus, which is defined in the text as originating in a mantra that Shiva bestowed on saints, who transmitted it through their bhakti.[91] Bahinabai received the mantra from Tukaram (1608–1649), a famous low-caste (shudra) saint from Maharashtra: "Because Bahini placed her undivided devotion at the feet of Tukoba [Tukaram], she received (the *mantra* through him)."[92]

According to her autobiography, Bahinabai was a profoundly spiritual woman who persisted in the devotional path in spite of the obstacles of poverty and a jealous and violent husband. Born to brahman parents in the town of Devagaon, some fifty miles from the Ellora Caves in the region now known as the state of Maharashtra, even as a child she demonstrated special interest in places of pilgrimage, images of God, and songs and stories of the saints. When she was eleven years old, she had visions of the then-living saint Tukaram and his chosen deity Panduranga: "Says Bahini, 'Tuka is my good *guru*, and my brother. Could I but meet him, it would be supreme happiness.'"[93] In successive visions, the saint gave her a mantra as well as spiritual instruction (v. 25.7).

Her husband responded violently to her spirituality. In contrast to the *Yoga Vasishtha* and the *Tripura Rahasya*, in which the husbands and wives had been from the royal, warrior caste—although revealingly, Chudala had taken the form of a male brahman to in order to teach her husband—Bahinabai's own caste and that of her husband was brahman. What happens when the wife of a brahman—a man who is skilled in the Vedas—seeks to teach him about the devotional path, taking a low-caste saint as her guru? He resents it, and a backlash occurs. She represents her husband as responding thus:

> The people thought all this [her visions of Tukaram in dreams] as very strange, and came in crowds to see me. My husband, seeing them, gave me much bodily suffering. He could not endure seeing the people coming to see me. And moment by moment his hatred increased. He exclaimed, "It would be well if this woman were dead. Why do these low people come to see her?" . . . My husband now be-

gan to say, "We are Brāhmans. We should spend our time in the study of the Vedas. What is all this! The *shudra* Tukā! Seeing him in a dream! My wife is ruined by all this! What am I to do? . . . Who cares for saints and *sādhus*! Who cares for the feelings of *bhakti*?"[94]

Their conflict has many levels, including the disobedience of a wife toward her husband; the tradition of the brahmans as knowers of the Vedas, in contrast to the path of bhakti; the low-caste status of Tukaram; and the gathering of people to witness Bahinabai's spiritual experiences.

When her husband threatens to leave her, she reflects on her wifely dharma: "My duty is to serve my husband, for he is God to me. My husband himself is the Supreme Brahma[n]. . . . The Vedas in fact say that it is the husband who has the authority in the matter of religious duties, earthly possessions, desires, and salvation. . . . My husband is my *sadguru*. My husband is my means of salvation."[95] Bahinabai unhappily remains with her husband for many years, conflicted by the disjuncture between her overwhelming bhakti and her life circumstances, including the fact that her husband and his family are learned in the Vedas yet devoid of bhakti (vv. 59.1–2, 65.1–3); that she is a woman, and thus closed off from the Vedic orthodoxy (vv. 63.1–4, 64.1–6); and that it is against the Vedas to neglect one's husband for any reason, including devotion.

Even though she indicates that she prays to the Lord that she will be able to accomplish devotion to both her husband and the Lord (v. 68.4), she does not represent such a reconciliation as occurring. The last event in her life that she describes, which probably occurred midway through her life, is her experience of the god Pandurang at a temple in the small village of Dehu on the banks of the Indrayani River. She and her family are staying at a pilgrims' rest house there, and, when her husband goes to Poona on business, she receives permission from her mother to go alone to the temple (vv. 74.1–4, 75.1–8, cf. v. 98.26). Contemplating Tukaram's feet, she remembers the mantra he had given her, and she feels him placing his hands on her head (v. 76.1–4). She experiences total joy and immersion in God, and she says that she is driven to silence, which is understood to mean that she observed a vow of silence for the rest of her life.

In the concluding section of her autobiography, which immediately follows her description of her experiences at Dehu, Bahinabai is seventy-two years old, and, certain that death will be upon her soon, she writes a letter to her son, urging him to leave his work and come to her (vv. 79–81). Her son, understanding his mother to be his guru, comes to her. Bahinabai recounts her twelve former lives in order to teach her son the path of bhakti; in all of them she exhibits profound spiritual discipline, as does her son, who appeared in many of her previous lives (her daughter is left out of the conversation). As her lives progressed, she had educated husbands who were supportive of her spirituality, until the present, thirteenth birth, in which: "My husband was simply the image of rage" (v. 98.25). Yet in this last birth, she is told by "someone in the form of Tukaram" that she should worship her husband (vv. 98.30–

32). In eight of her former lives she was unmarried; in two of them she was able to harmonize her religious activities with her wifely dharma.[96] Serving her husband is not a dominant theme in her verses that are teachings on religious topics; the section on wifely duty constitutes merely seven verses out of 473. Although her autobiographical verses directly address the conflict between devotion and wifely dharma, with the aim to reconcile them, ultimately they serve to reinforce dharma, even when the woman is a guru.

Stories of female gurus from the eighteenth and nineteenth centuries approach the controversy in a different way: Echoing the story of Sita Devi, they have the husband die earlier than the wife. Gauribai (1759–1809) was an upper-caste woman from Giripur, on the Gujarat and Rajasthan border.[97] When she was just a child, her betrothed died from disease. As a widow, she learned to read and write and spent her time singing and composing devotional songs in Gujarati, as well as reading sacred literature. Her spiritual discipline became known, which attracted the attention of a holy man, who compared her to Mirabai in a way that distinguishes guru from saint: "You are an incarnation of Saint Mīrābāī. Mīrābāī, though a great devotee, had not so much knowledge as one would desire in a saint. You are born to correct that defect. I have come to instruct you and give you the necessary knowledge."[98] Acting as a guru to her, he taught her about *brahman* and *atman*, and gave her an image of Krishna as a baby. Subsequently, she would frequently become absorbed in *samadhi*, or periods of deep meditation.

A prominent theme in her story is that many maharajas, or royal rulers, honored her as a spiritual adept. Raja Shivasimhji, who ruled the region in which Giripur lay, built a temple in her honor. The maharaja of Jaipur tested her by asking her to describe the ornamentation of an image of Krishna behind the closed doors of his private shrine; when she correctly told him that the crown had fallen off, he offered her a palace, which she declined. The maharaja of Benares accepted her as his guru. Her contact with these royal figures demonstrates the public acceptance and legitimation of her spirituality (although not necessarily by the brahman community), and it permits demonstration of her purity of motive, for she used the riches they insisted on giving her for charity. She expressed her spiritual insights in poetry in the Gujarati langage, as well as a few songs in Hindi.

Tarigonda Venkamamba (popularly Venkamma; fl. 1840) was a brahman woman from Tarigonda on the Andhra Pradesh and Tamilnadu border.[99] In contrast to the story of Gauribai, her widowhood is problematized in her story. When her betrothed died early on, the villagers insisted that her head be shaved, as was the custom, to signify publicly the inauspiciousness of widowhood. Venkamma refused, however, drawing a distinction between outward signs and internal purity: "So long as our inclinations are pure, the merciful Lord will not be offended with us even when we set aside worldly customs and manners. And if our inclinations are impure, though we may pay all homage to customs and manners, the Lord will not spare us. So please leave me alone."[100] Challenging authority, she refused a brahman religious leader's demand that she shave her head. He had it shaved by force, but when she subsequently bathed while praying to Krishna, she miraculously recovered her full head of hair.

Venkamma received spiritual initiation from a renowned male guru, Rupavataram Subrahmaniya Shastri, whom she reverently mentions in one of her texts. After several years of solitary religious practice, she began to write. "Venkammā found that for the regeneration of both men and women in her homeland, Āndhra-dēśa, the spread of ethical religious and philosophical teachings in a simple style was of paramount importance."[101] Claiming that she had never been educated but instead drew on God's grace and her own devotion, she wrote poetry, songs, and accessible compendia of Sanskrit originals, including the *Bhagavata Purana*, the *Venkatachala-mahatmya*, the *Raja-yoga-sara*, and the *Vasishtha-Ramayana*; in the latter, she tells the story of Chudala and Shikhidvaja from the *Yoga Vasishtha*.

The early female gurus from the sixteenth through nineteenth centuries advanced women's religiosity by becoming publicly recognized gurus. Like earlier female religious adepts, these gurus demonstrated steadfast commitment to the spiritual path. Indeed, two of these early female gurus self-consciously related themselves to previous female religious adepts; for example, Gauribai was compared to Mirabai, and Venkamma reiterated the story of Chudala. The two others, Sita Devi and Bahinabai, were connected to guru lineages. Like earlier female religious adepts, the female gurus of the sixteenth through nineteenth centuries are portrayed as experiencing the real and challenging authority, and their purity is highlighted.

Unlike earlier female adepts, however, the early female gurus are understood to have publicly assumed the role of teacher; for example, Sita Devi taught two disciples; Bahinabai taught her son directly, plus many others through her expository verses on religious topics; Gauribai taught members of the royal class; and Venkamma taught others through moral stories. This public role invokes the conflict of female bhakti saints, for it is deemed threatening if a woman views God, much less another man, even a guru, as a greater guide than one's husband, as is illustrated in the story of Bahinabai. If the guru role had been kept private, between husband and wife, as in the cases of Chudala and Hemalekha, then the husband could have been brought around to realize his wife's superior knowlege. This is not the case in these later stories, however, which are more like the stories of female bhakti saints in that the womens' spirituality is publicly recognized. However, unlike the bhakti saints, there is a great diversity in the ways in which the female gurus approach the conflict between wifely dharma and spirituality, which suggests that the category of publicly recognized guru provided a new creative space to address inherited issues of women's spirituality. Sita Devi was a loyal wife for many years, and then was reluctant to assume her husband's mantle of guruship upon his death; Bahinabai was in constant conflict between her devotion to her husband and her devotion to the Lord; and Gauribai and Venkamma were widowed early in their lives. The authority of female gurus, which rested on the authority of teaching as well as the authenticity of their religious experience, allowed for multiple models in addressing the deeply rooted conflict between devotion and duty.

Female Gurus in the Twentieth Century

In contrast to earlier periods, the twentieth century was an era in which the phenomenon of female gurus became widespread. Female gurus were appointed in many distinctive traditions within Hinduism, and they played public leadership roles. Linda Johnsen provides a list of female gurus in the twentieth century:

> Early in the 1900's the controversial tantric adept, Upasani Baba, reinstituted the Vedic tradition of *kanyadin*, a sort of Hindu supervision of male priests. He taught that women are capable of faster spiritual evolution than men, and that male devotees needed to cultivate "feminine" qualities like egolessness and purity in order to progress. He passed his lineage to the late Godavari Mataji, who presided over the Kanya Kumari Sthan in Sakori.
>
> Ramakrishna (world renowned devotee of the goddess Kali) passed his spiritual authority to his wife, Sarada Devi; Paramahansa Yogananda (who carried the Kriya Yoga lineage to the West) to the American-born Daya Mata; Shivananda (yogi and prolific author of Rishikesh) to the Canadian Shivananda Radha; Swami Paramananda (the first swami to settle in America) to his niece, Gayatri Devi; Swami Lakshmana (one of the peerless Ramana Maharshi's premier disciples) to the rebellious young Mathru Sri Sarada; Dhyanyogi Madhusudandas (long-lived exponent of kundalini yoga) to Anandi Ma; and Swami Muktananda (world travelling ambassador of Siddha Yoga) to Gurumayi Chidvilasananda.
>
> Papa Ramdas, one of the most homey of the popular Indian saints of this century, shared his mission with his spiritual consort, Krishna Bai. Sri Aurobindo, the influential philosopher/saint of Pondicherry, deferred to the French woman Mirra Alfassa Richard, whom he called "The Mother" and who administered Auroville, the community he founded in India, after his passing. Meera Ma (born in 1960 in Chandepalle, Andhra Pradesh), who had visions of Aurobindo since her childhood, has moved to Germany where European students have given her a warm welcome. Her legend continues to grow. And to everyone's surprise, the arch conservative shankaracharya of Sringeri empowered a woman (Lakshmi Devi Ashram, Jewish by birth) to found the first American temple to the Divine Mother in Stroudsburg, Pennsylvania.[102]

In the early decades of the twentieth century, very traditional rationales were used in support of women's leadership. For example, Upasani Baba emphasized "feminine" spiritual qualities (echoing male bhakti poets); Ramakrishna shared power with his wife, and appointed Gauri Ma as a leader of female-directed activities and services. The social context of these power transfers was the attempt by some elite males, including Mahatma Gandhi, to promote women as an emblem of virtue in the construction of an authentic "Indian" national identity, and to encourage their participation in selected nationalist agitations and events. Women were invested with a conservative meaning, which enabled, or even permitted, them to engage in significant and current struggles and positions of power.[103]

A fascinating example of this dynamic is Sri Aurobindo's validation of a foreign woman as a guru through his appeal to the traditional religious idea of shakti:

> In my own case it [the coming together of him and Mirra, the Mother] was a necessary condition for the work that I had to do. If I had to do my own transformation, or give a new yoga, or a new idea to a select few people who came in my personal contact, I could have done that without having any Shakti. But for the work that I had to do it was necessary that the two sides must come together. By the coming together of the Mother and myself certain conditions are created which make it easy for you to achieve the transformation. You can take advantage of those conditions.[104]

Sri Aurobindo's extension of the paradigm to a foreign woman parallels his expansion of the traditional teachings to the international community. Yet in this statement, he emphasizes not her foreignness but her femininity as necessity to promote his teachings beyond himself and personal acquaintances. Although her leadership was not uncontroversial in the early years, the Mother was the sole guru for many years following Sri Aurobindo's passing away. Both the Mother and Anandamayi Ma are important examples of early- to mid-twentieth-century women in India who definitively expanded the public role of guru to women, and who greatly internationalized the following of the guru.

Female gurus have been instrumental in bringing Hindu-based traditions to the West and maintaining them there. Hinduism has become established in the United States through a series of encounters over the past 150 years.[105] The nature of these encounters includes Americans' exposure to and increasing familiarity with Indian cultural traditions; contact between Americans and Indian immigrants; and relationships forged among cultural traditions in a society that is self-consciously pluralistic.

Two distinct forms of Hinduism have contributed to these encounters. In recent public lectures, Vasudha Narayanan of the University of Florida has classified Hindu institutions in America today into two categories from Hindu tradition: organizations that promote self-help practices (such as yoga and meditation), and organizations that provide the means for formal ritual worship (such as temples).[106] In Hindu Indian tradition, the paths of self-help and ritual worship are coexisting classical paradigms and present-day realities. The path of self-help is traditionally realized in the intense relationship between the guru and disciple; the path of ritual worship is traditionally realized in liturgical activities in temples performed by priests on behalf of worshipers. These are not mutually exclusive ways of worship; for example, there is often a temple at a guru's ashram, and temple priests have personal client relationships with worshipers. In India, what has separated the two paths until very recently is the participation of women as gurus in contrast to their exclusion from the priesthood in temples. Over the last ten years however, women have been studying to become priests, and achieving that status, at the Dyanaprabhodhini Centre in Pune.[107]

Today, the streams of self-help and temple coexist in America; however, the historical establishment of Hinduism in America reveals a distinctive pattern. For the first hundred years of Hinduism in the United States, its followers have mainly practiced the self-help approach; during the last thirty years, building Hindu temples in the United States has become a dominant focus.

"Self-help" describes well the paths of yoga, meditation, and the guru in Hindu tradition; however, it is one that is likely to be confusing in the American context. For example, there are a number of "self-help" organizations that deal with people who are trying to overcome specific problems, making the phrase something of a codeword for people in trouble. In addition, as I discussed in the first section of this essay, the meaning of "self" differs radically in the American and Hindu contexts. However, the designation "self-help" does apply to specific Hindu methods that emphasize that the participant herself must engage in activities of intensive discipline in order to achieve self-awareness, or the realization of the divine within.

Writing in 1977, Harvey Cox suggested that it is this participatory mode that distinguishes the guru traditions of the 1960s and 1970s from earlier Hindu formulations in the United States:

> The influence of Oriental spirituality in the West is hardly something new. . . . But there is something new about the present situation. In previous decades, interest in Oriental philosophy was confined mostly to intellectuals and was centered largely on ideas, not on devotional practices. There is no evidence that Emerson ever sat in a full lotus. Today, on the other hand, not only are large numbers of people who are in no sense "intellectuals" involved, but they appear more interested in actual religious practices than in doctrinal ideas. The recent wave of interest in Oriental forms of spirituality seems both broader and deeper than the ones that preceded it.[108]

In the 1960s and 1970s, the context of the mass marketing of the guru was the veritable marketing of the mystic East, with India and Indian gurus as a dominant product. Young Americans traveled to India in search of alternative lifestyles, some more spiritually inclined than others.[109] In the United States, Indian male gurus embraced mass-marketing techniques to promote their spiritual paths, including Maharishi Mahesh Yogi of Transcendental Meditation, A. C. Bhaktivedanta Swami Prabhupada of the International Society for Krishna Consciousness (ISKCON), and Swami Muktananda of Siddha Yoga.

Their emphasis on mass appeal represented a new, and conflicted, direction for the guru tradition. Traditional stories from India attribute two main vices to false gurus: the acquisition of money and sexual exploitation.[110] Past and present male gurus in India have been criticized and labeled as "false gurus" precisely on the issue of purity of motive, a critique that emerges from many corners, including those suspicious of "new religions" and gurus who maintain a rivalry with other gurus, as well as people involved in a "rationality movement" and those who attribute political and economic motives to gurus.[111] This suspicion appears within gurus' teachings as well. For example, Ma Jaya says that Swami Nityananda (of Siddha Yoga) warned her: "There is always a chance that one will use the serpent power—as shakti is sometimes known—for personal gain, thus limiting oneself to the feeling of power instead of bliss" (see Narayanan article in this volume). Since the gurus in the United States would have been aware of "the healthy cynicism maintained by anti-ascetic folklore in India" toward gurus who gather wealth, it is important to note what steps they took to counteract this criticism.[112] Generally speaking, their response included their assertion that a greater number of enlightened people improves our world, and that their methods are based on established, traditional practices, including chanting, vegetarianism, and gatherings of enlightened people (*satsang*); notably, social service works are prominent in the biographies of twentieth-century female gurus.

The current female gurus profiled in this volume are basically a "third wave" of gurus in the United States, with Ma Jaya Sati Bhagavati spanning the second and third waves, since she and her disciples had thirteen ashrams in Queens, New York, by 1975. These female gurus are a youthful group: Ammachi, Meera Ma (in Germany), Karunamayi Ma and Gurumayi are all in their forties, and Shree Ma, Ma Jaya Sati Bhagavati, and Jayashri Ma are slightly older. Gurumayi is the only one to have inherited an established ashram complex in the United States; the others fashioned their own centers, in their own styles (including the decentering tendencies of Shree Ma, Meera Ma, and Jayashri Ma). All of them are understood to be ascetics: Ammachi controversially declined to be married; Meera Ma is said to have married a German, but her husband does not play a public role in her mission; Ma Jaya Sati Bhagavati was married and has children; the issue of marriage arose in Shree Ma's life, but it was quickly dropped because she was a gifted student; and the issue seems never to have arisen in lives of Karunamayi Ma, Jayashri Ma, and Gurumayi.

All of the gurus attract followers who seek to experience the real for themselves, under the guidance of one who has experienced the real, and who can effectively lead others. The effectiveness of their leadership is often described as a transmission of shakti to the students, which awakens powerful cosmic energies in the subtle body. In this way, female gurus are also distinguished from the earlier male gurus, for as women they are the classic embodiment of shakti. Like their male predecessors, however, the female gurus of today are established enough to incur the criticism of some former followers; one can find such criticisms in discussion groups on the Internet.

In the United States, by far the largest group of followers of current female gurus are affluent, educated Euro-American women. A number of factors pertain to this group's dominant presence, including their value and validation of a woman leader; the fact that women traditionally participate in religion in higher numbers than men; and the chance to participate meaningfully in a welcoming spiritual path, based on the female gurus' tendency to avoid calling their paths "Hinduism" in favor of a path of spirituality open to all. An additional factor may be the approach captured by John Updike in his novel S., in which the protagonist is attracted to Indian traditions because they give her a language through which to understand her emotions and experiences; they are an important analytical tool in her commitment to self-growth.[113] It is also possible to understand this space for self-growth and self-awareness on feminist terms, for the majority profile of the women followers of female gurus matches the profile of women involved in feminist spirituality groups.[114] In addition, the "social expectation of the equality of women" in the United States may be a key factor in "legitimating [women's] presence in religious leadership roles," and thus their acceptance in those roles.[115]

The female Euro-American following of female gurus, as well as the gurus' inclusive perspective on the path, both serve to highlight the distinctive context of this "third wave" of gurus in contradistinction to the "second wave." For today in the United States, there is a new claim to Hindu spiritual authenticity in the American context: Hindu temples. As noted earlier in this section, the path of the guru and the path of temple liturgy are not mutually exclusive in India, nor are they necessarily in the United States, for early Hindu temples in the United States were constructed by guru-based organizations. For example, the Vedanta Society is credited with building the first Hindu temple in the United States, in San Francisco in 1906; others followed, such as the Hollywood temple in 1938, and the Santa Barbara temple in 1956. In keeping with the image of Hinduism Vivekananda had presented to Americans, the focus in these temples tended to be on understanding scripture. In addition, ISKCON built temples in cities across America, with the most famous being the elaborate Palace of Gold in New Vrindaban, West Virginia. Prabhupada's vision included both the guru-disciple relationship and temple worship, combining the personal spiritual quest, embodied by the guru, with traditions of ritual worship. However, the phenomenon of building temples in America that reproduce temple styles in India, including a full-time staff of brahman priests to conduct the worship services, began in the 1970s and was directly related to the presence of Hindu Indian immigrants in America.

In 1965 the Immigration Act liberated the long-frozen immigration of Asians to America by removing the national origins quota system and permitting the immigration of foreign professional people to the United States. In addition, the act's "family reunification" policy facilitated a second wave of Asian immigration. In the 1970s, the older generation of successful Indian professionals in the United States began to devote their wealth to building Hindu temples, which they viewed as cultural and spiritual centers for the education of the younger generation. The earliest temples of this type are the

Sri Ganesha Temple in Flushing, New York, and the Sri Venkateswara Temple in Pittsburgh, Pennsylvania, which were both dedicated in 1977.[116] In contrast to the ISKCON temples, which were built for a specific devotional community that includes both Euro-Americans and Indian-Americans, the Indian-style temples, most of which were built in the 1980s and 1990s and continue to be built, are by and for the Hindu immigrant community, and tend to incorporate diverse ways of worship as they attempt to bring ethnic Indian Hindus together as a cultural community.

It seems clear that currently gurus and Indian-style Hindu temples have marked off very different spaces in the United States. The guru path tends toward inclusivity, with its emphasis on self-power in relation to the guru's guidance, acceptance of participants from all ethnic and religious backgrounds, congregational modality of worship, and a tendency to dissociate itself with organized religion. As such, the guru path in the United States displays characteristics of the globalization of Hinduism. In contrast, the Indian-style Hindu temples tend toward specificity, with an emphasis on the ritual worship of a distinctive and often sectarian-defined God, ethnic Indian Hindu clientele, priestly modality of worship, and explicitly Hindu self-identification. As such, the Hindu temples in the United States tend to represent themselves as directly related to Hindu orthodoxy. Contributing to the tension is the tendency among followers to understand the female guru to be the Goddess, with whom they can interact directly and personally; their spiritual path toward self-discovery opens when the Goddess comes to life as the graceful guru. Still, there remains much common ground between the guru path and the way of temple worship, which could provide a basis for the interaction and mutual understanding among people of different backgrounds, for those who would commit themselves to such an endeavor.

NOTES

1. For example, Catherine Wessinger, ed., *Women's Leadership in Marginal Religions: Explorations outside the Mainstream* (Urbana: University of Illinois Press, 1993); Susan Starr Sered, *Priestess, Mother, Sacred Sister: Religions Dominated by Women* (New York: Oxford University Press, 1994); Susan Jean Palmer, *Moon Sisters, Krishna Mothers, Rajneesh Lovers: Women's Roles in New Religions* (Syracuse: Syracuse University Press, 1994); and Elizabeth Puttick, *Women in New Religions: In Search of Community, Sexuality and Spiritual Power* (New York: St. Martin's, 1997).

2. For example, Lisa Lassell Hallstrom, *Mother of Bliss: Ānandamayī Mā (1896–1982)* (New York: Oxford University Press, 1999); and Catherine Clémentin-Ojha's study of a contemporary female guru in Varanasi, Shoba Ma (b. 1921), *La divinité conquise: carrière d'une sainte* (Nanterre: Société d'Ethnologie, 1990). Besides this volume, other scholarly studies of several female gurus are in progress, such as Marie-Thérèse Charpentier's study of forty-five female gurus, with a focus on five of them, for her dissertation, tentatively entitled "The Thousand Faces of the Divine Mother," at Åbo Akademi University in Turku (Finland).

3. For example, Linda Johnsen, *Daughters of the Goddess: The Women Saints of India* (St. Paul, Minn.: Yes International Publishers, 1994); Timothy Conway, *Women of*

Power and Grace: Nine Astonishing, Inspiring Luminaries of Our Time (Santa Barbara: Wake Up Press, 1994); and Marcus Allsop, *Western Sadhus and Sannyasins in India* (Prescott, Ariz.: Hohm, 2000).

4. Miranda Shaw found evidence of women gurus in Indian and Tibetan tantric Buddhism in Sanskrit and Tibetan texts from the eighth to twelfth centuries; see her *Passionate Enlightenment: Women in Tantric Buddhism* (Princeton: Princeton University Press, 1994). I discuss stories of Hindu wives as gurus later in this introduction.

5. I discuss female saints later in this introduction. On the other types of participants, see the diverse articles in Laurie L. Patton, *Jewels of Authority: Women and Textual Tradition in Hindu India* (New York: Oxford University Press, 2002).

6. Kathryn Hansen, "Heroic Modes of Women in Indian Myth, Ritual and History: The Tapasvinī and the Vīrāṅganā," in Arvind Sharma and Katherine K. Young, *The Annual Review of Women in World Religions*, vol. 2: *Heroic Women* (Albany: State University of New York Press, 1992), p. 4.

7. Johnsen, *Daughters of the Goddess*, p. 61.

8. Ibid., p. 48.

9. Conway, *Women of Power and Grace*, p. 192.

10. Both quotations are from Catherine Clémentin-Ojha, "The Tradition of Female Gurus," *Manushi* 6 no. 1 (1985): 2–8; p. 2. Monier-William's Sanskrit Dictionary indicates that "guru" works for both genders, and it also lists a feminine form for "guru" as "guruvi" (thanks to Rebecca Manring for our personal discussion of these terms). Note that the contemporary guru, Gurani Anjali of Yoga Anand Ashram, uses the terms "gurani" and "Guru Ma" as titles to indicate "female guru," on the Web site http://www.santosha.com/dhyana/meditation.html. See also Katherine K. Young's mention of the terms *ācāryaṇī* and *upadhyāyinī*, "Oṃ, the Vedas, and the Status of Women with Special Reference to Śrīvaiṣṇavism," in Patton, *Jewels of Authority*, pp. 84–121; p. 115, n. 35.

11. Catherine Wessinger's edited volume "is primarily concerned to discover if there are factors supportive of the routine, noncharismatic religious leadership of women"; *Women's Leadership in Marginal Religions*, p. 2. Susan Starr Sered identifies characteristics of women leaders of women-dominated religions in her *Priestess, Mother, Sacred Sister*. Susan Jean Palmer presents case studies of women participants in religions new to North America in her *Moon Sisters, Krishna Mothers, Rajneesh Lovers*.

12. Elizabeth Puttick, *Women in New Religions*, esp. pp. 74–100, 175–95.

13. Rita M. Gross, *Feminism and Religion: An Introduction* (Boston: Beacon, 1996), p. 108.

14. Jeffrey J. Kripal, "Inside-Out, Outside-In: Existential Place and Academic Practice in the Study of North American Guru-Traditions," *Religious Studies Review* 25 no. 3 (July 1999): 233–38; p. 237.

15. See Hallstrom, *Mother of Bliss*, pp. 32, 70, 74, 80, and photographs between pages 106 and 107. See also the articles on Sita Devi and Gurumayi in this volume on the theme of hair.

16. See Vasudha Narayanan's discussion of bhakti, shakti, and women: "Brimming with *Bhakti*, Embodiments of *Shakti*: Devotees, Deities, Performers, Reformers, and Other Women of Power in the Hindu Tradition," in Arvind Sharma and Katherine K. Young, eds., *Feminism and World Religions* (Albany: State University of New York Press, 1999), pp. 25–77; esp. p. 65.

17. For example, on shakti and goddesses in Hinduism, see John Hawley and Donna M. Wulff, eds., *Devī: Goddesses of India* (Berkeley: University of California Press, 1996); Elisabeth Bernard and Beverly Moon, eds., *Goddesses Who Rule* (New

York: Oxford University Press, 2002); C. Mackenzie Brown, *The Devī Gītā: The Song of the Goddess* (Albany: State University of New York Press, 1998). On shakti and women in Hinduism, see Nancy A. Falk, "*Shakti* Ascending: Hindu Women, Politics, and Religious Leadership during the Nineteenth and Twentieth Centuries," in Robert D. Baird, ed., *Religion in Modern India* (New Delhi: Manohar, 1995), pp. 298–334; Julia Leslie, ed., *Roles and Rituals for Hindu Women* (Rutherford, N.J.: Fairleigh Dickenson University Press, 1991); and the classic, Susan S. Wadley, ed., *The Powers of Tamil Women* (Syracuse: Syracuse University Press, 1980).

18. Madhu Khanna, "The Goddess-Women Equation in *Śākta* Tantras," in Mandakranta Bose, ed., *Faces of the Feminine in Ancient, Medieval, and Modern India* (New York: Oxford University Press, 2000), pp. 109–123; p. 116. Khanna cites June McDaniel, "The Embodiment of God among the Bauls of Bengal," *Journal of Feminist Studies in Religion* 8 no. 2 (1992): 36.

19. Current studies of women's empowerment through possession by the Goddess include Mary Hancock, *Womanhood in the Making: Domestic Ritual and Public Culture in Urban South India* (Boulder, Col.: Westview, 1999); Kathleen Erndl, "The Goddess and Women's Empowerment: A Hindu Case Study," in Karen L. King, ed., *Women in Goddess Traditions* (Minneapolis: Fortress, 1997), pp. 17–38; and Lindsey Harlan and Paul Courtright, eds., *From the Margins of Hindu Marriage* (New York: Oxford University Press, 1995).

20. Johnsen, *Daughters of the Goddess*, p. 26. The nature and role of feminism in third-world countries, especially in the context of power relations among nations and the cultural applicability of perspectives that have had their genesis in the West, is an ongoing discussion in India and elsewhere. See Madhu Kishwar, *Off the Beaten Track: Rethinking Gender Justice for Indian Women* (New Delhi: Oxford University Press, 1999); Uma Narayan, *Dislocating Culture: Identities, Traditions, and Third World Feminism* (New York: Routledge, 1997); Irene Gedalof, *Against Purity: Rethinking Identity with Indian and Western Feminisms* (London: Routledge, 1999); Chandra Talpade Mohanty, Ann Russo, and Lourdes Torres, eds., *Third World Women and the Politics of Feminism* (Bloomington: Indiana University Press, 1991). For a scholarly critique of Western feminism's construction of the Goddess, see Katherine K. Young, "Goddesses, Feminists, and Scholars," in Arvind Sharma and Katherine K. Young, eds., *The Annual Review of Women in World Religions*, vol. 1 (Albany: State University of New York Press, 1991), pp. 105–179.

21. Hallstrom, *Mother of Bliss*; discussion is throughout the book, but see especially chapter 7, "Ānandamayī Mā and Gender," pp. 199–222.

22. In her study of American feminist spirituality, Cynthia Eller has observed that women who left traditional religions often turned to "alternative religions," including Asian traditions; *Living in the Lap of the Goddess: The Feminist Spirituality Movement in America* (New York: Crossroad, 1993), pp. 32–33.

23. See Patrick Olivelle's discussion of dating in *Upaniṣads, Translated from the Original Sanskrit by Patrick Olivelle* (New York: Oxford University Press, 1996), xxxvi–xxxvii.

24. Eknath Easwaran, trans. *The Upanishads* (Tomales, Calif.: Nilgiri Press, 1995), pp. 65–66.

25. Olivelle, *Upaniṣads*, p. xxiii.

26. This is convincingly argued by Ellison Banks Findly, "Gārgī at the King's Court," pp. 37–58, esp. pp. 38–42, in Yvonne Yazbeck Haddad and Ellison Banks Findly, eds., *Women, Religion, and Social Change* (Albany: State University of New York Press, 1985).

27. Vasudha Narayanan lists the Vedic poets in "The Hindu Tradition," in Willard G. Oxtoby, ed., *World Religions: Eastern Traditions* (Toronto: Oxford University Press, 1996), p. 26. Sushil Kumar De adds Vishwavara, Godha, Shashwati, and Romasha to the list in "Great Women in Vedic Literature," in Swami Madhavananda and Ramesh Chandra Majumdar, eds., *Great Women of India* (Mayavati, Almora: Advaita Ashrama, 1982), pp. 129–139; p. 130.

28. *Brihadaranyaka Upanishad* (hereafter *Br Up*) 3.8; Olivelle, *Upaniṣads*, pp. 44–45. The words for imperishable are *akshara* (m), "non-transitory," and *akshayan* (m), "without depriciation." Hereafter, page numbers accompanying references to *Br Up* will refer to Olivelle's translation.

29. *Br Up* 3.8.12 (p. 46).

30. Findly, "Gārgī at the King's Court," pp. 49–50. In her discussion, Findly draws on the evaluation of Gargi by the famous philosopher Shankara, whom I discuss in the next section.

31. Ibid., p. 45.

32. This important discussion is located in 2.4 of the text (pp. 28–30) and is repeated with slight variation in 4.5 (pp. 69–71).

33. This qualification occurs only in *Br Up* 4.5 (p. 69).

34. *Br Up* 2.4.3 (p. 28) and 4.5.4 (p. 69).

35. *Br Up* 2.4.5 (p. 28), 4.5.6 (p. 69).

36. *Br Up* 2.4.12 (p. 30).

37. Findly, "Gārgī at the King's Court," p. 40.

38. Eliot Deutsch provides an accessible discussion of the philosophy of Advaita Vedanta on this issue in chapter 3 of his *Advaita Vedānta: A Philosophical Reconstruction* (Honolulu: University of Hawai'i Press, [1969] 1973), pp. 27–45; esp. pp. 30–32.

39. For example, one of the Dharmashastras mentions "female guru" as the wife of a guru, in the context of discussing a "fallen man": "That man falls who has connection with a female friend of a female Guru, or with a female friend of a male Guru, or with any married woman"; *Apastamba Prasna I*, patala 7, khanda 21 of Georg Buhler, trans., *Apastambadharmasutra, or Apastamba's Aphorisms on the Sacred Law of the Hindus*, Bombay Sanskrit Series nos. 44, 50 (Poona: S. K. Belvalkar, 1932); reproduced on the Web at http://www.sacred-texts.com/hin/sla/apao121.htm.

40. "Social" does not necessarily mean that the teaching is verbal; for example, the first Siddha Yoga guru, Bhagawan Nityananda, was a great teacher of few words. See Swami Durgananda, "To See the World Full of Saints: The History of Siddha Yoga as a Contemporary Movement," in Douglas Renfrew Brooks, et al., *Meditation Revolution: A History and Theology of the Siddha Yoga Lineage* (South Fallsburg, N.Y.: Agama, 1997), pp. 3–161, esp. pp. 15–22.

41. The *Yoga Vasishtha* (hereafter, *YV*) has been dated as early as the sixth or seventh century C.E. and as late as the fourteenth century. T. G. Manikar has convincingly argued that the text was composed in Kashmir between 1150 and 1250; see Christopher Chapple's introductory comments in Swami Venkatesananda, *The Concise Yoga Vāsiṣṭha*, with an introduction and bibliography by Christopher Chapple (Albany: State University of New York Press, 1984), pp. x–xi. The *Tripura Rahasya* is possibly contemporaneous, or slightly later. Swami Sri Ramanananda Saraswathi, trans., *Tripura Rahasya or the Mystery beyond the Trinity* (Tiruvannamalai: T. N. Venkataraman, 1971).

42. As Christopher Chapple notes, the main protagonists of the *Yoga Vasishtha* are Rama, familiar as the kingly hero of the Ramayana epic and incarnation of Vishnu, and Vasishtha, a sage whom Shankaracarya referred to as the first sage of the

Vedanta school; Vasishtha, who teaches Rama in the *YV*, thus links the text with the Vedanta tradition. However, Chapple also remarks upon the diversity of traditions in the text: "Threads of Vedānta, Jainism, Yoga, Sāṃkhya, Śaiva Siddhānta, and Mahāyāna Buddhism are intricately woven into the *Yoga Vāsiṣṭha*; it is a Hindu text *par excellence*, including, as does Hinduism, a mosaic-style amalgam of diverse and sometimes opposing traditions" (p. xii). I tend to put the emphasis on bhakti, because the *YV* insists that Rama, enhanced by higher knowledge, then resumed his royal duty of ruling; thus, the text's emphasis on action in the world makes what the *YV* does for the epic Ramayana parallel with what the *Bhagavad Gita* does for the epic *Mahabharata*.

The *Tripura Rahasya* text is in praise of the Goddess, which associates it with the tantric Shakta theology, which I discuss in greater detail below. The frame story is that a sage named Dattatreya teaches Parashurama higher wisdom; tradition views both of these characters as incarnations of Vishnu.

43. Venkatesananda, *The Concise Yoga Vāsiṣṭha*, pp. 333–383. The *YV* has other stories that involve women who attain higher knowledge; for example, Queen Lila, who is taught by the goddess Saraswati (pp. 51–77); the demoness Karkati, who attained higher knowledge by her own meditation ("She had gained direct knowledge of the supreme causeless cause of all by her own examination of the intelligence within her. Surely, direct inquiry into the movements of thought in one's own consciousness is the supreme guru or preceptor, O Rāma, and no one else," p. 80), then heard teachings by a king and his minister (pp. 77–87); and a very interesting take on the Ahalya story (pp. 89–96).

44. Ibid., p. 333. In Hinduism, marriage is sacramental, as it is in Christianity; on a general level, this means that the ceremony metaphysically joins the two participants as one, which is the reason that divorce is controversial in both religions.

45. Ibid., p. 334.

46. Ibid., p. 336.

47. Ibid.

48. Ibid., p. 337.

49. Ibid., p. 349.

50. The series of quotations is ibid., p. 380.

51. Ibid., p. 381.

52. Saraswathi, *Tripura Rahasya*, 3: 47–59, pp. 24–26.

53. Ibid., 4: 1–3, p. 26.

54. This section of the story is found ibid., 4: 4–15, pp. 26–27.

55. Ibid., chaps. 5–8, pp. 34–62.

56. Ibid., 10: 15–27, p. 73.

57. On the prince, see ibid., 10: 43–61, pp. 75–76; on the princess, see ibid., 4: 96, p. 33.

58. Ibid., 10: 43–61, p. 76.

59. There are numerous studies of female bhakti saints; many I have listed in the bibliography. Female bhakti saints existed in all regions of India; it is not my intention here to represent all of them in this selective discussion of issues relevant to the emergence of Hindu female gurus.

60. Findly, "Gārgī at the King's Court," p. 39.

61. Ibid., pp. 40–41.

62. For a further discussion of bhakti, see Karen Pechilis Prentiss, *The Embodiment of Bhakti* (New York: Oxford University Press, 1999), especially the introduction and chapter 1.

63. Ram Dass, *One Liners: A Mini-Manual for a Spiritual Life* (New York: Bell Tower, 2002), p. 63.

64. C. Mackenzie Brown, *The Devī Gītā: The Song of the Goddess. A Translation, Annotation, and Commentary* (Albany: State University of New York Press, 1998), pp. 18–19.

65. Douglas R. Brooks, an expert on tantra, discusses "Śākta forms of Tantrism . . . [as] Hindu Tantrism par excellence," in his *Secret of the Three Cities: An Introduction to Hindu Śākta Tantrism* (Chicago: University of Chicago Press, 1990), p. 72; cited in C. Mackenzie Brown, *Devī Gītā*, p. 21.

66. Rita M. Gross discusses the validity of embodiment as a major theme in feminist understandings of religion in *Feminism and Religion*, pp. 237–40.

67. See "A Second Rabia: Lal Ded of Kashmir," in *Manushi* 50–52 (January–June 1989): 103–108. The unnamed author says that the account of Lal Ded's life discussed therein, as well as the translations of her poetry, are from Jayalal Kaul's *Lal Ded* (Delhi: Sahitya Akademi, 1973).

68. "There is a great deal of controversy regarding Lalla's philosophy. Some call her a follower of Shaivism; others claim that she was influenced by hatha yoga, Buddhism, or Shankaracharya. There are also long-standing legends, recorded in Persian chronicles, that she accepted Islam, and was a follower of Shah Hamadan, who had taken refuge in Kashmir from the persecution of Timur. Many remember her as a sufi and a *wali*, and she is often called a second Rabia. In 1885, Pir Ghulam Hasan summed up the argument in his *Tarikh-i-Hasan*: 'The Hindus say that she is one of them. The Musalmans claim that she belongs to them. The truth is that she is among the chosen of god. May god's peace be upon her' "; ibid., p. 106.

69. In Jayalal Kaul's translation from the Kashmiri, one of her poems explicitly mentions Shaiva tantra: "Whatever work I did became worship of the Lord;/ Whatever word I uttered became a *mantra*/Whatever this body of mine experienced became the *sadhanas* of Saiva Tantra"; ibid., p. 107.

70. From *Lalleshwari: Spiritual Poems by a Great Siddha Yogini, Rendered by Swami Muktananda* (South Fallsburg, N.Y.: Gurudev Siddha Peeth, 1981), p. 47. According to the preface by Swami Prajnananda, "In this book, the verses have been collected from different sources, arranged and rendered into Hindi by Baba [Muktananda], and translated into English by Yoginī Shrī Malti Devi [today, Gurumayī]," p. xi.

71. See John S. Hawley's thorough discussion of Mirabai's historicity in Hawley and Mark Juergensmeyer, *Songs of the Saints of India* (New York: Oxford University Press, 1988), pp. 122–29.

72. Ibid., p. 119.

73. Ibid., pp. 138–39; translated from Parashuram Caturvedi's *Mīrābāī kī Padāvalī* (see ibid., p. 205). There is a final verse to poem no. 117 that I have omitted here.

74. I am drawing on Hawley's insight: "Rather than accepting the loving profligacy that official *saguna* theology designates as the appropriate avenue of escape from mundane, domestic involvements—a theology, of course, designed by men—she may try something new. She may attempt to forge categories that give new bite to *bhakti* from a woman's point of view. This is what Mira did in demanding for herself a marriage with the world's most eligible and unmarriageable bachelor and in imagining this marriage as taking a form the world regards as impossible: the coupling of two yogis" (ibid., p. 133; for other distinctive features see pp. 130–32).

75. See A. K. Ramanujan, "On Woman Saints," in John Stratton Hawley and Donna Marie Wulff, eds., *The Divine Consort: Rādhā and the Goddesses of India*

(Berkeley: Graduate Theological Union, 1982), pp. 316–24; and Uma Chakravarty, "The World of the Bhaktin in South Indian Traditions—the Body and Beyond," *Manushi*: 50–52 (Jan–June 1989), pp. 18–29, esp. pp. 26–27.

76. Hawley and Juergensmeyer, *Songs of the Saints of India*, p. 126. In the case of Mirabai, there is tension along caste lines in her biography and among communities in Rajasthan today, with some communities rejecting Mirabai though she is lauded all over the country; see Parita Mukta, *Upholding the Common Life: The Community of Mirabai* (Delhi: Oxford University Press, 1994). See also Nancy Martin's remarks on caste and Mirabai, "Mirabai," in *Encyclopedia of Women and World Religion*, edited by Serinity Young (New York: Macmillan Reference, 1999), pp. 664–665.

77. In her balanced and interesting discussion of the application and meanings of the term *saint* in Hinduism, Lisa Hallstrom notes that many of Anandamayi Ma's devotees do not choose to refer to the guru as a "saint" because they view her as the embodiment of God rather than a human being; see her *Mother of Bliss*, pp. 87–92. See also two comparative studies of sainthood: John Stratton Hawley, ed., *Saints and Virtues* (Berkeley: University of California Press, 1987) and Richard Kieckhefer and George D. Bond, eds., *Sainthood: Its Manifestation in World Religions* (Berkeley: University of California Press, 1988).

78. Brown, *Devī Gītā*, pp. 8, 26. Note Brown's discussion of translating Supreme Ruler into English.

79. Ibid., p. 54 n. 5.

80. Ibid., pp. 58–59, 62 (vv. 1.26, 1.31).

81. Ibid., p. 81 (vv. 1.72–73).

82. Ibid., pp. 52–53.

83. Brown, ibid., p. 7, characterizes the authorship of the text as follows: "Sometime after the eleventh century, one ardent follower of the Goddess, or he and a small group of like-minded friends, decided to rectify the situation [of mythological texts devoted only to male gods] and compose a great Purāṇa dedicated solely to the object of their devotion, conceived of as the supreme power (*śakti*) of the universe, consort of none, subject to none."

84. Ibid., pp. 35–7.

85. In chapter 5, ibid., pp. 179–96; Brown's copious notes explain the connections with other texts.

86. "Above that is the Coiled Serpent appearing like a flame, blood-red in color. She is said to be the very essence of the Goddess, expanding with rapturous passion, O Mountain Chief" ibid., p. 184 (v. 5.33).

87. Hallstrom, *Mother of Bliss*, p. 92.

88. See Paul Muller-Ortega, *The Triadic Heart of Śiva* (Albany: State University of New York Press, 1989). See also the translation of a Kaula Tantric text, which offers a meditation to a female guru (*stri guru*), by Mike Magee, at http://www.clas.ufl.edu/users/gthursby/tantra/guru.htm.

89. In addition to her article in this volume, see Rebecca J. Manring, "At Home in the World: The Lives of Sītādevī," *International Journal of Hindu Studies* 2 no. 1 (April 1998): 21–42. In this latter article, Manring notes the leadership of two women in Gaudiya Vaishnavism: "Sectarian records mention no women among the leaders of the first generation. However, in the next generation, leadership shifted to (among others) two women who were so close to the founders that in retrospect their roles seem obvious, although at the time the community itself could not have anticipated their rise to power. These were . . . Sītādevī and Jāhnavī, primary wife of Nityānanda (one of Caitanya's closest associates)" (p. 22).

90. Sources in English for the study of Bahinabai include: Piroj Anandkar, "Bahiṇābāī," in Swami Ghanananda and John Stewart-Wallace, eds., *Women Saints East and West* (Hollywood, Cal.: Vedanta, [1995] 1979) pp. 64–72; Anne Feldhaus, "Bahiṇā Bāī: Wife and Saint," *Journal of the American Academy of Religion* 50 (1982): 591–604; and Justin E. Abbott, trans., *Bahiṇā Bāī: A Translation of Her Autobiography and Verses*, The Poet-Saints of Maharashtra No. 5 (Poona: Scottish Mission Industries, 1929). The numbering and order of verses differs in Felhaus' article from that presented in Abbott's translation.

91. The mantra originated with Shiva, who gave it to his wife Parvati; Matsyendra heard it from within the belly of a fish, "thus through him the supreme *mantra*, that Shiva held in His mind, became effective through *bhakti*"; he passed to it Goraksha (Gorakhnath), who passed it to Gahini, then Nivrittinath, then Dnyaneshvar, then Satchidananda; then Vishvambhara gave it to Raghava (Chaitanya), then to Keshava Chaitanya, who passed it to Babaji Chaitanya, to Tukoba (Tukaram), and through him to Bahinabai. See Abbott, *Bahiṇā Bāī*, p. 1 (vv. 1.1–9).

92. Ibid., chapter 1, 1.8.

93. Ibid., p. 18 (Autobiography v. 21.12).

94. Ibid., pp. 23–23 (vv. 31.1–4, 32.1–2, 4).

95. Ibid., p. 25 (vv. 35.4, 7, 11).

96. Verses 90–98. In the first seven births she was unmarried, in the eighth her husband died ["but that was an advantage to me" (v. 94.7)], in the ninth she was unmarried, in the tenth she was married with three children, in the eleventh her husband was a *siddha* skilled in yoga who became a guru to her, and in the twelfth she served her husband "while constantly in the act of contemplation" (v. 96.18).

97. Sarojini Mehta, "Gaurībāī," in Ghanananda and Stewart-Wallace, *Women Saints East and West*, pp. 73–79.

98. Ibid., p. 75.

99. Swami Chirantanananda, "Tarigoṇḍa Venkamāmbā," in Ghanananda and Stewart-Wallace, *Women Saints East and West*, pp. 86–93.

100. Ibid., pp. 86–87.

101. Ibid., p. 90.

102. Johnsen, *Daughters of the Goddess*, pp. 22–23.

103. See, for example, Lou Ratté, "Goddesses, Mothers, and Heroines: Hindu Women and the Feminine in the Early Nationalist Movement," in Yvonne Yazbeck Haddad and Ellison Banks Findly, *Women, Religion, and Social Change* (Albany: State University of New York Press, 1985), pp. 351–376. See also Tanika Sarkar, *Hindu Wife, Hindu Nation: Community, Religion and Cultural Nationalism* (Bloomington: Indiana University Press, 2001). A famous fictional exploration of the theme of woman as an emblem of the nation is Rabindranath Tagore, *The Home and the World*, translated by Surendranath Tagore (London: Penguin Books, [1915] 1985).

104. Sri Aurobindo, *On Himself*, Sri Aurobindo Birth Centenary Library 26: 455. Cited in Georges van Vrekhem, *The Mother: The Story of Her Life* (New Delhi: HarperCollins Publishers India, 2000): 205.

105. Research in this section is drawn from an essay entitled "The Pattern of Hinduism and Hindu Temple Building in the U.S." that I wrote for my affiliates Web page on the Harvard Pluralism Project site, http://www.fas.harvard.edu/~pluralsm/affiliates/pechilis-prentiss.html. An excellent resource is the CD-Rom "On Common Ground," a lucid discussion of religious pluralism in America from research conducted by the Pluralism Project at Harvard University under the direction of Diana L. Eck.

106. Dr. Narayanan presented these ideas at a keynote lecture during the annual Conference on Religion in South India held in Toronto, June 12–15, 1997. She has continued working with these ideas on her affiliate Web page for the Harvard Pluralism Project http://www.fas.harvard.edu/~pluralsm/affiliates/narayanan .html.

107. Lovejit Dhaliwal, "Hindu Women Spread the Word," BBC News Online, Thursday April 26, 2001. The Dyanaprabhodhini Centre in Pune is headed by Jayavantrao Leile; he began the course for training priests about ten years ago, and estimates that a third of the students are women. Web address: http://news.bbc.co.uk/hi/ english/world/south_asia/newsid_1298000/1298208.stm.

108. Harvey Cox, *Turning East: The Promise and Peril of the New Orientalism* (New York: Simon and Schuster, 1977): 9. A notable exception to the early emphasis on textual study promoted by Emerson and Thoreau, as well as Vivekananda's Vedanta Society, would be Swami Paramahansa Yogananda's emphasis on the practice of Kriya Yoga. Paramahansa came to America in 1920 as a delegate to the International Congress of Religious Liberals held in Boston, then settled in America and founded the Yogoda-Satsang (Self-Realization Fellowship), which surpassed the Vedanta Society as "the most influential Hindu movement in the country" in the 1930s. See Thomas A. Tweed and Stephen Prothero, *Asian Religions in America: A Documentary History* (New York: Oxford University Press, 1999), pp. 161–62 and 182–83 (on Paramahansa), and surrounding chapters on other gurus.

109. Interesting trade books on this phenomenon include Gita Mehta, *Karma Cola: Marketing the Mystic East* (New York: Fawcett Columbine, 1979); and Cleo Odzer, *Goa Freaks: My Hippie Years in India* (New York: Blue Moon Books, 1995).

110. Kirin Narayan, *Storytellers, Saints, and Scoundrels: Folk Narrative in Hindu Religious Teaching* (Philadelphia: University of Pennsylvania Press, 1989), p. 156.

111. On the establishment of new religions, note that the Buddha is said to have rejected the wisdom of Hindu gurus, which led up to his self-enlightenment; Sikhism accepted the guru ideal, but applied it very distinctively. On the rivalry among gurus, see Kirin Narayan's humorous telling of the "Nose-Cutters" story, and its application to Swami Dayananda and the Swami Narayan sect, in her *Storytellers, Saints, and Scoundrels.* pp. 132–59. On the Indian Science and Rationalists' Association, self-described "guru busters," see "India's 'Guru Busters' Debunk All That's Mystical," by John F. Burns, *New York Times*, October 10, 1995, International Section. For a political and economic analysis of contemporary male gurus in India, see Lise McKean, *Divine Enterprise: Gurus and the Hindu Nationalist Movement* (Chicago: University of Chicago Press, 1996).

112. Narayan, *Storytellers, Saints, and Scoundrels*, p. 158.

113. John Updike, *S.* (New York: Fawcett Columbine, 1988). The protagonist uses language from Indian traditions throughout the book, but seems most self-conscious of it when she says that her experience with yoga "gave me a vocabulary" (p. 11), and when she says that through her stay at the ashram she has achieved "a whole new vocabulary to frame the perennial problems in, and a way of looking at them that makes them almost vanish" (p. 235).

114. Eller, *Living in the Lap of the Goddess*, pp. 18–23.

115. Wessinger, *Women's Leadership in Marginal Religions*, p. 140. The other factor she deems important are images of the divine: "The history of Hinduism and Buddhism demonstrates that androgynous, neuter, or female conceptions of the divine are not sufficient in and of themselves to promote equality for women. But once there is a social expectation of the equality of women, conceptions of the divine that de-

emphasize the masculine prove attractive to women and support them in legitimating their presence in religious leadership roles"; pp. 139–40.

116. For a discussion of these two temples, see Tweed and Prothero, *Asian Religions in America*, pp. 289–98. See also the Web sites of the temples: The Ganesha Temple Web site is www.indianet.com/ganesh/ (including a section on "Temples On-line" with links to other temples); the Sri Venkateswara Temple Web site is www .svtemple.org/. Also relevant is a fascinating film, "Pilgrimage to Pittsburgh," by Fred Clothey and Ron Hess for the Department of Religious Studies, University of Pittsburgh. These earliest temples were built during the "second wave" of gurus in the United States; for example, at that time Swami Muktananda developed the Siddha Yoga ashram in South Fallsburg, New York. The widespread practice of building Indian-style temples across the United States in the 1980s and 1990s is the context of the "third wave" of female gurus in the United States.

SUGGESTED READINGS

Women in Religion: Feminist Studies and Comparative Studies

Christ, Carol P., and Judith Plaskow, eds. *Womanspirit Rising: A Feminist Reader in Religion*. San Francisco: Harper and Row, 1979.

Eakin, William R., Jay B. McDaniel, and Paula Cooey, eds. *After Patriarchy: Feminist Transformations of the World Religions (Faith Meets Faith)*. Maryknoll, N.Y.: Orbis Books, 1991.

Eck, Diana L., and Devaki Jain, eds. *Speaking of Faith: Global Perspectives on Women, Religion, and Social Change*. Philadelphia: New Society Publishers, 1987.

Eller, Cynthia. *Living in the Lap of the Goddess: The Feminist Spirituality Movement in America*. New York: Crossroad, 1993.

Falk, Nancy Auer, and Rita M. Gross, eds. *Unspoken Worlds: Women's Religious Lives*. Belmont, Cal.: Wadsworth, 1989.

Gedalof, Irene. *Against Purity: Rethinking Identity with Indian and Western Feminisms*. London: Routledge, 1999.

Gross, Rita M. *Feminism and Religion: An Introduction*. Boston: Beacon, 1996.

Haddad, Yvonne Yazbeck, and Ellison Banks Findly, eds. *Women, Religion, and Social Change*. Albany: State University of New York Press, 1985.

King, Ursala. *Women and Spirituality: Voices of Protest and Promise*. University Park: Pennsylvania State University Press, 1993.

———, ed. *Feminist Theology from the Third World: A Reader*. Maryknoll, N.Y.: Orbis, 1994.

———, ed. *Religion and Gender*. Oxford: Blackwell Publishers, 1995.

Nabar, Vrinda. *Caste as Woman*. New Delhi: Penguin Books India, 1995.

Palmer, Susan Jean. *Moon Sisters, Krishna Mothers, Rajneesh Lovers: Women's Roles in New Religions*. Syracuse: Syracuse University Press, 1994.

Ruether, Rosemary, and Catherine Keller, eds. *In Our Own Voices: Four Centuries of American Women's Religious Writing*. San Francisco: Harper and Row, 1995.

Sered, Susan Starr. *Priestess, Mother, Sacred Sister: Religions Dominated by Women*. New York: Oxford University Press, 1994.

Sharma, Arvind, ed. *Today's Woman in World Religions*. Albany: State University of New York Press, 1994.

———, ed. *Women Saints in World Religions*. Albany: State University of New York Press, 2000.

Sharma, Arvind, and Katherine K. Young, eds. *Feminism and World Religions*. Albany: State University of New York Press, 1998.
_____, eds. *The Annual Review of Women in World Religions*. Multivolumed. Albany: State University of New York Press, 1991–.
Wessinger, Catherine, ed. *Women's Leadership in Marginal Religions: Explorations outside the Mainstream*. Urbana: University of Illinois Press, 1993.
Young, Serinity, ed. *An Anthology of Sacred Texts by and about Women*. New York: Crossroads, 1993.
_____, ed. *Encyclopedia of Women and World Religions*. 2 vols. New York: Macmillan Reference, 1999.

Women and the Goddess in Hinduism

Bernard, Elisabeth and Beverley Moon, eds. *Goddesses Who Rule*. New York: Oxford University Press, 2002.
Bose, Mandakranta, ed. *Faces of the Feminine in Ancient, Medieval, and Modern India*. New York: Oxford University Press, 2000.
Brown, C. Mackenzie. *The Devī Gītā: The Song of the Goddess: A Translation, Annotation, and Commentary*. Albany: State University of New York Press, 1998.
Chakravarty, Uma. "The World of the Bhaktin in South Indian Traditions—The Body and Beyond." *Manushi* 50, no. 2 (Jan.–June 1989): 18–29.
Denton, Lynn Teskey. "Varieties of Hindu Female Asceticism." Pp. 211–231 in Julia Leslie, ed., *Roles and Rituals for Hindu Women*. Rutherford, N.J.: Fairleigh Dickinson University Press, 1991.
Falk, Nancy A. "*Shakti* Ascending: Hindu Women, Politics and Religious Leadership During the Nineteenth and Twentieth Centuries." Pp. 298–334 in Robert D. Baird, ed., *Religion in Modern India*. New Delhi: Manohar, 1995.
Feldhaus, Anne. "Bahiṇā Bāī: Wife and Saint." *Journal of the American Academy of Religion* 50, no. 4 (1982): 591–604.
Findly, Ellison Banks. "Gārgī at the King's Court: Women and Philosophic Innovation in Ancient India." Pp. 37–58 in Yvonne Yazbeck Haddad and Ellison Banks Findly, eds., *Women, Religion, and Social Change*. Albany: State University of New York Press, 1985.
Ghanananda, Swami, and Sir John Stewart-Wallace, eds. *Women Saints East and West*. Hollywood, Cal.: Vedanta, [1955] 1979.
Gupta, Lina. "Kali, the Savior." Pp. 15–38 in William Eakin et al., eds., *After Patriarchy: Feminist Transformations of the World Religions*. Maryknoll, N.Y.: Orbis Books, 1991.
Gupta, Sanjukta. "Women in the Śaiva/Śākta Ethos." Pp. 193–209 in Julia Leslie, ed., *Roles and Rituals for Hindu Women*. Rutherford, N.J.: Fairleigh Dickinson University Press, 1991.
Hansen, Kathryn. "Heroic Modes of Women in Indian Myth, Ritual and History: The Tapasvinī and the Vīrāṅganā." Pp. 1–62 in Arvind Sharma and Katherine K. Young, eds., *The Annual Review of Women in World Religions*, vol. 2: *Heroic Women*. Albany: State University of New York Press, 1992.
Hawley, John Stratton, and Mark Juergensmeyer. *Songs of the Saints of India*. Oxford: Oxford University Press, 1988.
Hawley, John Stratton, and Donna Wulff, eds. *Devī: Goddesses of India*. Berkeley: University of California Press, 1996.

Hiltebeitel, Alf, and Kathleen M. Erndl, eds. *Is the Goddess a Feminist?: The Politics of South Asian Goddesses*. New York: New York University Press, 2001.

Khanna, Madhu. "The Goddess-Woman Equation in Śakta Tantras." Pp. 109–123 in Mandakranta Bose, ed., *Faces of the Feminine in Ancient, Medieval, and Modern India*. New York: Oxford University Press, 2000.

King, Ursula. "The Effect of Social Change on Religious Self-Understanding: Women Ascetics in Modern Hinduism." Pp. 69–83 in Kenneth Ballhatchet and David Taylor, eds., *Changing South Asia: Religion and Society*. Volume 1 of papers presented to the Seventh European Conference on Modern South Asian Studies. London: Centre of South Asian Studies, School of Oriental and African Studies, 1984.

Leslie, Julia, ed. *Roles and Rituals for Hindu Women*. Rutherford, N.J.: Fairleigh Dickinson University Press, 1991.

Llewellyn, J. E. "The Autobiography of a Female Renouncer." Pp. 462–472 in Donald S. Lopez, Jr., ed., *Religions of India in Practice*. Princeton: Princeton University Press, 1995.

Madhavananda, Swami, and Ramesh Chandra Majumdar, eds. *Great Women of India*. Mayavati, Almora: Advaita Ashrama, 1982.

McDaniel, June. "A Holy Woman of Calcutta." Pp. 418–425 in Donald S. Lopez, Jr., ed., *Religions of India in Practice*. Princeton: Princeton University Press, 1995.

McDermott, Rachel Fell. *Mother of My Heart, Daughter of My Dreams: Kālī and Umā in the Devotional Poetry of Bengal*. New York: Oxford University Press, 2001.

Muktananda, Swami. *Lalleshwari: Spiritual Poems by a Great Siddha Yogini*. South Fallsburg, N.Y.: SYDA Foundation, 1981.

Narayanan, Vasudha. "Brimming with *Bhakti*, Embodiments of *Shakti*: Devotees, Deities, Performers, Reformers, and Other Women of Power in the Hindu Tradition." Pp. 25–77 in Arvind Sharma and Katherine K. Young, eds., *Feminism and World Religions*. Albany: State University of New York Press, 1999.

———. "The Hindu Tradition." Pp. 12–133 in Willard G. Oxtoby, ed., *World Religions: Eastern Traditions*. Toronto: Oxford University Press, 1996.

Ojha, Catherine. "Feminine Asceticism in Hinduism: Its Tradition and Present Condition." *Man in India* 61, no. 3 (September 1981): 254–285.

Pandharipande, Rajeshwari V. "Janabai: A Woman Saint of India." Pp. 145–179 in Arvind Sharma, ed., *Women Saints in World Religions*. Albany: State University of New York Press, 2000.

Patton, Laurie L., ed. *Jewels of Authority: Women and Textual Tradition in Hindu India*. New York: Oxford University Press, 2002.

Ramanujan, A. K. "On Women Saints." Pp. 316–324 in John Stratton Hawley and Donna Wulff, eds., *The Divine Consort: Rādhā and the Goddesses of India*. Berkeley, Cal.: Graduate Theological Union, 1982.

Ratté Lou. "Goddesses, Mothers, and Heroines: Hindu Women and the Feminine in the Early Nationalist Movement." Pp. 351–376 in Yvonne Yazbeck Haddad and Ellison Banks Findly, eds., *Women, Religion, and Social Change*. Albany: State University of New York Press, 1985.

Robinson, Catherine A. *Tradition and Liberation: The Hindu Tradition in the Indian Women's Movement*. New York: St. Martin, 1999.

Robinson, Sandra P. "Hindu Paradigms of Women: Images and Values." Pp. 181–215 in Yvonne Yazbeck Haddad and Ellison Banks Findly, eds., *Women, Religion, and Social Change*. Albany: State University of New York Press, 1985.

Sinclair-Brull, Wendy. *Female Ascetics: Hierarchy and Purity in an Indian Religious Movement*. Richmond, Surrey: Curzon Press, 1997.

Wadley, Susan S., ed. *The Powers of Tamil Women*. Syracuse: Syracuse University Press, 1980.

Young, Katherine K. "Women in Hinduism." Pp. 77–135 in Arvind Sharma, ed., *Today's Woman in World Religions*. Albany: State University of New York Press, 1994.

The Guru in Hinduism

Babb, Lawrence A. *Redemptive Encounters: Three Modern Styles in the Hindu Tradition*. Berkeley: University of California Press, 1986.

Baumer, Bettina. "The Guru in the Hindu Tradition." *Studies in Formative Spirituality* 11, no. 3 (1990): 341–53.

Clémentin-Ojha, Catherine. "The Tradition of Female Gurus." *Manushi* 6, no. 1 (1985): 2–8.

_____. *La divinité conquise: carrière d'une sainte*. Nanterre: Société d'Ethnologie, 1990.

Conway, Timothy. *Women of Power and Grace: Nine Astonishing, Inspiring Luminaries of Our Time*. Santa Barbara: Wake Up Press, 1994.

Dhavamony, Mariasusai. "The Guru in Hinduism." *Studia Missionalia* 36 (1987): 147–74.

Fort, Andrew O. and Patricia Y. Mumme, eds. *Living Liberation in Hindu Thought*. Albany: State University of New York Press, 1996.

Gold, Daniel. *The Lord as Guru: Hindi Sants in North Indian Tradition*. New York: Oxford University Press, 1987.

_____. *Comprehending the Guru: Toward a Grammar of Religious Perception*. Atlanta: Scholars Press, 1988.

Hallstrom, Lisa Lassell. *Mother of Bliss: Ānandamayī Mā (1896–1982)*. New York: Oxford University Press, 1999.

Johnsen, Linda. *Daughters of the Goddess: The Women Saints of India*. St. Paul, Minn.: Yes International, 1994.

Kripal, Jeffrey J. "Inside-Out, Outside-In: Existential Place and Academic Practice in the Study of North-American Guru Traditions." *Religious Studies Review* 25, no. 3 (July 1999): 233–238.

Manring, Rebecca. "At Home in the World: The Lives of Sītādevī." *International Journal of Hindu Studies* 2, no. 1 (April 1998): 21–42.

McDaniel, June. *The Madness of the Saints: Ecstatic Religion in Bengal*. Chicago: University of Chicago Press, 1989.

_____. "The Embodiment of God among the Bauls of Bengal." *Journal of Feminist Studies in Religion* 8 no. 2 (1992): 27–39.

McKean, Lise. *Divine Enterprise: Gurus and the Hindu Nationalist Movement*. Chicago: University of Chicago Press, 1996.

Mlecko, Joel D. "The Guru in Hindu Tradition." *Numen* 29, fasc. 1 (1982): 33–61.

Padoux, André "The Tantric Guru." Pp.41–51 in David Gordon White, ed., *Tantra in Practice*. Princeton: Princeton University Press, 2000.

Pujyaśri Chandraśedharendra Sarasvati Swami. *The Guru Tradition*. Bombay: Bharatiya Vidya Bhavan, 1991.

Sooklal, Anil. "The Guru-Shishya Parampara: A Paradigm of Religio-Cultural Continuity." *Journal for the Study of Religion* (Association for the Study of Religion, Southern Africa) 3 (September 1990): 15–30.

White, Charles S. J. "Mother Guru: Jnanananda of Madras, India." Pp.15–24 in Nancy Auer Falk and Rita M. Gross, eds., *Unspoken Worlds: Women's Religious Lives*. Belmont, Cal.: Wadsworth, 1989.

Hinduism in the West

Clarke, Colin, Ceri Peach, and Steven Vertovec, eds. *South Asians Overseas: Migration and Ethnicity*. Cambridge: Cambridge University Press, 1990.

Coward, Howard, John R. Hinnells, and Raymond Brady Williams, eds. *The South Asian Religious Diaspora in Britain, Canada and the United States*. Albany: State University of New York Press, 2000.

Cox, Harvey. *Turning East: The Promise and Peril of the New Orientalism*. New York: Simon and Schuster, 1977.

Eck, Diana L. *A New Religious America: How a "Christian Country" Has Become the World's Most Religiously Diverse Nation*. San Francisco: Harper San Francisco, 2001.

———. "On Common Ground: World Religions in America." CD–ROM. New York: Columbia University Press, 1997.

Ellwood, Robert S. *Religious and Spiritual Groups in Modern America*. Englewood Cliffs, N.J.: Prentice-Hall, 1973.

Fenton, John Y. *Transplanting Religious Traditions: Asian Indians in America*. New York: Praeger, 1988.

Hutchinson, Brian. "The Divine-Human Figure in the Transmission of Religious Tradition." Pp.92–124 in Raymond Brady Williams, ed., *A Sacred Thread: Modern Transmission of Hindu Traditions in India and Abroad*. Chambersburg, Pa.: Anima, 1992.

Iwamura, Jane Naomi, and Paul Spickard, eds. *Revealing the Sacred in Asian and Pacific America*. New York: Routledge, 2003.

Leonard, Karen Isaksen. *The South Asian Americans*. Westport, Conn.: Greenwood Publishing, 1997.

Lessinger, Johanna. *From the Ganges to the Hudson: Indian Immigrants in New York City*. Boston: Allyn and Bacon, 1995.

Sharpe, Eric J. "Some Western Interpretations of the Bhagavad Gītā, 1785–1885." Pp. 65–85 in Peter Slater and Donald Wiebe, eds., *Traditions in Contact and Change*. Waterloo, Ont.: Wilfrid Laurier University Press, 1983.

Tweed, Thomas A., and Stephen Prothero. *Asian Religions in America: A Documentary History*. New York: Oxford University Press, 1999.

Vivekananda, Swami. "Hinduism." Pp.968–978 in John Henry Barrows, ed., *The World's Parliament of Religions*. Vol. 2. Chicago: Parliament Publishing, 1893.

Wessinger, Catherine. "Woman Guru, Woman Roshi: The Legitimation of Female Religious Leadership in Hindu and Buddhist Groups in America." Pp. 125–146 in *Women's Leadership in Marginal Religions*. Urbana: University of Illinois Press, 1993.

Williams, Raymond Brady. *Religions of Immigrants from India and Pakistan: New Threads in the American Tapestry*. Cambridge: Cambridge University Press, 1988.

———, ed. *A Sacred Thread: Modern Transmission of Hindu Traditions in India and Abroad*. Chambersburg, Pa.: Anima, 1992.

I

Sita Devi, an Early Vaishnava Guru

Rebecca J. Manring

The little over a century since Vivekananda's visit to the first Parliament of World Religions, held in Chicago in 1893, has seen a steady stream of South Asian gurus pouring in to the United States. Prior to this influx, Americans untrained in Indic languages who were interested in "Hinduism" had to rely on the often bewildered writings of foreign colonizers, or on the words of such spiritual pilgrims—still outsider to the traditions they described—as Paul Brunton and Helena Blavatsky. Some of the newly immigrant teachers came as envoys from their own gurus, and some were attracted by the promise of greater material comforts and more relaxed social conventions than they had known in India. Some belonged to long-established lineages, and some were "freelancers." Others came at the behest of American seekers who had the means to bring them home. Conspicuous by their nearly complete absence among these gurus, however, were women. And yet if we dig deeply into Sanskrit religious literature, we can and do find evidence for the presence of female teachers. From the Buddha's first nun Mahaprajapati to Queen Chudala of the *Yoga Vasishtha*, there are a few—admittedly a very few—feminine voices to be heard.

Gaudiya Vaishnavism traveled to the United States in the late 1960s with the late Swami A. C. Bhaktivedanta Prabhupada (1896–1977). Prabhupada transplanted his branch of the movement (which he named the International Society for Krishna Consciousness, or ISKCON) in toto, bringing what struck young Americans of the time as a very conservative code of personal morality along with his devotional teachings. He and his students not only followed the daily ritual schedule but adhered to the Bengali monastic dress code and standards of personal hygiene, and even ate, to the extent possible in a much colder climate, the same foods Prabhupada and his family enjoyed in Kolkatta. Thus it is hardly surprising that, in accord with sectarian teachings, Prabhupada also insisted that women belonged in the kitchen and at the back of the temple, and certainly never in the forefront of religious or community activities. In time, though, some long-term ISKCON members have begun to search for female voices in their adopted religion's history.[1] This search is apparent from titles of articles appearing in the past two decades in *Back to Godhead*, the glossy monthly magazine published by ISKCON, and from somewhat more scholarly articles in the *ISKCON Communications Journal*. Kunti, mother of the Pandavas, the heroes of India's national epic the *Mahabharata*, has long been held as a role model for ISKCON women, but now a number of these women have begun to seek someone more recent to emulate, or perhaps someone whose life more closely parallels the life female ISKCON devotees have chosen. In Sita Devi, wife of one of the founding triumvirate of Gaudiya Vaishnavism, they may have found the model they were seeking.[2] Thus it is only very recently that Prabhupada's followers, since his death now spread among a number of splinter groups, have discovered their spiritual foremothers. Sita Devi constitutes the anchor for the project of this volume, and in her refusal to defy feminine stereotypes and roles of her time and station, she will differ significantly from many of those to follow.

A complicating factor in the emergence of knowledge about earlier women devotees was Prabhupada's strong recommendation that his disciples read only "authorized" translations of Indian texts, authorized either by Prabhupada himself or by his immediate guru. The list of sanctioned texts was a very short one, so most ISKCON members were not well informed about Indian literature that might, to scholars, seem relevant to their interests.[3] Further, because the lineage of Advaita Acharya (elder statesman and herald of the new brand of Vaishnavism, married to Sita Devi), like Nityananda's, is parallel to but somewhat separate from Chaitanya's, from which Prabhupada claimed descent for his ISKCON, members of his young movement would not have had access to such peripheral and hitherto untranslated works as *Sita Charitra* (to be discussed below).[4] And consequently Sita has had virtually no impact in the New World.

The Vaishnava movement in Bengal has probably generated the most voluminous body of hagiographical literature in South Asia, beginning during Chaitanya's own lifetime and continuing to the present day. Gaudiya Vaishnavism came to be so called because this devotional stream arose in northeastern India in the area now known as Bengal, historically called Gauda, and now divided between the nation of Bangladesh and the Indian state of West Bengal. Though the movement derives its name from that of the god Vishnu, this variety of Vaishnavism, unlike many of the others that developed in other parts of the subcontinent, places Krishna in the supreme position as the ultimate reality, and relegates Vishnu to subsidiary status as a minor manifestation of Krishna. Gaudiya Vaishnavism does not have, nor has it ever had, a central authority. The movement has come down through history through several parallel lineages descending from its ecstatic founder Chaitanya (1486–1533), Chaitanya's right-hand man and elder Advaita Acharya (purportedly ca. 1434–1559), his left-hand man Nityananda (ca. 1473–mid sixteenth century), and a few other first-generation leaders.[5] Thus doctrinal competition seems not to have been a factor in the spread of Gaudiya Vaishnavism, though there has been a certain amount of vying for numbers of followers.[6] The Advaita Acharya lineage, for example, has produced more literature than any other branch except that of Chaitanya himself, perhaps in response to its dwindling numbers and perhaps also motivated by a fear that their leader would lose his place in history as their branch faded away. To ensure that Advaita Acharya maintained his pivotal position even as the numbers of his descendants receded, they generated accounts of his life, and that of his primary wife, full of tales of majesty and mystery that no one would easily forget. Hagiographies of such figures, perhaps more than those of religious leaders whose status remains unchanged through time, allow us to develop a reasonable idea of what the writers of the biographies were concerned with at a given point in their own religious history. Biographies of Chaitanya were the first to appear, with works on Advaita Acharya, his forerunner, showing up shortly thereafter. Some time later biographies of Nityananda and the leaders of the second and third generations also appeared.

Specific women do appear frequently in the Chaitanya biographies, but these women do not play major roles. The women discussed are clearly important to the lead figures in the works but take no part in shaping sectarian policy or dogma. Chaitanya's mother Shachi and his second wife Vishnupriya, for example, are consistently portrayed as dutiful women, fulfilling all the expected obligations of social positions narrowly defined by their relationships to Chaitanya.[7] After his renunciation, Chaitanya seems to have done his best to avoid contact with women to whom he was not related, and according to his definitive biography, the *Chaitanya Charitamrita* (3.2.101–164), actually banished one devotee from his presence after that man had begged some special rice for Chaitanya from a woman.[8] And after Chaitanya's death, his mother and his widow both properly retreated into seclusion, never again to be seen in public.

Similarly, in the Advaita Acharya corpus certain women receive frequent mention because of their relationships with notable men: Shachi, Vishnupriya, Jahnavi (wife of Nityananda, the third member of the founding triumvirate), and of course Sita Devi.[9]

This article will discuss Sita Devi, one sanctioned, premodern South Asian female guru, in the attempt to ground this volume solidly in India's past. I hope thereby to demonstrate that the current seeming profusion of female gurus in the West is not merely the product of contemporary feminist indignation (though such feelings may play a part in these gurus' ability to attract western female followers today), nor entirely culturally anomalous, but a phenomenon, however unusual, backed by centuries of history.

Sita Devi, senior wife of Advaita Acharya, elder statesman of the Gaudiya Vaishnava movement, is one of the earliest female gurus in South Asia for whom we have literary evidence. Sita, whose husband was the leader of an ostensibly conservative wing of the movement, became de facto leader of that subgroup after her husband's death in the mid-sixteenth century. Her leadership constituted the next stage in that particular Gaudiya Vaishnava lineage which continues, through the couple's second son Krishna Mishra, to the present day in Shantipur, West Bengal.[10] She occupies a significant if problematic role in Gaudiya Vaishnavism as its first female leader.[11]

We know of her mostly through two works describing her teaching career, Lokanatha Dasa's *Sita Charitra* and Vishnu Dasa's *Sita Guna Kadamba*, and the two lengthy hagiographical treatments of her husband, Ishana Nagara's *Advaita Prakasha* and Haricarana Dasa's *Advaita Mangala*.[12] Gaudiya writers unanimously hail her husband Advaita Acharya as the instrumental cause for the advent of Krishna Chaitanya,[13] and the relationship between those two men makes Sita, by association (and aside from anything she may have done independently), a legitimate member of the group. *Except for the fact that she was not a man.* All of the literature that discusses Sita in any detail is clearly wrestling with its authors' perceived need to account for a strong leader who did not fit previously established models of leadership, and whose authority might therefore be questioned.

How then do the various texts talk about Sita Devi? The little description of Sita found in the Chaitanya biographies centers around her culinary skills. But the literature devoted to Sita and Advaita shows her vital role in the newly developing movement on several different levels, usually in metaphorical terms. Krishnadasa Kaviraja, author of the *Chaitanya Charitamrita*, explains repeatedly that one of Krishna's reasons for taking birth in this age (as Chaitanya) was to taste the sweetness that Krishna's favorite consort Radha enjoys in his embrace. Many view Chaitanya as a dual embodiment of both Krishna and Radha. Chaitanya introduced a new variety of devotionalism into what was already a dualistic religion that places great importance on the individual's personal relationship with the divine. Erotic love is the most intimate among all possible human relationships. Chaitanya urged his followers to grow as close as humanly possible to their lord, envisioning him as their divine lover. Advaita Acharya, however, as a member of the "old school," is usually described as worshiping from a more distant vantage point. This representative of the old guard of brahmanical scholarship and praxis stands not only first in the history of Gaudiya Vaishnavism but also at the head of a continuum of devotionalism that describes the range of possible attitudes toward Krishna. This continuum of devotion begins with the majestic (*aishvarya*) and then progresses through servitude (*dasya*), friendship (*sakhya*), parental affection (*vatsalya*), and finally, erotic sweetness (*madhurya*), the relationship embodied in the androgynous incarnation of Radha and Krishna in the single body of Chaitanya.

Some schemas also include *shanta*, peace or serenity, between *aishvarya* and *dasya*. Each successive point on the continuum includes all previous points, so that all possible relationships to the divine are contained in the erotic relationship.

Different members of the first generation of Gaudiyas relate to Krishna, and to Chaitanya, in different ways, illustrating the various types of relationship available to them. Advaita Acharya is usually depicted firmly and respectably at the *aishvarya* point, and will usher in Chaitanya, who as the physical embodiment of Krishna with the emotional makeup of Radha, stands at its opposite extreme along the continuum. And because Advaita is the agent responsible for Krishna's, that is to say, Chaitanya's, advent in Kali Yuga, and is in a sense the point of origin for the new movement, he must stand at the starting point of that continuum.

Advaita's wife, his female counterpart, must not only be similarly irreproachable but must also have a compatible theological identity, as the two function together to form the base of the new structure created by Chaitanya. Each of the authors of works treating Advaita or Sita describes this partnership in his own terms, all based on sectarian doctrine. Let us begin with Advaita's own status within the movement.

Advaita Acharya seems to have been a charismatic figure. The texts tell us he was constantly bringing some new and interesting acquaintance home for dinner. And he had a sizeable following of his own in the young community. Judging by the number of residences he maintained in two or three separate cities, and the huge feasts he frequently offered to the other devotees, Advaita Acharya was a wealthy man. His household would have included many servants as well as his family members. As his wife, Sita would have been largely responsible for supervising employees and keeping the house running smoothly. These duties would have fallen to the wife of any wealthy pillar of the community, and there is nothing remarkable about her fulfilling them properly.

The hagiographical corpus tells us that Advaita Acharya lived a long time.[14] Although he married a rather young woman quite late in his own life, Sita would have been well beyond her childbearing years when her husband died. Throughout her married life she seems to have remained in her husband's shadow politically. She performed all the proper wifely duties, raised the couple's six sons, fed the family and frequent large numbers of guests—but never, so far as we know, took any sort of active role in the theological or political activities of the new movement during her husband's lifetime.

Haricarana Dasa, author of the *Advaita Mangala*, describes Sita as an extraordinary individual, claiming her to be the goddess Lakshmi. Lakshmi, goddess of wealth, is the consort of Mahavishnu, with whom Advaita Acharya has been identified in that text.[15] Mahavishnu, the Great God Vishnu, is for most Vaishnavas (those outside of Bengal) the supreme being and source of all other divine incarnations. It is entirely fitting for the man responsible for the arrival of Chaitanya/Krishna in the new age to be identified as the source of all. Chaitanya's teachings will then place Krishna in that supreme position, replacing Mahavishnu, but first his advent itself needs to be accounted for. This parallel assertion is deliberate and significant, for Mahavishnu and his wife are awesome representations of divinity, majestic and unapproachable, as the continuum of devotion discussed above illustrates. Their entrance into the phenomenal world of necessity precedes that of the more approachable and adorable child Krishna, whom his devotees worship in friendship, with parental affection, or, ultimately, in an erotic relationship.

Although Haricarana reports nothing out of the ordinary regarding Sita's birth aside from its being heralded with music and joy, Ishana Nagara describes the birth as a supernatural event in chapter 8 of his *Advaita Prakasha*. Ishana writes that the fragrance of lotuses (sacred to Vishnu) drew the pious Brahmin Nrisimha Bhadudi to a marsh, where he decided to pick some of them to offer to Vishnu in his morning worship. But as he began to gather the blossoms, Nrisimha noticed one particularly beautiful flower, gleaming like gold and with a hundred petals. A tiny girl sat in the middle of this lotus, emitting streams of light. He recognized this child as Lakshmi and took her home with him, lotus and all. He and his wife raised this child as their daughter, along with their biological daughter Shri, born that same day.[16]

Later, in the section leading up to the marriage of Advaita and Sita, Ishana gives us some further theological postulations. He identifies Sita as Paurnamasi and as Yogamaya, clear indications that she is mythologically suited, indeed, intended, to be Advaita Acharya's wife. Both identifications show her theological relationship to and suitability for her husband, as well as her position vis-à-vis Krishna, now embodied as Chaitanya. Paurnamasi is the old woman in Vraja who arranges the secret trysts of Radha and Krishna that epitomize the intense and intimately passionate relationship with the divine which the Gaudiyas advocate. That is, Paurnamasi is the individual who brings Krishna and Radha together, a union that ultimately produces the androgynous dual incarnation known as Chaitanya. This assertion of Ishana's is metaphorically consistent so long as we view Advaita and Sita as a unit, with Sita functioning as a part of her husband in causing Krishna's birth in this time and place.

Yogamaya is the personification of Krishna's magical powers, who always precedes him into the world. Both characters are essential to Krishna's activities, and both are older than Krishna. Thus Sita is the perfect mate for the older man who will eventually invoke Krishna to take birth in Nadiya. Ishana also has Advaita deliberately reveal (with the unmistakable imagery of his four-armed form, seated on a crystal throne in a huge palace) his own majestic nature in this episode, thereby sanctioning the match Nrisimha is initially hesitant to allow for his daughters. The Krishna with whom devotees are encouraged to form an erotic attachment is the two-armed Krishna (for how can mere mortals attain true intimacy with someone who does not at least appear to be human?). Yet Advaita, who represents the earlier notion of god as distant and awe-inspiring, from time to time displays the appropriate (to his position) and clearly nonhuman four-armed form. Advaita had already admitted his own ambivalence about marriage when his friends first broached the subject, but in both Ishana's and Haricarana's accounts, his reluctance to wed dissolves.[17] Briefly put, in Haricarana's story he simply falls in love, while in Ishana's his theophany confirms the theological appropriateness of the match.

The authors usually depict Sita in the same majestic mode as her husband.

On one occasion, Haricarana Dasa tells us, Sita's hair came unbound while she was serving food to an assembly of Vaishnavas.[18] But since her hands were full with the serving dishes, she could not tie her hair back. Two extra hands appeared to take care of the problem, and then disappeared again, and she continued to serve her guests as if nothing unusual had occurred. In displaying this four-armed form, Sita revealed herself to be Ishvari (the female counterpart to Advaita's majestic Ishvara). Advaita, Haricarana writes, explained his wife's display by announcing that he himself had been Krishna in Vraja. However, the Krishna of Vraja never appears in majestic form in the company of Radha, whose relationship with Krishna is the closest possible human relationship. Sita does not appear in this episode as Radha, whom we expect to find with Krishna in Vraja, but as Ishvari; why then does Haricarana have Advaita announce himself the Krishna of Vraja in response?

Vaishnavas recognize Chaitanya as the playful Krishna of Vraja, the one who has marvelous adventures with the cowherd boys and erotic interludes with the cowherd girls. The author is making the dramatic assertion through this equation that Advaita is Chaitanya's theological equal! If Advaita proclaims himself to be the same Krishna as Chaitanya, then Krishna is incarnating not only serially (to prepare the way for his eventual full appearance) but, remarkably, completely, rather than in progressively greater increments, with the arrival of each successive partial manifestation. Although Vaishnavas would agree that there are no limitations to what god can do, including producing multiple selves that coexist temporally, few would consider Advaita the theological equal of Chaitanya. And yet, according to Vaishnava thinking, had it not been for Advaita's prolonged efforts to force Krishna to take birth in Nadiya at that particular time and place, Chaitanya might not have been born at all. One could argue, as I believe Haricarana comes dangerously close to doing, that Advaita is therefore even more important than Chaitanya, since without him there would have been no call (literally) for a Chaitanya. Haricarana cannot make such an assertion directly, as to do so would approach heresy, and so he must use this oblique technique to make his claim.

Let us now examine Haricarana Dasa's treatment of Radha vis-à-vis Advaita. The author repeatedly equates Sita with Radha, but not with Radha as we usually envision her in Vraja. Immediately following the hair-tying episode described above, Advaita announces that he had pledged to bring Radha and Krishna, together in a single body, to Navadvipa. Haricarana has thus asserted that Krishna first incarnated in Advaita (who then became a condition for Chaitanya's advent), and so implies that he was necessarily accompanied by Radha in the form of Sita, because Krishna never incarnates without his female counterpart. But whereas Radha is usually associated with erotic love, Haricarana's assertion of Sita as Radha is clearly something different, situated as Sita must be at the distant, majestic point at the other end of the devotional spectrum. We find a follow-up assertion later on, at another feast, when multiple Sitas are serving the guests, much as multiple Krishnas had danced with the cowherd girls in the moonlight of the famous circle dance described in Book 10 chapters 29–33 of the *Bhagavata Purana*, a seminal text for all of the

Vaishnava devotional traditions. Chaitanya comments on this occasion that few people realize Radha's majesty,[19] but that this present group has been granted a rare vision of that aspect of her divinity for themselves. And this is as it should be, and fits the overall scheme, for *that* Radha—the majestic one—is indeed the appropriate partner for Advaita Acharya, the first Krishna to enter the scene. Chaitanya seems to be reversing the direction of the continuum, and placing a majestic Radha at its head. The metaphor is now clear.

Ishana Nagara in his *Advaita Prakasha* has much more to say about Sita than does Haricarana in his *Advaita Mangala.* Ishana portrays Sita simultaneously as the perfect brahman housewife and as a divine manifestation. As the perfect housewife, Sita not only fulfills the customary obligations of a woman of her social class but she also demonstrates through her behavior that she understands and accepts this traditional role. Sita's acquiescence to social expectations forms the base for her character in Ishana's work. Her exemplary domesticity anchors her firmly in respectability, just as her husband's erudition did for him, and provides a parallelism in the images of the couple. Once Ishana has clearly established Sita as a proper brahman woman who knows her place in society, he can then establish her as divine and capable of extraordinary feats and roles. Yet at no time does Sita abandon her societally sanctioned role as she expands into other realms.

In both the Advaita Acharya hagiographies, Sita's remarkable abilities are in evidence only until she is married. She also appears in other Gaudiya Vaishnava works, where every author emphasizes her culinary abilities but has little else to say about her. In the two works dedicated to her, however, she continues to function on supranormal levels even after her marriage. Sita is there identified with Lakshmi, as she is in both *Advaita Prakasha* and *Advaita Mangala*, and as a goddess, she is clearly no ordinary housewife.[20] Later in life, after she is widowed, when she announces to two male would-be disciples that she can only teach other women, she acknowledges her social limitations, and her divine power is again contained: it is limited to the female realm.

Although sectarian records mention no women among the leaders of the first generation of Gaudiya Vaishnavas, Sita's occupation of such a venerated position in and of itself seems not particularly problematic for the Gaudiyas.[21] We can easily imagine that the many students who regularly frequented Advaita Acharya's home would have become accustomed to seeing Sita Devi, and would probably have treated her with the respect and deference, and affection, they would show their own mothers. The author of the *Advaita Mangala* even describes the first feast Advaita Acharya held after his marriage, to introduce his disciples to his new wife. The texts in fact state that Sita treated these boys and young men as if they were her own sons. And so it would not have been much of a stretch for these students to take the next leap of faith, once their guru had departed, to align themselves with the person who was closest to that guru in some clearly visible ways—his widow. That is apparently exactly what happened: Her husband's students, her foster sons, in a sense, shifted her into the position of authority recently vacated by her husband.[22] What seems to have bothered the Gaudiyas is the possibility of her conferring initiation upon

male devotees. Initiation—the conferring of sectarian mantras and practices—
is the vehicle for the continuity of the lineage, and has historically been the
domain of male gurus. (Apparently her initiating female students would not
raise hackles, and when she tells would-be disciples that she can only provide
spiritual instruction to other women, this suggests that she actually did so.)

According to Lokanatha Dasa's *Sita Charitra*, her problems begin when
two male seekers—Yajneshvara and Nandarama—approach her for instruction, and she is obligated to refuse them on gender grounds.[23] Their story is
rich in clues to Sita's theological identity and the ways her movement chose
to accommodate and contain that identity.

Nandarama is a brahman, and his friend Yajneshvara is a shudra (the
fourth major caste group) from a farming family.[24] Both are great devotees of
Krishna, and have decided to seek out a suitable guru. Nandarama remembers
having been given a mantra some time previously by Sita, in Shantipur, so the
pair set out in search of her. Sita greets them warmly, but tells them that she
can only teach other women. Nevertheless she gives them the Radha mantra
and some rudimentary advice: to worship Radha and Krishna, visualizing
themselves as attendants in the divine couple's trysting place. Apparently gender is of greater significance than caste, because Sita, a brahman, again reminds them of her inability to teach men, but seems to have no qualms about
Yajneshvara's lowly shudra status.[25]

The two disappear, only to reappear a short time later dressed as *gopis*, the
young cowherd women of Vraja who were Krishna's close friends and lovers,
complete with braided hair, anklets, bangles, skirts and bodices. They announce that the practice of repeating Radha's mantra has effected a sex change
in them. This is an amazing claim! We have no reports of others who use
Radha's mantra experiencing similar transformations. We must conclude then
that this change has come about through the pair's deep faith and their firm
conviction that Sita is the proper guru for them. Not satisfied simply to take
their word that the two men are now women, Sita examines the evidence,
Lokanatha writes, and then agrees that she can now instruct them. And from
this time on Nandarama and Yajneshvara are known as Nandini and Jangali,
and live out the remainders of their lives as women. So great was their devotion
and their desire to learn from Sita rather than from any other guru that these
two were willing to relinquish their very maleness to do so. In a culture where
women are by definition inferior to men, this is no small matter.

In fact, however, seemingly transgressive gender roles are to a point normative in the Gaudiya tradition, some of whose advocates take the notion of
Krishna as the only male in Vrindavan quite literally. These practitioners follow
the model of Krishna in the above-mentioned *rasa lila*, the circle dance under
the full moon during which the god projected himself in such a way that each
of the thousands of young women dancing in the meadow believed herself
alone to be partnering Krishna. Since Krishna is the supreme being, and the
highest relationship to be cultivated with him is the erotic one, and since we
are operating within a heterosexual world view, all of Krishna's devotees must
necessarily be female. Most of the male devotees are content to accomplish

this merely by visualizing themselves as female participants in Krishna's eternal activities. Many Gaudiyas practice *manjari sadhana*, visualizing themselves as members of the inner circle of Radha's and Krishna's very young female companions (the *manjaris*, or flower buds) who wait on the divine couple during their erotic encounters.

Other groups engage in more overt expressions of femininity. One such, the *sakhi bhavas*, adopt the mood and manners of Radha's girlfriends (her *sakhis*). The *sakhi bhavas*, however, carry the imagery far beyond mere visualization, dressing and behaving as women throughout their lives. Some even sacrifice their physical *purushatvam* (maleness) by castration to do so. Sectarian lore considers Jangali and Nandini, whose sexual identities through Vaishnava literature are mysteriously ambiguous, to have been the first *sakhi bhava* practitioners.

We can never say with certainty that Sita is the deliberate founder of this Gaudiya offshoot, the *sakhi bhavas*. This marginal group, its membership consisting entirely of originally male practitioners who live as women, however, has chosen to name Sita Devi, an archetypically proper brahman housewife, as their leader and founder. The *sakhi bhavas* clearly found it useful to appropriate her name and identity to themselves, and their doing so strengthens the claim that these devotees of Krishna comprise a group of female worshipers, for, as we have already seen, Sita very properly refused to instruct men. That very appropriation as an act of legitimation demonstrates the high regard in which Sita Devi has been held over the centuries.

The descriptions of Sita are in every case written by men who were intimately linked to their contemporary Gaudiya Vaishnava power structures, and probably all writing with political agendas of their own. This leads one to suspect that Sita had indeed enjoyed an amount of sectarian power herself and that other devotees, formerly attached to her late husband, aligned themselves with her following her husband's death. This shift may have been perceived as a threat to the rest of the Gaudiya Vaishnava community and would help to explain the emphasis on Sita's "proper" statement that she can instruct only women. Limiting her teachings to one group (a group that has virtually no role in the larger community) effectively contains the power that her hagiographers describe. Conveniently, artificial women—that is, men who perform their worship of Krishna in female guise, either through meditative visualization or in actual physical manifestation—are considered proper devotees of Krishna.[26] Perhaps Sita's male followers were thus forced to choose subversive means to maintain their relationship with their guru by disguising themselves as women. We have no material mentioning her connections with any female disciples, nor do we know how many men, if any, followed the example set by Jangali and Nandini. Surely Sita had women among her circle of devotees, though clearly none of them rose to any prominence.

The issue further suggests continued communal discomfort over leadership at the (uncertain) time these works were produced, as evidenced by the different agendas we find in the different works. The author of the *Advaita Prakasha* writes to establish the legitimacy of a particular lineage through Advaita's second son, citing Sita's mythological birth and identity with Lakshmi as part of his proof. The author of the *Sita Charitra*, writing at a time when the *sakhi bhavas* were coming under sectarian assault, used Sita's hagiographical image to define the *sakhi bhavas* as women and then to connect their sect to a venerable branch of the greater Gaudiya Vaishnava community.

In conclusion, let us recap some of the issues under consideration in this volume. Sita Devi is clearly affiliated with an important lineage in a widely recognized tradition. In fact the very unorthodox *sakhi bhavas* appear to have made use of that status in their own attempts at sectarian legitimation. Sita was a married woman, mother of several sons, and was living as any other householder. And of course she did not remarry after her husband's death. Sita Devi's followers, like those of many others described in this volume, did identify her with a specific goddess.

Second, attention is drawn to her gender, and in fact her gender was problematic for the Vaishnavas in Bengal. Later writers had to find a way to talk about her that would make it clear that her case is very unusual, lest other women develop similar aspirations.

Her documented leadership role is not intended to provide a model for other women in the Gaudiya Vaishnava community, but female devotees are exhorted rather to emulate her devoted service to her family. And although she was permitted to provide religious instruction to other women, she was not preparing these women to serve a function similar to her own within the community. Sita had no message of her own to propagate, and is consistently portrayed as merely carrying on her husband's mission of spreading the joint worship of Radha-Krishna. She was not bucking the system, but merely fulfilling an obligation that had landed on her shoulders unsought, and she did so, apparently, in ways intended to attract as little attention as possible. Sita Devi, or at least the Sita Devi of literature, is an early example of a female guru who remained firmly planted in the Gaudiya Vaishnava tradition, despite the anomaly of the role in which she found herself.

NOTES

1. During most of ISKCON's history in the United States, the vast majority of initiated members, as well as noninitiated regular participants in temple services, were Americans of European or African heritage. In the last decade, however, many diaspora Hindu families have joined ISKCON congregations, largely as a means to ensure that their children are exposed to their own religious heritage. This phenomenon appears at the same time as increasing interest among the same community in temple construction, and usually in cities where there is no other Hindu temple.

2. The word *devi*, or goddess, is often attached to a woman's name as a courtesy title. In some sectarian literature the wife of Advaita Acharya is also called Sita Thakurani, or Mrs. Sita. The word *thakurani* denotes a female brahman. A more detailed treatment of Sita Devi can be found in my article, "At Home in the World: The Lives of Sita Devi."

3. Since Prabhupada's death, a number of ISKCON members have undertaken

serious study of Sanskrit and other Indian languages, and several have earned Ph.D.s in religious studies in various universities. Their efforts have led to the translations of more Gaudiya Vaishnava texts. All of these that I have seen, however, show the standard ISKCON tendency to meld translation with commentary, a style that makes it difficult for the neophyte to recognize what is original text and what is the translator's or editor's own commentary.

4. In point of fact, it would appear that Prabhupada's lineage comes through Nityananda. Prabhupada's guru Kedarnath Dutta Bhaktivinode received his initiation from Bipin Bihari Gosvami, a grandson of Vamshivadana Thakura. Bipin Bihari was at the time head of the Baghnapada Vaishnavas, a group established in the late sixteenth century by Ramachandra Gosvami. This Ramachandra was a foster child of Jahnava (sometimes called Jahnavi) Devi, wife of Nityananda. Hence it makes more sense to derive Prabhupada's spiritual heritage from Nityananda than from Chaitanya himself. Since Prabhupada's death his movement has splintered, and it is certainly possible that one or more of these newer groups may trace itself to Advaita's branch of Chaitanya's "tree," though I am not aware of any to do so. Tony Stewart kindly directed me to the works of Kānanvihārī Gosvāmī (*Bāghanāpāra-Sampradāya o Vaiṣṇava Sāhitya*), and Bruce D. Marvin ("The Life and Thought of Kedarnath Dutta Bhaktivinode") on this subject.

5. Krishnadasa Kaviraja in his *Chaitanya Charitamrita* repeatedly uses the metaphor of a tree whose trunk is Chaitanya and whose branches are Chaitanya's various lieutenants, with their followers as the leaves growing from their respective branches. My description is based on the iconography, which usually depicts the three with Chaitanya in the center, Nityananda on his left, and Advaita on his right. I must also mention that Nityananda is often associated, at least in popular imagination, with left-hand, or impure, practices, whereas Advaita is always the bastion of propriety for the group.

6. As Tony Stewart has pointed out in "Strategies of Persuasion," Gaudiya Vaishnavism has always been characterized by its strategy of nonconfrontation and noncontradiction, with the result that a place is made for everyone. The various lineages produced their own hagiographies, both of Chaitanya and of their own leader, and so each such text reflects a different *parampara*, or guru-disciple lineage.

7. Chaitanya's first wife, Lakshmi (Lakshmipriya), died not long after their marriage.

8. See Edward C. Dimock, Jr., *Caitanya Caritāmṛta of Kṛṣṇadāsa Kavirāja*, and Tony K. Stewart, *The Final Word*. The *Chaitanya Charitamrita* not only became the official word on the life of Chaitanya but, equally important, set out what was involved in being a proper Vaishnava. With its characteristic citation from previous sources, the text effectively tells the reader what other works and writers are to be considered "authentic" and bear the sectarian seal of approval. Conversely, omitted texts and authors are denied this official sanction.

9. Jahnavi was a much younger woman than Sita (her husband was about the same age as Chaitanya) and is similarly credited with having taken over for her husband after his death. Some people confuse Sita Devi with Jahnavi Devi, perhaps because of their similar positions with respect to Gaudiya Vaishnava founding fathers.

10. A small town in Nadiya District, about ninety kilometers north of Kolkatta.

11. She shares this position to some extent with Jahnavi Devi.

12. Since I was unable to obtain a copy of the *Sita Guna Kadamba*, that text will not be discussed herein.

13. Gaudiya Vaishnava authors tell us that the elderly scholar had from a young age been very disturbed by what he perceived to be a state of areligiousness and chaos

that prevailed in the region. He performed rigourous austerities and rituals to attract Krishna's attention and force him to take birth in Bengal to remedy the situation.

14. Ishana Nagara, the author of the *Advaita Prakasha*, claims that Advaita Acharya lived to the age of 125, an apparently standard attestation not necessarily to be taken literally.

15. Advaita has also been identified as Ishvara and as Sadashiva. For a more detailed discussion of these theological identifications, see chapter 2 of my *Reconstructing Tradition*, forthcoming from Columbia University Press.

16. Shri was also married to Advaita, along with her sister, but is nowhere credited with the same sorts of achievements as Sita, and so is not discussed here.

17. Various of Advaita's associates had long been urging him to marry and produce the sons needed to help him in his mission.

18. Loose hair is more than a hygiene problem, as it is culturally understood to indicate a "loose" woman of poor character. Thus it is imperative that Sita retie her hair immediately.

19. The text uses the word *aishvarya* (majesty) here.

20. It is worth noting that even though most of the authors describe Advaita Acharya as a dual incarnation of Vishnu and Shiva, his wife is never identified as Shiva's wife Parvati, but always maintains her purely Vaishnava identity.

21. We can be reasonably certain that Sita Devi did indeed come to occupy such a position in the community, because mention of her in such a role appears in many Gaudiya Vaishnava sources, including some generated by groups other than her husband's.

22. Of course we can never know *exactly* what happened in historical terms, and fortunately the precise historical details are not what is of interest here; rather we are interested in learning how and why the community describes itself as it does. And specifically, in this example, what is of interest is why the community reports that Sita did indeed slide into that leadership role.

23. Some questions arise as to the provenance of this text, extant in two manuscripts and one 1926 published edition. The published text contains significantly more material than either manuscript, and one manuscript is longer than the other. As this issue does not bear directly on the present discussion I simply refer interested readers to chapter 7 of my forthcoming *Reconstructing Tradition*.

24. Traditionally only members of the highest three caste groups are entitled to receive most types of religious instruction. Shudras are normally denied this access.

25. This disregard for caste boundaries is at first glance surprising, since all the early leaders of the movement were brahmans. Ishana Nagara, however, in his *Advaita Prakasha*, devotes a great deal of space to Advaita Acharya's close friend and disciple Haridasa, who had been raised in a Muslim family and converted to Vaishnavism as a young man. Advaita Acharya repeatedly proclaims that becoming a Vaishnava, regardless of one's background, removes all impurity and elevates the individual to the same purity and status brahmans enjoy.

26. And yet real biological women are not!

REFERENCES

Brzezinski, Jan. "Women Saints in Gaudīya Vaiṣṇavism." *Journal of Vaiṣṇava Studies* 3 no. 4 (Fall 1995): 57–84.
Caudhurī, Acyutacaraṇa Tattvanidhi, ed. *Lokanātha Dāsera Sītā Caritra*. Calcutta: Bhaktiprabha, 1926.

Dimock, Edward C., Jr., *Caitanya Caritāmṛta of Kṛṣṇadāsa Kavirāja*. Edited by Tony K. Stewart. Harvard Oriental Series No. 56. Cambridge: Harvard University Press, 1999.

Ghosa, Mrnalkanti, ed. *Īśāna Nāgarera Advaita Prakāśa*. 3rd ed. Calcutta: Visvakosa Press, 1933.

Gosvāmī, Kānanvihārī. *Bāghnāpaṛa-Sampradāya o Vaiṣṇava Sāhitya*. Calcutta: Ravindrabharati Visvavidalaya, 1993.

Maiti, Ravindranatha, ed. *Haricaraṇa Dāsera Advaita Maṅgala*. Barddhaman: Barddhaman University, 1966.

Manring, Rebecca J. "At Home in the World: The Lives of Sītā Devī." *International Journal of Hindu Studies 2*, no. 1 (1998): 21–42

―――. *Reconstructing Tradition: Advaita Ācārya and Gauḍīya Vaiṣṇavism at the Cusp of the Twentieth Century*. Forthcoming 2004, Columbia University Press.

Marvin, Bruce D. "The Life and Thought of Kedarnath Dutta Bhaktivinode: A Hindu Encounter with Modernity." Ph.D. dissertation, University of Toronto, 1996.

Nātha, Rādhāgovinda, ed. *Śrīla Kṛṣṇadāsa Kavirāja Gosvāmīviracita Śrīśrī Caitanya Caritāmṛta*. Calcutta: Sadhana Prakasani, 1994.

―――, ed. *Śrīlavṛndāvanadāsa-Ṭhākuramahodāya-viracita Śrī Caitanya Bhāgavata*. Calcutta: Sadhana Prakasani, 1981.

Stewart, Tony K. "The Biographical Images of Kṛṣṇa-Caitanya: A Study in the Perception of Divinity." Ph.D. Dissertation, University of Chicago, 1985.

―――. *The Final Word: Creating the Gaudiya Vaishnava Tradition in Seventeenth Century Bengal*. In production.

―――. "Strategies of Persuasion, or How the Gauḍīya Vaiṣṇavas Survive without Centralized Authority." Paper presented at the annual meeting of the Association for Asian Studies, San Diego, California, March 12, 2000.

2

The Life of Gauri Ma

Carol S. Anderson

Gauri Ma was born in the environs of Calcutta in the middle of the nineteenth century. In the course of her eighty years, she was initiated by Ramakrishna Paramahamsa at the age of ten, left her upper-caste family when she was eighteen to live as a religious renouncer, and returned to Calcutta at forty to found the Sri Sri Saradeshvari Ashram. The ashram is larger and stronger today than it was during her lifetime, with two formally established branches in India—one in Navadvip and the second in Giridih—and other less formal relationships with centers in the United States, one of which is located in Ganges, Michigan. It was there that I was introduced to Gauri Ma several years ago through the Mother's Trust/Mother's Place interfaith center. The story of Gauri Ma's life is fascinating in its own right, but it also provides us a window into an ashram whose sole purpose is to provide a place of refuge, aid, and education for women.

I open this chapter with a sketch of the first forty years of Gauri Ma's life to provide a background for the questions that frame this paper. Those questions are: What set Gauri Ma on her life of intensive meditation and ascetic practice as a *tapasvini*? What induced her to shift her attention and effort to "serving women"? Finally, to what extent was this woman unique in both her life and her establishment of a women's ashram in 1895? The life of Gauri Ma intersects with the lives of other female gurus at a number of points. First, she should be considered a "reformer" instead of a "revolutionary," to use the categories suggested in the introduction of this volume. Second, we will see that Gauri Ma exemplifies a certain use of ascetic ideals and practices in ways designed to work with but also to challenge the Hindu concept of women's duly (*stridharma*). Her accomplishments as an ascetic enabled her to be the charismatic leader of the early ashram, and thus invites us to reconsider the role of charisma in women's leadership within the comparative study of religions. Like other women examined in this volume, Gauri Ma studied with a male teacher (although she never lived in the same compound); she never married; she focused her service on the education and training of women in northern India and set up institutions designed for this purpose; and her ashram today has various ties to individuals and centers in the United States. The locus of Gauri Ma's authority as a female guru resides in her divinity and embodiment of the Mother within the Vaishnava Ramakrishna lineage and in her pragmatic vision of what it meant to "serve women" in late-nineteenth- and early-twentieth-century Calcutta.

Gauri Ma's Life as an Ascetic

The biographies of Gauri Ma bear all the features of a classic hagiography.[1] Gauri Ma was born as Mridani in 1857 or 1858.[2] Her parents were both of orthodox brahman families; her father's family was originally from Sibpore, west of Calcutta, and her mother's family had land in Bhawanipur in south Calcutta. Her father, Parbati Charan Chattopadhyaya, was known to be pious in his devotions. Her mother was Giribala Devi (Mukhopadhyay), who was both practical and compassionate; she knew Sanskrit and Bengali, as well as some English and Persian. Mridani's maternal grandmother, Kalidasi Devi (Mukhopadhyay), was also considered a devout and learned woman. Like her mother, Giribala was a devotee of Kali; the Mukhopadhyay family of Bhawanipur had a room in the Kalighat temple to prepare their offerings to Kali. Later in her life, Gauri Ma would say that her mother and her grandmother inspired her own devotional interests at a very young age. Mridani was born to Giribala "after a dream in which the Divine Mother [that is, Kali] had smilingly handed over to her a beautiful baby, accepted by the mother with reverent gratitude as a divine gift."[3] She was their fourth child and their second daughter; in the future, Mridani would have two younger sisters. They named her Mridani, which is another name for Gauri, Durga, or Parvati—that is, Shiva's wife.

Mridani was educated during the 1860s, and attended a school that was opened in 1868 by Anglican Bishop Robert Milman (1816–1876) and his sister, Miss Frances Maria Milman (1825–1888). The school was located near St. Paul's Cathedral and was designed to educate upper-caste girls of devout Hindu families.[4] Mridani quickly distinguished herself with her curiosity and keen mind. Miss Milman remarked on one occasion that she wished to take Mridani to England for further education, but such an option was not a possibility for the young girl at the time. It is unclear how long Mridani attended this school; one biography tells us she left over religious differences to "receive more valuable instruction in other ways."[5] Those other ways included learning about religious practices from her mother and grandmother. Mridani learned to conduct the daily puja, as did nearly all young Hindu women of her time, and she also memorized large passages from various Hindu scriptures and grammars. Her biographers credit her uncle with inspiring her attraction to and fascination with travel when he told Mridani of the sacred sites he had visited all over India. He was also something of a palmist and predicted that Mridani would become a great yogini. Mridani was, in all, a well-educated girl, trained in the family traditions of nineteenth-century Hinduism. She is described as a "quiet, self-contained child . . . she had, however, a core of strong, unbending purpose curiously combined with a mild and pliable temper."[6]

When Mridani was almost ten years old, she met a "stranger, a tall Brahman with a lofty bearing" who approached her as she watched her friends playing a game. He asked her why she wasn't playing, and she responded, characteristically, that she wasn't interested. "An inexpressible feeling came over her" at this moment, and she longed to throw herself at his feet, but she simply bowed to him and received the usual blessing: "May you be devoted to Krishna." Sometime later, Mridani found out where this stranger stayed and went to him during the Rasa-Purnima holiday, which falls one month after Durga-puja. She approached his cottage, waited until he had completed his meditations, and asked him to initiate her into the path of devotion.[7] She spent the night with a neighboring family and, after bathing in the Ganges the next morning, was initiated by this stranger. Immediately after this, her brother found her and chastised her for leaving the family; the stranger defended Mridani, saying that she was simply doing what she needed to do. After the stranger told Mridani that they would meet again on the banks of the Ganges, Mridani and her brother departed.

Not too long after this incident, a female renunciant (sannyansini) committed to Krishna came to the family home at Bhawanipur. Mridani's biographers never tell us this woman's name, but describe how she spent all of her time in meditation and devotional rituals. The object of her devotions was a *shila*, a round, black stone that was the embodiment of Krishna; the *shila* was called Damodar.[8] This woman became a close friend of Mridani, and one day she entrusted the *shila* to the girl, enjoining her to worship it every morning.[9] The sannyasini left Bhawanipur soon after she made this bequest.

Mridani was expected to marry when she turned thirteen, and suitors began to offer proposals to her family. As we might expect, Mridani knew she would never marry, for she was devoted to Damodar, who was "her only Lord." One afternoon during a visit from the family of a prospective husband, Mridani shut herself in a room, swore she would never come out, and threw things out the window at anyone who came near.[10] Giribala, her mother, realized that they would never convince Mridani to marry and "took the unusual step of giving her in marriage to the Lord of the Universe . . . through a holy prayer at the appointed hour."[11] Her mother slipped her out of the room and told her to go to the home of a widowed aunt to escape, but Mridani was caught and returned home. She was kept under strict watch for the next few years, until the family realized that she would not marry at all. They then thought that she could live a devout life of religious practice at home, but this, too, failed.

When she was eighteen, Mridani joined a group of sadhus in Gangasagar;

they included both monks and nuns who were headed for Hardwar. This was the start of Mridani's life devoted to intense meditation and ascetic practices that generate stored heat (*tapas*). Women who undertake such practices are called *tapasvini*. By the time she was forty, she would complete on foot the entire grand pilgrimage of India found in the *Mahabharata*.[12] On this first pilgrimage she began to be called Gauri-mayi or Gauri Ma—perhaps, her biographers suggest, because of her light skin and her resemblance to Gauri, the daughter of the Himalayas. Gauri Ma left the group of sadhus and spent three years on this pilgrimage, moving from Hardwar to Rishikesh, Kedarnath, and Vadrinarayan (Badrinarain, modern Badrinath), visiting Devaprayag and Rudraprayag along the way. She returned to Hardwar and then spent winters in the foothills, in Gangotri and Jumnotri. Throughout her travels, she "prayed to God to disfigure her body, because the outward beauty of a woman who had chosen to be a pilgrim and a devotee was in itself a great hindrance."[13] She spoke only when it was absolutely necessary; sometimes she appeared as if she were mad, with her hair cut off and her body smeared with ashes and dust. Other times she dressed as a man with a turban and a loose robe. She usually wore a red-ocher-colored robe, and carried pictures of Kali and Gauranga (Chaitanya) and copies of the *Chandi* and the *Bhagavad Gita*. She always wore Damodar around her neck, tied with a strip of cloth.

During her journeys, Gauri Ma was once rescued by a mysterious woman who pulled her out of a river in the dead of winter. On a different trek, as she was wandering lost in the hills and suffering from frostbite, another woman appeared and carried her to a nearby village. She met other sadhus on her travels and continued to explore, visiting sites in the Punjab, Kashmir, and western India, she started from Vrindavan, went through Rajasthan, seeing Pushkar, Prabhasa (modern Somnath), and finally arrived in Dvaraka.[14] Gauri Ma returned eventually to Vrindavan, where she was seized with a ferocious longing to see Krishna face to face: "she was mad with an intense passion for Him, without whom life appeared to her as a useless burden."[15] She went out to the Lalita pond in the middle of the night, intent on suicide if she could not see Krishna. The women of Vrindavan found her there, unconscious, the next morning. Gauri Ma lived in a state of semi-consciousness for a period of time, laughing or crying with no provocation, and awaking from states of insensibility "with cuts and bruises on her body, while tears streamed forth from her eyes."[16] After this experience of divine madness (*bhava*), Gauri Ma met some relatives in Vrindavan who persuaded her to return to Calcutta to see her mother; her father and grandmother had since died. It had been three years since she had escaped from the party on the pilgrimage to Hardwar.

Gauri Ma remained in Calcutta only long enough to see her mother. She went on to Puri, where she was enthralled with Jagannath in his temple.[17] Her madness in Vrindavan had deepened into a state of quiet ecstasy, and she was widely respected as an accomplished sannyasini for her devotion and renunciation. She returned to Vrindavan, where she met Balaram Bose, a close friend of her family. Balaram encouraged her to go meet the saint who lived at Daksineswar; this was the first time she had heard of Ramakrishna. She said that she had seen enough of saints, and she went on to Rishikesh with the intention of never returning to Calcutta or Vrindavan. But an old man at Rishikesh told her that her mother was ill and wished to see her; Gauri Ma returned to Calcutta, where her mother soon recovered. Gauri Ma went again to Puri, where she met yet another sadhu who spoke of a man at Dakshineswar; she returned to stay at Balaram's house. He still wanted her to meet Ramakrishna—Gauri Ma finally told Balaram that if his saint was so powerful, he could pull her to him by force! The next day, she was unable to complete her daily puja, and she began to wander aimlessly—feeling pulled in the general direction of Dakshineswar. Balaram's staff didn't want her wandering around the city in her deluded state, so Balaram himself took her directly to Dakshineswar. As soon as Gauri Ma lay eyes on Ramakrishna the feelings of being pulled disappeared and she regained her senses, realizing that Ramakrishna was the stranger who had initiated her over fifteen years ago—they had indeed met on the banks of the Ganges. Gauri Ma was now twenty-five, and it was 1882.

She spent the next three years with Ramakrishna and his wife Sarada Devi. Gauri Ma revered Sarada Mata as Ramakrishna's partner and as a "cosmic force" in her own right; in turn, Sarada Ma "on her part loved Gauri Ma like a daughter," and respected her as a erudite scholar as well as a close friend.[18] During this time, we are told that Gauri Ma came to regard Ramakrishna as "God incarnate"; on one occasion Ramakrishna induced in her the same intoxicated state that he himself knew.[19] Gauri Ma's biographies attribute the shift in her regard for Ramakrishna—she had once had enough of sadhus— to the man himself. Ramakrishna had, after all, pulled her to him by his own power, as she had joked to Balaram. In the three years she spent with him and Sarada Devi, Ramakrishna encouraged Gauri Ma to speak to groups of women, saying that her remarks would be beneficial to them, since women were "devotional by nature."

On one occasion Ramakrishna appeared with a pitcher of water in his hand and told Gauri Ma that "I am pouring the water, you must prepare the clay." Gauri Ma responded to this remark by asking him where the clay was—all she saw was gravel! He laughed and told her that he was referring to her work for women in India. This line is remembered today by devotees of the Saradeshvari Ashram and its branches as the moment when she realized that her life would not be spent as a solitary *tapasvini*. She acceded to Ramakrishna's repeated suggestions that she devote her life to serving women, but only after leaving in 1885 for Vrindavan to finish her solitary devotions. She spent nine months in seclusion, emerging from her cave only when she learned of Ramakrishna's death in August of 1886. She returned briefly to Calcutta, and then journeyed south to Kanyakumari at the southernmost tip of India.[20] Gauri Ma returned to Calcutta some nine years later, in 1895, to take up the charge given to her by Ramakrishna. The rest of her story will unfold as I take up the legacy she established.

Like other female gurus discussed in this volume, Gauri Ma clearly spent time as an ascetic and a wanderer, living as a *tapasvini*, a solitary woman devoted to rigorous ritual practices. There seems to be no single factor that set

Gauri Ma on this path, although we should certainly credit her uncle for telling her stories about the Himalayas and the stories of sadhus and sannyasis. Gauri Ma knew there were other women who had given up home and marriage for a life of meditation and pilgrimage; the woman who stayed with her family in Bhawanipur and bequeathed the Damodar *shila* to her was one such seeker.[21] The group that Gauri Ma had joined in Gangasagar to begin her journeys included women, and we learn that she met other sannyasinis during her own itinerant years.[22] It is worth noting that her successor, Durga Ma, used two examples of women who had taken *sannyasa* vows to convince her father that *sannyasa* was not forbidden to women: Gauri Ma and Bhairavi Brahmani, who was Ramakrishna's tantric teacher.[23]

In her study of Bengali saints, June McDaniel states that the most important criterion for holy women is the experience of *bhava*, or the "ecstatic state that comes with a direct experience of the divine."[24] Gauri Ma had many *bhavas* throughout her life, although her vision of Krishna was the most intense and striking; after that vision Gauri Ma suffered a period of madness, which is also characteristic of Bengali women saints. Aside from this, however, Gauri Ma does not fit the model of Bengali holy women that McDaniel describes. McDaniel cites A. K. Ramanujan's outline of characteristics common to Virashaiva women saints of south India, which include an early dedication to God, denial of marriage, defiance of social norms, initiation by a male authority figure, and marriage to the Lord as a divine bridegroom. In contrast, McDaniel notes that Bengali women saints usually display visions or trances at a young age (which leads parents to consider madness instead of true dedication to God); accept marriage, with various relationships to her husband; defy social norms; and be initiated, though initiation is not an essential factor.[25] Gauri Ma's experiences accord with Ramanujan's characteristics for Virashaiva women saints far more than with McDaniel's Bengali model, although Gauri Ma was never married to God at the end of her life, as Ramanujan describes. There are several women who received *sannyasa* initiation within Gaudiya Vaishnava circles; several of them were known to have taken up the life of a *tapasvini*. Of the women who renounced during the Hindu renaissance, Gauri Ma is the earliest.[26] As discussed in the introduction to this volume, female gurus follow a pattern different from those identified for women saints, for not all saints are gurus.

Kneading the Clay

One answer to the second question, "What induced her to shift her attention and effort to serving women?" is simply Ramakrishna. The stories of Gauri Ma's life explicitly tell us that Ramakrishna himself persuaded her to turn her efforts toward alleviating the suffering of women. However, the question of how Gauri Ma came to the decision to "serve women" is related to two larger issues: first, how Ramakrishna's friendship with Gauri Ma was related to his other relationships with women, as well as to Sarada Devi's friendship with

Gauri Ma; Sarada Devi was influential and offered substantial help to Gauri Ma in establishing the Sri Sri Saradeshvari Ashram. She was probably involved in persuading Gauri Ma to devote her life to aiding women during the three years that Gauri Ma spent with Ramakrishna. The second issue is to understand the task and conception of "serving women" in the context of the British Raj. Let us take up these topics separately.

We need only to crack the lid of the Pandora's box that contains the tangle of Ramakrishna's relationships with women to gain some perspective on his relationship with Gauri Ma. It is evident from all sources that Ramakrishna focused most of his attention on the men in his circles, although he is often portrayed by his devotees as supportive of women. Jeffrey Kripal's two independent but intersecting typologies of the householder/renouncer and the inner/outer circle enables us to grasp the shape and dimension of the group of Ramakrishna's followers, and thus to establish the social location of women. Membership in the inner circle was made up of both householders and renouncers, and it was always shifting. The outer circle comprised largely householders, and was a fairly well-defined group. Kripal writes that he is not aware of "a single woman ever being described as a member of the inner circle."[27] It is interesting to compare the descriptions written by Gauri Ma's biographers to those written by Ramakrishna's biographers; according to the former, Gauri Ma, Ramakrishna, and Sarada Devi shared a close friendship from 1882 until 1885. The latter, however, scarcely mentions the presence of Gauri Ma in Ramakrishna's life. There is a reason for this; although Gauri Ma's activities have not been deliberately erased within the Ramakrishna lineage, neither was her initiation by Ramakrishna recognized by the Belur Math tradition, the monastic order established by Vivekananda.

The academic debate over Ramakrishna's regard for women occurs between two groups, according to Kripal: "one sees Ramakrishna as a misogynist who hated and feared women; the other sees Ramakrishna as an infallible saint who loved all human beings and who worshipped women as embodiments of the divine."[28] Characteristically, Kripal's analysis is more complex than either of these two opposing points of view. Kripal suggests that Ramakrishna divided women into two now-familiar stereotypes, distinguishing women who led men into the trap of *maya* with marriage and fatherhood, who were to be feared, from those women who could lead men to knowledge of God. Women who could teach were certainly not be hated or even feared. Kripal persuasively shows that this distinction makes sense of Ramakrishna's attitudes toward women, and points out that Ramakrishna's followers did not always recognize this difference, and thus wrestled awkwardly with the master's attitudes toward women.

Among Ramakrishna's disciples as well as in the subsequent lineage of Belur Math and the Ramakrishna Mission, there are only a few references to Gauri Ma and no references to other sannyasinis initiated by Ramakrishna.[29] Whereas Ramakrishna's biographers have at least struggled to understand how Ramakrishna regarded women, however, the absence of any substantive discussion of the role of independent women belies the disregard for women that has characterized the Order.[30] There are, of course, women held up as examples: Sister Nivedita is widely recognized, and the Holy Mother is revered above all others. But it was not until the early 1950s that Belur Math and the Mission recognized the need for a women's order and established Sri Sarada Math, despite Vivekananda's urgings to do so soon after the turn of the century.[31] From the point of view of the Ramakrishna Missions in the United States, the existence of the Saradeshvari Ashram is scarcely acknowledged; far less are their resources able to shed light on Gauri Ma's relationship with Ramakrishna. However, by drawing on Kripal's work, we can understand how Ramakrishna would have enjoyed Gauri Ma's friendship, since she was a woman who could lead men to spiritual knowledge; but we are left with no sources outside of Gauri Ma's biographies that might provide a different perspective on the relationship that Ramakrishna shared with Gauri Ma.

In contrast, the biographies of Gauri Ma, Sarada Devi, and Ramakrishna do provide evidence for us to know that many women sought an audience with Ramakrishna. Although Ramakrishna did see some of these women, it is more precise to say that the women who sought out the company of Ramakrishna and Sarada Devi constructed a separate circle around Sarada Devi that grew after Ramakrishna's death. Some of these women were married, others were not. Gauri Ma, and Durga Ma after her, were sannyasinis. There were other disciples of Sarada Devi, including Sarala Devi.[32] Unlike Gauri Ma, who is remembered today as a rather sharp, daunting, and discriminating teacher, Sarada Devi is known for her compassion, her open welcome to those who approached her, and her willingness to grant initiation to anyone who requested it.[33] Udbodhan (the Holy Mother's house in Bagbazar) is recognized as a center for a circle of friends and followers who gathered to hear Sarada Devi talk and just to socialize. This circle was composed of both men and women, foreign as well as Indian.[34]

The friendship between Sarada Devi and Gauri Ma also embraced her niece Durga Ma, who was born in 1896 to Gauri Ma's youngest sister Brajabala. Durga Ma's name at birth was Jugal Kishori. From the outset, Gauri Ma was concerned about her successor at the ashram, and this young woman was promised to the religious life at her birth. Gauri Ma took charge of her at a very young age to train her as the second guru of the ashram; Sarada Devi assisted Gauri Ma with Durga Ma's education and spiritual training. Jugal Kishori took *sannyasa* initiation from Sarada Devi when she was thirteen years old, and was given the name of Durga Ma. The relationship shared by these women was often as humorous as it was serious; for example, Durga Ma's biographer tells a story about one occasion when Gauri Ma arrived in Jayrambati to see the Holy Mother wearing a turban, a man's saffron-colored robe, and carrying a stick in her hand; she was accompanied by a young girl dressed as a young attendant disciple. Her companion was Durga Ma. Sarada Devi, Gauri Ma, and Durga Ma constituted a triumvirate of sorts that provided a stable transition for the leadership of the Sri Sri Saradeshvari Ashram in its early days. Durga Ma received her authority to grant initiation from Sarada

Devi, having been chosen by Gauri Ma to assume the position of guru at a young age.

Thus there was a network of relationships that shaped Gauri Ma's efforts to "serve women," as Ramakrishna enjoined her. She shifted her life's work away from her own solitary practices to establishing and running an ashram that would educate women. Gauri Ma had only a minor role in Ramakrishna's life from the point of view of his own followers and biographers, but her biographers describe how extensively she worked with Sarada Devi following Ramakrishna's death. Sarada Devi was a supporter who worked with Gauri Ma to make her vision and charge into reality, and her authority provided the ashram with the prestige it needed to prosper. Sarada Devi conveyed her support of the ashram through her friendship with Gauri Ma, her initiation of Durga Ma, and by her advocacy of their work. These questions are significant in light of the very few resources available to students and scholars that shed light on the question of how institutions that support and educate women are established in traditionally patriarchal societies and religious traditions.

Sri Sri Saradeshvari Ashram

The third question I posed at the outset was: "To what extent was this woman unique in both her life and her establishment of a women's ashram in 1895?" The simple answer is that she was in fact unique; a more extensive response leads us into the network of friendships that Gauri Ma had with other women that ensured the success of the Sri Sri Saradeshvari Ashram. Gauri Ma was welcomed back by Sarada Devi after her nine years of wandering that followed Ramakrishna's death. With Sarada Devi's help, the ashram that Gauri Ma wanted to establish opened its doors in Barrackpore in 1895—and it was named Sri Sri Saradeshvari after Sarada Devi.

There was a number of stories that documented the sacred nature of the ashram's location; one follower, Surendra Nath Sen, described how "One morning . . . an astonished Gauri Mata found in the precincts of the Barrackpore Ashram small footprints emerging from the shore of the Ganga and ending at the temple door. It was ascertained by the mother that no little girl had come to the Ashram in the early morning. So, concluding that the Mother of the Universe had visited the Place, Gauri Ma began to roll upon the holy footprints and cry."[35] The women at the ashram recalled how, on another occasion, Gauri Ma slipped into *samadhi* while singing a song she had composed for Ramakrishna in the *panchavati*, and remained there all night. (A panchavati is a grove that traditionally consists of five different kinds of trees, each of which is valued for various medicinal properties.) Gauri Ma had a growing reputation for her spiritual achievements—her experiences of various forms of *bhava*—as well as her "disinterested zeal and incessant activity."[36] Her blend of the spiritual and the eminently practical provided the ashram with the leadership it needed. From the outset, Sarada Devi provided spiritual advice and sent many donors to Gauri Ma to ensure the success of the ashram; the mutual respect and friendship that Sarada Devi, Gauri Ma and, later, Durga Ma shared made the ashram possible through mutual consultations, advice, and conversations with influential members of Calcutta society.

We learn from her biographers that Gauri Ma was well acquainted with the plight of Hindu women from her days as a solitary *tapasvini*. She had seen the problems caused by ignorance, the hardships caused by too many mouths to feed, and "the speechless hearts of women crushed under awesome burdens."[37] She chose the environs of Calcutta specifically to reach the women who required such assistance as the ashram could provide. Gauri Ma's mission dovetailed with the establishment of a girls' school since the ashram would eventually be able to house a few girls from the school as well as those who chose to take *brahmacharini* vows. Subrata Puri Devi (Durga Ma's biographer and third Mother of the ashram) explains that it was difficult at the start to find girls who would devote themselves to the ashram. Living an ascetic life was not an acceptable option for young Hindu girls at the turn of the century—despite Gauri Ma's own escape into the Himalayas. Stories of this time describe not only how Gauri Ma went from house to house to raise funds for the ashram but also how she persuaded parents to entrust their daughters to the ashram for their education and training. The successes that Gauri Ma had were followed by Durga Ma's persuasiveness; the fact that Durga Ma had received initiation from Sarada Devi conferred on the ashram the prestige it needed to become a respected institution.

Gauri Ma and Durga Ma, in consultation with Sarada Devi, provided the ashram with its current structure. They established a solid reputation for the school and set up an advisory committee of devotees from the upper classes and castes of Bengali society. By the time the Sri Sri Saradeshvari Ashram was established in its current location in 1925, Gauri Ma had established a community of women *matri-sangha*) who were committed to the ashram, with Durga Ma as its head.[38] There were (and are) three different groups of women at the ashram: the girl students (most of whom are day students who live at home), *brahmacharini*s, and sannyasinis. The formal rules and regulations for the *matri-sangha* were framed and established in 1928. These guidelines were strictly followed; life in the ashram today seems to follow a pattern that is as well worn as the narrow stairway that leads up to the shrines on the upper levels of the building. The residents of the ashram are proud that their traditions and procedures today are the same as those established at the time of the ashram's founding.

Devotees of the ashram take initiation (*diksha*) from the Mother (Mataji) at their own request. Being initiated by the Mother signals a certain kind of "membership" among the lay visitors. This membership denotes a shared realization of the significance and spiritual sanctity of the ashram and its sisters. At the time of initiation, the devotee arrives with the *dakshina* (gift) for the guru, and receives instruction in how to repeat his or her mantra 108 times by counting rosary beads or on the fingers. This practice of *japa* is traditional within Ramakrishna circles, and particularly at the Sri Sri Saradeshvari Ashram.[39] Initiation signifies that one is truly a devotee, committed to serving the ashram.

The authority to grant initiation comes not from Gauri Ma but from Sarada Devi, who granted Durga Ma *sannyasa* initiation when she was thirteen. After teaching her how to look into a supplicant's heart to reveal the appropriate mantra, Sarada Devi told Durga Ma that she was ready for her first *brahmacharini* initiation at the age of eighteen. That initiate was Subrata Puri Devi, who was the third Mother of the ashram.

Gauri Ma, Sarada Devi, and Durga Ma deftly negotiated the religious, class, and caste politics of Calcutta in order to ensure that the ashram prospered. It was, and is, a unique institution. One author wrote about the "special feature of this institution," namely, that this Ashram that was designed to serve women was also supported by women: "from the beginning most of the sympathy, help, and financial support came from women."[40] Gauri Ma's reputation and news of her work at the ashram were spread by women's conversations and support. Subrata Puri Devi's biography of Durga Ma indicates that these strategies were self-consciously designed to establish the ashram as a respectable school for girls that would aid women in need. The guidelines and rules of the ashram guaranteed that its reputation would not be jeopardized by inadvertent misconduct among its members; the ashram's good standing was, and is, the bedrock on which the institutions stands. With her decision to provide aid to young women and widows of respectable families, Gauri Ma recognized that the security she desired for the ashram depended on establishing a niche within traditional Hindu Bengali society.

Instituting Women's Learning

One of the central questions in the study of women as religious leaders and teachers is the relationship between the power they command by virtue of their charisma and the power that may be traced to other sources. Gauri Ma, as I have sought to demonstrate, was a charismatic woman. Catherine Wessinger has defined "extraordinary charisma" as "any sort of direct revelation defined as being available to the leader and not generally accessible to other members of the group. The leader with extraordinary charisma is, therefore, set apart from and over the followers."[41] Gauri Ma clearly possessed this quality of "extraordinary charisma." She distinguished herself with her spiritual accomplishments, her wisdom, and her "dispassionate zeal." However, the success of her ashram cannot and should not be attributed solely to this characteristic of her leadership; her drive, pragmatic grasp of the details, and her support from Sarada Devi were equally important. Her biographers unequivocally credit the establishment of the ashram and the girls' school to Gauri Ma's focus and sense of purpose. That drive led her to create an institutional basis for Durga Ma's authority as well as her own. The vehicle she used to institutionalize her work was women's education.

Education for Hindu women was not just a means to an end for Gauri Ma. The girls' school was an element thoroughly integrated into her vision of "serving women." Gauri Ma had four distinct goals for this work: first, to teach girls about Hinduism and its relevance for their lives; second, to establish an ashram so that such teaching could take place; third, to provide shelter for "unhappy girls from respectable families as well as for widows"; and fourth, to assist women to live their own lives in such a way so that they would find "inner peace conducive to their spiritual growth."[42] In order to realize these goals, Gauri Ma recognized that she required a structure within which committed women could work toward the benefit of women. We have already seen how that institution was established; it grew from twenty-five women who resided at the ashram with seventy-five students in 1911 to fifty residents with three hundred students by 1925.[43] The ashram had its mission and students to teach, and it managed to tuck itself into the conservative responses to the debates over "the woman question."

It is no coincidence that Gauri Ma's goals included the education of girls and women, a place of refuge for girls of good families who could not live at home, and widows. Women's education, age of consent for marriage, and treatment of widows were at the forefront of political and social debates throughout nineteenth-century India. The Hindu renaissance is typically described as a campaign against "the practices of child marriage, sati, polygamy, the ban on widow remarriage, female infanticide, the lack of education and property rights, seclusion, and violence against women. Largely a movement led by Brahman men, its primary goal was to challenge the imperialistic British Raj."[44] Although such generalizations overlook the fact that the reform of women's social status in India was used both as an argument for British intervention into Indian social affairs and as evidence to reject British authority, the fact remains that the social reform of women's lives was an integral if not pivotal component of the nationalist movement. Similarly, the strategies employed by British and American women in the same cause have been the subject of new arguments over the degree to which these white women were complicit in the racist and imperialist Raj and the extent to which sexism constituted an "other burden" for these activists.[45] Gauri Ma's philosophy of women's education could not fail to reflect these debates.

The stereotype of an educated Hindu woman was a familiar subject for satire in the songs and jests of the marketplaces of Calcutta in the middle of the nineteenth century. For example, the following song displays a distinct unease with any change in women's traditional roles:

> Housewives no longer have any sense of shame,
> They always dress in Anglicized fashion.
> They've left cooking and are fond of knitting.
> Wearing gowns they move around,
> Singing all sorts of nonsense.
> Men have lost their power,

They're tied to their wives' apron-strings
It's a world of women all around.[46]

Similarly, the rejection by Ramabai Ranade, wife of Bombay high court justice
M. G. Ranade, of the Hindu practices regarding child marriage, widows, and
sati, along with her subsequent conversion to Christianity, is the manifestation
of another fear of "what might happen" if Hindu women received an education:
that they would cease to be Hindu. Despite these threats, the act of providing
education for women and girls—once that education was extracted from the
hands of Christian missionaries—was adopted by many as a positive step for
India. In Bengal, Debendranath Tagore, Keshab Chandra Sen, and other members of the fragmented Brahmo Samaj movement had long been advocates for
women's education, raising the age of consent, and widow remarriage.[47] Even
within these liberal circles, however, the need for an ideal Hindu woman remained strong. Few of these debates, among conservative nationalists or liberal
reformers, examined the benefits of education to women themselves.

Gauri Ma spoke with many leaders over the years, both men and women,
who occupied widely varying positions on the question of nationalism and
women's education, including Ramabai Ranade, Bal Gangadhar Tilak, and Mahatma Gandhi.[48] Closer to home, Gauri Ma was certainly influenced by Ramakrishna and Vivekananda, both of whom were fairly conservative on issues
of social reform.[49] Amiya Sen has pointed out in a recent set of essays that
both of these men were "keen to promote female education . . . but far more
reluctant to concede the individuality that was bound to grow with such education."[50] Vivekananda certainly idealized Hindu women: "In India," he said
on one of his tours, "a woman is the mother first and the mother last." On
other occasions, he defended child marriage and enforced widowhood.[51] Like
the other reformers noted above, Vivekananda sought to enhance the status of
the ideal Hindu woman. Gauri Ma's philosophy of women's education was
equally conservative; she too held onto the Hindu ideal for women. She is
reported to have said: "No society can prosper without education for its women.
By treating women as the lowest caste, how can you consider yourself to be
great? Keep in mind that women are a part of shakti. If you don't raise them
to the level of *vidya shakti* [educated power], they will end up being *avidya shakti*
[ignorant power]. That is not conducive to their welfare, to your welfare, or to
the nation's welfare."[52] Despite the fact that Vivekananda seemed threatened
by the thought of women's independence, that issue was not a serious one for
the ashram. Education was tempered with duty: duty to the ashram, duty to
family, and duty to a woman's own spiritual path.

Thus Gauri Ma did not reject the notion of an "ideal Hindu woman."
Neither did she strongly promote the notion that all Hindu women should be
mothers, as did Sister Nivedita and Sister Christine Grenstidel. As a close
associate of Vivekananda, and also as an Irish nationalist converted to the
Indian nationalist cause, Sister Nivedita had a rather romantic view of the
mother in Hindu society: "The mother in India, says Nivedita, is a 'goddess

enthroned in her sons' worship—she is the bringer of sanctity and peace.' "[53] In much the same tone, Sarada Devi often remarked that girls should pursue their studies for "enlightenment," but that girls should not "possess sharp and piercing intelligence. Women should be pure and simple in nature."[54]

The ideal for Hindu women appealed to Gauri Ma as well, as one of her biographers notes: "The models of Sita, Savitri and Arudhati, with their chastity and sacrifice, of Gargi and Maitreyi, their divine knowledge and renunciation were to be held up before the present age." But Gauri Ma diverged from Vivekananda's position as well as those of Sarada Devi and Sister Nivedita. The same passage in her biography declares that "iron turned into steel can in all conditions function like sharp weapons, and woman can work for the good in any circumstances once her ignorance is dispelled by true education." Gauri Ma recognized that even though wives and mothers remained the traditional roles for women, education provided other possible options: "A sound education will awaken her soul and then she will choose her own way and seek to make her life successful."[55] Gauri Ma had little use for the religious and political debates that marked the Hindu renaissance, a point that further distinguished her educational philosophy from that of Sister Nivedita's.[56] We learn that she regretted that some well-intentioned volunteers at the ashram had no faith in God: "She had grave misgivings about the ultimate good of such work as they sought to do," calling it "godless work."[57] The Hinduism of the ashram was, and is today, bhakti—worship, ritual, and devotion.[58] One should be wholly devoted to God.

Sisters followed, and follow today, strict rules of purity, learning how to clean the floors, vessels, and implements properly so they may be used correctly in daily worship. There were and are fixed schedules for the various pujas. Today students recite the *Gita*, singing entire chapters from memory, and sing *bhajans* after the evening *arati* service. Gauri Ma is said to have taught regularly out of the *Gita*, emphasizing the need to act without regard or attachment for the result. In short, Gauri Ma's Hinduism was a Hinduism of devotion, of total and absolute surrender to God in all walks of life—albeit with a good education.[59]

This is the environment that Gauri Ma provided for young women and widows, and for women who lived outside the ashram. She constantly offered knowledge, advice, and support that women required for their own spiritual growth. The same was offered to men; there are many anecdotes about how men and women "bowed down by sorrow and suffering" would listen to her "inspired words and find new life, joy, and strength." Education, assistance for young women and widows, and spiritual counsel were all grounded in total devotion to God.

The question remains of the degree to which Gauri Ma's authority as a female guru was a function of her "extraordinary charisma." This is not an easy question to answer, for Gauri Ma or for other female gurus who are identified with the theological "Mother" such as Anandamayi Ma, Meera Ma, Ammachi, or Karunamayi Ma. Much of her authority was rooted in her initiation by Ramakrishna, a male teacher. Her travels as a *tapasvini* and her assiduous ritual practice further consolidated her authority and position as a learned and enlightened teacher. Sarada Devi's support of Gauri Ma and the ashram strengthened Gauri Ma's position in the community as a leader as well as the status of the ashram. Gauri Ma's charisma was, finally, inseparable from the authority she derived from Ramakrishna and Sarada Devi; without "passing the test" as a guru, she would not have been accepted as a leader of an ashram. Gauri Ma required the proper lineage and support of one of Calcutta's most widely revered holy women—Sarada Devi—to consolidate her position as a guru of the Sri Sri Saradeshvari Ashram. Had she not established the ashram she would have been a highly respected holy woman, but not necessarily a guru.

In discussions about the nature of women's leadership within religious communities, we need to focus on the means by which institutions are established and reformed within particular religious traditions. We need to ask about the relationship between female gurus, for example, and the women within those communities. This is precisely the legacy of Gauri Ma's efforts: serving women, she resolved, meant establishing a center that would be a place of refuge for lay women as well as ordained sisters, a place for education, a place that nurtures spiritual growth, and, a finally, a place where all people, men and women alike, may seek guidance and insight into their lives.

NOTES

1. There are two biographies that have been translated into English: *Gauri Mata*, published by the Sri Saradeshvari Ashram in 1944; and *Gauri Ma: A Monastic Disciple of Sri Ramakrishna*, published by Mother's Trust/Mother's Place in 1994. This second biography was translated from a series of articles written by Swami Shivatatvananda, published serially in a Marathi journal sponsored by the Ramakrishna Mission during 1960. There is a Bengali biography of Gauri Ma, which is much longer than either of the two English biographies, but I have not had the opportunity to use it. Nearly all of the biographical information contained in this paper is drawn from these two sources; I have provided page numbers only for quotations.

2. The biographies do not provide a specific date for her birth. *Gauri Ma* says "around 1857" and *Gauri Mata* claims that she was born in 1858. Subrata Puri Devi's biography of Durga Ma notes that the centennial of Gauri Ma's birth was held on February 12, 1957, which, she wrote, was "the day the ninety-ninth year of Gauri Ma's advent was completed and the day the one hundredth year began." February 12, 1957 was the 29th of Magh of the Bengali Era 1363; Subrata, *Durga Ma*, p. 252.

3. *Gauri Mata*, p. 5.

4. The school was located just off Chowringhee Road in the southern portion of the Maidan. The resident head of the school was a woman named Miss Hurford; the Committee of the Ladies Association of the Society for the Protection of the Gospel organization sent Miss Cameron to assist her. Jessie Robertson Hoare, *The Life of Angelina Margaret Hoare* (London: Wells Gardener, Darton, 1894), cited in *Gauri Mata*, pp. 7–8, note.

5. *Gauri Mata*, p. 8; see also *Gauri Ma*, p. 14.

6. *Gauri Mata*, p. 10.

7. *Gauri Mata* says only that his village was near Dakshineswar.

8. Shalagrama stones (*shilas*) are widely recognized for their sanctity throughout West Bengal. They are round black stones found near the Gandiaki River used in daily tantric devotions. They may not be bought or sold; the smaller it is, the more auspicious; the worship of a shalagrama is said to be more efficacious than thousands of Shiva-lingas; and, finally, even women and shudras are entitled to worship shalagramas. These practices are described in a manual apparently codified by Gopala Bhatta, one of the six Gosvamin disciples of Vrindavan and the author of the earliest and most important Bengali biography of Chaitanya. The manual is the *Hari-bhakti-vilāsa*, composed sometime before 1541. See S. K. De for a comprehensive discussion of this text's authorship; De, *Early History of the Vaiṣṇava Faith and Movement in Bengal*, pp. 137–141 and 467–469.

9. We never learn the name of this woman in the biographies. There is a story associated with Ganga Mata Gosvamini that illustrates how such *shilas* circulated. This woman lived in the eighteenth century and was perhaps the first woman in Chaitanya Vaishnavism who established her reputation as a devotee of Chaitanya solely on the basis of her own learning and spiritual achievements. She went on to establish her own lineage. Ganga Mata Gosvamini moved into the home of Sarvabhauma Bhattacarya in Puri, who was probably Chaitanya's most important disciple in Puri, and "when she came there, there was only a shalagramashila named Radha-Damodara being served at this house." This is the closest reference that I have found to Gauri Ma's Damodar *shila*, or to the unnamed sannyasini who gave it to her. Brzezinski, "Women Saints in Gauḍīya Vaiṣṇavism," pp. 73–74.

10. *Gauri Ma* says that she shut herself into the room on her wedding day.

11. *Gauri Mata*, p. 17. Similarly, Gauri Ma's successor, Durga Ma, was married to Lord Jagannath at a young age to circumvent marriage to a human husband; this was not uncommon.

12. Bhardwaj, *Hindu Places of Pilgrimage in India*, pp. 30–88, passim.

13. *Gauri Mata*, p. 22.

14. *Gauri Ma*, p. 23, and *Gauri Mata*, pp. 24–26.

15. *Gauri Mata*, p. 25. This is the state of divine madness known as *bhava*; see McDaniel, *The Madness of the Saints*, pp. 6–25.

16. *Gauri Mata*, p. 26.

17. She went to Jagannath Puri, Sakshigopal, Buvaneshwar, and then back to Vrindavan; this was her third pilgrimage; her second pilgrimage had taken her to Dwarka on the east coast in Sanrashtra. *Gauri Ma*, p. 25 and *Gauri Mata*, p. 28.

18. *Gauri Mata*, p. 34.

19. *Life of Sri Ramakrishna*, cited in *Gauri Mata*, p. 36.

20. This was her fourth pilgrimage. She began at Puri, then went to Vidyanagar (Vijayanagar?), Madura, Srirangam, Pakshitirtha, Shivakanchi, Vishnukanchi, Rameshvaram, and then Kanyakumari. Gauri Ma made her fifth pilgrimage to Pandharpur, Pune, Belgaum, and Bombay a few years after the ashram was established, between 1895 and 1900. *Gauri Ma*, pp. 40, 42–43, and *Gauri Mata*, pp. 44–45.

21. June McDaniel documents the wandering of female Bauls throughout West Bengal and Bangladesh today, and it appears evident from Gauri Ma's biographies that a few such women existed in the second half of the nineteenth century. Brzezinski indicates that there may be fewer such women today than in the past. McDaniel, "The Embodiment of God among the Bauls of Bengal" Brzezinski, "Women Saints," pp. 59–60; and McDaniel, *Madness of the Saints*, p. 198.

22. There are very good studies of the history of female asceticism in Hinduism. See Ojha, "Female Asceticism in Hinduism." Robert Gross also mentions a reference

to an ascetic named Salabham, who appears in the *Mahabharata* in conversation with King Janaka. She was apparently a brahmani, or a brahman woman in the *sannyasa* stage. But Salabha herself says in the text that she was really a kshatriya woman who took up the ascetic life when no suitable husband could be found for her; Gross, *The Sadhus of India*, p. 33. For an excellent discussion of the origins of asceticism in India, see Bronkhorst, *The Two Sources of Indian Asceticism*. Two more studies must be included in this list of studies of female asceticism; the first is by Ursula King, and the second is an excellent collection of articles that explore women disciples with a comparative approach; four of the ten articles focus on renunciation in Hinduism. See King, "The Effects of Social Change on Religious Self-Understanding"; and Puttick and Clarke, *Women as Teachers and Disciples in Traditional and New Religions*.

23. Her father was concerned that if Jugal Kishori (who became Durga Ma) took *sannyasa*, it would harm his family. Jugal Kishori convinced him otherwise with Gauri Ma's example. Subrata, *Durga Ma*, p. 54.

24. McDaniel, *Madness of the Saints*, p. 6.

25. See Ramanujan, "On Women Saints." Ramanujan's article is also discussed by McDaniel in *Madness of the Saints*, pp. 231–232.

26. Jan Brzezinsky discusses a disciple of Sita Thakurani (Advaita Acharya's wife) by the name of Jangali who took up the renouncer's life; two daughters of Narottama Das's chief disciple Ganganarayani Chakravarti, Krishnapriya and Vishnupriya, who also took up residence at Radhakund to live as ascetics; and Ganga Mata Gosvamini. Brzezinsky, "Women Saints," pp. 66, 73–75. For contemporary women, see McDaniel, *Madness of the Saints*, pp. 191–240. See also McDaniel, "A Holy Woman of Calcutta," and Llewellyn, "The Autobiography of a Female Renouncer." Both of the women described by McDaniel and Llewellyn were younger than Gauri Ma: Archanapuri Ma (1902–) is also the leader of a large ashram in Calcutta, and Miram (1929–) renounced within the Arya Samaj movement.

27. Kripal, *Kālī's Child*, p. 11.

28. Ibid., p. 278.

29. Gauri Ma is generally considered in the literature and among contemporary followers to be the only female disciple of Ramakrishna. However, Nancy Falk once met a woman who said that she was a direct disciple of Ramakrishna; this sannyasini was the last of four women who ran their own ashram in Kerala. I have also heard several rumors of other women disciples, but upon further investigation they prove to be disciples of Sarada Devi or of other teachers in the lineage of Sarada Math. Nancy Falk, personal communication, November 5, 1999.

30. This is a complex and complicated issue that has received very little open discussion. From the point of view of many of the devotees of the Sri Sri Saradeshvari Ashram, there is no real conflict or clash with the Ramakrishna Mission or Belur Math. The center of the ashram's life is the ashram itself, the women who have taken vows, and lay initiates. Similarly, the Institute of Culture schedules talks on the Holy Mother, holds a copy of Gauri Ma's biography in its library; and, on the surface, one would not recognize any overt rejection of Gauri Ma or the Sri Sri Saradeshvari Ashram. However, while the publications of the Sri Sri Saradeshvari Ashram mention the work they have done with swamis associated with Belur Math, the ashram receives little mention in the publications of the Ramakrishna Mission or the Institute of Culture. For example, Subrata Puri Devi (who was the third Mataji of Sri Saradeshvari Ashram) talks about how Gauri Ma and the young Durga Ma (the second Mataji) rushed to see Vivekananda before he died, wanting to say goodbye to a man who had been a good friend of both of them. To the best of my knowledge, there are only pass-

ing mentions of the relationship between Gauri Ma and Vivekananda in his biographies.

31. Several sisters, including a woman named Asha, and in consultation with several monks of the Ramakrishna Order, rented an apartment in late 1944 as an embryonic Sri Sarada Math. Slowly supported by Belur Math and the Ramakrishna Order, the trustees of Belur Math granted *brahmacharya* vows to seven women who had worked in different centers of the mission on December 27, 1953. Sri Sarada Math was formally opened on December 2, 1954, by Swami Shankarananda in the presence of senior officials of Belur Math. On December 31, 1958, the *brahmacharanis* were granted *sannyasa*. Brahmacharini Asha was initiated as Pravrajika Muktiprana, and served as Sri Sarada Math's general secretary for over forty years. The math was granted full independence from Belur Math in 1959. Atmaprana, *Pravrajika Muktiprāṇa*, pp. 24–26.

32. Sarala Devi was later named Pravrajika Bharatiprana, and served as the first president of Sarada Math. Atmaprana, *Pravrajika Muktiprāṇa*, p. 11.

33. "Gauri Ma was rather choosy in such matters and, like Gouranga Dev, preferred to follow the principle of sifting the grain from the chaff. She used to send many for initiation to the Holy Mother, or to Svami Brahmanandaji, instead of adopting them as direct disciples." Subrata, *Durga Ma*, p. 201.

34. Ibid., pp. 39f. Sister Nivedita, Miss McLeod, and Miss Christine Grenstidel are among the Western women who were part of this circle.

35. Ibid., p. 57.

36. *Gauri Ma*, p. 49.

37. Ibid., p. 34.

38. The ashram moved in 1915 to Goabagan Lane, and then moved two more times before settling in its current location in north Calcutta.

39. References to the significance of *japa* within the Ramakrishna lineage may be found in Ramakrishna, *The Gospel of Sri Ramakrishna*, vol. 2, pp. 588f., and Atmaprana, *Pravrajika Bharatiprāṇa*, p. 128.

40. *Gauri Ma*, p. 47.

41. Wessinger, *Women's Leadership in Marginal Religions*; p. 17 n. 12.

42. *Gauri Ma*, p. 72.

43. *Gauri Ma*, pp. 54 and 62.

44. Young, "Women in Hinduism," p. 79.

45. See Burton, *Burdens of History*, and Kumari Jayawardena's more nuanced reading of the topic in *The White Women's Other Burden*.

46. Banerjee, *The Parlour and the Streets*, p. 111.

47. Sen, *Hindu Revivalism*, pp. 30–42.

48. *Gauri Ma*, pp. 42–43 and 73; *Gauri Mata*, pp. 55 and 66. Judge Ranade was in favor of the British government's intervention on behalf of social reform for women; Tilak was staunchly opposed. See Jayawardena, *Other Burden*, p. 27.

49. Most studies of the Ramakrishna Order fail to distinguish between Ramakrishna's attitude toward religious pluralism and Vivekananda's. I am persuaded by Kripal's argument that the roots of Ramakrishna's Hinduism lay in Tantrism, and also by Amiya Sen's suggestion that Vivekananda's universalist Vedanta glossed over Ramakrishna's concern with ritual. Ramakrishna, despite his experiences of Christianity and Islam, tolerated the truths of other religions; he did not go nearly as far as Vivekananda did in proclaiming that all religions are one. See Kripal, *Kālī's Child*, pp. 2–7 and 25; Sen, *Hindu Revivalism*, 308–309; and, for an example of a failure to distinguish between these two attitudes, see Jayawardena, *Other Burden*, p. 177.

50. Sen, *Hindu Revivalism*, p. 293.

51. Jayawardena, *Other Burden*, p. 189.

52. *Gauri Ma*, pp. 69 and 72.

53. Sister Nivedita (Margaret Elizabeth Noble), "Kali the Mother," vol. 1, p. 464, cited in Jayawardena, *Other Burden*, p. 190. See also Sister Nivedita, *The Master as I Saw Him*, pp. 135–167.

54. Subrata, *Durga Ma*, p. 62.

55. *Gauri Mata*, pp. 68–69. All of the quotes on Gauri Ma's ideas about women's education come from these pages in *Gauri Mata*. The author of this biography states her educational principles even more strongly, although it is not clear whether the words are those of the biographer or Gauri Ma: "The aim of education is the unfolding of power; the greater such unfolding the more grows a woman's fitness for taking up heavy responsibilities."

56. Sen, *Hindu Revivalism*, pp. 8–10. Sister Nivedita's school scheduled time for adult women to come in and learn to read and write, and thus became a center for political discussions. Later in her life, her relationships with more revolutionary figures in Bengal became a source of a great deal of speculation. Jayawardena, *Other Burden*, p. 187.

57. *Gauri Mata*, pp. 66–67.

58. I have chosen to call the practices at the ashram bhakti instead of *gurubhakti* (devotion to the guru) on the basis of my observations, although this is a tentative conclusion. Service and donations are given to the ashram, not to the Mataji. One evening, a sister told me that Bandana Ma, the current Mother, was quite diligent about turning over all money offered to her to the ashram; residents may accept donations from devotees directly for their personal use. I have observed a marked difference between the attitudes toward the current Mataji at the ashram and other discussions of the guru's authority. McDaniel, *Madness of the Saints*, pp. 241–252.

59. *Gauri Mata*, pp. 61–62.

REFERENCES

Atmaprana, Pravrajika. *Pravrajika Muktiprāṇa*. Dakshineswar: Sri Sarada Math, 1994.

Banerjee, Sumanta. *The Parlour and the Streets: Elite and Popular Culture in Nineteenth-Century Calcutta*. Calcutta: Seagull Books, 1989.

Bhardwaj, Surinder Mohan. *Hindu Places of Pilgrimage in India: A Study in Cultural Geography*. Berkeley: University of California Press, 1973.

Brzezinski, Jan. "Women Saints in Gaudiya Vaisnavism." Pp. 59–85 in *Vaiṣṇavi Women and the Worship of Krishna*, edited by Steven J. Rosen. Delhi: Motilal Banarsidass, 1996.

Bronkhorst, Johannes. *The Two Sources of Indian Asceticism*. Delhi: Motilal Banarsidass, [1993] 1998.

Burton, Antoinette. *Burdens of History: British Feminists, Indian Women, and Imperial Culture 1865–1915*. Chapel Hill: University of North Carolina Press, 1994.

De, Sushil Kumar. *Early History of the Vaisnava Faith and Movement in Bengal*. Calcutta: Firma KLM, 1986.

Gauri Ma: A Monastic Disciple of Sri Ramakrishna. Michigan: Mother's Trust/Mother's Place, 1994.

Gauri Mata. Calcutta: Sri Saradeshvari Ashram, 1944.

Gross, Robert Lewis. *The Sadhus of India: A Study of Hindu Asceticism*. Jaipur: Rowat Publications, 1992.

Jayawardena, Kumari. *The White Women's Other Burden: Western Women and South Asia during British Rule*. New York: Routledge, 1995.

King, Ursula. "The Effects of Social Change on Religious Self-Understanding: Women Ascetics in Modern Hinduism." Pp. 69–83 in *Changing South Asia: Religious and Society*, edited by K. Ballhatchet and D. Taylor. Hong Kong: Asian Research Service, 1984.

Kripal, Jeffrey J. *Kālī's Child: The Mystical and the Erotic in the Life and Teachings of Ramakrishna*. Chicago: University of Chicago Press, 1995.

Life of Sri Ramakṛṣṇa. Almora: Advaita Ashrama, n.d.

Llewellyn, J. E. "The Autobiography of a Female Renouncer." Pp. 463–472 in *Religions of India in Practice*, edited by Donald S. Lopez, Jr. Princeton: Princeton University Press, 1995.

McDaniel, June. "The Embodiment of God among the Bauls of Bengal." *Journal of Feminist Studies in Religion* 8 no. 2 (1992): 27–40.

———. "A Holy Woman of Calcutta," pp. 418–425 in *Religions of India in Practice*, edited by Donald S. Lopez, Jr. Princeton: Princeton University Press, 1995.

———. *The Madness of the Saints: Ecstatic Religion in Bengal*. Chicago: University of Chicago Press, 1989.

Nivedita, Sister (Margaret Elizabeth Noble). "Kali the Mother." Vol. 1. in *The Complete Works of Sister Nivedita*, 5 vols. Calcutta: Advaita Ashrama, [1900] 1982.

———. *The Master as I Saw Him*. 9th ed. Calcutta: Udbodhan House, 1963.

Ojha, Catherine. "Female Asceticism in Hinduism: Its Traditions and Present Condition." *Man in India* 61: no. 3 (September 1981): 254–285.

Puttick, Elizabeth and Peter B. Clarke, eds. *Women as Teachers and Disciples in Traditional and New Religions*. Studies in Women and Religion. Vol. 32. Lewiston: Edwin Mellen Press, 1993.

Ramakrishna. *The Gospel of Sri Ramakrishna*, Edited by Mahendranath Gupta, translated by Svami Nikhilananda. Mylapore: Sri Ramakrishna Math, c. 1944.

Ramanujan, A. K. "On Women Saints," pp. 316–324 in *The Divine Consort: Rādhā and the Goddesses of India*, edited by John Stratton Hawley and Donna Marie Wulff. Berkeley: Graduate Theological Union, 1982.

Sen, Amiya P. *Hindu Revivalism in Bengal, 1872–1905: Some Essays in Interpretation*. New Delhi: Oxford University Press, 1993.

Subrata Puri Devi. *Durga Ma: Only Sannyasini Disciple of Sri Sri Sarada Devi*. Edited by Sri Bandana Puri Devi. Calcutta: Sri Sri Saradeshvari Ashram, 1966.

Wessinger, Catherine, ed. *Women's Leadership in Marginal Religions: Explorations outside the Mainstream*. (Urbana: University of Illinois Press, 1993).

Young, Katherine. "Women in Hinduism," pp. 77–135 in *Today's Woman in World Religions*, edited by Arvind Sharma. Albany: State University of New York Press, 1994.

3

Anandamayi Ma, the Bliss-Filled Divine Mother

Lisa Lassell Hallstrom

On August 28, 1982, in the foothills of the Himalayas, a funeral procession made its way between the Indian towns of Dehradun and Kankhal. It took longer than usual to make the twenty-seven-mile trip because the procession had to stop every few minutes to allow crowds of mourners to have their last darshan, or glimpse of the divine, of the one whom they simply called Ma, or Mother.

By the time the body of eighty-six-year-old Anandamayi Ma, or the Bliss-Filled Mother, had reached its final destination at her ashram in Kankhal on the banks of the Ganga, an unending stream of people had begun to gather to pay their respects. *India Today* reported, "One could see them coming as far as the eye could see. They came in cars, rickshaws and on foot. Many were in a state of dazed shock." While some kept up the twenty-four-hour chanting of the divine name, mourners continued, hour after hour, to *pranam*, or bow, in front of Ma's body, many weeping profusely. Among them was Indira Gandhi, who had flown in by helicopter and who considered Ma her spiritual mother. On that day Mrs. Gandhi left the following message of condolence at the ashram: "Anandamayi Ma was the living embodiment of devotion and love. Just with a glimpse of Her, countless problems are solved. She considered humanity Her true religion. Her spiritually powerful personality was a source of great guidance for all human beings. I offer my homage to Her!"

On Sunday, August 29, Anandamayi Ma was buried as a realized being according to strict scriptural injunctions presided over by some of India's most renowned brahman priests. Her shrine has become a place of worship and pilgrimage renowned for its spiritual power. Her twenty-eight ashrams, a charitable hospital, schools, and dispensaries continue to be administered by the nonprofit society established in her name. Yet, although nearly every Hindu in India knows of Anandamayi Ma as a *mahatma*, or great soul—a saint—those who consider themselves to be her devotees, her disciples, who number in the hundreds of thousands, worship her as an avatar, as God who came in the form of a woman for the sake of her devotees.[1]

Anandamayi Ma was born as Nirmala Sundari to a poor brahman family in rural Bengal in 1896. She was married at the age of twelve, but lived with her husband until his death in 1938 not as his "wife," as Hindu dharma, or sacred law, would define it, but as his guru. As her sacred biographies recount, early in their marriage Nirmala withdrew more and more from everyday activities and spent a large part of her day in states of spiritual ecstasy. She began to attract devotees who saw her as an extraordinary spiritual being. Her husband, while bewildered at first, soon became convinced that his wife was a manifestation of the Goddess. He received spiritual initiation from her and spent the rest of his life following her spiritual instruction, mediating between her and her growing number of devotees, and caring for her physical well-being, as she seemed completely disinterested in her body.

In fact, in 1926 Ma, or "Mother" as Nirmala had come to be called, completely stopped feeding herself and for the rest of her life was fed by the hands of her close devotees. That same year Ma completely abandoned her dharma, or sacred duty, as a Hindu wife and began her endless travels around India, accompanied by her husband and attracting devotees wherever she went. Thousands came to receive her blessings and bathe in her ecstatic spiritual state. Many reported that one glance from Ma awakened in them a spiritual energy so powerful as to redirect their entire life.

After her husband's death, Anandamayi Ma continued to grow in stature and influence. Paramahamsa Yogananda, referring to Ma in his book, *Autobiography of a Yogi*, says "never before had I met such an exalted woman saint." Heads of state as well as the intellegensia of India considered her their guru and, in some cases, their deity. In the last decade of her life, Anandamayi Ma's devotees numbered in the hundreds of thousands, and ashrams, schools, and hospitals were established in her name all over India. By the time of her death in 1982, this illiterate woman, who called herself simply "this body," had become the spiritual guide and focus of reverence for people all over India. It was my good fortune to spend 1990–1991 traveling throughout India interviewing close devotees of Ma, or divine Mother as she was called, in particular the women among them who described enjoying a rare privilege—that of intimately caring for the body of God as Mother.

Although Anandamayi Ma's devotees insisted that she was neither a saint nor a guru, she easily fulfilled the requirements of both categories. The primary condition for Hindu sainthood is that one live a life of *sannyasa*, or "casting off" of the material world. Although Ma never took formal vows of *sannyasa*, she was the paramount renunciant. She deeply embraced the logic of homelessness, calling no place home yet seeming comfortable everywhere, describing herself as "a bird on the wing." She had no interest in material possessions and always wrapped herself in a simple white cotton cloth. Apparently effort-lessly, she practiced austerities and self-denial throughout her life; she was a lifelong celibate, went through periods when she would eat as little as a grain of rice per day, and engaged in periods of *mauna*, or silence lasting as long as three years. Ma's egolessness is well documented. She called herself simply "this body" and seemed devoid of the manifestations of ego—anger, desire, greed. She was said to follow only her *kheyal*, or the reflection of the divine will, in any action. She was always one-pointed in her devotion to and absorp-tion in God. When asked if she did not feel annoyance at the thousands of devotees who crowded to touch her feet or receive her blessings, she replied, "Why would I feel bothered by these things? I feel they are simply parts of this body, like my hands or feet."

The other two identifying characteristics of Hindu sainthood are the ability to manifest states of spiritual ecstasy and God absorption, or *bhavas*, and the existence of miraculous powers, or *siddhis*. Every interview that I conducted with Anandmayi Ma's devotees was replete with stories of Ma's extraordinary states and her spiritual powers. For example, Sita Gupta, a householder devotee witnessed the following *bhava* of Ma in 1928, when Sita was eighteen:

> In the evening Ma came. The *kirtan* [devotional chanting session]
> was almost over. Everyone was getting more enthusiastic and an
> echo started resounding. Ma started dancing in a circle. We all
> caught hands and made a circle around Ma. Ma took five to six
> rounds. Suddenly she lay on the floor and started rotating like the
> earth moves round the sun, like a dry leaf. The *kirtan* came to an
> end. Everyone was gazing at Ma, amazed. Ma was still rolling; after
> ten minutes, she sat up. Her face looked like the sun, there was
> such a reddish glow, and her eyes had an eternal gaze. She started
> reciting verses in something like Pali, something close to Sanskrit.
> It was as if she were listening to some very sweet melodious music
> very far off. Then she said some mantras for five or ten minutes.
> Then gradually she started to come back. At that time everybody
> touched her feet. Didi took her inside her room.[2]

Forty-three out of forty-four of my interviews with devotees of Anandamayi Ma contained stories of miraculous events associated with Ma. Most typical were stories of miraculous hearings, of Ma's ability to read the minds of her devotees, of her appearance in dreams or visions, her protection of devotees, her fulfilling of devotees' desires, and even her interventions in global conflicts. There were many stories demonstrating her *siddhis*, or miraculous powers, such as her knowledge of the past, present, and future, her materialization of objects, and her omniscience. One of my favorite stories was told to me by an elderly renunciant (*brahmacharini*) woman as I was leaving Ma's ashram in Kankhal to board a train to Varanasi:

> One day when I was a young woman, I was drawn to meet Mother.
> I went to where she was staying in Brindavan and as soon as I saw

her I was filled with devotion. I began to throw myself at the feet of Mother. It was natural. But some girls near Mother chastised me, saying, "No one is allowed to touch Mother's feet!" That night I had a dream. In the dream Ma was sitting so sweetly on a cot in a beautiful garden. When I approached her, she garlanded me with a *mala* of flowers and motioned for me to touch her feet, which I did. I awoke with a beautiful feeling. It was so sweet. Many years later I was preparing for Ma to visit the house of my elder brother in Calcutta. When Ma arrived, she seated herself on a cot in the midst of my brother's beautiful garden. Ma beckoned me forward. She took the *mala* from around her neck and placed it around my neck. Then Ma said, "Isn't there something else you long for?" She pointed to her feet. I *pranamed* [bowed down] to touch Ma's feet. I was full of amazement.

Anandamayi Ma's devotees insisted that she was not a guru. They maintained that unlike a guru, Ma had nothing to attain in this lifetime, that she was born a perfected being and was, in fact, an avatar, or incarnation of God. Yet Ma certainly fulfilled the functions of a Hindu guru for her close devotees. My interviews demonstrated that Ma did, indeed, give powerful initiation, or *diksha*, to most of her lifetime devotees and even some people who met her only once through the classical modalities of touch, spiritual gaze, word (mantra), and even thought. Devotees who received this initiation told stories of a complete redirection of their lives after that moment, from the material to the spiritual, from outer direction to inner direction. For example, in an interview in Kankhal, Swami Jnanananda, a former French physician, describes his initiation as a classic experience of *shaktipat*, or awakening, during his first darshan with Ma in 1951:

Meeting Ma was not something very important to me, it was very secondary. . . . So I went to the ashram and just then Ma Anandamayi came out and she looked at me. You know, she had this special look. It looked at you, inside you, and through you to beyond you. Like seeing your past, your future, your destiny. I felt something strange inside. So instead of going away, I said, "Let's sit a little more." So I sat and there was *kirtan. Kirtan* I like very much. Then I went back to my hotel, to my room. And there was an inner explosion, a revolution within myself, you see? A feeling of unearthly love, unearthly love. And the solid conviction, without a shadow of a doubt, that this was the guru I was looking for. . . . And it lasted, it didn't go away. Next morning I came to the ashram, asked permission to stay in the ashram. She agreed and since [then] I'm there.

Anandamayi Ma's teachings can be reduced to one statement, "God alone exists." The Divine Absolute veils him/herself in order to enjoy the divine play of life in the world of form, the world of duality in which everything is impermanent and illusory. The person who has forgotten that he or she is God suffers as things change and eventually turns within to find that which is permanent, the Self of All. Ma recommended that people begin the process of turning within at whatever point they are, and she prescribed many different practices depending on an individual's inclination and capacity. Yet always the message was one of restraint of the senses, one-pointedness on the Divine, and repetition of one's chosen name of God. Ma was tireless is stating her conviction that anyone can know God, indeed can become God, if only they possess the desire.

I did not come to India in the summer of 1990 prepared to do research on someone considered a female incarnation of God. I had my own agenda, which was to study a woman saint who might serve as a powerful model for her women devotees, offering them an inspiring alternative to the sometimes oppressive paradigm of the devoted Hindu wife. Yet the book that came out of this research, *Mother of Bliss: Ānandamayī Mā (1896–1982)*, reflects a dramatic change of focus that was foreshadowed by the following incident.

In September 1990, full of anticipation and excitement, I was traveling on a train from Banaras to Allahabad. Things were beginning to come together. I was about to meet and interview the most prominent biographer of Ananda-mayi Ma, Bithika Mukerji, emeritus professor at Banaras Hindu University, with whom I had been corresponding for several years. From the train station in Allahabad, I took a horse-drawn wagon to the grand Victorian house which is Bithika's family home. We were greeted very graciously by Bithika-ji, who is a strikingly handsome, brilliant yet serene woman, and told that dinner was almost ready.

I was quite nervous to be sitting down to a meal with the person whom I expected would be central to my research in India. As the first course was being cleared, Bithika-ji, wasting no time, asked me to tell her about my work. I said, "Well, I am very excited to be doing this study on Ma. You know, I have been interested in women saints for a long time." A look of alarm and even horror came over Bithika's face. "My dear Lisa," Bithika said emphatically, "Ma was neither a woman nor a saint!" She added, "Once I was invited to give a talk on Ma at a conference on women saints. I refused! They obviously did not have an understanding of who Ma was!" I was speechless.

Indeed, this interaction was central to my research on Anandamayi Ma. Although I had considered myself particularly respectful of Hindu tradition, as of that moment I was being called upon to deconstruct and transcend the categories of "woman" and "saint" and to entertain new and less familiar cat-egories.

As Norman Cutler notes, in spite of the twentieth century's romance with the concept of God as "symbol" and its aversion to the concept of concrete divinity, India still fully embraces God as possessing an embodied reality and valorizes a personal relationship with an embodied God. "In India," says Cutler, "a 'personal' relationship between deity and devotees is possible as a conse-quence of the embodiment of both. Deprived of a body, neither human nor deity is capable of particularized, 'personal' interactions."[3] In the course of my interviews with Anandamayi Ma's closest devotees, I asked twenty-eight people

"Who is Ma?" and, not surprisingly, the answers were as diverse as the devotees themselves. Narendranath Bose said, "You see, for everybody, Ma was a very different person because she responded to individual vibrations. You will have to draw your own conclusions." But the most common reply to the question was, "Ma was God." Nearly all devotees were interviewed in English and, although some went on to give equivalent Sanskrit terms such as Parabrahman or Devi, the first word that came to them to describe Ma was God.

One celibate female renunciant, or *brahmacharini*, Malini-Di, spoke poignantly about knowing Ma since birth, having been born into a devotee family:

> When I was in school, I was about seven or eight years old, the Christian nuns over there, they said that God never comes on earth. And so, I was very upset. I said, "No, I have spoken to God!" And they said, "You can't speak to God. There is no such thing. God never comes to earth. Only Jesus Christ can and no one else!" They said unless you believe in Jesus Christ, you can never reach God. So I was very perturbed. All these things I was told. And when I came back home, I cried and cried. So my mother asked, "What is the matter?" So I told her. "They have been telling me that unless I become a Christian, I won't reach God. And I told them, 'No, I have met God I have talked to Her. I have seen Her. For on our holidays, we go to God!' How can they say those things?" So my mother said, "Don't worry, they won't understand this. But, yes, your God talks to you."

When I asked Malini-Di, "Did your family have a chosen deity?" she replied, "No, we believe in Krishna and Ram and things like that, but as children we were taught that Ma was everything. For us Ma was Krishna, Ma was Ram, Ma was Shiva, Ma was everything. To us the name of God was Ma." Sita Gupta, a housewife, reiterated this theme when she said, "My children and grandchildren know of no other God except Mother. You say Ram or Krishna or Shiva or Devi, they think Ma. They don't know these others, just Ma."

Naren Bose, a sophisticated young Calcutta businessman, trained at Boston University and Harvard, who also grew up in a family devoted to Ma, put it this way, "For me, Ma is God. I have no deep knowledge of the Hindu scriptures or any scriptures. So my conviction in any one established religion is not there. All my convictions are what I have seen through Ma. All my belief is only Ma. And God for me is Ma. Ma is my life. Very simple. Everything."

For some devotees, recognition of Ma's divinity took time. Uma Chatterji said, "After I met Ma, I could not immediately associate Ma with God. But after some time, it became Ma and God, the duality. It took years to identify Ma with God as One. And it took place because of fantastic experiences and dramatic situations. But for Ma there is no beginning and end to the story. It is all her *lila* [play]."

One such fantastic experience that obviously became a part of the family's perception of Ma was reported by Gita-Di Bose:

My grandfather was a doctor from the medical school in Calcutta. There were only ten of them at that time sitting around Ma. All of a sudden grandfather started feeling drowsy and he thought, "Why am I feeling like that? I just got up from an afternoon sleep." His eyes just closed all of a sudden. And then he opened them forcibly and he saw there was no Ma. And in the place of Ma, there was one of the ten avatars of Devi The form he saw was Chinnamasta. You know, the body was here and the head she is holding in her hand. He saw that form, and the nine other people, they each saw a different form. And another devotee was a judge. He saw all ten forms. And after that the drowsiness went away. And everybody asked each other, "What have you seen? I don't know what to think!" And the judge said, "I saw all ten forms." And they ran to him and said, "You are so lucky!" My grandfather told me this when I was little.

Regardless of whether devotees thought of Ma as an incarnation of Devi, of Krishna, or of the formless *brahman*, she was considered by each of them to be a divine incarnation, both the means and the goal of spiritual life.

In this article we will explore how Anandamayi Ma's devotees, particularly her women devotees, have been affected by having had what they consider to be a personal relationship with God in a woman's body. More important, we ask whether or not we can assume that a relationship of this kind necessarily empowers women. We will see that the answers to these questions are complex and fraught with ambiguity. As Caroline Walker Bynum would say, Anandamayi Ma, in her full complexity as a gender-related symbol, is certainly polysemic and in some ways might be " 'about' values other than gender."[4] We entertain the possibility that there are ways in which Ma's being born in a woman's body particularly inspired and benefited women and ways in which it was irrelevant, and we ask why that is so. For example, how can Ma's renunciant women devotees, who have apparently followed in her footsteps, maintain that Ma can never be a model and that they could never identify with her? How could Ma have lived such an unconventional life compared to most Hindu women and have advised certain women devotees to stay at home and devote themselves to their husbands and children? In the course of reflecting on this multidimensional issue, we will consider briefly the subject of the cultural construction of gender as it relates to the spiritual path within the Hindu tradition and as it is reflected in the community of Anandamayi Ma. We will examine Ma's words on the relevance of gender to spiritual life as well as the words of other contemporary Hindu religious figures.

Why Did Ma Take Form as a Woman?

To initiate our exploration of gender and Anandamayi Ma, we begin by consulting the voices of Anandamayi Ma's women devotees themselves. In twelve of the interviews with my female contributors, after I had asked who they thought Ma was and received the nearly unanimous answer that Ma was not a woman, not a saint, not a guru, but was God incarnate, I asked, "Why do you think Ma took form as a woman?" My interview with Sita Gupta, for which Rupa Vishvanathan was the translator, was representative of the various dimensions of the issue. At first Sita had some difficulty even relating to the question. Her first response was, "For Ma, female or male, it made no difference. For Ma, woman's body, man's body, it made no difference." When I asked, "If she could have chosen any form, why did she choose this one?" Sita-Di replied, "That is for Ma to say." At that point, Rupa interrupted to say, "I feel like this—every now and then, God takes sometimes the form of a father, sometimes a mother, because some feel more comfortable with a father than a mother. I feel some of us are more comfortable with Mother. I'm more comfortable with Mother than Father." Then Sita said, "Didi [Ma's closest female disciple] explained, 'This time Ma has come for the ladies.' Didi said this!" Rupa added, "Because we can do personal service for Ma." Sita elaborated:

> We can touch, go ahead, massage her legs. You can't do that with a man. In Vindyachal, Ma used to lie down and one person would be massaging her arm and one person her leg, massaging and talking to Ma and Ma would be laughing. She took off all her clothes and her petticoat used to be there. And she would be laughing and talking. You see, that intimacy you cannot get except with the Mother. So soft, just like a new-born baby, so soft to massage, so smooth. That's a personal feeling. . . . The ladies understood her better and felt closer to her than the men.

These themes—Ma's blindness to gender, the special intimacy possible between female devotees and Ma and, thus, between women and God, the preference for Mother over Father, and the relative inaccessibility of Ma to male devotees—were mirrored in most of the responses. A number of women agreed with Sita Gupta that Ma, as an incarnation of ultimate truth, was neither male nor female and that as such she did not have an eye for gender distinctions. At the same time, however, they emphasized that because they were women, they could enjoy a special intimacy with Ma. Due to the cultural prohibitions governing the relationships between unrelated men and women in India, only women could spend time in close proximity to Ma. For example, Vasudha-Di, now age fifty-four, described a special moment with Ma when she was eight:

> When we came from Assam in 1944, Ma was staying on a boat on the Ganges. And my father would bathe in the Ganges three times a day. We used to go with him. We used to see Ma's boat and we would go to it to get *prasad* [blessed food]. We would wash our hands in the Ganges. And Ma would talk. Ma used to swim very nicely and sometimes Ma would jump into the Ganges. I was only

eight years old, but I learned to swim. And sometimes I would hold Ma's feet. And we played. The gentlemen kept their distance from Ma. And Didi did not swim, so she stayed on the deck. And afterwards, in the full moonlight, Ma would sing on the boat and we would have ice cream.

This incident is reminiscent of an incident described by *brahmacharini* Nirmala-Di in which Ma orchestrated a *lila*, or divine play, for a few young women, costuming them as pairs of gods and goddesses and dancing with them. At the end of that story, Nirmala-Di emphasized, "And it was only women!"

Interestingly, two male devotees mentioned the disadvantage of being a man around Ma, one of them expressing the longing to have been more intimate with Ma. Swami Premananda, who had met Ma nearly a half-century ago as a twenty-five-year-old university graduate, made this poignant statement about the fate of being male around Ma:

> When I came to stay with Ma, I could not accept that it was not possible to be near the body of Mother. Her being a lady and I being a man, there were certain limitations. I couldn't be involved with her. There are certain things one shouldn't do. . . . Then I was a foolish boy, because I didn't know all these things one should and shouldn't do. Ma had to teach me. For example, there is this Kanyapith, this girl's school. Ma went there one day, but she didn't take me. So sometime later, I went there. I went inside. Now, in India, the boys and girls are separated. I went inside the Kanyapith and Ma scolded me, right there. She said, "Have you gone insane!" I said, "Ma, I went along with you." She said, "It is all right that you went along, but you should not come in here." I was crying. I said, "I have not done anything wrong!" Then one day, Ma was sleeping there and I said I also wanted to sleep there. And Ma did not take food herself, she had to be fed. So, she was being fed by someone and I said, "I also want to feed you." And her hair, she had very long black hair and I just wanted to comb that. . . . It took me a long time to accept.

What Premananda was longing for, then, was the intimacy that Ma's close women devotees enjoyed when caring for Ma's physical body as they apparently engaged in the mundane activities of life. However, when engaging in these activities with Ma, her women devotees tell us that these activities were hardly mundane. If we imagine, as Ma's community imagines, an opportunity to swim with God, to sleep next to God, to feed God, or to comb God's hair, we can understand why the men around Ma felt envious.[5]

Several women emphasized, in particular, that the cultural context into which Ma came was one in which women were extremely cloistered, to the extent that they were unable to participate fully in spiritual life. Because Ma took a female form, she offered protection to women wanting to pursue *sadhana*. Malini-Di explained:

In U.P. [Uttara Pradesh], people are very strict about this. They
don't let you go to any sadhu. They don't let you go to any person
like that. It was only because Ma had come in the form of a lady
that we were allowed to go near Ma. Otherwise, we were not. In
U.P., they were very strict about this. . . . And you see, women were
always suppressed. But Ma brought out the personalities of the
women. . . . And the life of *brahmacharya*, it would never have been
allowed, because it is considered very, very wrong not to get the girl
married. . . . At the time, things had become so immoral that you
couldn't leave girls unmarried.

This point of view is echoed in other responses. Lalita Kumar said: "Ma came
in this form especially for the women of this land, because there have been so
many rascals masquerading in the form of *mahatma*s, in the sannyasin garb,
and taking advantage of women, that it was so utterly safe to be with Mother,
for women of all ages." Gita-Di Bose believes that Ma "became Ma" because
women prayed to the Divine Feminine: "In India, the women are very much
suppressed by the men. That is why she became Ma. Most of the women at
the time must have prayed to Shakti. So she came in like a woman. But she is
not a woman, she is not a man."

Other women spoke more specifically about Ma's taking form as a woman
in order to enable women to have greater spiritual equality and freedom.
Lakshmi Shrivastav, a university professor, speaks of Ma's helping women gain
access to formerly male spiritual practices. She said, "I have read history and
also a little bit of anthropology, and I think that in India especially, if the woman
changes, then it is easier to change the whole society. I feel that. At the time
Ma came, it was 1896. In East Bengal there weren't even trains, just boats. So
it was only her coming that introduced women to *kirtan*, the all-night chanting.
She introduced women to that. She said, 'Why can't the women do that?' There
were many things like that. She gave them courage." Lakshmi was one of many
to mention Ma's arranging for women to be allowed to perform *kirtan*, something that was not accessible to Ma as a young wife. Lakshmi went on to give
an example of Ma's inspiring women to be more courageous: "Once Mataji
was in Banaras staying at the house of a lady. One night Ma went out and she
hadn't returned. That lady said to herself, 'As a woman, I can't go out at night
in a sari.' It was quite late. So she just put on a man's dhoti, put on a *dushala*
[a shawl], put her hair up in a turban, took a *lathi* [a stick] and she went to that
place to get Ma. So this is the sort of courage Ma gives." This example is
particularly interesting because it seems clear that Lakshmi saw the "lady" in
question as inspired by Ma's fearlessness and refusal to behave in a conventional manner. Ma herself always wore a white cotton sari wrapped around her
in an unconventional way and surely was not afraid to go out at night.

By contrast, Swami Brahmananda, the head of the Kankhal Ashram, who
voluntarily brought up the question of why Ma was born as a woman, had a
different slant on Ma's mission, not surprisingly one involving the uplift of
men. In the process of explaining his "idea," he nuanced Ma's gender in a

different way. He said, "Ma was a lady. She was not male or female. But because she was a lady, whenever she went into a household, she was accessible to the females. Now what happened, she came to this world to change, to bring change. Now who can change the world? The mother. The household mother can change the boys, not the father. You know, the boy stays twelve, fifteen years with mother. These ladies are future mothers, so they can teach whatever Ma used to teach." Having just interviewed four female renunciants whom he had told me would help me understand Ma, I asked for clarification. "Did Ma encourage those women to stay in the household or to become *brahmacharinis*?" Brahmananda replied, "No, no, she encouraged them to stay in the house and change their sons and their husbands. That was the idea. And in the future, thirty years after Ma's passing, there will be a new generation. That is my idea. And I have seen the boys who came in touch with Ma. They are more forceful than the people of this generation, the younger ones. And they got their teaching from their own mother who got it from Ma." Not surprisingly, there were no women devotees who believed that Ma's purpose in coming into the world as a woman was to raise a generation of more "forceful" men.

Ma's Accessibility to Women

There seem to be three main ways in which Ma's being a woman particularly benefited and inspired women. The first, which has been well documented in the interviews throughout this study, is that because Ma was in a female body, women had greater access to her and, therefore, greater intimacy with her. In watching the films and videotapes of Ma, it is striking to see the number of women, both householders and *brahmacharinis*, surrounding Ma at public events. I have been able to see the faces of many of the women devotees whom I interviewed hovering around Ma. I can only imagine that in Ma's private moments, there was a total absence of men and the opportunity for many women to serve God as Ma very closely. It is easy to understand how those women who physically cared for Ma might have been particularly devastated by her death. Chitra, a *brahmacharini*, movingly expresses the grief of many women close to Ma in an article in *Ananda Varta* written in 1984. She says, "My pained heart cries out in anguish to take shelter in the pure haven of love that was our Mother's lap."[6]

While women devotees' privileged access to Ma offered them a rare spiritual opportunity to have a personal relationship with God as Ma, caring for her and being cared for by her, it also offered them an emotional opportunity. Most Hindu marriages, and certainly Bengali ones, require a young woman, who is often a mere teenager, to leave her own mother and spend the rest of her life in the household of her husband, receiving what motherly attention is available, which may be little or none, from her mother-in-law. The heart-wrenching separation of a daughter from her mother at marriage is sung about and ritualized in the time preceding a traditional Hindu wedding, so that nearly every young girl, although prepared for it, also dreads it.[7] After the marriage, depending upon regional and caste customs, a young bride is allowed to visit her own mother only at specific times of the year and, depending upon distance, perhaps only once a year or less. For married devotees, in the absence of a continuous and nurturing relationship with their own mother, Ma fulfilled that motherly role. Women often mentioned that the kind of intimacy that they enjoyed with Ma mirrored their relationship with their biological Ma. For example, Krishna Bhattacharya, presently in her sixties or seventies, reminisced about a time when Ma invited her to come to Naimisharanya:

> Just like a daughter who after so many days goes to her parents' house, I was looked after by everybody with care. In that way I was. Naimisharanya is a very quiet and peaceful place, and Ma used to ask me every day whether I have seen everything there, and whether I have taken my food, lunch, etc. Ma would let me take her hair down and lie on the cot. We would chat, just as mothers and daughters do. She would say, "What did they feed you? Was the food good?" And I used to ask her about the proper way I should make my rituals and things. And at that time, she used to ask everybody to leave the room, so I could be alone with Ma.

For Ma's *brahmacharini* devotees, the choice to live with Ma as celibate women meant that they could have a lifelong relationship with both mothers, their own biological mother and their spiritual mother. For example, when I interviewed the brahmacharini Malini-Di, I also met her mother, who was living in the Kankhal Ashram with her. Mother and daughter seemed to be enjoying an intimacy and a proximity not usually possible when a daughter leaves home for her husband's household. In addition, as Malini intimated, whereas an unmarried daughter is considered an embarrassment and a potential disaster, a *brahmacharini* daughter, safe in the confines of Ma's ashram, can be a source of pride.

Ma as an Advocate for Spiritual Equality for Women

The second way in which Ma's being a woman benefited women was that Ma, because of women's accessibility to her, was in a better position to be an advocate for their spiritual equality with men. In particular, she was able to inspire some of them—the ones whom she determined were suited—to take a vow of lifelong celibacy and become *brahmacharinis*, pursuing full-time *sadhana*. We have already mentioned that eight out of the twenty-five women whom I interviewed for this study had taken such a vow. This act of renunciation apparently had both associated difficulties and boons. On the one hand, "Ma's girls," as they were called, lived a cloistered life in which they had few personal possessions and little or no privacy, were told what to do and where to do it, and engaged in various levels of *tapasya*, or austerities, such as sleeping on a thin mat on the floor. On the other hand, they were just that, "Ma's girls," and as such they enjoyed the enviable position of living and traveling with Ma most of the time. Certainly many of them must have been motivated to become *brahmacharinis* for this reason. While women householder devotees came and went, based on their husband's permission and their family responsibilities, "Ma's girls" stayed on, caring for Ma.

Although it would be tempting to think of "Ma's girls" as doing more combing of Ma's hair than meditation, it is apparent that along with physical proximity to Ma came Ma's close scrutiny of their spiritual progress. Swami Gitananda, the only sannyasini whom I interviewed, described the benefits as well as the demands of the "girls' " relationship with Ma:

> [The girls] who wanted to be closely related to Ma were treated differently by Ma. She was open with them. She liked to scold them in front of the assembled people. Ma had a free, unrestrained relationship with us and took pleasure in speaking to us. And we girls took pride in our status. Ma would scold us in public for the smallest infractions. . . . It was only for show and then she would say later, "Now, I can scold you with all my heart. I can be very direct with you. I do not have to hide anything." This was our pride that Ma thought we were special. . . . With us Ma felt every little, tiny behavior had to be so fragrant and fruitful as a rose in full bloom. You see, Ma wanted us to blossom into perfection. So she pointed out even the smallest failing so that we will improve and make our life beautiful like a rose.

Even deeper insight into the blessings as well as the challenges inherent in the relationship between Ma and her *brahmacharinis* can be gained by reading the article entitled "Let Us Be Filled with Sweet Memories," written in 1984 by the *brahmacharini* Chitra.[8] In this article, Chitra reproduces a letter dictated by Ma to her and five of Ma's other "older friends," whom Ma had left in Kishenpur Ashram in Dehradun during the "three severe winter months to practice intensive *sadhana*." Although Chitra frames the article by saying that "there is no one now who lavishes grace and compassion on us as did our adored Ma," one can only imagine that practicing sadhana in the bitter cold of the Himalayan foothills in December and January without central heating, coupled with Ma's absence, was pure *tapasya*.[9] Ma, indeed, acknowledges this in her letter, saying that "we are told that for the sake of concentrated *sadhana*, sadhus and sannyasins [both terms for male practitioners] often stay in cold places since this is congenial to meditation." She says that spending too much time traveling with Ma and "meeting too many people becomes an obstacle." Thus, for their "spiritual welfare," Ma has had the *kheyal* (alignment with divine will) that they should be away from "this body." Ma chastens, "Therefore, this splendid opportunity should not be wasted. The aroma of the *sadhana* of these *tapasvinis* [female ascetics] must be noticed in their looks, their way of speaking; each movement should manifest their progress towards Truth. Every effort must be made to speak the truth, to remain steeped in the spiritual, to advance toward immortality."[10]

The letter goes on to address each *brahmacharini* individually with both motherly advice and compassion as well as gurulike corrections. For example, Ma is happy to hear that Pushpa's and Chitra's inflammation of the throat has subsided. Yet Ma says, "Udas is growing old, wrinkles have started on her face. When will you concentrate on *sadhana*? Are you going to spend your whole life attending to this body? Complete your *japa* [reciting a mantra] and do your *sadhana* with enthusiasm and steadiness."[11] She cautions against drinking too much tea in winter and recommends hot water instead. At the same time she says, "Many a day have you spent watching the sights of the world, joking and laughing in the worldly way; now, friends, be pilgrims on the journey to your real Home! Do not think that just because you have not felt His presence and the touch of Him you are free to while away your time in frivolities, this can never lead to your real welfare."[12] Ma closes with detailed instructions for daily recitation of sacred texts, *japa*, and meditation.

This letter belies any impression we might have gotten that the *brahma-charini* close to Ma did not really engage in *sadhana*, but only cared for Ma as one would a *murti*, or statue of a deity. Yet Ma seems to be acknowledging that tendency. She seems to be calling them to turn their focus away from her and back to themselves and their own spiritual progress, maintaining that "patience and forbearance are necessary for all. How can the foundation be laid without endurance?"[13]

The second evidence of Ma's advocacy for the spiritual equality of women is her establishment of the Kanyapith, the Sanskrit school for girls from ages five to twelve, in Banaras. Although it is firmly maintained that Ma never affiliated herself with any institution established in her name, both my interviews and the literature available on Ma point to her active involvement in the school. Swami Samatananda told me, "Our Kanyapith girls are famous in Banaras. They speak in Sanskrit. Ma used to watch the girls speaking in Sanskrit, doing dramas from Sanskrit literature. They have received much respect and Mataji founded this institution . . . for girl's education, for the uplifting of the girls." Uma Chatterji told me that the Kanyapith was technically started by Gurupriya Devi in order "to provide protection for girls who did not desire marriage and education for those who do." Parents, she said, used to send their girls to get a good, spiritual education, but now there are also "economic and domestic reasons." But remarkably, even today, 25 percent of the girls stay on to be lifelong *brahmacharinis*, teaching in the school. Certainly Ma's support of and involvement in the school reflects her commitment to spiritual educa-tion for girls and to the institution of *brahmacharya* and its availability to Hindu girls as an alternative to marriage.

A third demonstration of Ma's advocacy for women's spiritual equality is her arranging for certain women to participate in the Vedic ceremony of *upan-ayana*, or the investiture with the sacred thread, an initiation available only to boys for nearly two thousand years.[14] The *upanayana* has traditionally marked the passage of a boy of the highest three castes into the period of celibate study in which he was to master the Vedas. According to Gurupriya Devi's journal, which is corroborated by my interviews with Ma's devotees, sometime in 1929, in Dacca, "the subject of investing women with the sacred thread had arisen in Ma's *kheyala* and she herself had taken on a sacred thread."[15] Keshab Bhattacharya, in the midst of telling me about Ma's enthusiasm upon hearing about his *upanayana* in 1971 at the age of eight or nine, said, "Yes, it was Ma who started the ancient practice of giving the sacred thread to brahman girls. There's a very interesting story of how she was playing with a gold chain of hers and one day, it had three strings, she started putting it around her neck and putting the other end under her arm. She kept it like that for some time, telling Didi, 'Look, I'm now a dvija, a twice born.' "[16] According to Gurupriya Devi, sometime thereafter at the Ramna Ashram in Calcutta, Ma gave Bhaiji, who was not a brahman, the sacred thread because she had "the feeling that he was a brahman."[17]

In 1934, according to Didi, right after Ma had given her the name Gurupriya along with some yellow clothes and the instruction to live as a *brahmacharini*, Ma "raised one more point":

> "Find out from the scholars in Kashi [Banaras] whether the ritual of conferring the sacred thread on women is mentioned in our scriptures or not. . . ." At Kashi we made exhaustive inquiries, from many scholars, about investing with the sacred thread. The unanimous reply was, "This tradition was prevalent in ancient times, but we cannot find an opinion for modern times." Finally we decided we could get the best solution from Mahamahopadhyaya Pandit Sri Gopinath Kaviraj and so we approached him. Ma also had suggested his name to us. He did some research on the subject and found many examples of instances where women had received the sacred thread. He proposed, "If Ma so desires, she can give the sacred thread to women even now. Ma's will is scriptural. No other opinion is necessary."[18]

And so, in 1935, Ma had Gurupriya Devi invested with the sacred thread, along with Bholanath's grandniece, Maroni. Swami Samatananda spoke about the same sequence of events:

> There are some things that created history. People went against her down in Banaras. People were very much against her. Gopinath Kaviraj was the most learned person in Banaras in those days. He has given me a draft in favor of sacred thread [for women]. I have a copy. I will show it to you. He said, in those days, in the ancient days, a guru can give a sacred thread to any lady or anyone. If guru thinks he or she sees fit, since Mataji is the greatest guru, if she sees fit, he did not think she did anything wrong.

Malini-Di told me the rest of the sequence. She said after Gurupriya Devi received the sacred thread, Ma had Pumananda, Chandan, Udas, Nirukma, Jaya, and Dika take it. I asked if these people asked for the sacred thread. Malini replied, "No, Ma asked everybody. She asked Padmaji—all these people—'Will you take? Will you take?' Some said 'No,' because it meant you had to shave off your hair and take the sacred thread. Then you had to follow a bunch of rules and regulations, and some people felt because of their health they couldn't do." I asked Malini if Ma had asked her and she said, "No, I am not a brahman. She did ask Swami Paramananda, 'Do non-brahmans also . . . can we give them?' and Swamiji said, 'Amongst the men folk, there is, but I don't know about the ladies.' So on that basis."

In a *satsang* in Dehradun in 1980, Ma talks about the issue of the sacred thread for women and a conversation she had with the Mahamandaleshvara, an important regional head of a order of sannyasis. She says that the Mahamandaleshvara came to her respectfully but concerned, saying, "You have taken this sacred thread. Will you please tell me something about it?" Ma relates the argument that ensued between the two of them in which Ma argued strongly that the true meaning of the scriptures is that Kaliyuga, the present, most degenerate age, is no different from Kritayuga, the perfect age, and, therefore, women deserve to be treated equally. She says that finally the Mahamandaleshvara relented, saying, "Ma what you have said and done is all correct." In closing the story, Ma says:

> Why did he say so? The reason is that this body put on that sacred thread by herself. She started reciting *Gayatri* [mantra] on her own. She did not make any guru. She did not listen to that *Gayatri* from anybody. It automatically came from her heart. That is why this body says, "This mantra does not exist in any educated person alone. It is not the property of any scholar. It exists in everyone and when it comes forth, it seems to be flowing from *Apaurusha* [Not-Man], not from a man but from God."[19]

There is one other phenomenon that demonstrates Ma's advocacy for women's spiritual equality: the planning for the construction of a *yajnashala*, or building dedicated to the performance of the sacred fire ritual, at Kankhal Ashram, which was done entirely by a committee of women selected by Ma. I found out about this while touring the ashram with the *brahmacharini* Malini-Di. She asked me, "Has anyone shown you the *yajnashala*?" I said that I hadn't even heard of it. She smirked and said, "I'm not surprised. The girls built it." We walked over to the large, formal building and Malini-Di began to explain:

> *Atirudra Mahayajna* took place from 6 May 1981 until 16 May 1981. And 135 learned *pandits* took part in it. All the *mahatmas* of significance at the time were present for that function. . . .*Atirudra Mahayajna* is performed for the welfare of the world. There were eleven *kunds* [enclosed pits] in which the fire was ignited. . . . There was a committee that Ma formed to design this building. The president was Padma Mishra, the vice president was Parul Banerji, the treasurer was Nirmala Nahandu, the secretary was Shanta Patak, known as Pushnananda. And she is the daughter of the vice president of the country, Mr. G. S. Patak. And myself. We were five. We ap-

proached an architect and he designed it for us according to the rules of the shastras. . . . We researched everything. We enjoyed ourselves and we learned a lot about the *yajna*.

Malini-Di was obviously very proud of the building and remembered every detail of the planning and construction as well as every detail of the fire ritual itself. Lakshmi Shrivastav, another *brahmacharini*, remembers the process similarly. In telling me about it she emphasized that "we had control of the accounts, of everything. The treasurer handled that. There were lakhs of money. We arranged everything."

It is obvious from these examples that Ma was an advocate for her women devotees, particularly for her *brahmacharinis*. She held them very close, gave them a great deal of support and guidance, and offered them many opportunities for spiritual advancement. In addition, particularly in the case of the construction of the *yajnashala*, Ma empowered the women close to her to learn new skills and take charge of things that were normally within the male domain. In this way, she nurtured a certain kind of independence in her celibate women devotees, which I felt when I interviewed them. The seven *brahmacharinis* and one sannyasini whom I met were, as a group, very strong, outspoken, and independent. Although Ma was clearly the center of their lives, they were hardly shrinking bhaktas. One can imagine them arguing with Ma, pleading with her, and being fully engaged with her as individual personalities. Perhaps this is what Ma intended to foster in them as they developed into "pilgrims on the journey to their real Home." Regardless, she gave them every opportunity to develop spiritual parity with men.[20]

Ma as the Perfect Householder, the Perfect *Sadhika*, and the Perfect Sannyasini

The third way in which Anandamayi Ma's being born in a female body might have particularly benefited women was that different women could identify with different stages of her life and be inspired. It has been established that Ma was in no way the "perfect wife" according to the *dharmashastra* paradigm. However, one could imagine that Ma's life with Bholanath might inspire housewives to make time in their day for *sadhana* and the pursuit of God. Clearly Ma's priority during the years of her "lila of *sadhana*" was not her relationship with her husband but her relationship with God. I did meet many housewives who, at least since their children were grown, have devoted large parts of their day to puja, *japa*, and meditation. I met women in that phase of life who had left husbands to live in Kankhal Ashram for part of the year. In fact, Brahmacharini Chandan says, "The lesson that we have received in this context of the veiled *bahu* [Nirmala as a young bride] is that, though we complain about our inability to sit for *sadhana* due to our household responsibilities, yet, if there is a real awakening of the desire for attainment even from the worldly point of view, then, despite remaining in the midst of all, an effort can

be made to undertake the journey toward that Supreme State."²¹ We will discover in the following section, however, that Ma's advice to housewives was
largely traditional and that her example was probably lost on most householder
women. She certainly did not seem to be saying, "Be the kind of *sadhika* I was
when I was married."

There is no question that Ma's life as a renunciant was one of the factors
in inspiring many women to leave the worldly life and become *brahmacharinis*.
However, it may be that Ma's definition of *sadhana* and that of her *brahmacharinis* were not the same. It may have been difficult for many *brahmacharinis*
to separate their desire to do *sadhana* from their desire to be with Ma. In some
ways, being with Ma was their *sadhana* and try as Ma might have to get the
focus off her and onto their own spiritual growth, many women saw the goal
of life as being as physically close to Ma as possible. We know that very few
women looked up to Ma as a model, because, as Malini-Di said, you would
have to look "way, way up." We turn now to the ways in which Ma's having a
woman's body and leading an unconventional life relative to most Hindu
women did not seem to be a major factor in how devotees, particularly women,
lived their lives and why this was so.

"Do as I Say, Not as I Do"

Although it is apparent that Anandamayi Ma's life presents a radical challenge
to the orthodox concept of marriage, there is a way in which Ma communicated
the message, "Do as I say, not as I do." In spite of Ma's advocacy for the spiritual
equality of women, Ma seemed to hold many orthodox views on how women,
particularly householders, should live their lives. She approved of arranged
marriages and, in spite of her husband, Bholanath's, extreme concern, insti-
gated the betrothal of Bholanath's eight-year-old grand-niece, Maroni (who
lived with them), and her marriage at the age of twelve.²² Ironically, Ma suggested that it was time for Maroni to marry the man to whom she had been
betrothed right after she arranged for Maroni to receive the sacred thread along
with Didi. Mukerji maintains that Ma had Bholanath marry off Maroni so that
he could "discharge his obligations" to her and "resume again his life of *sadhana*."²³ Lipski says that Ma also "counsels: 'There is only one marriage,' and
never advises a second marriage even for widows."²⁴

Ma's advice to women householders was quite conventional. In 1936 Ma
was asked "What *sadhana* can a housewife do?" Ma replies, "*Seva* [selfless
service] and *japa*. All duties can be performed in a spirit of service and dedication. God himself appears to you in the guise of your various obligations in
the world. . . . If you sustain the thought, 'this also is one of the many aspects
of the Divine,' then there need be no conflict between what is worldly and what
is religious."²⁵ It must be said, however, that although she, like the authors of
dharmashastra texts, advised a wife to treat her husband like a god, she also
advised a husband to treat his wife like a goddess. For example, when asked if
renunciation is a prerequisite to communion with God, Ma says:

You are not called upon to retire to the forest, nor to become inert, like a stone, unresponsive to what goes on about you. You have to start life from the position God has placed you in. Be His servant. If you are at home, look upon your son as Balagopal [infant Krishna], your little daughter as Uma [Divine Mother], and your consort as Narayana [God in one form] or Lakshmi [Divine Mother, daughter of Durga]. Do not do harm to anybody. Let the little attachment you have developed to people about you continue within its minimum limit. This world is but a *dharmashala* [a lodge for pilgrims where they may stay for a short time]. When the call will come for your final exit, all the ties of life will have to be snapped and you won't have a moment's reprise.[26]

It is interesting to note in this statement that Ma does seem to be saying that one ultimately needs to progress from householder to sannyasi or sannyasini, if not in this lifetime then in a future one.

It seems that Ma asked most housewives, especially those with husbands unsympathetic to spiritual practice, to fulfill their daily duties, to serve their husband and children as God and to keep their *sadhana* to themselves. Mukerji says that Ma would say, "The efforts you make for your spiritual welfare are to be carefully hidden. Guard them as closely as a miser guards his wealth. You do not have to advertise the fact that you are engaged in *sadhana*. It is between God and you only. . . . You may do your work with your hands, but nobody can prevent you from keeping your mind on God."[27] Ma's conservative attitude toward married women was reflected in that fact that although Ma instituted *kirtan*s (chanting) for women in Dacca, a radical idea for that time, she also made sure they were in the middle of the night so they would not interfere with the daily duties of *stridharma*, or the righteous behavior of a wife. We know that Ma herself neither kept her *sadhana* nor her *bhava*s to herself, nor fulfilled the duties of *stridharma*. It seems as though the kind of piety that Ma recommends for married women mirrors the kind of piety Caroline Walker Bynum sees in medieval Christian women. Bynum calls it an "inner-worldly asceticism" as opposed to a "world-rejecting asceticism," a piety that unites action and contemplation in such a way as to provide continuity in women's lives as they become more spiritualized.[28] This perspective certainly allows for a more positive reading of Ma's message to married women.

More challenging is Ma's apparent attitude toward the practice of *sati*, or the ritual immolation of a wife on her husband's funeral pyre. Ma, along with her mother, Didima, speaks of the honor of having a *sati* in their family lineage.[29] Lipski quotes Ma as having spoken at some length on the reverence due to one who is able to unflinchingly ascend the funeral pyre. He says:

Once a male devotee asked Anandamayi Ma whether by committing suicide upon the death of his beloved wife he would be able to join her. In the strongest possible terms she condemned suicide: "To whom belongs the body that you speak of destroying? Is this the way a human being talks? For shame!" And She added that suicide is nothing but a foolish attempt to escape from harvesting one's karma. It only further retards spiritual progress. However, She does not consider that a woman who had become a *sati* [literally chaste woman], i.e., a widow who had burnt herself on her husband's funeral pyre, had committed suicide. As far as Anandamayi Ma was concerned, *sati* was a ritual death, a confirmation of a wife's unconditional loyalty to her husband and an expression of true chastity. "A real *sati* has to be completely steady in mind and body. If entering the fire she suffers, she cannot be called a *sati*." If thus her conduct in life has been totally unblemished, she will be fearless at the time of immolation. In this connection Anandamayi Ma tells about one of Her ancestors who put one of her fingers into the flame of a candle to test whether she would be able to endure the pain of being burnt. She experienced no pain. Subsequently she ascended her husband's funeral pyre, lay down and remained completely motionless while the flames consumed her body.[30]

Lipski goes on to say that, although Westerners will undoubtedly be shocked by Ma's approval of *sati*, it is important to understand that, from her perspective, "motive is all-important. The true *sati* is not escaping from life but is willing to do her duty according to the dharma [right way of living] prevailing within her cultural milieu at the time. She is acting selflessly and shows that she is not attached to this delusive body." Lipski closes the subject by saying, "It must be said that Anandamayi Ma does not advocate sati in the present age."[31]

Although I was unable to find the original source of Ma's remarks on *sati*, I have no reason to doubt Lipski's rendering. I believe that Ma's attitude toward *sati* derives from a tendency to spiritualize the phenomenon, to idealize asceticism and detachment from the body. It completely disregards the double standard involved in the practice of *sati* and the cultural pressures that have brought women throughout history to consider *sati* as an option. Ma is seeing it purely as the act of an ascetic and, as such, as an act to be honored. Ma's attitude reflects her ability to separate the spiritual liberation of women, with its required asceticism and disengagement from attachments, from their social or political liberation. For Ma, it seems that the end of spiritual liberation justifies the means. As Lipski reminds us, according to Ma, "suffering is really a means to end suffering," and, as such, "should be welcomed."[32]

We can conclude that although Anandamayi Ma was an advocate of women's *spiritual* equality, in many ways she reinforced the *dharmashastra* ideal for women that her life contradicts. Catherine Ojha, having studied thirty-eight female ascetics of Banaras, one of whom was Ma, concludes that although these women are considered to be rebels because of their refusal to live within the bounds of marriage and their adoption of a "masculine type of behavior," they "do not profoundly question the established order." Ojha goes on to say:

The influence [these rebels] get is not used as a platform in order to criticize such or such fundamental aspect of the social model. . . .

When they speak, it is to encourage people to respect their *sva-dharma*, to urge them to adopt dharmic behavior. When, more particularly, they address themselves to women, it is to ask them to follow with more dignity the rules of this *stridharma* which their own life belies. The defense of the caste system, and of all the exclusive types of attitudes involved in it is also their preoccupation. They admit themselves that in their private life they may disregard certain rules but that in public it is their duty to keep their distance in order to educate people. In this respect they are not at all different from the majority of *sadhus* who, though they have left the norm behind, are taking the part of *dharma-raksaka*, or protectors of the *dharma*. . . . In the case of female ascetics, it may sometimes amount to discouraging other women from doing what they have done themselves. But by strengthening the most orthodox socio-religious values, they are assured to maintain a good reputation.[33]

Although it would be difficult to determine the extent to which Ma was motivated by a need "to maintain a good reputation," it does seem that, indeed, she often functioned as a "protector of the dharma," and, in doing so, she did not expect or even want married women to follow in her footsteps. Rather, she expected them to follow her instructions for living an orthodox life as "inner-worldly ascetics."

The Cultural Construction of Gender and Anandamayi Ma

There is one significant factor that seems to inhibit the potential of Anandamayi Ma, as a gender-related symbol, to serve as a model for women, and that is the ambiguity surrounding her gender. We have seen in the interviews with her devotees that Ma is repeatedly described as neither a man nor a woman, or as neither male nor female. In fact, Brahmacharini Chandan relates in detail an incident that she considers critical to the life story of Anandamayi Ma, which communicates the same thing. She says that she heard from Ma's mother, Didima, that when Ma was nine or ten months old, a "lustrous figure," a *mahatma*, was seen standing very close to little Nirmala. After meditating next to her and performing puja to her, the *mahatma* pointed to Nirmala and said, "This is Ma, neither solely woman nor solely man. You will certainly not be able to keep Her bound in family ties. She will definitely not remain here."[34] Regardless of the historicity of this event, its inclusion speaks to the fundamental nature of the community's claim that Ma is neither man nor woman.

There has been considerable recent scholarly focus on the cultural construction of gender.[35] Shelly Errington defines "gender" as a "cultural system of meaning pertaining to the differences and similarities between men and women as they are lived and interpreted in particular contexts."[36] She explains that whereas sex refers to human bodies, gender refers to what different cultures make of sex.[37] Using the analogy of a frosted cake, Errington says that whereas the body has sometimes been thought of as a cake and the culture as the frosting, on the contrary, the biological givens are the ingredients and the socializing process of a given culture is the cooking process. Human bodies are "asked to bear . . . the culture's gender ideology, its mythologies of the person with specific reference to men and women."[38] Moreover, a person assigned to a gender category may not hold onto that assignment indefinitely. Rather, "a person's gender must continually be affirmed and expressed in social practice," an activity some refer to as "doing gender."[39]

Within the Hindu context, although male and female difference among ordinary people is highly marked, it seems that in the realm of extraordinary people, such as saints, gurus, and renunciants, male-female difference may not be so highly marked. In fact, for reasons that we will discuss below, it may be that the gender of a Hindu saint, guru, or sannyasin or sannyasini is seen as a kind of third gender, that certain male and female holy people are seen as more like each other than they are like other men and women. This may in part be a by-product of the process of initiation into the life of renunciation. Charles Keyes notes that although most anthropologists see initiation processes as van Gennep does, as a rite of passage in which a child is transformed from an asexual into a sexual person, in Theravada Buddhist society in Southeast Asia, for example, a man emerges from the renunciant initiation process with an ambiguous gender identity, "a sexual-social identity that is in tension with an ideal [ordinary] male religious identity."[40] Certainly a man who has become a renunciant is not going to be in a position in the future to "do gender" to affirm his masculinity, and thus may lose his male identity.

Within both the tantric and Advaitin frameworks, however, the ambiguity of the gender of extraordinary Hindu personalities seems to have more to do with the conceptualization of the path to self-realization. In both traditions this path is conceived of as a process of transcending the limitations of one's sexual identity, which is itself only a reflection the limited, dualistic world, into the realm of ultimate reality that is envisioned as having either a perfectly balanced male-female gender (the union of Shiva and Shakti) or a formless, sexless gender (*nirguna brahman*).[41] Particularly if one wants to embark on the Advaitin path to liberation, one must begin by understanding "I am not this body" before one can progress.

The theme "I am not this body" is a thread that runs strongly through the Hindu tradition from the Upanishads onward. One of the most important conversations of the Upanishads occurs in the *Katha Upanishad* 1.2.18–19, when Lord Yama, the lord of death, reveals the secret of liberation to the boy, Nachiketas, saying, "The knowing self is never born, nor does he die at any time. He sprang from nothing and nothing sprang from him. He is unborn, eternal, abiding and primeval. He is not slain when the body is slain."[42]

This upanishadic truth has been central to the teachings of Hindu gurus right up to the present day. For example, the contemporary Hindu Advaitin Ramana Maharshi (1879–1950) taught that only by getting rid of *dehatma buddhi*, or the consciousness of "I am this body," can a person realize his true nature. Once he was asked how to root out the sexual impulse. He replied, "By dhi. Gandhi's ideal seems to reflect one aspect of the larger Hindu ideal of the *homo religiosus* as well as the *femina religiosa*. Indeed, the true guru, whether possessing a male or a female body, is propitiated as both mother and father, having supposedly attained the state beyond distinctions.

The ambiguity within the Hindu tradition about the gender of Self-realized beings, then, reflects an ambiguity within the tradition about the gender of God. This ambiguity, however, is less a product of confusion or contradiction than it is a product of the inclusiveness of the tradition. Just as there is great flexibility and interchangeability about the names of God, the faces of God, and the perspectives from which God can be understood, so there is flexibility about God's gender. God is sometimes conceived of as masculine, as Bhagavan, Shiva, Krishna, sometimes as feminine, as Bhagavati, Shakti, and Radha. Sometimes God is seen as a third androgynous, balanced male-female gender—Shiva-Shakti or Krishna-Radha. However, there is a sense in which whatever form of God a Hindu worships, he or she sees that god as encompassing both the form of Ultimate Reality as well as its formlessness. Thus, worshipers of Devi, while they see her as manifesting countless feminine forms, at the same time see her in her most ultimate sense as formless *brahman*, a sexless gender.

Anandamayi Ma on Gender

Not surprisingly, Anandamayi Ma's position on the gender of ordinary people, of extraordinary people, and of God mirrors the ultimate irrelevance of gender. If we examine Anandamayi Ma's statements on gender, we find that she, too, maintains that from the perspective of the Self there is no male and female, and that one needs to transcend these distinctions to make any spiritual progress. Once Ma, reportedly in a trance state in Dehradun, echoed the words of Ramana Maharshi, saying, "All the time, everybody is engaged in bearing a body and feeding it everything that it wants. But there is also a vibration inside and it tells us to be free from this *dehatma buddhi* [this consciousness that "I am this body"]. The main thing is to remove this *dehatma buddhi*."[50] According to Ma, the body is part of and depends on this illusory world. In the following statement she creates a pun on the Bengali word *sharira* (body), comparing it to the verb *shara*, which means to move on and slip away, " 'Body' signifies that which slips away, which is constantly changing. If there is no want, no desire, then this kind of body that is ever in the process of perishing does not persist. Thus, after God-realization one can no longer speak of such a body for the Self stands revealed."[51]

Although Ma alternated her use of the names of God as well as the masculine and feminine pronouns to refer to God, she maintained that the Absolute, whether called the Self, Bhagavan, *brahman*, or even Devi, is neither male nor female. In Vrindavan, in November 1967, Ma said, "You are the Self, you are He. He is neither masculine nor feminine. Therefore here, too, there

rooting out the false idea of the body being Self. There is no sex in th
... Only when differentiation ceases will the sexual impulse cease."
Hindu woman saint Mother Jnanananda of Madras, on the other hand, :
more in terms of the tantric goal of balancing male and female in or
transcend sexual gender. According to Charles White, when asked if me
women have exactly equal spiritual characteristics, Jnanananda said:

> Have you ever seen the statue of Shiva Ardhanari? He is depicted i
> two sexes but in one body. It is primarily at the gross physical level
> that we must perceive precise distinctions. When the male and fe-
> male elements are completely developed and complement each
> other in the same individual, the soul is fully realized. It is certainly
> true that men and women have different characteristics. The woma
> tends to be more emotional, also motherly and loving; whereas the
> man is more intellectual, perhaps braver. But we cannot rely abso-
> lutely on these distinctions. For myself I no longer feel that I inhabi
> a body of a particular sexual gender. In fact, I sometimes refer to
> myself with the masculine pronoun.[44]

Within the lives of the bhakti saints, as well, according to A. K. Raman
"the lines between male and female are crossed and recrossed so many ti
as to render them "a kind of third gender."[45] He notes that many male s
wish to become women in order to have the intimacy with Shiva or Kri
that women saints enjoy. Several famous saints are renowned for their
scendence of gender. The Vaishnava saint Chaitanya, according to W
O'Flaherty, cultivated a kind of androgyny so that he could experience wh
would be like to make love to both Krishna and Radha, at times dressing
a woman and retiring each month during menstruation.[46] In explaining
cross-dressing of Ramakrishna Paramahamsa, Isherwood says that "if the
otee can make himself seriously believe for a while that he belongs to
opposite sex, he will be well on his way to overcoming the illusion of
distinction altogether; for he will then know that the distinction is not absol
as he supposed."[47] Thus, in the process of exploring being the lover of G
one can overcome superficial distinctions and attain the absolute, which
beyond sexual gender.

Mahatma Gandhi also minimized the importance of distinctions betwe
men and women. In his letters to the women of the ashram, Gandhi respond
to a letter from one ashram sister requesting him to return to protect them
saying, "In the ashram we all desire to have experience of 'the soul'. Now t
soul is neither male nor female, neither young nor old."[48] Gandhi, himself,
renowned for having attained a balance of masculine and feminine charact
istics. In another letter, he said, "My ideal is this: a man should remain a m
and yet should become woman; similarly a woman should remain woman ar
yet become man."[49]

It seems that the ideal of a person who exhibits a balance of male ar
female characteristics accompanied by a transcendence of identification wi
the body can be considered to be more than simply an ideal particular to Ga

is no question of man or woman. In all men and women, it is He alone. The Self in everybody is genderless. And that Self is He."[52] In other words, the genderlessness of the Absolute is reflected in the genderlessness of human beings.

However, Ma, like Jnanananda of Madras, also seemed to recommend a *sadhana* in which one learns to balance their masculine and feminine qualities as a step toward embracing the genderless Self. In a *satsang* in Poona in 1969, Ma said, "If the manhood in a woman or the womanhood in a man is awakened, the question of sexual difference does not arise. . . . Then He does reveal himself."[53] In Banaras in the same year, Ma made a statement, apparently in reference to a certain woman, that reveals that one of the characteristics of the womanhood of which she speaks is a kind of weakness. Yet, she says that it can be overcome: "Where is there a difference between a man and a woman? There is womanhood in a man and manhood in a woman. They called her *abala* [weak]. Yes, you are *abala*, without strength, til the time you nurture the desire, need the support. Once manhood is awakened in you there is no question of being *abala* any more. So there is no question of a man or a woman. Whether you are a man or a woman you must recite the syllable *Om*."[54] I was unable to find a corresponding example in which Ma spoke about a quality that a man might have to nurture in himself in order to awaken his womanhood and, therefore, be in a position to have God reveal himself.

It is difficult to determine whether Ma's conviction that both men and women need to become fully male and fully female in order to embrace the Absolute implies that she also believes that the Absolute is fully male and fully female, an androgynous third gender as well as *brahman*, a third sexless gender. Since Ma often spoke of the Absolute as both ice and water, as both *saguna* and *nirguna*, it is more likely that she did conceive of the Absolute as both *saguna*, possessing a perfectly balanced Shiva-Shakti nature, and as *nirguna*, without any qualities. If so, she may have thought of herself in the same way.

Regardless of how Ma thought about her own gender, it is not surprising that her devotees would say that she was not a woman and not a man. As Ultimate Reality, she would have to be thought of as either a perfect union of Shiva and Shakti or as formless *brahman*. In any case, if we acknowledge the many ways of understanding the gender of God within the Hindu tradition, as well as the importance placed on a seeker's disidentification with the body, it is not difficult to understand why Ma's women devotees fail to identify with Ma as a woman. If they have listened to Ma well, they have come to believe that they, too, are neither woman not man, but are, instead, the Self of All.

Anandamayi Ma as Deity: "Looking Way, Way Up"

There is a second important but related factor that seems to inhibit Anandamayi Ma's potential to serve as a model for women, and that is the very fact of her being considered a deity, albeit a deity in female form. We have seen that women devotees had a difficult time even relating to the question of whether or not Ma had been a role model for them because they saw her as the divine "other." When I asked Ma's *brahmacharini* devotee Malini-Di if Ma was her role model, she replied, "No, you see, to model yourself on Ma was very, very difficult because Ma was the embodiment of perfection." I pushed her a bit further, saying, "But you had somebody to look up to?" Her answer reflects what most of Ma's devotees see as the unbridgeable gulf between the human and the divine: "Really look up! Way, way, up!" While we might have expected that Ma's women devotees would have imitated Ma's life in both minor and major ways, from wearing their hair loose and displaying *bhavas* to casting aside all worldly goals to pursue Self-realization, we have found that most women felt, as Malini-Di did, that what Ma did was not applicable to them. Those who chose a life of renunciation did not report that they chose it because Ma lived such a life. Instead, they cited other reasons: because Ma had suggested it, because Ma's spiritualizing presence inspired them to renounce the world, or because they wanted to be close to Ma's side.

We have seen that there are ways in which Ma encouraged her women devotees to see her and the things that she did as beyond imitation. She made statements such as: "The behavior of saints is not to be copied by ordinary people. But one should endeavor to carry out in one's life the teaching or advice received by them." She participated in the creation of their conviction that she was not a human being, speaking of her life in terms of *lila* (play). She encouraged devotees to take the path of bhakti and surrender themselves unconditionally to the Almighty "like a besieged garrison," having already intimated that she herself was an incarnation of that Almighty.

Yet, although Ma was establishing herself as beyond emulation, she was also telling her devotees that she went through what seemed like the stages of life, from householder to *sadhika* to sannyasini for their sake, by which she seemed to have meant in order to set an example. It appears, however, that the existence of the conception of Ma as deity inhibited the potential of Ma, the extraordinary woman, to serve as a model for her devotees. It seems that once devotees accepted Ma as embodied deity, no matter how many times she told them that they, too, were God, it was difficult for them to believe her, since they naturally assumed that she was more God than they were. Instead of devotees being inspired by the process through which Ma came to know she was God, they marveled at her "*lila* of *sadhana*," which by its mere name communicates that a human being cannot identify with it. Although Ma may have wanted to be available to her devotees as the model of perfect householder, the perfect *sadhika*, the perfect renunciant, it seems that they persisted in seeing her as "way, way up" and out of reach.

Anandamayi Ma is surely not the only female Hindu religious figure whose "otherness" stood in the way of women identifying with her. Madhu Kishwar and Ruth Vanita note that even in the case of the medieval saint Mirabai, who was considered simply an extraordinary woman and not an avatar, her "otherness" stands in the way of ordinary women applying her norm to themselves. They say,

Mirabai had not only to live an extraordinary life, but to prove her extraordinariness by going through ordeals. . . . Having thus proved herself, dared all, broken all barriers, she is exalted and revered, and regains in far greater measure the honor and repute she lost or seemed to have lost by flouting the norms of womanly behavior. She is now perceived as existing beyond such norms. But, by being compelled to be so far beyond the ordinary, she becomes a not easily imitable model. Her way remains literally *anuthi* [unfollowable]. Like Kali who may tread on her husband, like certain south Indian goddesses who behead their husbands, she becomes an object of adoration rather than a model or a guide to action for other women. . . . Being perceived as extraordinary, she is by definition considered to be in a different category from other women and the freedom allowed her will not be extended to them.[55]

We have seen that Ma was not seen by her devotees as an extraordinary woman as was Mirabai, however, but rather she was seen as a divine being who was beyond extraordinary, beyond compare. As such she was even more likely to be an "object of adoration rather than a model or a guide to action for other women." Yet a devotee of Ma might respond to this by saying, "The fact that I cannot identify with Ma is not important. Ma is my Mother, my God incarnate, and, therefore, my association with her, my recognition of her, will carry me to rest with her eternally. I need only sit in the lap of Mother to have it all, both worldly and spiritual fulfillment." For the bhakta of Ma, Ma's being "way, way up" is hardly a hardship. He or she undoubtedly feels that sitting in the lap of the divine Mother is far preferable to walking behind an extraordinary woman, following in her footsteps.

Concluding Remarks

To explore the phenomenon of Anandamayi Ma is to explore the complex terrain of the worlds of the Hindu woman, saint, guru, and avatar. None of these worlds is discrete and each is replete with ambiguity and paradox. Although Ma's devotees maintain that she was not a woman, they also insist that she was the "perfect wife." Her life story, on the other hand, reveals a relationship between husband and wife that is highly unconventional from the perspective of *dharmashastra*, and more closely resembles that between disciple and guru. Yet although this kind of marriage is unusual within the Hindu tradition at large, there is a paradigm within a Shakta culture, such as that in Bengal, in which a conventional marriage can evolve into a relationship between a bhakta husband and a wife whom he and a larger community has come to worship as an incarnation of the Goddess.

When we explore the world of Hindu sainthood, we see that although Ma's devotees reject the use of the term "saint" to define her, Ma manifested the moral ideals and charismatic qualities sought in identifying a Hindu holy person. Her life was a tribute to the spirit of *sannyasa*. She rejected the notion of her existence as separate from others, seeing "all persons as organic members of this body." Yet although Ma is said to have seen the whole world as her garden and been blind to gender and caste, her ashrams hold to strict brahmanical purity regulations and a certain kind of division of labor based on gender. Ma's powerful presence has been well documented by her devotees in descriptions of her ecstatic states and her miraculous powers. She appeared to be at all times the paramount bhakta, or devotee of the Lord, totally immersed in a celebration of the One, which she called by different names. The list of her *siddhi*s, or miraculous powers, confirms her as an accomplished yogini. Yet Ma's devotees insist that referring to Ma by any of the terms used to describe a Hindu holy person would relegate her to the level of a perfected being, when, in fact, she is a divine being, perfect from birth.

In the same way, Ma's devotees insist that Ma was not a guru, a person who attains the status of master by following to perfection the path of his or her guru, and is thus able to guide others along that same path. The main reason they cite for maintaining that Ma was not a guru is the apparent fact that she did not give *diksha*. However, through my research it became clear that Ma did indeed give *diksha*, both directly or indirectly, and instructed each devotee as to their individual *sadhana*, or spiritual practice. We are therefore left wondering why it seems so critical for devotees to convince others that Ma was not a guru. It seems that there may be two reasons. First, the inner circle of *shishya*s, or disciples, who received initiation from Ma, whether directly or indirectly, may see themselves as an esoteric group who were "special to Ma," and, therefore, especially blessed. They may see the power of their special connection as sealed by the secrecy surrounding it. Second, they may see that although they received their initiation from Ma, her role as their *ishta devata*, or chosen deity, supersedes her role as guru. They see their living master, then, as the Divine Absolute and therefore they require no mediation.

When Anandamayi Ma's devotees were asked, "If Ma was not a woman, not a saint, and not a guru, who is Ma?" they responded, "Ma is God." There is a multiplicity of concepts reflected in that assertion: Ma is the incarnation of formless *brahman*, Ma is the avatar of Devi, Ma is the avatar of Vishnu, or simply Ma is my *ishta devata*, my chosen deity.

Regardless of what concept lies behind the term "God," however, devotees seem to hold a common vision that the Divine Absolute came to earth as Ma to be accessible to his or her devotees. The centrality within the Hindu tradition of the concept of God's accessibility, or *saulabhya*, both in descending as human avatar and even more intimately as *archa*, or divine image, is articulated and praised by the thirteenth-century Shrivaishnava philosopher Lokacharya. In a fourteenth-century commentary on Pillai Lokacharya's verse 38 in the *Shrivacana Bhushanam*, Manavala Mamunikal describes God, who is himself full and independent, as allowing himself to be bathed, to be dressed and fed, seeming "to be like one who has no independence."[56] In his commentary on the verse 39, Mamunikal explains that it is God's accessibility "which helps us to be attached to the Lord."[57] So Ma allowed herself not only to walk among her devotees but also, like an *archa*, to be fed, dressed, and massaged by those women devotees who were fortunate enough to be in close proximity to her. Therefore, although all of Ma's close devotees believed that they were relating to the divine in human form, occasionally even receiving God's spiritualizing touch, it was the women who saw themselves as having had the opportunity to "handle" God, and, therefore, to become particularly attached to her.

Narendranath Bose has remarked, "For everyone Ma was a different person." Indeed, in the case of each of the extraordinary aspects of Anandamayi Ma, there is the sense that Ma as saint, as guru, and as avatar, was willing to be whatever people wanted her to be. She manifested a particular aspect only if she was called upon to do so. One of her favorite aphorisms was, "As you play, so you shall hear."⁵⁸ Swami Jnanananda, in talking about Ma's miracles, said that miracles "come from the *bhava* [in this case, attitude or state] of the people. It's the people who drag it from the saint." Ma, herself, in responding to a devotee who asked her to speak to them as a guru, said, "There is no case for the *guru-shishya* relationship if the *shishya* is not there. The guru will only speak if the *shishya* is there." In reference to Ma's identity as a divine incarnation, Swami Samatananda reminds us that Ma always said, "You called for me. You prayed for me. You got this body. As long as you want this body, it will stay. If you don't want this body, it will vanish." In a similar vein, Ma said, "I never say, 'I will do this, I will not do that.' It is you who make me carry out whatever work lies in your power to induce me to perform."⁵⁹ We might conclude from these statements that Ma is as we see her, that when an ordinary person holds the possibility that these extraordinary aspects of Anandamayi Ma exist, they manifest.

Personal Postscript

When I first undertook this study, I welcomed the opportunity to explore the world of a Hindu mystic. However, I was also drawn to exploring the impact that a female saint, guru, or avatar would have on women's lives. Similarly, I was interested in understanding the worldview of men and women who worship God as the divine Mother. Therefore, what I have drawn from Ma is just this—her mystical, charismatic presence, her influence on women devotees, and the vision of the world as a manifestation of the divine Mother. As Gurupriya Devi expressed it, "Ma came for the ladies," and being a woman, what excited me most about this study was the ways in which Ma apparently came for me.

Lina Gupta, in her article entitled, "Kali the Savior" in *After Patriarchy: Feminist Transformations of the World's Religions*, says that women need both alternative models of Ultimate Reality that will emphasize the female experience as well as positive role models "that reassert the importance of the 'feminine' in all religious experience."⁶⁰ Gupta suggests that the goddess Kali might provide such a model, since in her fierce independence, her motherly compassion, and her creative power, she gives "birth to a wider vision of reality than the one embodied in the order of patriarchy."[61] There are definitely ways in which Anandamayi Ma also provides such a model. There is no question that she was fiercely independent, by any culture's standards. She refused to be restricted by the bonds of family, she traveled wherever and whenever she wanted, and she apparently took action only out of her *kheyal*, or alignment with the divine will, not out of limited ego. She was the embodiment of motherly love and compassion. Sara Ruddick, the author of *Maternal Thinking: Towards a Politics of Peace*, would undoubtedly find Ma displaying all four elements of "maternal thinking," the practice of which, by mothers and nonmothers alike, she believes can lead to global transformation: holding one's children close while at the same time welcoming change and growth, understanding the particular needs of each child, "attentive love" and acceptance focused on the child as she is, and telling stories intended to strengthen values.[62] Ma's creative power, or shakti, is apparent in her single-handed orchestration of a large community, each member of which was committed to following her every direction. When I hear how Ma manifested these qualities I am reminded of that potential within myself.

As a woman who, though not a devotee, is drawn to Ma, I can select from my understanding of Anandamayi Ma as a female religious symbol that which inspires me. I can lift up the fact that Ma, in Joseph Campbell's terms, "followed her bliss," that she manifested complete equanimity and fearlessness, and that she flouted the expectations of others. I can contemplate Ma's absorption in the divine and her vision that everything, from animate to inanimate, is a manifestation of divinity, and strive to respect and care for the world as my garden and to see the divine in each person. I can listen to Ma's words on the importance of *sadhana* and rededicate myself to my spiritual practice. At the same time, I can also choose to live a life in which I celebrate my body and gender as inseparable from my path, to God/dess, seeing part of my work as helping other women do the same. Throughout this process, I can imagine any kind of relationship with Ma that serves me on my path, keeping in mind that "As I play, so I will hear."

As a member of the global community, I have a unique opportunity to be moved and changed by the faith of others. Process theology, inspired by the Buddhist idea of dependent origination, maintains that a human being is not same person from moment to moment.[63] From that perspective, the person I was the moment before I heard about Anandamayi Ma is not the same person I am after having heard of her. There is no question that imagining that God could come to earth as Anandamayi Ma has stimulated my imagination to envision and embrace the possibility of God as Mother. As a creative thealogian, having encountered the possibility of God as Ma, I can better embrace the richness of a worldview in which the visible world is alive with the energy of God, our Mother. According to Ma, having at one time been drawn to her, even in my imagination, I am ever changed. As I bring this article to a close, I wonder in what ways I have been and will be changed, remembering Ma's words: "You may want to banish this body from your mind. But this body won't leave you for a single day—it does not and never will leave your thought.

Whoever has once been drawn to love this body will never succeed in wiping out its impression even despite hundreds of attempts. This body rests and shall remain in his memory for all times."[64]

NOTES

1. My contribution to this volume is part of a larger work on Anandamayi Ma entitled *Mother of Bliss: Ānandamayī Mā (1896–1982)*. For the purposes of this chapter I have emphasized the material on Anandamayi Ma and gender, which is the focus of chapter 7 of the book. In order to fully understand the phenomenon of Anandamayi Ma, however, it is important to explore the categories of Hindu women, saint, guru, and avatar in relation to Ma, subjects that are the focus of the earlier chapters of *Mother of Bliss*.

2. As in *Mother of Bliss*, I have used pseudonyms for the subjects of my interviews to protect their privacy.

3. Cutler, "Conclusion" in *Gods of Flesh, Gods of Stone*, pp. 169–170.

4. Bynum et al., eds., *Gender and Religion*, p. 2.

5. It is interesting to note at this point that caring for Ma as if she were a child—combing her hair, feeding her, and helping her dress—must have called up in the women performing these services what the Vaishnava tradition would call *vatsalya*, or the maternal attitude of devotion. Most commonly *vatsalya* refers to worship of Lord Krishna as Gopal, the baby and young boy.

6. Chitra, "Let Us Be Filled with Sweet Memories."

7. For traditional songs about the impending separation of mother and daughter, see Archer, *Songs for the Bride*. See also Sax, *The Mountain Goddess*, for a study of a pilgrimage in Garhwal that traces the trek of the goddess Parvati from her parents' home to the home of her husband, Shiva, and back again for periodic visits. See especially the section entitled, "A Female Perspective on Residence," pp. 115–126, in which Sax speaks of the anguish of young brides as they leave their natal home and the eagerness with which they await their periodic visits back home. Sax documents this perspective with interviews and translations of traditional songs.

8. Chitra, "Let Us Be Filled with Sweet Memories."

9. Ibid., p. 59.

10. Ibid., p. 60.

11. Ibid., pp. 60–61.

12. Ibid., p. 62.

13. Ibid., p. 61.

14. According to Altekar, *The Position of Women In Hindu Civilization*, p. 9, brahman girls did have a *upanayana* initiation until the turn of the common era.

15. Devi, *Sri Sri Ma Anandamayi*, vol. 2, p. 160.

16. This incident is reported ibid., pp. 8–9.

17. Ibid., p. 154.

18. Ibid., pp. 160–161.

19. *Satsang* tape no. 89, Dehradun, June 1980, pp. 3–9.

20. In this way, Ma could be seen, in the words of Paula Arai, as an "innovator for the sake of tradition." Arai's thesis, "Zen Nuns," speaks of contemporary Zen nuns in this way, highlighting their striving to attain spiritual equality in order to preserve Zen tradition, which is eroding at the hands of modernity. Anandamayi Ma, as well, was committed to women's spiritual parity with men in order to insure the continuity of ancient spiritual traditions. Her innovations were intended, I believe, to

bring men and women back to a more inspired, ideal time, when spiritual education was part of everyone's early life and all phases of life lead toward one's eventual turning within.

21. Chandan, *Svakriya Svarasmrita*, vol. 3, p. 223.

22. Mukerji, *From the Life of Anandamayi Ma*, vol. 1, p. 159; and vol. 2, p. 50.

23. Ibid., vol. 2, p. 51.

24. Lipski, *The Life of and Teaching of Anandamayi Ma*, p. 56.

25. Mukerji, *From the Life of Anandamayi Ma*, vol. 2, p. 57.

26. Ganguli, *Anandamayi Ma, The Mother Bliss-Incarnate*, pp. 145–146.

27. Mukerji, *From the Life of Anandamayi Ma*, vol. 1, p. 198.

28. Bynum, *Fragmentation and Redemption*, pp. 50–73.

29. Bhaiji, *Mother as Revealed to Me*, p. 8.

30. Lipski, *The Life and Teachings of Anandamayi Ma*, pp. 45–46. I have been unable to find the original source of this story, although I have no reason to doubt Lipski, as I have been able to locate many of his other references.

31. Ibid., p. 46.

32. Ibid., p. 53.

33. Ojha, "Feminine Asceticism in Hinduism," pp. 280–281.

34. Chandan, *Svakriva Svarasamrita*, vol. 2, pp. 9–12; vol. 3, p. 32.

35. See, in particular, Errington, "Recasting Sex, Gender, and Power," and Atkinson, "Review Essay: Anthropology."

36. Errington, "Recasting Sex, Gender, and Power," p. 8.

37. Ibid., pp. 26–27.

38. Ibid., pp. 13–14, 15.

39. Errington notes here that when women in America "do gender," they reveal themselves to be nonpowerful (p. 22).

40. Keyes, "Ambiguous Gender," p. 68.

41. Here we note that the word *brahman* itself is neither masculine nor feminine, but neuter.

42. *Katha Upanishad*, 1.2.18–19, pp. 616–617.

43. Ramana Maharshi, *Talks with Sri Ramana Maharshi*, pp. 143–144.

44. White, "Mother Guru," pp. 29–30.

45. Ramanujan, "Talking to God in the Mother Tongue."

46. O'Flaherty, *Women, Androgynes, and Other Mythical Beasts*, pp. 298–299.

47. Ibid., p. 112.

48. Gandhi, *Bapu's Letters to the Ashram Sisters*, p. 26.

49. Ibid., p. 95.

50. *Satsang* tape no. 34, Dehradun, November 1974, p. 3.

51. Anandamayi Ma, *Mātri Vani*, Atmananda, translator (Shree Shree Anandamayee Charitable Scoiety, 1982), no. 16, p. 9.

52. *Satsang* tape no. 20, Vrindavan, November 1967, pp. 9–10.

53. *Satsang* tape no. 25, Poona, June 1969, p. 27.

54. *Satsang* tape no. 8, Banaras, 1969, p. 38.

55. Kishwar and Vanita, "Poison to Nectar," p. 92.

56. *Śrivacanapūṣaṇa viyakkiyanam*, sutra 38, in *Śrīmat Varavaramunītra krantamalai*. I am indebted to Vasudha Narayanan for translating this beautiful sutra by Pillai Lokacarya and its commentary:

Diminishing his fullness and independence, [the Lord in his archa form] seems to care for those who do not care for him.

(Fullness:) All his desires are fulfilled. Diminishing this [quality], he comes to his [the human being's] place and appears as though he is needy and has to be satisfied. (Independence:) Having the essential nature (*svarupa*) of being in control of himself. Diminishing this he assumes the nature and the state of becoming dependent on the devotee (*ashrita*). "The Most Brilliant one who is full of motherly love for his devotee (*ashrita vatsala*) stands to be worshiped because of [the devotee's] wish (*icca*). The Lord of the universe (*jagatpati*) has a bath (*snana*), drinks [for his thirst] and goes on journeys (*yatra*). Even though independent, this Lord of the universe (*jagannatha*), seems to be like one who has no independence. Even though he is omnipotent (*sarvashaktopi*) the creator of the universe seems to act as though he is powerless (*ashakta iva*). [*Visvaksena Samhita*, citation not known]

57. *Śrīvacana Bhūṣaṇam*, sutra 39, in Narayanan, "Arcāvatāra," p. 63.
58. Ganguli, *Anandamayi Ma*, p. 181.
59. *Matri Darshan*, p. 24.
60. Gupta, "Kali, the Savior," p. 16.
61. Ibid., p. 38.
62. Ruddick, *Maternal Thinking*, p. 95.
63. For an introduction to process theology, see Cobb and Griffin, *Process Theology*.
64. Ganguli, *Anandamayi Ma*, p. 170.

REFERENCES

Altekar, A. S. *The Position of Women In Hindu Civilization*. Delhi: Motilal Banarsidass, 1991.
Arai, Paula. "Zen Nuns: Living Treasures of Japanese Buddhism." Ph.D. dissertation, Harvard University, 1993.
Archer, W. *Songs for the Bride: Wedding Rites of Rural India*. New York: Columbia University Press, 1985.
Atkinson, Jane Monnig. "Review Essay: Anthropology." *Signs: Journal of Women in Culture and Society*, 8 no. 2 (1982): 236–258.
Bhaiji, *Mother as Revealed to Me*. Translated by G. Das Gupta. Calcutta: Shree Shree Anandamayee Charitable Society, 1983.
Bynum, Caroline Walker. *Fragmentation and Redemption: Essays on Gender and the Human Body in Medieval Religion*. New York: Zone Books, 1991.
Bynum, Caroline Walker, Stevan Harrel, and Paula Richman, eds. *Gender and Religion: On the Complexity of Symbols*. Boston: Beacon, 1986.
Chandan, Brahmacharini. *Svakriya Svarasmrita*. 3 vols. Kankhal: Shree Shree Ma Anandamayi Ashram, 1981–1983.
Chitra, "Let Us Be Filled with Sweet Memories." *Ananda Varta*, 21 no. 1 (January 1984): 59–63.
Cobb, John, and David Griffin. *Process Theology: A Introductory Exposition*. Philadelphia: Westminster, 1975.
Cutler, Norman. "Conclusion." Pp. 159–170 in *Gods of Flesh, Gods of Stone: The Embodiment of Divinity in India*, edited by Joanne Waghorne and Norman Cutler. Chambersburg, Pa.: Anima, 1985.
Devi, Gurupriya. *Sri Sri Ma Anandamayi*, Translated by Tara Kini. 4 vols. Calcutta: Shree Shree Anadamayee Charitable Society, 1984–1990.

Errington, Shelly. "Recasting Sex, Gender, and Power." Pp. 1–58 in *Power and Difference: Gender in Island Southeast Asia*, edited by Shelly Errington and Jane Monnig Atkinson. Stanford: Stanford University Press, 1990.

Gandhi, Mahatma. *Bapu's Letters to the Ashram Sisters*. edited by Kaka Kalelkar. Ahmedabad: Navajivan Publishing House, 1952.

Ganguli, Anil. *Anandamayi Ma, The Mother Bliss-Incarnate*. Calcutta: Eureka, 1983.

Gupta, Lina. "Kali, the Savior." Pp. 15–38 in *After Patriarchy: Feminist Transformations of the World's Religions*, edited by Paula Cooey, William Eakin, and Jay McDaniel. Maryknoll, N.Y.: Orbis, 1991.

Hallstrom, Lisa Lassell. *Mother of Bliss: Ānandamayī Mā (1896–1982)*. New York: Oxford University Press, 1999.

Katha Upanishad. In *The Principal Upaniṣads*, translated by S. Radhakrishnan. London: George Allen and Unwin, 1953.

Keyes, Charles. "Ambiguous Gender: Male Initiation in a North Thai Buddhist Society." Pp. 66–96 in *Gender and Religion: On the Complexity of Symbols*, edited by Caroline Walker Bynum, Stevan Harrell, and Paula Richman. Boston: Beacon, 1986.

Kishwar, Madhu, and Ruth Vanita. "Poison to Nectar: The Life and Work of Mirabai." Pp. 74–93 in *Manushi: Women Bhakta Poets*, reprint of *Manushi* nos. 50, 51, 52, (January-June 1989).

Lipski, Alexander. *The Life of and Teaching of Sri Anandamayi Ma*. Delhi: Motilal Banarsidass, 1977.

Matri Darshan. Edited by Doris Shang, Stuhlingen, West Germany: Mangalam Verlag S. Schang, 1983.

Mukerji, Bithika. *From the Life of Anandamayi Ma*. 2 vols. Calcutta: Shree Shree Anandamayi Ma Sangha, 1980, 1981.

Narayanan, Vasudha. "Arcāvatāra: On Earth as It Is in Heaven." Pp. 53–66 in *Gods of Flesh, Gods of Stone*, edited by Joanne Punzo Waghorne and Norman Cutler. Chambersburg, Pa.: Anima, 1985.

O'Flaherty, Wendy Doniger. *Women, Androgynes, and Other Mythical Beasts*. Chicago: University of Chicago Press, 1980.

Ojha, Catherine. "Feminine Asceticism in Hinduism: Its Tradition and Present Condition." *Man In India* 6 1 no. 3 (1981): 254–285.

Ramana Maharshi. *Talks with Sri Ramana Maharshi*, Edited by T.N. Venkataraman. Tiruvannamalai: Sri Ramanashram, 1989.

Ramanujan, A. K. "Talking to God in the Mother Tongue." Pp. 9–14 in *Manushi: Women Bhakta Poets*, reprint of *Manushi* nos. 50, 51, 52, (January–June, 1989).

Ruddick, Sara. *Maternal Thinking: Toward a Politics of Peace*. New York: Ballantine, 1989.

Sax, William. *The Mountain Goddess: Gender and Politics in a Himalayan Pilgrimage*. New York: Oxford University Press, 1991.

Śrīmat Varavaramunītra Krantamalai. Kāñchi: Śrī Kāñci Pirativātipayanikaram Aññānkarācariyar, 1966.

White, Charles. "Mother Guru: Jnanananda of Madras, India." Pp. 15–24 in *Unspoken Worlds*, edited by Nancy Falk and Rita Gross. Belmont, Cal.: Wadsworth, 1989.

4

Fusion of the Soul:
Jayashri Ma and the
Primordial Mother

June McDaniel

In this chapter, we shall look at an unorthodox female guru, Jayashri
Ma, who is understood by her disciples to be a living incarnation of
the goddess Adya Shakti Kali. Jayashri is an underground practitioner, as are most Shakta tantrika practioners in West Bengal. The
fact that she is female is not unusual for a tantric practitioner, nor
are her periods of stress and illness, nor is the faith of her devotees
in her abilities to bless, heal, and predict the future. There are many
small-scale female gurus with groups of devotees in modern West
Bengal. What makes her unusual is her continual state of spiritual
merger with a goddess who gained widespread attention in the early
twentieth century, Adya Shakti Kali.

Adya Shakti Kali was popularized by a visionary saint named
Annada Thakur. She commanded him to find her hidden statue, to
set up her worship, and eventually to build a major shrine in her
honor, named Adyapitha. Along with Belur Math and Dakshineswar,
Adyapitha today makes up the "holy trinity" of sites north of Calcutta most visited by Bengali Shaktas.[1]

Bengali Shaktism or goddess worship is an ancient religious tradition in India that is currently commercialized in its exoteric and
devotional aspects, and that has gone underground in its mystical
dimensions. The tradition of the Kali-kula, the tantric worship of the
dark goddess Kali as primordial mother (especially by tantric sadhus), has been suppressed by the Communist government in the
state of West Bengal, India. They accuse tantrikas of being supersti-
tious and primitive, malingerers who are counterrevolutionary.
Many modern Shakta tantric practitioners are women. I interviewed
several of them in 1993–1994, during nine months of Fulbright

research in India. One female guru that I interviewed while I was in West Bengal was Jayashri Ma.

Jayashri Ma is a holy woman (*sadhika*) believed by her disciples to be an incarnation of a form of Kali known as Adya Shakti Kali.[2] She describes herself as one with the Mother. Sometimes she is fully aware of the goddess's presence, but she states that her deepest soul (*atma*) is eternally fused with Adya Shakti Kali. She is a visionary and medium, who speaks the goddess's words in trance. Her health is very bad and she is subject to crippling abdominal pain, but her trances kill the pain and identification with the goddess brings a state of bliss. She eats little and has never married. She teaches elementary school, and none of her colleagues know of her religious experiences or her role as Ma (spiritual leader or holy mother) to her devotees.

Jayashri was born in 1948, in Darjeeling, West Bengal. She came from a Shakta family, and her father was a deputy magistrate and practitioner of tantra (*tantra sadhaka*). He was a disciple of Taraksepa of Basirhat (in South 24 Parganas) and a visionary who had many religious experiences.

When she was eight years old, Jayashri met a friend of her father, named Sudin Kumar Mitra. He was an officer of the Indian Administrative Service (IAS) posted to Darjeeling, who came originally from Calcutta. He was also a tantric practitioner, and a year after she met him, Jayashri took initiation (*diksha*) from him. She said that he chose her as a disciple for her spiritual gifts, and she was his first disciple. She was fascinated by her guru, and described her love for him, which later was transformed into a love of Adya Shakti Kali.

Her guru Sudin claimed that he had been initiated directly by Adya Shakti Kali. At the age of seventeen years, he wished to have the respected Shakta practitioner Nagin Bagchi of Tarapith initiate him, but Bagchi refused.[3] He said, "The Mother herself must decide, I am not your guru." After repeated requests, Bagchi finally told Sudin to bathe, fast, and remain alone in a room for the whole night. If Sudin were willing to do this, then Bagchi said he would initiate him the next morning. He went into the room at night, and at 2:00 A.M. the room was filled with brilliant light. He saw a vision of Adya Shakti Ma, who said to him, "Chant these mantras along with me." He did so, and then she disappeared. He did not realize this was his initiation (*diksha*).

The next morning, he ran to Nagin Bagchi to get initiated. Bagchi told him, "Don't you realize, you were already initiated by Ma at 2:00 A.M.!" Nagin Bagchi gave him two photographs, one of Bagchi himself and another one of Adya Shakti Kali. He told him to do a simple ritual of worship, offering incense to the photo and praying for universal blessings. He was to say, *Tomar jaya hok*, all victory to you, before her photograph. Jayashri and her mother were both initiated by Sudin Mitra, but her father was not. Mitra told him that he was due to be initiated by another person, a renunciant (*sannyasi*), who later turned out to be Taraksepa.

During her school life, Jayashri was close friends with her guru, and also with Swami Bhavesananda. By the age of ten years she would visit them and do meditation with them. Mitra told her that Adya Ma was always with him, and that he had trouble sleeping at night because Adya Ma would keep him awake. He said that Jayashri would grow up to be a powerful woman, who would help many people.

At the age of thirteen, when Jayashri began going to temples for worship, she would fall into trances (*samadhi*). During worship she would see images of the goddesses Tara Ma and Adya Ma before her. She was "drowned in *dhyana* [meditation]," subject to frequent visions and trance states. When Adya Ma would come, she would see the world turned to light, and she would lose track of the physical world. Jayashri would then see the goddess before her. She says that sometimes Adya Ma looks like her picture (there is a set iconographic image of the goddess), and sometimes she appears in the image of Jayashri's body, so that it is like looking in a mirror. However, when the form (*rupa*) looks like Jayashri, it is really the goddess beneath that form. Adya Shakti cannot be described in words, but her power can be felt.

When Jayashri was seventeen or eighteen years old, Sudin Mitra was transferred to Allahabad for his IAS posting, and she went along with him. She stayed with him for a year. He instructed her in spiritual practice (*sadhana*), and they did meditation with tantric mantras and visualizations before Adya Ma on matching *panchamunda asanas* (seats made of five skulls: four animal skulls and one human skull). She sat next to him, and he transmitted his power to her. The power came directly from heart to heart, and could only be felt; it was not mediated by sight or touch. After this meditative practice with her guru, Jayashri said that Adya Shakti took up permanent residence within her.

About a year later, her father was transferred to Birbhum District in West Bengal, and she came there to live with her family. She had wanted to take renunciant vows (*sannyasa*), but her guru said that she had already become a sannyasini inwardly, so no outward renunciant initiation (*sannyasi diksha*) was necessary. She was to be a householder holy woman, a *grihi sadhika*.

When she moved to Birbhum District, she became seriously ill with dysentery. She soon developed ulcerative colitis and heart trouble, which have stayed with her to the present time. She got a college degree and studied classical music, but the illnesses restricted her movement and eventually made her stop her education.

She stayed in Birbhum District after her father's death, but never married. She is now a primary school teacher, working with children from five to nine years of age. She is weak from her illnesses, and eats little food. The doctors she saw at the time she first developed the symptoms of colitis and heart trouble told her that she would be dead in ten years, but she has survived for twenty-five years thus far. This is understood as a miracle by her devotees. Her guru prayed to Adya Ma to allow her to survive and help others, and she credits them both for her survival.

After her *sadhana* with her guru, she also developed some abilities at mediumship. She said that she has had the saints Mira Bai, Annada Thakur, Trailanga Swami, and Ramakrishna Paramahamsa speak through her. Adya Shakti Kali is always there, in the background, and the god Shiva often visits. These gods and goddesses give information and suggestions to her disciples; she keeps a journal of their words (the entries are often written by her disciples, as she may be unable to write). She says that they speak a variety of languages, including fluent English, whereas Jayashri speaks little English (and none during her discussions with me).

She also continues to have a close relationship with her guru, though he is dead. Several female gurus I have interviewed maintain relationships with their dead gurus, who are believed to travel in spiritual bodies. She says, "Whenever I feel love, he comes to me. When I am sleeping, the guru comes and strokes my head. If I wake, I try to grab his hand, but I cannot. I always speak with him and see him. I feel that he has come now, even while we are speaking, and he is watching us. He always knows when I am in pain from my illnesses, and this causes him pain because of his love for me." One of her disciples described a past event, when she was writhing in pain from the colitis. Suddenly the pain ceased and she began to speak—but it was the guru's words coming from her mouth. She was not aware of this, but she was aware that the pain had ceased. Instead of pain, she felt *ananda*, bliss, which showed its power by being able to erase her pain.

Another disciple described a time when the Shakta saint Vamaksepa came to speak through Jayashri. He told the disciple that when he went to Tarapith, he should not eat at a certain hotel because the brothers who owned the hotel were evil people who had murdered their own father. Instead he should fast, and go directly to speak to Nagin Bagchi, the respected tantric sadhu at Tarapith. He told him of the story that Vamaksepa told through Jayashri as medium, and Bagchi told him that the story was accurate, though not well known: the brothers had indeed murdered their father.

Jayashri often feels distant from the world. She said, "Now, I do not feel that I am really in a human body. Instead, I am pure Shakti, I feel that I am Adya Ma. I am the universal mother, and all of creation is my child. If you do meditation, you too can realize that you are really Adya Ma. Ma divided herself throughout creation, and everybody has a piece of the goddess inside. In the end, all will come back together again, and when everybody realizes this, they will all become the goddess." This is to occur at the end of the Kali Yuga, the time of universal destruction. The end-time may only come when there are no more sadhus to pray and meditate. Because this time is coming, Adya Kali has been withdrawing Shakta sadhus and sadhikas (holy men and women) from the world—their prayers and meditation avert the time of destruction. Jayashri also noted that Adya Shakti Kali is a goddess who appeared recently—she did not wish to appear earlier, it was not her desire (*iccha*).[4] Jayashri believes that Adya Shakti Kali has come to earth to preside over the end of the yuga. As such, she is understood to be the goddess of the Indian apocalypse.

Jayashri is both a tantrika and a devotee (*bhakta*), and her *ishtadevi* (chosen form of the divine) is Adya Shakti Kali. She finds tantra to be a good practice, for it ignores the concerns with caste status and impurity found in more mainstream dharmic Hinduism (though she is herself upper caste). Tantra accepts everybody and everything. She performs neither materializations (which are often seen with holy people in India) nor initiations. She avoids publicity, partly because most people who have visited her on the basis of her reputation have wanted favors—children, good marks on exams, new jobs. She spends her private life surrounded by photos of saints and pictures of gods, and finds her greatest happiness in meditation. She believes she has remained alive in spite of her illness and the pain it brings because her disciples need her presence and guidance.

Jayashri must live in relative secrecy, because of the activist students and the antisuperstition clubs organized by communist groups at the high schools in her area. They disturb yogis and sadhus in meditation, accusing them of being social parasites and preaching false beliefs, and several known to Jayashri have been chased out of town. Indeed, she says that if her colleagues at school knew of her spiritual practice, she would be dismissed from her job. West Bengal is a Communist state that was once rich in religious traditions, and a major center of goddess worship in India, but much has been suppressed over the past few decades. Indeed, overt politicizing begins in the elementary schools, where children join political clubs sponsored by the various parties. This politicizing has been especially prominent over the past ten years; in 1984, the Shakta tantric group Kali-kula was still a living tradition with many members, whereas in 1994 I could find few members remaining, and local informants said that the practitioners had either been killed or had disappeared from the area without a word.

Jayashri Ma is in many ways typical of the holy woman in the Bengali Shakta tradition. There is no set religious institution or organization in Shaktism, and women mystics become valued for their states of ecstasy (*bhava* or *devabhava*), their trance states (*bhor*),[5] and their close relationship with a guru or other religious figure. Women gurus are often charismatic figures, who tend to gather relatives and friends around them as devoted followers.

Like many holy women whom I interviewed in West Bengal, Jayashri described her religious experiences as *bhava* or *devabhava*, divine states of mind, rather than *bhor* or mere possession trance. *Bhava* implies a conscious union with a deity, a merger in which the individual mind is opened to the deity's mind, and usually filled with devotional love (bhakti or *prema*), during this process. *Bhor*, on the other hand, implies that the practitioner has a weaker or more primitive mind, unable to stand the surge of divine energy that occurs during the deity's visit. When the person is in a state of *bhor*, or trance descends (*bhor nama*), the mind disappears or sleeps, and the person is taken over by the deity without participating consciously in the event. The person becomes merely a tool for the deity to use, and is submissive before the deity's power. This is unlike the active cooperation involved in *bhava*, in which both centers of consciousness work together within a single body.[6]

Jayashri Ma describes her relationship to the goddess Adya Shakti as *ekatmika bhava*. The notion of *ekatmika bhava* or "single fused-soul state" is dependent upon a religious anthropology that divides the self into two major parts. The *atma* (or *atman*, or sometimes *paramatman*), the deeper soul, is an eternal part of the divine ocean of consciousness—indeed, from a certain perspective it is the entirety of that ocean. The *jiva*, or individual soul, is the culturally determined soul or self that carries karma from life to life, the aspect of the self bound up in time, relationship, and history. The *atma* in the devotional or bhakti tradition is pure spirit. It is like Augustine's idea of the "god-shaped hole"—there is a place in its center where the powerful *atma* or *svarupa* (true form) of a god may dwell, permeating the human *atma* with divine light and personality. In the state of *ekatmika bhava*, the fusion or permeation of the human *atma* by the divine *atma* causes a continuous awareness of the deeper and more powerful god-identity within the human identity. Sometimes this state is called *akhandatma* (undivided *atma*), *ekprana* (one shared life energy), or *abhinna hridaya* (not-separate or not-different hearts).

The *bhava* of union with a god or a goddess may be full (*purna*), in which the person is considered to be a complete incarnation of the deity (*purna avatar*), or partial (*amsa*), in which there is a temporary conscious fusion that recurs but falls away. In the Indian devotional tradition, the people in the highest spiritual states are often called full avatars (though Jayashri's disciples did not refer to her in this way, calling her *guru ma* instead).

The state of full fusion described by Jayashri Ma gives continual access to the divine light and personality. This allows consolation in misery and diminution of pain, which is replaced by joy. It is not easy to attain, however. It is typical of Indian holy women, especially those with strong devotional or tantric experiences, that adolescence is a time of chaos, full of uncontrolled trances, visionary experiences, emotional intensity, and sensory confusion (in Bengali terms, the senses literally "go away"). The bond with the god is not easily made, and in Jayashri's case, it was stabilized by her guru during his "heart-to-heart" transmission of power. The *panchamunda asana*, the seat of five skulls, is traditionally used by tantrikas who are involved in the conquest of instinct and the passions. In this case, the guru's attainment of detachment was transmitted to the disciple in the symbolic setting in which spirit conquers desire.

Although this *bhava* of fusion with the Mother may be attained by both genders, it appears to be more frequent among women. In Bengali Shaktism, women are understood more often than men to be incarnations of the goddess, whereas the male devotee or saint is more frequently called the goddess's son, and his religious experience is one of relationship rather than identity. Women are believed to have more natural religious sensitivity than men, who are limited by their pride and power. As a woman can hold a child inside her, near her heart, so can she hold a god or goddess. Whereas male possession is often marked by strength and the endurance of pain, female possession is more often marked by healing and by statements of love of the guru and compassion for the world.

This may have to do with the deities involved in the possession. In the tantric tradition, it is said that "All men are (the god) Shiva, and all women are (the goddess) Shakti."[7] This also tends to hold true for the religious practitioners. Men unify with Shiva, lord of detachment, lord of the burning ground, of yoga, of the dance, and of endurance. They demonstrate Shiva's presence by enduring ordeals. Women unify with Shakti, mother of the world and the essence of power, goddess of creation and destruction. In the Hindu saint Ramakrishna Paramahamsa's famous image, she stands with a baby in one hand and a sword in the other, showing the fertility and death that are part of the natural world. Female possession often involves materialization of food or medicine, as well as healing and prediction of the future. Such mediumship may incorporate the imagery of a benign or wrathful Mother, but the benign side is seen much more frequently. The destructive side may involve predictions of death, illness, and apocalyse.

Bhakti or devotional mysticism, often mixed with tantric and folk elements, seems to be the most prominent form of mysticism in modern India. The older traditions of Vedanta and Patanjali's raja yoga are known to scholars but rarely practiced in the towns and villages. Instead, we see devotion, especially among older people. In the dharmic tradition, life after retirement was intended for spirituality, and devotion to home and family is later transformed into devotion to god and goddess.

Among renunciants and serious practitioners, there is a variety of possible relationships with the deity. Most are devotees, who often practice austerities (*tapas*) to rid themselves of bad karma and the *vasanas* (traces of past actions) from previous lives by undergoing suffering. Among practitioners that I have encountered, male *tapas* tends to focus on actively causing that suffering, especially by means of ordeals and vows, whereas female *tapas* tends to involve passive endurance of suffering, especially that due to disease, isolation, family obligations, and the jealousy of others. Both male and female practitioners often have to undergo exorcism, but I have heard of it used more frequently on women. The notion of exorcism in India is different from the idea of it in the West. In India, it is not used to get rid of demons (as there are no Christian-style demons who are followers of Satan in Indian thought), but rather to expel ancestors and angry ghosts. If the person can get through an exorcism and continue his or her religious claims, then those claims are believed to be proved by the person's resistance to the exorcism. The cause of the visionary experience and possession is shown not to be a ghost or ancestor but rather a deity. With holy women, exorcisms are usually paid for by her natal family or her in-laws. Jayashri avoided this by not marrying and by coming from a religious family in which her trance states and visions were accepted. Such tolerance is rare in Indian families.

Jayashri is unusual for an Indian holy woman, for she is a working woman with independence—she earns her own money and has her own apartment. She is therefore not subject to the kinds of harassment and testing normally given to women who claim special religious status. In older, more traditional areas, women gurus and mystics either lived in large families, were tied to ashrams and guru/disciple relationships, or gained independence by claiming madness and wandering alone. A religious calling was not usually sufficient reason for a woman to gain independence. The modern world of West Bengal forces Jayashri to live a double life, keeping her spiritual life largely underground, but it allows her an independence not seen among women living in joint families or in ashrams. Her money comes from her job—she does not accept money from disciples, and she would not accept an offering from me.

As a guru, Jayashri Ma sees people coming and asking for boons and blessings. People hear about her by word of mouth, but the number who know of her must be limited. She maintains a low profile in order to keep her job and avoid harassment.[8] People ask her for good marriages, success in lawsuits, new jobs, raises in pay. She despairs at this, and wishes that they would ask for spiritual knowledge, but very few do. She becomes exhausted from sending spiritual blessings to people, and her brother controls the secular traffic, acting as doorkeeper. When she is exhausted, he tells people to wait.

Jayashri Ma is a celibate Shakta tantrika and bhakta. The Western assumption that all tantric practice involves sexuality is not accurate for West Bengal—the field of tantra has been sensationalized and distorted by Westerners who teach it as a path to increased pleasure. The major focus of Bengali Shakta tantra is transcendence of death, overcoming karma, and gaining immortality in the paradise of the goddess. Pleasure binds people to the world of illusion, and it is something to overcome and reject. Sexual ritual is accepted as *stridharma*, or a women's moral obligation, if her husband wants to do tantric meditation and needs a consort. It is also accepted as a subcategory of prostitution, a specialty like sado-masochism, for women who are desperate and need money (especially mothers who must raise children alone). But for average Shakta women and Shakta tantrikas, it is not a part of initiation, nor is it a part of daily life. It is a special *sadhana* or spiritual practice, used to overcome particular problems. One female Shakta tantric informant compared it to antibiotics—only used for specific diseases. Another said that women lost energy or shakti to their male partners, who then used it for their own spiritual development, so it was a sort of sacrifice on the part of women rather than a spiritual path. In the popular view of mainstream Bengali Shaktas, it was the lower-status female tantrikas who performed such rituals, while the higher-status ones did not, for they were not compelled to do so.

In the tantric texts most widely used in West Bengal (such as the *Kali Tantra*, the *Maya Tantra*, and the *Mundamala Tantra*), sexual ritual is performed by men to overcome lust, or to develop supernatural powers (*siddhis*). Most female gurus and *sadhikas* interviewed stated that uncontrollable sexual desire was primarily a male problem. Women learned to overcome desire as children, when their brothers were given preference on food, toys, clothing, and education. In many poorer Hindu families, sons could hope to fulfill desires, and would feel free about expressing them, whereas daughters traditionally kept silent and were expected to renounce selfish thoughts. Girls learned renunciation early.

When I asked Jayashri Ma about *lata sadhana* (sexual ritual), she was horrified. She said that she was *kanya*, a virgin, and that was one reason why Adya Shakti Kali had chosen to dwell in her. Other forms of Kali would dwell in women of other types.[9]

Though Jayashri Ma clearly states that she has avoided sexuality, we may note that she studied with a male guru, was initiated by a man, and now lives with a man (her brother). Her disciples are primarily male, and she works in a school where the administration is largely male; it is part of an organization known for its charitable work.

She has never traveled outside of India, speaks little English, and has no Western devotees. She gives darshan (she lets people come and be in her presence, and looks kindly on them), and devotees may touch her feet, but she does not get any closer to those who come to her. Her devotees range from local merchants and businessmen to professors and doctors.

Though I cannot give more specific information about her location, as I respect her concern for confidentiality, I can mention how I came to find her. I was looking for a professor who taught at Vishvabharati University in Shantiniketan, and accidentally walked up to the wrong house. It turned out to belong to another professor who asked me about my research and invited me in for tea. He taught in another field, but he had long been interested in religion. He said that he had searched for a true guru all of his life, and that only one person seemed to him honest, humble, and with genuine religious insight and experience. This was Jayashri Ma. He said that it was not an accident that I had come to the wrong house—it was the working of karma. I was meant to see her.

Whether or not this was the case, I did see her. She lived far away, in a small apartment. I went to speak with her in March 1994, and spoke with her on and off all during the day, as groups of disciples came and went, and people came with questions and requests for blessings. I spoke with her, with her brother, and with about a dozen of her disciples.

She felt that her major role was to tell people that Adya Shakti Kali lived within them—she was not unusual, she had just realized this fact, while others had not. The goddess lived within her, and she could radiate the goddess's love and knowledge to all who came to visit her.

NOTES

1. The term "holy trinity" came from Calcutta informants.

2. In this paper, I use the name Jayashri Ma, which is her spiritual name, for this woman. I do not use the name by which she goes at her job, for she asked me not to repeat it, and I respect her desire for confidentiality.

3. Tarapith is a center of worship for the goddess Tara, usually viewed as a form of Kali. It is debated whether her origin is Hindu or Buddhist. Many Shakta practitioners have done meditation in this town, which is understood to be sacred to the goddess because it is a Shakta *pitha*, in which a part of the goddess dwells.

4. Adya Shakti Kali appeared in the form of a statue to a man named Annada Thakur at the turn of the century. He publicized her power, and her worship began due largely to his efforts.

5. This term is pronounced bhor, but would be spelled in correct transliteration as *bhar*.

6. For greater detail on these issues, see my book *The Madness of the Saints*, especially chapter 5 on holy women.

7. This statement is widely bandied about, but it is likely that it comes from the *Kularnava Tantra*, a text of the Kula Shakta tradition, which is several centuries old (its exact dating is much debated). It is generalized out from its initial application, which is only in the ritual context. As the *Kularnava Tantra* states, "Whether they

(men and women) are seated in a row or a circle in the midst of the ritual circle (*chakra*), all of them should be worshipped as forms of Shiva and Shakti" (8.105).

8. Tantrikas in West Bengal who are employed professionals have told me of organized harassment both by threatening calls to employers and by *goondas*, who threaten bodily harm. I have heard this from tantrikas in many areas of the state, but most complaints have come from Calcutta and the Birbhum area.

9. Adya Shakti Kali is not a goddess dedicated to virgins in Annada Thakur's writings, but Jayashri Ma seemed to interpret her in that way. There is an English translation of Annada Thakur's autobiography *Swapnajiban* (literally, a life of dreams) entitled *A Life of Visions*; it talks about his experiences with Adya Shakti Kali.

REFERENCES

Kulārṇavatantram: Mūla, Ṭīkā o Bangānubādsaha. Edited by Upendrakumār Dās. Calcutta: Nababhārata Press, 1383 BS [1975]. In Bengali and Sanskrit.

McDaniel, June. *The Madness of the Saints: Ecstatic Religion in Bengal.* Chicago: University of Chicago Press, 1986.

Thakur, Shree Shree Annada. *A Life of Visions.* Adyapeath Dakshinswar Ramkrishna Sangha, 1968.

5

Mother Meera, Avatar

Catherine Cornille

Among the many female gurus who in the past few decades have become celebrities in the West as well as in India, Mother Meera may be regarded as one of the most enigmatic. She has no ashram, no teachings, no rituals, and no inclination to travel or to proselytize. But an estimated 40,000 people visit her every year at her center in Thalheim, Germany. They line up in silence four nights a week to receive darshan of the woman they believe to be the incarnation of the divine Mother. They come from all walks of life and from a variety of different countries, predominantly Western. Most have heard of Mother Meera by word of mouth, or through New Age networks. Each comes with distinct expectations and hopes, and in spite of or because of her silent presence, Mother Meera seems to fulfill them all.

Because most of the evidence is in the experience of the follower, the researcher is left with minimal resources: one hagiography called *The Mother*, two collections of questions from disciples and answers by Mother Meera called *Answers I* and *Answers II*, and a few records of experiences with Mother Meera by Andrew Harvey and Martin Goodman.[1] Mother Meera is kept at a distance from all but her most intimate followers, and there is little or no opportunity for interviews with either her or her entourage. The only possible relation to the guru is a devotional one, and even frequent visitors and faithful believers are kept from entering into personal contact and conversation with her. Focus on her disciples offers little relief since no records are kept (or divulged) of people visiting Mother Meera, and those who do visit rarely call themselves disciples or followers.[2]

To these practical limitations may be added the larger hermeneutical questions that apply to any research on new religious movements, especially as they insert themselves in the global culture. Numerous are the new religions, not only of Indian but also of Japanese, Korean, and Chinese origin which have settled in the West. These religions may be studied in continuity and discontinuity with their culture of origin and/or with their host culture. A full understanding of these movements thus will have to take both into consideration, keeping in mind that out of the mixture of cultures and elements of continuity and contrast, something genuinely new or distinct may emerge. This is particularly the case when one also attends to the element of female religious leadership, a relatively new phenomenon both in India and in the West.

The figure of Mother Meera may be understood from within the context of the Hindu devotional or bhakti tradition, as a disciple and self-acclaimed successor to Aurobindo and Mira Alfassa, as a female version of the silent saint Ramana Maharshi, or as one of the many female gurus who seem to give evidence to women's spiritual emancipation in India during the past century. Although all of these contexts will shed some light on the person and meaning of Mother Meera, it must be remembered that for most of her Western followers, the Indian background of this female guru is probably secondary to her ability to answer to a spiritual hunger or need that must be understood primarily from within the Western social and religious context of most of her devotees.

The Making of Meera

As is the case with most gurus in the history of Hinduism, Mother Meera owes her reputation and fame to her first mentor and/or disciple, Balgur Venkat Reddy, who "discovered" her at the age of twelve, and paved the way for the religious honor and veneration with which she is presently endowed. He is regarded in his own right by Mother Meera and her followers as "a rishi, a great saint and a divine messenger."[3]

Records portray Venkat Reddy as a lifelong seeker for the divine Mother. He successively became a disciple of Saradadevi (wife of Ramakrishna), the yogini Mannikyamma (who lived on the top of a hill without food or water), the *avadhuta* [completely free of worldly attachments and distinctions] Chinnamma, and Sweet Mother (Mira Alfassa, the female consort and successor of Aurobindo). Beginning in 1956, Venkat Reddy lived with his family in the ashram of Aurobindo, returning from time to time to his village Chandepalle in Andhra Pradesh for family business. It was on one of these visits in 1972 that he met Kamala Reddy. Since her own parents were very poor and unable to provide for her, Kamala went to live as a servant in the Reddy family (no direct family relation) at the age of eight. Books on Meera mention her very early propensity for supernatural experiences. At the age of six, she is said to have had her first experience of *samadhi* when "She fell senseless for a whole day."[4] Upon seeing her, Venkat Reddy believed himself to have come face to face with the incarnation of the original and supreme divine Mother, the Adi-parashakti. The confirmation of her divinity came when he is said to have had an experience of her omnipresence. "Ma had gone to stay fifty miles away. I was lying on my cot one evening. I heard her low, soft voice calling me and I was amazed. How should she come all that way? I got up and looked for her. She went on calling me. I could not find her anywhere. Later I went to where she was. She said: 'I came to you and you did not notice anything. I called out to you and you did not hear.' I asked her how she had come to me. She said with her mischievous smile, 'There is another way of travelling. Don't you know?' "5

This discovery of the divine Mother incarnate was for Venkat Reddy the fulfillment of his life's search and purpose. One of his previous gurus had foretold his eventual encounter with the ultimate source of divine energy and light in the form of a young girl. And on a more worldly level, it is said that "Mr. Reddy had always had a strong wish in his youth to take care of a small child from his village and show her to the world in such a way that the whole world would respect that Child."6 After having failed to introduce his wife and subsequently his daughter as incarnations of the divine Mother at the Auro-bindo ashram, he felt that he had finally encountered the real divine Mother.

Although it is often said that it is the disciple who makes the guru, this seems to apply in an almost literal way in the case of Mother Meera. In *The Mother*, it is said that Venkat Reddy left his wife and daughter to devote himself to Kamala Reddy,7 who then came to be called Mother Meera after the medieval saint Mirabai, whose devotional songs he often sang.8 Although Venkat Reddy regarded himself as Meera's disciple rather than her teacher, he did play a crucial role in the development of her self-understanding as a divine incarna-tion and a guru. In this, the process of formation of Mother Meera is not very different from that of other female gurus (such as Gauri Ma, Jayashri Ma, and Chidvilasananda) who were discovered at a young age by male gurus who took them into their school (*gurukula*). In the case of Mother Meera it was to the ashram of Aurobindo that Venkat Reddy took her in 1974, one year after the death of Mira Alfassa, and it was there that her self-understanding as a divine messenger came to develop fully.

One of her first disciples in the ashram was Adilakshmi Olati, a woman who had left home after her studies in philosophy, and become a disciple of Sweet Mother and of Venkat Reddy (who had become a spiritual guide in his own right). After the death of Sweet Mother, Adilakshmi came to recognize Mother Meera as a divine incarnation and has remained her closest disciple and associate until this day. Adilakshmi may be regarded as both a shield and a channel between Meera and the world. It is she who watches over the dar-shan, who runs the sale of books and pictures, who screens all requests for personal interaction with Mother Meera, and who wrote her first hagiography, entitled *The Mother*. In this book she records the numerous supernatural ex-periences that Meera had between 1974 and 1983, followed by personal testi-monies by followers of Mother Meera. Recurring themes in Mother Meera's own experiences are: merging with various gods (Durga, Kali, Saraswati,

Lakshmi), being in assemblies with seers, visions of "supramental beings," receiving the light of Paramatman, walking and talking with Sri Aurobindo and Sweet Mother, and receiving her mission from them.[9] This sense of continuing in the footsteps of Aurobindo and Mira Alfassa seems to have arisen soon after her arrival at the ashram of Aurobindo. In one of her early experiences in 1974, Mother Meera states:

> I was very sad because I had lost my soul. Then Sri Aurobindo called me and asked me why I was sad. I told him that I had lost my soul. He said "Your soul is not lost and could never be," and then he showed me the flower he had stolen. Then he replaced Sweet Mother's rose with a golden rose and told me that this golden rose was his soul and that it would stay with me always. And then he blessed me. I merged in Sweet Mother and Sweet Mother merged in me. I was told by Sweet Mother that I must look after the affairs of the whole world, that I must bear very heavy responsibilities and work unceasingly for the Divine.[10]

A few months after joining the Aurobindo ashram, Venkat Reddy felt that Meera needed some formal education and enrolled her in school in Hyderabad. This, however, lasted no more than two years. During this time, Meera had her first experience of the so-called "light of Paramatman" and came to be progressively absorbed in the experience of *samadhi*. Venkat Reddy relates that in 1975 "She would often go into Samadhi, sometimes for fourteen hours without a break. She would sleep and eat very little. Eventually, She would learn to be in trance continually, which She is, with open eyes, and able to do anything which needs doing."[11] Meera then came to be regarded by her devotees as continuously in a state of *samadhi* or divine consciousness. Her own accounts of this experience are filled with mythical themes from which a hierarchy of worlds and beings gradually emerges. Whereas gods and supramental beings often figure in her early experiences, the emphasis gradually shifts to Paramatman, which is identified with light and regarded as the Ultimate Reality. In 1978, Meera speaks of experiences of the light entering her body and of calling down the light into the world. "Great forces and lights from the Supramental Planes descended into me continuously from March 17 to April 15. Before this descent my subtle personality was that of the Goddess Lakshmi, my character that of Durga. After the descent my subtle personality was replaced with white light. The forces themselves were like white clouds, changing into blue and gold. They came day and night. I received from them like a flood, knowledge, light, ananda and peace.[12] This experience of being possessed by the light, which occurred at regular intervals in the following years (and in a particularly intense way in April-May of 1983), seems to have been accompanied by a state of physical weakness and dependency. However, it also marked the beginning of Meera's public role. Whereas people had come to see her in *samadhi* before, the first real darshans took place in 1978. In June of 1979, Meera for the first time speaks of herself as an avatar, sent by Paramatman to save the world.[13]

From 1978 on, Meera's fame started to spread, both in India and abroad. An Indian government newspaper (U.N.I.) reported the fact of her darshans in the Aurobindo ashram, and two of her earliest devotees were a Canadian seeker called Jean-Marc Frechette and the English poet and writer Andrew Harvey. Against the hopes and expectations of Venkat Reddy, Mother Meera did not succeed in gaining the trust and devotion of the Aurobindo ashramites. As Martin Goodman reports, "many ashramites come and pay a visit or two and are never seen again. The excited buzz that greeted her second stay in Pondicherry is now touched with words of scorn."[14] Between 1979 and 1983, Mother Meera, Venkat Reddy, and Adilakshmi lived in various places in India and traveled to Canada and Germany. In 1981 Venkat Reddy was diagnosed in Germany with malfunctioning kidneys and decided to stay in Germany to undergo dialysis treatment. In 1982, Mother Meera married a German, who is never mentioned by name and who does not feature at all in her public life and mission.[15] In 1983 a house was bought in Thalheim, and Mother Meera settled in Germany. Since the death of Venkat Reddy in 1985, her travels have been limited to occasional visits to India and one trip to the United States. Mother Meera lives a seemingly secluded, quiet, and simple life in which she participates in all sorts of domestic work in the house as well as in the garden, and in which she has also given herself to painting. In many of her paintings, Mother Meera depicts herself in union or fusion with Venkat Reddy, the images suggesting the intimacy of a mother and child.[16] These paintings (or copies of them) are sold in the gift shop and have become an important product in the devotional ambiance surrounding Mother Meera.

As the numbers of devotees grew through the years, the precincts in Thalheim became too small, and in 1999 a more sizable manor was purchased at Schloss Schaumburg. This is where Mother Meera currently gives darshan four evenings a week. Although these darshans were originally held in a rather informal and open style, visitors must currently book a place in the darshan hall weeks or even months in advance, and the frequency and length of the visits is regulated. The darshan itself seems to have kept its original form throughout the years. Meanwhile, Mother Meera and Adilakshmi have also purchased property in their respective hometowns in India, which is managed by relatives.

Mother Meera as Avatar

Mother Meera is regarded by her disciples and by herself as a divine incarnation or avatar. In the Hindu tradition, this belief, based on the *Bhagavad Gita* 4:6–10, involves a deliberate act of descent of God to the world to destroy evil, restore righteousness, and save the world. Whereas tradition has tended to a certain fixation of the number and identity of the avatars, the earlier texts manifest a great flexibility in this matter. Avatars have been animals, mythical beings, humans, and founders of other religions, but the recognition of women as avatars is a recent development. Whereas some myths recount the appearance of Vishnu as the beautiful Mohini who will lure the demons away during the churning of the cosmic waters, this may be regarded as a minor and secondary or derivatory appearance of God (who in this story is mainly incarnated as the tortoise upon which the churning stick is placed). All the human avatars who have come to figure in the Hindu tradition are male, even though in time their consorts might have acquired a more important role than the avatars themselves.[17]

The fact of a woman claiming the status of avatar may thus be regarded as an anomaly in the history of Hinduism. This is the case not only because of the female gender of Mother Meera but also because of her self-proclamation as avatar. Even Mira Alfassa, who might be said to have been the first female to be called an avatar, was pronounced such by Aurobindo. For Aurobindo, an avatar is "the divine leader of humanity and the exemplar of a divine humanity."[18] He wrote, "It is the manifestation from above of that which we have to develop from below; it is the descent of God into that divine birth of the human being into which we mortal beings must climb; it is the attracting divine example given by God to man in the very type and form and perfected model of our human existence."[19] He thus emphasizes both the divine nature of the avatar and his (or her) ethical and spiritual function to uplift humanity to its divine status. Whereas the divine nature of every person is emphasized, the avatar is regarded as being of a distinct nature and status. Whereas ordinary mortals are born with and from karma, the avatar is divine and without karma in origin and essence.[20] This is the conception of the avatar adopted by Mother Meera. She clearly distinguishes herself from gurus. Whereas the latter are humans who gradually became enlightened, she herself claims never to have been human and to have known since childhood that she was an avatar: "I knew who I am [sic] at birth. There has never been any separation between me and the divine."[21] The state of divine consciousness in which Mother Meera is believed to dwell is said to be far beyond the human states of waking, dreaming, sleeping, and even *samadhi*, and to require no special spiritual exercises such as meditation.[22]

Whereas the notion of avatar was originally connected to the god Vishnu, other gods have in the course of time been believed to descend as human beings to fulfil a particular salvific function. Mother Meera regards herself to be the incarnation of the female divine essence called Adiparashakti, a generic term that refers to the primordial and supreme power of the universe. In line with the Hindu tradition, she claims no particular exclusivity as avatar. Whereas the avatar occupies a unique position with regard to ordinary humans, he or she is only one of many descents that have come at different historical periods or that exist within the same period. Thus, Mother Meera acknowledges the importance of Jesus Christ as avatar,[23] and she recognizes the existence of other incarnations of the divine Mother on earth at this time. However, she also insists that "the work of each is different. Each expresses a different aspect of the Divine Mother. My scope is very broad and more integral. I help people in all stages of life, and I also work with Sri Aurobindo and Divine Mother."[24]

Mother Meera thus vacillates between an emphasis on her own unique salvific mission and role and the recognition of other saviors. Every avatar in the Hindu tradition is believed to descend with a particular mission. Mother Meera understands her own as that of bringing what is called the "light of Paramatman," as expressed in the words of Adilakshmi: "The whole purpose of Mother Meera's work is in the calling down of the Light, it is for this that She came; it is to open our hearts to this Light that her mission on earth was begun. Our entire purpose, as her devotees, and as lovers of the world, is to open with all our being to this Light. If we open to it, She has promised, it will work with amazing swiftness and force within us; its miracle of transformation will be achieved within us. That is Her promise and Her will."[25] The notion of divine light as the source and means of salvation is borrowed from Aurobindo, who gradually came to develop a more explicitly instrumental view of his role and that of the Mother in the history of salvation:

When we speak of the Mother's Light or my Light in a special sense, we are speaking of a special occult action—we are speaking of certain Lights that come from the Supermind. In this action the Mother's is the White Light that purifies, illumines, brings down the whole essence and power of the Truth and makes transformation possible. But in fact all Light that comes from above, from the highest divine Truth is the Mother's.

It is not balls or flashes of light, but a flow or sea of Light entering into the body and surrounding it and illuminating the whole field of consciousness . . . Light or rays of Light are always Light of the higher consciousness working in the being to illumine or to awaken the consciousness or attune it to the Truth.[26]

Whereas Meera is said to have been divine from birth, her ability to receive and channel the light seems to have emerged only gradually. In her biography, it is said that she already saw the light as a child, that she then went to search for the light in the heavenly worlds, that she started to receive the light in 1974, and that this process was completed in 1979. In 1980, Meera speaks of her experience of transmitting the light in the following terms: "The Light is bursting out from me as a tremendous sound like thunder and dazzling like bright sunlight. . . . I am sensing Light like this everywhere three times a day. The Light is covering the whole earth. When the Light leaves my body, it leaves it with such an enormous sound that I cannot hear for two or three hours afterwards. This process is going on."[27] Adilakshmi reports that in the years that followed the full merging with the light, Meera had more intense eperiences of the descent of the light in which "She was 'somewhere,' we don't know where. If we called Her, She did not answer, for She was very far away. All the function of Her senses were stopped. The entire body was shaken, legs and arms moving in all directions."[28] Since 1983, when this latter experience took place, little has been reported in terms of supernatural experiences of the descending of the light, and more attention is given to the effect of the light on other human beings and on the world at large.

On an individual level, the light is said to bring "an unmistakable and extraordinary lightness and happiness and peace," and to heal all wounds and hardships: "The results of the Light entering are many. You experience happiness, even if you were suffering before. When you work you do so without strain and attachment. Although you don't feel that you are doing anything, the results of the work will be good. You have less enthusiasm for work, but you can accomplish more because the work goes easily."[29]

On a cosmic level, the light is believed to bring about a fundamental transformation of an eschatological or millenaristic nature. "I understand that the individual physical body and the earth consciousness change every moment in an inexpressible way. This is a crucial time for the earth; many changes will be brought about. It is a supremely auspicious time to receive light. That is why everyone must aspire for it and surrender to the divine."[30]

Whereas the world is believed to be constantly in a state of change and evolution, this evolution is quickened through the mediation of the light of Paramatman. The light is thus regarded as a transcendent cause of salvation for the individual as well as for the world at large, and Mother Meera is viewed as its vessel. Although the work of salvation is being carried out by Mother Meera regardless of the recognition of the world or the faith of disciples, humble devotion to her is believed to provide a direct access to the workings of the light. This takes place during darshan.

Darshan

The expression of the religious significance of Mother Meera is concentrated in the moment of darshan. It is darshan in the fullest sense of the word, the exchanging of the grace-filled gaze between god and the devotee. In the Hindu tradition, the term *darshan* is used for visiting the temple and seeing an image of a god in an icon, as well as for an audience (in private or in group) with a human guru or avatar. Since Mother Meera is believed to be the incarnation of god, seeing her, and being seen by her, constitutes a moment of grace and salvation. This is the heart of the teaching and practice of Mother Meera.

Darshan with Mother Meera takes place in complete silence. There is no chanting, no reading, and no teaching. Silence is regarded as the only way to reach a state of calm, receptivity, and insight. People are encouraged to practice silent *japa*, or the recitation of the (any) divine name. If people have no knowledge of or attachment to any divinity, the mantra "amma Meera" is suggested. The darshan hall itself has no icons, no incense, and no music. People are guided to sit on comfortable chairs provided with instructions on how to go for personal darshan. After waiting for a while, all are asked to stand and Mother Meera enters. Darshan begins immediately. First the immediate entourage of Mother Meera receives darshan, thus setting the model for others to follow. One person sits on a waiting chair while another kneels before

Mother Meera. The first moment of darshan is called *pranam* and consists of bowing down and putting the head between the hands of Mother Meera, who softly presses the sides and the front of the head. The meaning of this gesture is explained in *Answers I* and *Answers II*, and is loosely derived from the *nadi* system of traditional tantric physiology:

> On the back of the human being is a white line running up from toes to the head. In fact two lines start from the toes, rise along the legs, join at the base of the spine and then become a single line reaching to the top of the head. This line is thinner than a hair, and has some knots in it here and there which divine personalities help to undo. It is very delicate work and great care has to be taken to undo the knots, as there is danger for your life if the thread is broken. When I am holding your head, I am untying these knots. I am also removing other kinds of obstacles to your sadhana, your practice.[31]

The practice described here bears considerable resemblance to the tantric experience of *shaktipat*, or the awakening of the kundalini energy by the guru.[32] These terms are, however, absent from the vocabulary of Mother Meera, who either is unfamiliar with them or prefers to use less esoteric language. In addition to the white lines, there is also mention of red lines that start at the toes and that grow up on each side of the legs to meet the white lines at the bottom of the spine in the state of total detachment. These lines are at times presented as part of human physiology and at times as spiritual forces that must be cultivated. In addition to the therapeutic explanation of the act of *pranam*, it is also understood as a test or as a measure of the spiritual development of the person: "When I touch your head, the Light moves upward in the white line. It indicates, like a meter, the development of your sadhana. When there is no development, the Light moves downwards along the line, showing the degree to which your sadhana has deteriorated."[33]

After holding the head for five to ten seconds, Mother Meera loosens her grip, which is the signal to sit up straight and look into her eyes. This is darshan proper, the meaning and importance of which is explained by Mother Meera in the following terms: "I am looking into every corner of your being. I am looking at everything within you to see where I can help, where I can give healing and power. At the same time, I am giving Light to every part of your being, I am opening every part of yourself to the Light. When you are open you will feel and see this clearly."[34] Although people may feel the light on rare occasions outside of darshan, the moment of darshan is regarded as the privileged moment and chance to receive the light.[35] This experience of the light is then believed to bring about rapid spiritual growth, and blessings of all kind. In *The Mother*, a wide variety of testimonies are given of people experiencing sudden love and satisfaction, assistance in practical matters and needs, forgiveness and burning away old wounds, a sense of protection, healing, and all kinds of fantastic experiences of light.

Darshan is given four nights a week (Friday, Saturday, Sunday, and Monday) from 7 to 9 P.M. to about 150 to 200 people. So as to make darshan accessible to as many people as possible, one cannot attend more than two consecutive evenings.[36] No fees are charged for darshan, but gifts may be made in the collection box outside the darshan hall.

After darshan, visitors have a chance to buy books and souvenirs (pictures of Mother Meera, and so on), and to briefly speak with one of Meera's closest followers. There is little opportunity, however, to discuss deep spiritual problems or progress, and there are no practical instructions on how to pray or meditate. On the evenings of darshan, it is also possible to call Mother Meera on the phone with questions or to write to her. This, however, is not encouraged. The whole practice is oriented toward resolving one's questions and problems by listening to one's own inner voice. Thus it is said that it is possible to call Mother Meera without a phone, or that is possible to write to her without using a stamp. The religious meaning of Mother Meera thus seems to lie purely in her ability to function as a focal point and a catalyst for the spiritual needs of people.

Teachings

One of the characteristics of Mother Meera is the complete absence of any teaching or doctrine. The only message that she is said to bring to the world is that of the divine nature of each person and the need to discover that divinity within. Meera's teaching is said to take place in the silence itself. In this, Meera is often compared to the figure of Ramana Maharshi, a Hindu saint who spent most of his life in silent meditation in a cave on the sacred mountain Arunachala.[37] The only verbal interaction that he had with disciples was condensed in the famous question "who are you?" This apophatic way of teaching is usually associated in the Hindu tradition with the nondualistic philosophy and practice of Advaita Vedanta. However, from the bits and pieces of beliefs and teachings that emerge from the interviews with Meera, it is clear that she situates herself within the devotional or bhakti tradition of Hinduism. This is evident not only from her focus on God and her self-understanding as avatar but also from the practice of devotion to her person that is advocated.

Mother Meera's conception of the divine world appears mostly in relation to her own supernatural experiences of traveling through various divine and spiritual worlds. She speaks of merging with various Hindu gods, predominantly female ones such as Kali, and of encountering so-called "Supramental Beings":

> I noticed that the Supramental Beings were different from Gods and from men. They were very tall, and they had a white and rose-tinged complexion. Their bodies were soft, slender, delicate, shining like mirrors and transparent, without bones or nerves. There was no way of telling male from female. As an outer covering, instead of clothing, there was a substance clinging to their bodies as a part of it,

and it could be changed at will. Their language was different and
not even the Gods could understand it. The articles they used were
beautiful, soft and delicate as their bodies. I had thought they did
not feed themselves, but I saw a fruit tree and it bore seedless fruits.
The Supramental Beings were surprised and saddened by everything human, by the ugliness of man's skeleton, by the range of his
vices, by his laziness and unconsciousness and ignorance.[38]

The category of the "supramental" seems to have been borrowed from Aurobindo, who used it in a more spiritual or mystical sense as the "Truth-
consciousness" or "the full truth of consciousness in matter."[39] For Mother
Meera, as already for Mira Alfassa before her, the term acquires more mythical
connotations, and comes to represent a pure and transcendent way of existence. Whereas these supramental beings are often referred to in Meera's visions and experiences, their status in the divine hierarchy and their role in the
salvation of the world remains unclear.

Of much more importance in Mother Meera's conception of salvation is
the figure of Paramatman. This term is used at times to refer to a personal
god beyond all other gods in the Hindu pantheon, and at other times to refer
to the ulimate ground of the universe, equivalent to the notion of *brahman*. It
may be regarded as a variant or a personalization of Aurobindo's category of
Parabrahman, which is based on the Advaitic notion that the deepest ground
of the person (*atman*) is no different from the ground of the universe (*brahman*). Whereas Mother Meera's emphasis on the divine essence of every person might suggest an inclination toward the contemplative and nondualistic
tradition of Hinduism, the practice she advocates tends more toward the bhakti
or devotional tradition. She directs herself predominantly to lay people and
strongly discourages any form of retirement from the world: "I do not accept
that people do not work. Everyone must work. I am working. Everyone must
do what they can. This is not a time for people to withdraw from the world. It
is a time to work with the power and love of the Divine in the world. I don't
accept people of any age just coming here to be with me. I want people to
come and go. When people are really dedicated to the Divine, there is no
difference between action and prayer."[40] Mother Meera thus encourages her
followers to find jobs, marry, and dedicate themselves to their families. Systematic meditation techniques are regarded as harmful because "quite often
they increase people's spiritual pride instead of destroying it."[41] All that her
followers are required to do is work in the spirit of care and love of others and
dedication to God. In traditional bhakti terms, she declares that "action and its
results cannot be avoided, but when we offer our actions to God or to the
Divine with devotion and detachment, wholeheartedly and sincerely, then the
actions will be purified and the result is that we are free from our karma."[42]

Since Mother Meera is regarded as the incarnation of God, it is toward
her that the attitude of devotion and surrender should be expressed. Disciples
are encouraged to become like children and to approach her with an attitude
of "complete simplicity, complete surrender, humility and openness (without

too many thoughts)."[43] This attitude is said to lead to complete realization. Mother Meera compares a realized person to a "child at peace in the womb of the Mother, knowing he is sustained at every moment by the grace and Light of the Divine Mother." Humility and surrender are thus not only the means to but also the expression of realization. The state of realization is defined as "absolute feeling, absolute freedom to love everything and to know everything."[44]

Whereas realization is regarded as the ultimate goal of life, Meera also discourages too much attention to and preoccupation with this end, which according to her cannot be reached within a lifetime: "People put too much emphasis on realisation. In my view it will take lifetimes. Instead, it is better to love and remember the Divine." Realization is understood not so much as a once-for-all state, but rather as a journey and as an endless process. Rather than one's own liberation or realization, it is the love of God that is the central focus and pursuit for Meera, who admonishes her disciples to "do the practice for the sake of the Divine, not for the sake of liberation."[45]

Meera's teaching—if one may speak of it thus—may therefore be regarded as essentially derived from the bhakti tradition of Hinduism. It is in this tradition that the concept of the avatar finds its proper place. As avatar, Mother Meera also promises her own help with concrete problems and mediation in the process of salvation. Like other avatars in the history of Hinduism, she is believed to have power over nature and to save people from misfortunes. She herself, however, often adopts a more humble and common-sensical attitude toward her followers, discouraging them from projecting too much power and direct control upon her person.[46]

Meera in the West

Whereas the person and teachings of Mother Meera may be understood in continuity (and discontinuity) with the Hindu tradition, the question remains how to understand her appeal in the West, where she currently resides and where the majority of her disciples live. The Hindu philosophical and religious background against which we have interpreted her person and teaching are of little or no use in understanding her success in the West. Rather than a particular symbolic or philosophical background, it is the apparent absence of any concrete doctrinal content or ritual practice that may explain the appeal of Mother Meera among Westerners, for it takes away all barriers related to cross-cultural communication and understanding that limit or impede Western relationships to other non-Western teachers and teachings. There would seem to be virtually none of the difficult terms and theories to master, no alien symbols or rituals to overcome. But more than this advantage in communicating without words, the implied emphasis on experience as opposed to doctrines and practices resonates with the current antidogmatic and anti-institutional attitude toward religion in the West. The atmosphere around Mother Meera is highly individualistic and evocative of any number of thoughts and feelings, both between and within individuals. Ken, the Australian psychotherapist whom I interviewed, reported the following experiences of darshan.

> Every time is different. Sometimes it is euphoric, sometimes very uncomfortable. Sometimes I am filled with light, life, and bliss and, in fact, experience myself dissolving in that completely. At other times I am very preoccupied with physical stuckness or discomfort, emotional hassles. The first kind of experience has to do with my arriving in an open and available state and being able in the night to expand into that further and further. The second kind has to do with the way I arrive at times in a somewhat more contracted state and need to experience the contractions in my system in order to digest them and release them. I want to make clear that I know and understand at the time that whatever I am going through is clearing my system and making me more available to the fulfillment of my personal quest.

Accordingly, Mother Meera may be regarded as a catalyst for any thoughts or feelings that might be at work in the individual. With the absence of any teaching, icons, acts of communal worship, or personal interaction with Mother Meera, the mind of the individual is turned intensely upon itself. As Ken put it, "it is important to understand that this remoteness is a significant part of what she offers us. It gets us to relate to the reality behind her as a person and the trappings of the ashram and the darshan processes." If Mother Meera therefore seems to function as a living icon whose very silence permits her to answer to every person's needs, one may be tempted to understand the relationship with her in terms analogous to what psychoanalysis calls "transference," the investment of the power to satisfy a desire in someone who gives no outward sign of it. However, Ken is adamant about the mutuality and the authenticity of his relationship with Mother Meera:

> It is important to me to emphasize that what I am describing is not a figment of my imagination. I am familiar with these dimensions and am aware of a distinct difference between me creating a fantasy and me having a verifiable link with someone. I have trained in this for over four decades in various ways. So now, while there are times when I am uncertain, there are times when I am very clear that I am in a link with someone or sharing an experience with them, even though they are half a world away, and this is particularly so with someone like Mother Meera who is clearly very accomplished in these dimensions.

Ken emphasizes that every person he knows who has visited Mother Meera has been transformed. Yet even a quick internet search under the name "Meera" reveals stories of individuals who have failed to experience a much-anticipated transformation.

Although the appeal of Mother Meera may be seen mainly in terms of the apophatic nature of her person and teaching, there are certain distinctive characteristics that may explain her appeal in a more positive and restrictive sense. Two characteristics of Mother Meera that cannot be overlooked are her Indian background and her female gender. Whereas most followers of Mother Meera are not searching for a course in Indian philosophy or an initiation in Hindu ritual practices, Indian spiritual teachers still consciously or unconsiously benefit from the romantic Western image of India as the source and summit of all spirituality. Indian gurus are thus surrounded with a certain mystique that Western spiritual teachers may lack. Indian spirituality is also associated with the attainment of enlightenment here and now, and it is to this that many of the followers of Mother Meera seem to aspire.[47] A good number of those who visit Mother Meera already have some acquaintance with Hindu thought and practice. This would partly explain how visitors so easily adopt a posture of silent meditation during darshan even though no meditation practices are taught. Beyond the purely spiritual appeal of Meera, the belief in her supernatural powers to heal, protect, and resolve problems or difficulties may also be enhanced by her distinct look and the mystique that goes with it.

A second aspect of Mother Meera that probably plays a role in attracting attention and generating particular feelings is her femininity. Like many of the other female gurus of our times, she is regarded as the manifestation or the incarnation of the Goddess. Although goddesses in India may be worshiped as wives or consorts of the gods or as symbols of fertility, it is under the image of the divine Mother that the divine nature of most female gurus is conceived. As the divine Mother, the female guru incarnates the qualities of universal and unconditional love, warmth, forgivenness, and care. The image of Meera that is most explicitly advocated is also that of "The Mother," as her biography suggests with its title. Mother Meera herself speaks of her maternal characteristics in terms of patience, love, and power,[48] while her disciples may associate her motherhood with any number of particular qualities and feelings. Darshan is understood by many a disciple as falling under the loving gaze of the Mother, which burns away all limitation and sin.

What is probably the most detailed and reflective account of a relationship with Mother Meera has come in Andrew Harvey's *Hidden Journey*. For Harvey, Mother Meera represented the rediscovery of the mother whom he had lost as a child in India. "India gave me a mother, then took her away. Years later, I found in India another Mother in another dimension, and the love I had believed lost returned. Without that first wound I would have not needed love so much or been prepared to risk everything in its search. Without the memory of a human tenderness I might never have accepted the passion that awoke in my being when I met the woman who has transformed me.[49] Whereas Harvey is clear about the psychoanalytical dimension of his relationship with Mother Meera, he also points to the more universal dynamics of the relationship of a disciple to a female guru. What the divine Mother brings about in the disciple is a return to the state of childhood. In a conversation with his friend Jean-Marc, the latter confesses, "I never wanted to grow up. Why be thirty-six when you can be six? A much more inspired age."[50] In these words, one may detect a certain regressive tendency that perhaps lies at the origin of Mother Meera's appeal for a number of devotees. But the state of childhood and surrender to which the figure of the mother calls the disciple is also associated with the loss of pride and ego that are generally acknowledged to be the condition for enlightenment. Thus, Venkat Reddy tells Harvey in a conversation that "to give yourself fully to the mother is complete realization."[51] Harvey's journey may be regarded as a struggle to surrender completely to the Mother. Moments of doubt are alternated with very explicit visions and experiences of her divinity:

> Ma sat down, with her back to the storm. I sat on the edge of the roof next to her. We were looking into each other's eyes. . . . Suddenly the entire horizon behind her from one end to the other broke into a vast flame of lightning and a thunderclap so loud I wanted to cry out. What I saw, as clearly and precisely as I have seen anything, was that the great unfurling of lightning was in her body. In the second of the explosion of lightning I saw her in outline on the edge of vanishing altogether, but with the whole of the purple sky and the zigzag of lightning inside her.[52]

Throughout Harvey's struggle, Mother Meera herself refrains from any form of direction or reproach. Conversations with her consist mainly of her confirming particular suggestions Harvey makes of his own spiritual problems and progress. Although Harvey ultimately denounces Mother Meera, embittered by her refusal to embrace his homosexuality, his writings have exercised a great influence in the West, and have set the tone through which many a seeker have come to approach Mother Meera.[53]

Conclusion

Any encounter of religious phenomena belonging to a particular culture with a new cultural context raises questions of meaning, interpretation, and forms of inculturation. In the case of female gurus, we are dealing with a phenomenon that is new not only to the West but also to the culture of origin. To understand these women it is thus necessary to understand them first in continuity and discontinuity with their own religious heritage, to then focus on how their own (often precarious) self-understanding, religious practice, and teaching might be understood in the West.

Common to almost all female gurus is their identification with the divine Mother. This may be seen to establish a basic field of universal symbolic meaning. Beyond this identification with the divine Mother, however, every one of the female gurus has a distinct style and teaching. The style of Mother Meera is characterized by an extreme absence of teaching and ritual. From interviews, a certain self-understanding emerges that is clearly situated within the bhakti or devotional tradition of Hinduism. Meera regards herself as an avatar who has come to bring the divine light and who requires complete self-surrender from disciples. This self-understanding and teaching is built up not only from elements belonging to traditional Hinduism but also from ideas derived from Aurobindo, in whose footsteps she clearly considers herself to be walking. Although Meera's self-image as avatar is very strong, her teachings seem to be made up of ad hoc answers to particular questions of disciples, and do not constitute a systematic whole. The focus is clearly on the practice. This practice of darshan seems to have been established very early in her career, and cannot be said to be theoretically well founded. The physiological explanation of the red and white lines running from the toes to the head may be regarded as a popular version of the Hindu *nadi* system, while the act of looking the disciple into the eyes is also explained in the most elementary of terms. The result, whether intended or not, is a wide variety of possible interpretations available to the disciples, and a great cultural flexibility. Whereas Indian disciples may understand Meera from within their common religious culture and categories, Western disciples are left free to attribute to Mother Meera and her darshan gestures the meaning and importance that fit (or contrast with) their own cultural and religious framework.

The particular gestures that Meera employs during darshan seem to have a rather powerful effect upon many Westerners. The acts of bowing, of being touched and of being looked at (in a spiritual sense) may be understood as a powerful contrast-experience with the dominant alternative spiritual atmosphere of our times. Although the spiritual market is flooded nowadays with all kinds of practices, techniques, and therapies to reach enlightenment or realization, much of it is based on self-effort of some kind or the other. In the figure of Mother Meera, nothing is required but self-surrender and openness to her power and grace. Disciples are not required to leave the world and live in an ashram. Nor are they expected to master alien teachings or to practice long hours of meditation. The religious practice advocated consists of no more than a short daily prayer or repetition of the name and focus on the image of Mother Meera.

Whereas Meera discourages the development of an ashram or any formal institutional structure around her person, she does not eschew the devotion normally attributed to a God or to a divine person. Meera thus offers a clear sense of protection, support, and care, with a minimum of expectation from the disciple. In this, Meera does embody some sense of the unconditional love that the divine Mother is said to have for her disciples.

NOTES

1. *The Mother* was written by Mother Meera's closest devotee, Adilakshmi, and published in Thalheim in 1987; *Answers I* was published in 1991 and *Answers II* in 1997; Harvey, *Hidden Journey*; Goodman, *In Search of the Divine Mother*.

2. When I tried to interview Adilakshmi, the most intimate follower of Mother Meera, I was told that all the information I would need was in the literature. I did

interview two Australian psychotherapists, Ken and Elisabeth, who have visited Mother Meera repeatedly since 1996. In our conversation, they stressed that "We don't think of ourselves as 'followers' of Mother Meera. She is a highly evolved person who makes herself available to anyone who goes to her darshans and, as far as I know, to many people who telephone, fax, etc. who can't get to Germany. We go there because we can learn and grow from our contacts with her. We don't follow her as such. Since we have never spoken, I can't say what her perception of us is. However, ours of her is that she is a highly evolved senior colleague with whom we 'train.' "

3. *The Mother*, p. 69.

4. Ibid., p. 9. References to Meera in devotional literature are always in capital letters.

5. Andrew Harvey, *Hidden Journey*, p. 67.

6. *The Mother*, pp. 77–78.

7. Both his wife and daughter (Jyoti) suffered greatly from Venkat Reddy's neglect, and have few friendly words to say about him and about Kamala Reddy; see *In Search of the Divine Mother*, p. 169–177.

8. *The Mother*, p. 74. The inspiration for her name may have also come from Mira Alfassa, called "Sweet Mother," the female consort of Aurobindo, whose spiritual mission Mother Meera believed herself to be called to carry through.

9. In all of these experiences, the cosmic snake Nagendra features prominently.

10. *The Mother*, p. 12.

11. Ibid., p. 16.

12. Ibid., p. 22.

13. Ibid., p. 44.

14. *In Search of the Divine Mother*, p. 128. In *The Spiritual Tourist*, pp. 175–180, Mick Brown mentions several lifelong members of the Aurobindo ashram who continue to focus their devotion exclusively upon the original founders and refuse to recognize Mother Meera as their successor.

15. Martin Goodman writes that Mother Meera and Adilakshmi each married German disciples. About the marriage of Mother Meera to Herbert Bednarz, he states that "The nature of the marriage is never explained and is made public knowledge only some ten years later. It is presumed that the marriage is not a conventional one. It is certainly an unconventional step for a young woman to have taken, presuming the initiative was hers"; *In Search of the Divine Mother*, p. 135.

16. Their relationship seems to have been the cause for some scandal in her hometown, as well as in the Aurobindo ashram. There is no indication, however, that their relationship went beyond a profound mutual dependency. Mother Meera also painted various images of the journey of Venkat Reddy into the afterlife.

17. See Hawley and Wulff, eds., *The Divine Consort*.

18. Ghose, *Essays on the Gita* (Sri Aurobindo Centenary Library, vol. 13), p. 156. Henceforth, Aurobindo's writings will be cited with reference only to the title of the text, volume from the Sri Aurobindo Centenary Library collection of his works, and the page numbers.

19. *Ibid.*, p. 148.

20. Aurobindo spends many pages in vol. 13 of his collected works arguing for the logical possibility of such a divine birth.

21. *Answers I*, p. 24; *Answers II*, p. 25.

22. *The Mother*, p. 57.

23. This is said in response to a question from a disciple as to whether he or she

can still follow Jesus; *The Mother*, p. 89. To a disciple who stated that he or she had rediscovered Jesus after visiting Meera, she said: "It is a good thing that you returned to your faith in Jesus. That is important. It is not so important that you have lost faith in me. To regain the faith in Jesus is important. Pray to Jesus and surrender to God" (*Answers II*, p. 118).

24. *Answers I*, pp. 19–20.

25. *The Mother*, p. 40.

26. Ghose, *On Himself*, vol. 26, p. 456; *Letters on Yoga*, vol. 24, p. 1,205.

27. *The Mother*, p. 50.

28. This experience took place in April and May of 1983; ibid., p. 51.

29. *Answers I*, pp. 41, 42.

30. *The Mother*, p. 25.

31. *Answers I*, p. 54; *Answers II*, p. 38. According to the Tantric system, the cosmic body is constituted by various energy centers called chakras, and a complex whole of energy channels or *nadis*. Traditional tantra distinguishes three main energy channels: *susumna*, *ida*, and *pingala*. In addition to this, there are hundreds of smaller *nadis* running through the body.

32. This energy is believed to lie dormant at the bottom of the spine, and needs to be awakened by a guru during *shaktipat*.

33. *Answers I*, p. 54; *Answers II*, p. 38.

34. *Answers I*, p. 55; *Answers II*, p. 39.

35. *Answers I*, p. 40.

36. People from Europe can receive darshan at most twice a month, while visitors from outside of Europe can attend all four evenings of a weekend. Previous registration is necessary.

37. "I was captivated by the beauty of her eyes that reminded of the eyes of Bhagavan Sri Ramana Maharshi," *The Mother*, p. 197.

38. *The Mother*, p. 20.

39. Ghose, *Letters on Yoga*, vol. 22, p. 91.

40. *Answers I*, p. 95.

41. Ibid., p. 67.

42. *Answers II*, p. 107.

43. *Answers I*, p. 31.

44. Ibid., p. 91.

45. *Answers II*, p. 57.

46. One disciple who believed he had received a message or calling from Mother Meera in a dream was told not to attach too much attention to these kinds of projections. See *Answers II*, pp. 77, 99, 182.

47. In *Answers I* and *Answers II*, Mother Meera often criticizes her followers' thirst for enlightenment.

48. *Answers I*, pp. 18–21.

49. Harvey, *Hidden Journey*, p. 10.

50. Ibid., p. 100.

51. Ibid., p. 80.

52. Ibid., p. 71.

53. At first, Harvey believed that Mother Meera endorsed his homosexuality (see p. 41). This, he thought, was part of the all-embracing love of the Mother. It was when she suggested that he renounce his homosexuality and marry that he no longer believed in her divine and unconditional love.

REFERENCES

Adilakshmi. *The Mother*. Thalheim, 1987.

Answers I. Ithaca, N.Y.: Meeramma Publications, 1991.

Answers II. Ithaca, N.Y.: Meeramma Publications, 1997.

Brown, Mick. *The Spiritual Tourist*. New York: Bloomsbury, 1998.

Ghose, Aurobindo. *Essays on the Gita*. Vol. 13, Sri Aurobindo Centenary Library. Pondicherry: Sri Aurobindo Ashram, 1970.

————. *Letters on Yoga*. Vol. 24, Sri Aurobindo Centenary Library. Pondicherry: Sri Aurobindo Ashram, 1970.

————. *On Himself*. Vol. 26, Sri Aurobindo Centenary Library. Pondicherry: Sri Aurobindo Ashram, 1974.

Goodman, Martin. *In Search of the Divine Mother*. London: Thorsons, 1998.

Harvey, Andrew. *Hidden Journey: A Spiritual Awakening*. London: Rider Books, 1991.

Hawley, John Stratton, and Donna Marie Wulff, eds. *The Divine Consort: Rādhā and the Goddesses of India*. Delhi: Motilal Banarsidass, 1984.

6

Gurus and Goddesses, Deities and Devotees

Vasudha Narayanan

The Divine Mother has always been worshiped as the sustaining soul and force of the universe. Although some of the faces she wears are well known—Kali, the Virgin Mary, Isis, for example—many of Her embodied forms have chosen to work quietly in the world. In turbulent times such as these, several incarnations of the Divine Mother move among us, each with Her particular task of healing or protection, or transformation.

—Mother Meera's home page, March 2001

An Internet Web site explains the presence of many women gurus in the world by saying that they are manifestations of the divine female energy in a troubled world. The twentieth century has seen more women gurus with large circles of international adherents than any other time. With the advent of the Internet we are also more aware of Web pages for women gurus than ever before. Indian newspapers in the diaspora advertise visits, video tapes, and lecture series of visiting women gurus.

Some women gurus are of West European descent and others are from India. They range in age from the late thirties to the seventies. Although the teachings of these women fall in spaces broadly conceived as "Hindu," many of them were not born of Hindu parents. In what way can those important gurus who were born Christian or Jewish be considered to be Hindu? Are they considered to be goddesses who descended to earth, or are they human beings who ascended to an exalted state? Do women gurus empower and elevate the status of other women? Is gender important in how a guru is perceived? What kind of messages do they give? While there are many detractors and critics for all gurus (both male and female),

and it is important to note that one cannot give any empirically verifiable answers to the claims of the devotees, we can try to answer some of these questions by discussing the lives and messages of two very popular gurus, Ma Jaya
Sati Bhagavati and Karunamayi Ma, who is also known as Sri Sri Sri Vijayeswari Devi.

Since the last decade of the nineteenth century and Swami Vivekananda's
trip to the Parliament of World Religions, one important image of Hinduism
in Europe and the Americas has been that of "universality" and interfaith
traditions. Although this image has been modified radically in the latter part
of the twentieth century with the new Indian immigrants who emphasize the
ethnic context of the Hindu religious tradition, many gurus proclaim this message of "universality." This message addresses the centrality of meditation and
says that people of any religious tradition can be devotees of the teacher or
followers of the path they show. There is no focus on any particular temple
worship, though the teachers may participate in them. The divine truth is said
to be within oneself and many deities are honored. Many gurus do not highlight specific theistic orientations; if any philosophy is preferred, it is that of a
nondualist bent. Ordinarily, these teachings, which one can loosely include
under the rubric of "neo-Vedanta," are espoused by gurus who are not part of
any sectarian *parampara* or tradition in Hinduism. Almost all women gurus—
there are a few exceptions like Mate Mahadevi, a teacher in the Vira Shaiva
community—are "stand alone" figures, that is, not part of a sectarian community or tradition that wields orthodox power in traditional societies. These
women gurus, therefore, tap not into the orthodox lineages but into the themes
of universality and neo-Vedanta. These spaces offer ways in which a person
can be a transmitter of a divine truth and be perceived as divine by their followers. Karunamayi Ma and Ammachi (seen elsewhere in this volume) are
perceived as divine manifestations. Ma Jaya Sati Bhagavati, born into an American Jewish family, is seen as a teacher who elaborates on the messages of love
given diachronically by several male gurus in India.

I have used several sources in the writing of this chapter. Over the last few
years I have met a few gurus, including Ma Jyotishananda Bharati (from Long
Island); Ma Jaya Sati Bhagavati (Sebastian/Kashi Ashram, Fla.); Sivaya Subra-
muniya Swami (Kauai, Hawaii); and Karunamayi Ma (Andhra Pradesh, India).
Visits to communities that venerate women gurus like Gauri Ma (at Sri Sara-
deswari Ashram or "The Mother's Place") were helpful in considering the social impact that these leaders had on the community in general and women
in particular.[1] The followers of Ma Jaya Sati Bhagavati and Ma Karunamayi also
made materials available for this chapter, and I have used the videos and books
they gave me for both classroom discussion and for research. In particular, I
am especially indebted to Krishna Priya, who very kindly sent me an unpublished autobiography of Ma Jaya—a truly extraordinary story of an extraordinary life. Videos and books about and by these teachers have also facilitated
the work. Finally, there have been the ever-popular Internet sources, especially
useful in trying to understand other women gurus.

Hearing the gurus directly and reading their words were both very helpful in getting a feel for their teachings, and I will quote them directly so as to present an unmediated look at the gurus. Specifically, I shall quote quite extensively from Ma Jaya's autobiography, for two reasons. The more important is that her words are powerful and poignant; through them we hear her voice. Second, her autobiography is yet unpublished, and since it is not yet available for those who want to go beyond citations, it seems important to present the original words.

Ma Jaya Sati Bhagavati

Who is Ma Jaya? She introduces herself in her autobiography thus: "Who am I? I am simply Ma. I am a devotee of Neem Karoli Baba, the daughter of the black mother Kali, the chela [disciple] of Hanuman the god of service, and the poet of the River Ganga. I acknowledge my river in my own way, sometimes with bells and incense and oils, other times with the fury of a woman who faces injustice every moment of her life. I acknowledge my river by meeting those injustices with an open heart and a quiet mind."[2] The introduction provides a useful framework for understanding various facets of her life, and we shall turn to that momentarily. Ma Jaya is an energetic leader, an engaging speaker, moving easily between being extremely amusing and quietly profound. She is one who works tirelessly for the downtrodden, for those whose religions seem to have forgotten them. She cares for those with AIDS and those terminally ill. She is a guru to thousands, mother to all her followers, guiding them on a spiritual path, leading them through various exercises. She is described in her videos as a "lover of God."

The autobiography is a portrait with recollections of her childhood friends and protectors, the poor folk who lived under the boardwalk in Coney Island. We hear the voices of the people she speaks about: at times the Brighton Beach/ Coney Island dialect, at times African American, Jewish, or Sicilian, with a liberal sprinkling of four-letter words that were part of their daily vocabulary and the idiom of the culture she grew up in, all interwoven with words like stigmata and *samadhi* (absorption into God).

Ma Jaya's life

Ma Jaya was born as Joyce Green; her mother wanted to call her Joy, but someone in the hospital made a mistake and put her name down as Joyce. She has been called Joya, Joyala, Juicy, and Lady J by her family and friends. Her parents, Anna and Harry Green, lived in New York. Anna worked with the Internal Revenue Service, but Harry, an affectionate father, was always gambling away the family's money down the alleyway. They were Orthodox Jews, and Joyce was one of four children; the others were Shirley, Melvin, and Harvey. Growing up in utter poverty, Joyce lived in a cellar with her family, rats, and very little else. Although there are no miracle stories as such attached to her conception (we will note one with Ma Karunamayi), her birth itself was something of a medical miracle. Apparently her mother had a burst appendix when she was pregnant, and needed emergency surgery that was life-threatening to the baby. No one expected the baby to survive, and her live birth was considered to be medical history;[3] the doctor sent her mother flowers every day and she was written up in medical journals.

Growing up under the Coney Island boardwalk, Ma's close friends were four African Americans who taught her the enduring values of life. Their friendship seems to be extremely important—a good deal of the autobiography is filled with affectionate memories of Chews, Chicky, Big Henry, and Hudson, as well as her first boyfriend, who became her "blood-brother," a young African American called Joe Joe. Young Joyce seems to have had an ungoverned child-hood; her mother worked long hours, and her gambling father focused on his cards and was content to have his daughter running around on her own, just as long as she did not "cross the streets alone." She learned to survive on the streets and to eat with her friends on castaway food. "We were all urchins, we all lived in the streets, we all ate from the garbage pails behind Nathan's. We had the beach, we had the boardwalk, we had fireworks on a Tuesday night, we had life. It was rich. There was always somebody being murdered under the boardwalk, there was always somebody being mugged, there was always somebody being robbed, there was always somebody being happy, there was always somebody crying, there was always somebody laughing. Everything I know, I learned on those streets."[4]

Early in life, the word "Ma" kept echoing in her head. She also seems to have had an intimate relationship with God, whom she called "Mac," because everyone in Coney Island was called "Hey Mac."[5] Ma calls her mother her spiritual teacher for the first years of her life, but when Joyce was thirteen her mother died of cancer, and two years later, Ma—then fifteen—married Salvatore, a handsome young Sicilian boy.[6] She led a very happy life; her husband adored her, she had a thriving business selling "hot" goods, and had three children. She was a great homemaker and a wonderful cook, and we hear about the splendid and luscious details of making lasagne, meatballs, salads, and pancakes. Having put on weight over the years, she was upset when her husband told her one day—half teasing, half serious—to "eat a little." She tried to lose weight and as part of this decided to take up yoga. The breathing exercises connected with yoga led her to other states of consciousness, and in 1972 the events that were to change her life began.

According to the autobiography, the changes that began with her yoga classes eventually led her to visions, meetings with spiritual teachers who had been dead for many years, and other startling events. One day, she says, the Christ figure appeared in her foyer; only she could see him. He announced that he would appear four times to her and would finally find a place in her heart. Christ apparently told her that the secret of the universe is love, and that she must teach all ways, for all ways [to God] are his. He told her to follow the story of Luke; for that is the story closest to his life.[7] Christ's coming, she says, brought her a joy that she had never experienced before; his leaving her plunged her into the depths of despair. She was in love with Christ—"every way a woman could be in love." She loves him "as a lover, as a child, as a mother, and now He was gone."[8]

Joyce/Ma Jaya began to neglect her family and her home; it was during this time, sometime in early 1973, while she was doing her breathing exercises, that "Swami" Nityananda appeared to her in a vision that was like reality to her.[9] She thought she was going crazy. Ma's words here are striking:

> About 1 o'clock in the morning, breathing in and breathing out, holding my nose until there was no breath at all, Swami Nityananda came to me. Naked except for a little loincloth, a fat man in a diaper, he came and sat on top of my toilet bowl with the lid down. And by this time I was ready for Bellevue. I said, this could not be possible. I was so near death. . . . When Christ was before me, He told me many others would come, He told me they would be from different religions and different ways of life, He even described Swami to me, and told me that he too shall be God. But when Swami came to me, I did not believe him, I did not believe he was real. Therefore, I thought, I was crazy.[10]

Who was this man? In Ma's life, he was a teacher who was to apparently prepare her to receive the teachings of her guru, Neem Karoli Baba (c. 1900–1973). Neem Karoli Baba was the teacher who was to get her ready for her work and teaching in life. Swami Nityananda (d. 1961), a well-known Hindu guru, had been dead for a few years when he appeared in front of Ma in her bathroom. Nothing in Ma's life had prepared her for a vision of this man—she certainly had never seen anyone even remotely like him in Brooklyn. Nor was Nityananda in any hurry to explain who he was.

Ma says that he appeared to her every night in her bathroom (it was the only place where she had any privacy) while she, wearing her nightgown, sat in the bathtub, and instructed her on various aspects of Hindu scriptures, practice, and teachings. He taught her various mudras—hand gestures that a teacher does when instructing with body language. He taught her to sit straight for hours in meditation. It is during this time, she says, that he asked her to become celibate. We are not told what her husband's reaction was to this new phase of Ma's life, but his worry, concern, and love is evident through the process. The teaching continued; Swami instructed her on the meaning of Shakti:

> "Shakti is the female power of the Goddess herself," my Swami continued. "She has to go from one vessel to another; one gives and one receives. Shakti then rises in the one receiving, and his whole life changes. As She goes toward the different centers—or chakras—the receiver rises out of the place of indifference and enters into the world of God and the Mother. However, Shakti can be dangerous without teacher or Guru. There is always a chance that one will use the serpent power—as Shakti is sometimes known—for personal gain, thus limiting oneself to the feeling of power instead of bliss."

Ma explains it thus in her autobiography: "The simplest way to put it is that Shakti is the movement of the earth in the form of God the Mother. The stillness is, of course, God the Father. Shakti is the emptiness and the fullness at the same time."[11]

The lessons with Swami Nityananda apparently went on every night. He trained her with rigor; Ma Jaya writes:

> The body has to be trained to hold the power and love of God. Night after night Swami trained me like that, and night after night he pounded the scriptures into my head, and night after night I complained, because I never liked school, and how am I supposed to remember all this? We were halfway through the *Bhagavad Gita*, when I made a deal with him. I learned how to absorb the scriptures into myself without forcing wisdom through my mindless mind. . . . The hardest thing was learning to use my hands. There were all these mudras I had to learn, and I couldn't get them straight. Mudras are gestures of the hands and body that a teacher can use to help people, usually without their knowing anything has happened. Swami was trying to teach me all the things that a spiritual teacher should know, but I couldn't get it. Swami used to call me "stupid" and "idiot." I used to write things down, and I would look at this piece of paper and do my mudras. I would still get them wrong, and he used to slap my hands, and I'd slap him back.[12]

Ma's life seemed to be collapsing; she had a grown daughter, a son, and a six-year-old. Swami had told her that her guru was coming. It was at this time that the family went to the Poconos for the Jewish new year. It was 1974. Searching for God, and oblivious to all but the divine experience she craved, she went to a lake and started rowing; she almost drowned. It was at this time that she had a vision of a man with a bandana. This, she says, was Shridi Sai Baba; he had come to rescue her, and he left her with a small icon of himself. Shridi Sai Baba (d. 1918) had lived in a small village in Maharashtra, India; like Nityananda, here was another dead teacher who had manifested himself in front of Ma Jaya. His saving Ma Jaya from drowning seems to be for a reason—she had a mission to fulfil. Ma Jaya's words, musing on her choices, are poignant: "Here was a family, a home, a husband. And here was God. There were choices to be made, and yet there was never a choice. For here was God, and the rest was just floating away. It was never really a choice, for if you put God here, what else is there? Where are your choices? You have none. No matter how fierce the world seems to you, or how beautiful, no matter how it beckons you—No one, no man, no woman, no child can give you what God can give you."[13]

Swami Nityananda had told her she would lose everything: her family and himself, but she had to share the teaching with all people for the sake of the guru, God, and humanity. Ma Jaya says that while totally surrendered to Swami Nityananda, she was yet unable to separate from her family. Eventually, her "third eye" of wisdom apparently opened and she struggled to deal with all the issues it raised. We are led through several chapters of breathtaking phenomena, including her association with people involved in what one may call paranormal and spiritual exercises. In March 1974, Ma Jaya met Swami Nityananda's disciple Hilda Charleton, and Hilda became one of her teachers.[14] Hilda Charleton is portrayed as someone familiar with psychic phenomena and the Hindu pantheon, as well as several Hindu gurus. She was thus a kind of interpreter of the many almost shocking physical and psychic states that Ma is portrayed as going through. When Ma apparently got stigmata and started to bleed during Easter 1974, it was through Hilda's intervention that she was able to bring it under control and function for her family. Eventually, Ma's quest left Hilda behind; according to Ma's biography, Hilda apparently wanted to spend all her time exploring and playing with the psychic realm of the dead and not in the unrelenting search for God. There are more incredible happenings; during the same period, Easter 1974, Ma had visions of all the Hindu deities; she described them on the phone to Hilda who, hearing about their appearance, identified them by name. It is then that she first met the goddess Kali and Hanuman, the monkey-god.

A few months after these visions, on August 1, 1974, Ma's guru, Neem Karoli Baba, finally appeared before her. She was filled with immense love for him; she felt she had everything now: "I felt safe in my life of selling hot goods, feeding the kids in the neighborhood, and letting the street kids spend a night or two a week in my recreation room. I loved the way the kids called me Ma or Aunt Joyce. It seemed I had a million names and perhaps a million faces. I had Hilda and Mount Manressa, where I went to find my beautiful Christ. I had my Jesuits and my nuns. In other words, I had my life. Now I had what I'd been searching forever for, or maybe it was just in this life. 'My Guru.' I said the words over and over, 'My Guru.' "[15] This was a flimsy stability; the status quo did not remain. There was a choice between her life as she knew it and her life with God, teaching everyone. The choice between family and God, the world of known security and comfort versus the promise of eternal and boundless joy, is one that we come across many times in world religions. The struggle between her family and her God is a remarkable one; and yet, it is ultimately no choice at all for her. Swami Nityananda himself had once chided her, and Ma Jaya muses on this attachment:

"So you think you love your husband. So you think you love your children. What is this love? MY husband, MY children, MY home— this is not love, this is possession, attachment. You don't know the meaning of love." I who loved my husband and children so deeply could not understand. I stared in his eyes, this stern, hard, harsh man. In his eyes were pools and pools of love, and I knew for the first time that I had never loved in completion. Complete love is giving totally of yourself without ever looking to see who is taking. Swami was the first to show me the meaning of unconditional love.[16]

Her family tried to help her through this; knowing her father was afraid of anything non-Catholic, Ma's older daughter, Denise, tried to help her in many ways. And yet, here was Ma, talking to her teachers in the bathroom all night. At one point she observes: "My husband of twenty years who loved me so much, he sat with me night after night while I carried on with invisible men. What could he have thought except that I was crazy?"[17]

Ma now had to make a decision. She needed her husband to let her go, to set her free. They were young, in their thirties. Her husband, Salvatore, told her:

> "Listen, babe, I don't want to lose you. Do you hear me? I'm not gonna let you go to God or man. I'll fight—do you understand?"
>
> "Sal, I understand. Now it's your turn to understand. I love God." I began to cry. "I love God. Sal, please believe me. You've been the only man for me since we were just kids in Red Hook and Coney Island, but Sal, I need to be with God in a different way, not the way of man and woman. I need to serve, I need to nourish, I need to give. Will you let me?" I asked with hope in my voice and heart. "Will you let me?" I asked again; this time I found myself begging, a thing I thought I'd never do. "Will you let me?"
>
> He didn't answer. We were both crying now. I went into his arms and just held on for my life. "Let me go, Sal." He began to smile. I could feel that smile though I couldn't see his face. I could feel it in my heart. We both were remembering that song from years before, "Let Me Go Lover." It was big in the 50's. How many memories we shared, this young man and I, and both of us only in our 30's. He whispered to me with his face buried in my hair, "I thought we could grow old together, babe."
>
> My heart was breaking as I asked a question that would change our lives forever. "Will you share me, Sal, will you let me serve?"
>
> "I can't," he answered, "I can't."[18]

By the end of 1975, Ma and her disciples had thirteen ashrams in Queens, New York, and in 1976 she left her family. Her gurus had warned her that she would lose her family but that she would get them back later. Ma settled in Florida with her disciples, and Kashi Ashram was founded in 1976. A year later, in 1977, Ma visited India.

Ma's work with terminally ill AIDS patients has made her well known, and in 1993 and 2001 she was invited to the Parliament of World Religions. She is a close friend and colleague of many religious leaders including the Dalai Lama, and continues to work and serve on many fronts, including raising people's awareness about Tibet.

The Kashi Ashram

The beautiful enclave where Ma and her disciples live is called Kashi, after the city in India. The quiet pond is their Ganga; nearby is a stream, where the wood on the boardwalk has the names of the many who have died in Ma Jaya's arms. The large room where one hears and sees her has portraits of her teachers and gurus as well as several of her paintings. The ashram itself is named after her, her guru, and the place that she considers to be most sacred—Kashi. The place where she resides and which she calls home is called Ma Jaya Neem Karoli Baba Kashi Ashram.

Who is Ma Jaya? We can ask that question again and discuss facets of her life with the very categories she provides us with in the beginning of her autobiography; she says: "I am a devotee of Neem Karoli Baba, the daughter of the black mother Kali, the chela of Hanuman the god of service, and the poet of the River Ganga." There are four aspects of her life mentioned here: she is a devotee of the guru, she is a devotee of the goddess Kali, she is the disciple of the god of service and therefore serves humanity, and finally, she is connected with Mother Ganga in inextricable ways.

Many Teachers, One Guru

Ma Jaya distinguishes between having many teachers and just one guru. She says that she has been taught by many teachers; she was taught by the homeless, a prostitute, a hard-working mother and sister, a gambling father, and above all, many spiritual teachers who instructed and mentored her. In this last category come Hilda Charleton and the teacher par excellence, Swami Nityananda. Swami Nityananda, who taught her every night for more than a year, prepared her for the coming of her real guru. By looking at the dates, it seems that Swami Nityananda had evidently begun his instruction to Ma Jaya even while Neem Karoli Baba was still alive on earth. During all his teachings, however, he never does reveal to her who her guru is or when he would come; he just denies that *he* is her guru. Teaching alone, therefore, does not equal guruship for Ma. She lists the splendor and compassion of her many spiritual teachers: "I had many teachers, and I wouldn't trade those days of hardship and joy. I could not have lived without the touch of Mary, the beauty of Christ, the crazy laughter of Shirdi, or the softness and strength of Ramana Maharshi [who are revered male gurus in India], who knew how to combine his love for Shiva with his great love for the Mother. They were all there. The harshness of Swami Nityananda gave me strength, and I realized that harshness was indeed the softest teaching I have ever received."[19] She longs to meet her real guru; when he manifests himself to her during one hot August afternoon, in the middle of a barbecue (an incident that borders on the surreal), she has no doubt that he is the one. She does not know his name; her first response when she hears the name Karoli is to think he is Italian. Ma Jaya muses for at some length as as to why he kept her waiting, why she had to be taught by Swami Nityananda for so long before she gets her guru. The reason for the swami appearing before the guru is finally revealed. The teaching of the swami is said to be an exercise in detached action, an exercise of compassion. It was also to prepare Ma to teach:

"To teach you, knowing that your heart was some place waiting to be picked up, was the greatest act of transformation any Guru, any sad-dhu, any swami, could have ever done, for he taught you so completely, so utterly free of mockery, so utterly fierce and void of pride, he taught you only to put you in my arms. And that is true love of one God for another, one Guru for another, one swami for another." Then I understood—Always came Swami first, in every lifetime, to train the child for her beloved. For if I would have seen Baba first I would not have eyes for anything in the world, including my chelas [disciples] and you who read these words. I would not have learned anything. I would not have been taught anything, and I would have nothing to teach. I would have had ears full of cotton and a mouth sewn together, and eyes that could only see God. So I had to be taught how to take the cotton out of my ears, pull out the thread of my mouth, and open my eyes to all things. If I'd seen my Baba first, I would have gone straight into God, but who would understand? I'd either be dead or sitting crosslegged in total bliss, maybe in a re-mote cave in India or maybe on the back ward of some mental hos-pital. All my love of God would have flowed straight back to God, and me with it, and who would have learned? Swami had to be there, to teach me to teach.[20]

In Ma Jaya's understanding, if the guru were to come first, the disciple will not have the time or the inclination to teach, and the teaching would end with her. It was by example, by being the recipient of the compassion and instruction of many teachers, that she was trained to be a guru herself.

There is a sense of cosmic appropriation and appropriateness about the relationship between a guru and a disciple. Just as one can have only one biological mother, one can have only one guru. Ma Jaya's words about this are unambiguous: "Either you're someone's Guru or you're not, from the begin-ning of time. You don't get to pick and choose a Guru, although of course you can choose a teacher. You may have many teachers, but there's only one Guru."[21]

It is perhaps in the understanding of the guru that one can find several parallels in Hindu literature. There is an intensity and passion in the descrip-tion of who a guru is. Swami Nityananda describes the guru thus:

"Everything and nothing," he answered. "It is he you live for. It is he that you would die for. It is he that you acknowledge as goodness, and it is he that will show you how to consume evil. It is he that has given you the boon of using your eyes to take pain and heartache and even karma from those who will come and sit in front of you. It is he that will take that same pain from you. He is the heart that beats inside of you and the soul that occupies the flesh. He is the silence your soul longs for. He is you. You will go on in life always in the heat of your passion for your Guru and your God. Those who want the merge and oneness that we all come from will see it in you and ask to sit at your feet. And the time will come when you too will be called Guru and your name will come to mean Mother. You will be the Mother to all who are willing to give up attachment to the world."

Ma Jaya's response to this charge is simple—either she will be the Mother to all who need her, or to none. She will be the Mother to those whom the world considers to be unworthy: "I looked at my Swami and said, 'If this comes to pass, then I will become the Mother to all, not just the holy. I will call to me those I knew in my youth, those under the Boardwalk that the world was afraid of and therefore missed out in learning of the wisdom of the streets. I will be Mother to all, or no Mother at all.' "[22] It is after this proclamation of Ma Jaya's that Christ comes back to her. He says: "You are getting there." Ma Jaya laughs and says that when she did, "the Christ smiled at me and disappeared into my beating heart, a place He has never left."

Ma Jaya, then, identifies herself first as the disciple of the guru Neem Karoli Baba, and then proceeds to call herself "the daughter of the Black Mother Kali."

Daughter of Mother Kali

Ma Jaya is a devotee of Kali. And indeed, there is no missing this fact—there were striking images of this goddess in her inner chambers where she gave us darshan. There are Kali images all over Kashi Ashram. Symbols of Kali appear in Ma's arresting paintings. Even the roller hockey team of the River School is called "the Skulls."

Kali is the dark goddess whose terrifying image is loved by her devotees. Well known in some parts of India, she takes a form that is hard to understand by those who are not her followers. Whereas most Hindu goddesses are beautiful in a classical way and have a benign aspect—even when they are out to destroy evil—Kali is formidable in her darkness and in her appearance. Garlanded with skulls, haloed with disheveled hair, rolling a red tongue, she is most beloved of those who apprehend her divinity. She is considered to be the supreme mother in Kashi Ashram. On the home page of the Kashi Ashram, we find this prayer to Kali:

> Mother of all that is light and dark, show me your form. I shall hold my hands so close to your being that perhaps my fingers shall burn. I shall fill myself up with your purity and become aware of the Earth and all the pitfalls that can call a child away from its mother. You, Kali, are the mother of all. The All Good and All Powerful One, Kali is without beginning or end. Where her consort creates, she preserves and withdraws the world of extended matter. May She, the Black One of the Dead Night's Glory, forgive those who live in the silence and have never—due to lack of meditation—felt her Hand on their breast. I am Ma, and I beg you to go deeper into the place of the terrifying horror of the dying ego. I shall be there with you.[23]

Ma Jaya was evidently terrified when Kali first appeared before her in all her darkness. This was while she was still married and before her real guru had appeared in front of her. When Kali appeared in front of Ma Jaya, she called up her friend and mentor, Hilda Charleton. Hilda told her to ask Kali to "un-zipper" herself. Kali did so and inside was the most beautiful golden goddess. While Ma Jaya was terrified of her wild form earlier, she now says that there is no greater beauty than Kali in her horrific form. She says that in the old days she asked to see the golden form out of fear, but now "out of wisdom, I do not care to see the golden Kali any more." Kali is frequently seen as a destroyer; Ma Jaya simply says it is the destruction of the ego. It is Kali who kills the ego; it is she "who takes evil, devours it inside herself. Kali goes afer pain and evil."[24]

Despite the predominance of Kali in her worship, Ma Jaya also reveres all other goddesses. She writes: "I was born from the jetta hair of Shiva, and yet I too bow to Laxmi. I walk a blood path . . . and at the end of that path stands Mother Laxmi, spreading upon the ground the flower petals of a white rose. I who walk the bloodied path of Kali, need at times to step upon the sweet petals of Laxmi, and to hear that gentle laughter, and allow her coins to fall upon us gently, revealing our own desire to serve."[25] She juxtaposes the fortune of the goddess Lakshmi with the need to serve; the prosperity that Lakshmi gives, she says, is when she looks into one's heart and sees "what it is that you need to go on."

River of Love, Streams of Compassion

In the very first page of her autobiography, as in many of her other writings, Ma talks about the river Ganga:

> There is a sacred river in India called the Ganga. She's so brilliant
> in her love, this Mother Ganga, that she continuously flows toward
> every human being, and everyone that comes toward her is blessed
> and purified. All are greeted by an astonishing amount of beauty.
> Even those who are filled with corruption and hate are never judged.
> . . . My wish when I first got started in spirituality was that I could
> always be like that river. I wished only to reach out arms that will
> always hold and hands that will always touch. Now, in this time of
> AIDS and so much pain in the world, the whole river is in my heart,
> and the river has overflowed its banks.[26]

It is this river that forms the spiritual trope for Ma's teachings and life. Ganga appears on many levels in her life and in her message. On one level, it is the most sacred of rivers, on whose banks is Kashi, the city of light. For Ma Jaya, however, Brooklyn is also a sacred place, for that is where Christ appeared to her. Above all, it is Kashi (Benaras, modern Varanasi in India) on the banks of the river Ganga that is sacred to her. In India, the dying were taken to Kashi, for dying in its precincts assured one of liberation. The ashes of many Hindus who die in other parts of India and the world are taken and immersed in that river. For Ma Jaya, this sacred river is present in Florida, in her Kashi Ashram. Ma Jaya calls this ashram her own Kashi, and the pond her own Ganga. In the waters that flow through her ashram, the ashes of all those she loves, all those who die of AIDS, are immersed. When describing the dying Bruce (whom she affectionately refers to as Shiva Baba), we understand the importance of this sacred place in Sebastian, Florida: "Every once in a while he would turn to the window to see the water in our pond, our own sacred Ganga. He knew then, that this pond is a part of the sacred river, and this was where his ashes would be spread." She says that there is no place "holier than Kashi at the banks of the Ganga," but that this place is in Florida at the Connor's nursery where children dying of AIDS are cared for; this place where the children are unconditionally loved is a place as sacred as Kashi.[27]

Service

The river is the mother, the river is the love in service for Ma Jaya. This leads us to the final point in the way she describes herself—she is connected with Hanuman, the god who exemplifies service. Early into her spiritual awakening, Ma Jaya would go to hospital wards to give her love to the dying. She describes Shakti as the flowing essence of God: "It's the same thing that you can feel in a moment of giving, it's warm and liquidy. It was an expression of my love for my God, this love that flows through me and into people."[28] In one memorable conversation, Swami Nityananda explains this:

> "That, my dear Jaya, is Shakti. The joy you bring people and want to bring people is an actual substance that we all have dwelling within us, waiting for the holy to come and activate it and tease it alive." He continued, "When Shakti is silent, it melts one's resistance to love and affection. Judgment is drowned in the waters of the Mother."
>
> "Whoa!" I said. "What are you talking about? What are the waters of the Mother? Is it like the waters that the baby floats around in before birth?"
>
> "Yes, it's like the waters of a pregnant woman that protect her young. When you go and visit the sick, you bring them the mist of the Mother; that mist is an actual substance. It says to the one lying in the bed, 'You're a human being; you're not this disease that ravishes your body.' Service cannot be dry," he continued. "It must be, it has to be soaking wet, drenched in the love of God, and you, my Jaya, have the ability to bring this Shakti—or soul waters—to all who cross your path. Go out and initiate them into Shakti. She is the Divine One who dwells at the base of the spine. She stays asleep there until awakened by Her own Self in one who cares enough to want to touch humanity, withstanding the judgment of the world."[29]

The service, drenched with love, she says flows from her. Ma Jaya is most certainly unique in the intensity and passion with which she takes care of the AIDS victims. Near Kashi Ashram is the house for those dying of AIDS—a place where they can die with dignity, a place that can shake one's faith in the beauty of life and yet affirm it. Ma Jaya has been working in Florida, in San Francisco, and all over this country and the world, raising people's awareness of AIDS. She serves those with AIDS, those whose religions have rejected them, those homeless, those in poverty. Over and over again we hear her say: "there are no throwaway people."

In her story, she speaks many times of being able to take on the pain of others by looking at them:

> I was given the gift of being able to take pain into my eyes, as God in the form of my Guru takes it from me. As this happens, some-one looking into my eyes feels a buoyancy; the spirit rises. It took me many years to refine the process of consuming the suffering of another person without looking too weird. As the person gets lighter, giving up what he fears the most, my face gets darker, until the person closes his eyes. It is called the power of Kali, the black goddess of nighttime fears who stalks the cremation grounds of life's shores, protecting her children from evil. She becomes darker than evil, consuming it with a flick of her protruding tongue. I was given the blessing of the dark Kali. It brings to me those who suffer, with all their heartache. I hold my arms out and, with the knowl-edge of Mother Kali, I can take away pain.[30]

Ma Jaya's service extends to feeding the homeless regularly; she says it is Neem Karoli Baba who tells her: "Feed everyone, Ma. Everyone needs the Mother." In the large kitchen and dining facilities of the Kashi Ashram, there is a beau-tiful image of Annapurna ("she who is filled with food"), a form of the Hindu goddess Parvati, who nourishes all human beings.

As with the river, as with Kali, feeding is literal and metaphorical. It is the food of love, the food that makes people heal, the food that makes people whole that Ma Jaya refers to. She quotes Neem Karoli Baba: "I tell you, with my lips and my heart, feed everyone. The thirsty, give them to drink of the River's flow, wet their lips with her waters. The hungry, feed the food of love. You are the River's daughter. With your own hands, touch the leper and the sick, feed them all, reach their stomachs and their hearts. And when they cry out in grief, hold them to your breast, Jaya, give them the milk of relief. River child of my soul, feed everyone, make the moment whole."[31] Here we have many facets of Ma Jaya's identity merging—she is devotee of her guru, the river's daughter, she feeds and serves those who need it.

Although the guru is sacred to the devotee, Ma Jaya presents herself as one who serves and teaches humanity rather than a divine being. But although Ma Karunamayi also teaches and serves her flock, she is a guru who is directly apprehended and portrayed as a goddess by her devotees.

Ma Karunamayi, aka Bhagavati Sri Sri Sri Vijayeswari Devi

Karunamayi Ma ("one who is permeated with compassion"), also known as Bhagavati Sri Sri Sri Vijayeswari Devi (the goddess of victory), lives in India and visits the United States every year. Vijayeswari is her given name; the triple Sri (sacred, venerable, auspicious) before her name is an honorific prefix of respect. She has the title of Karunamayi. The home page introduces her thus: "Bhagavati Sri Sri Sri Vijayeswari Devi, revered as the incarnation of Sarasvati, Goddess of Knowledge, Music and the Arts, resides at Her ashram in India."

I met her in the Hindu Temple of Atlanta in May 1999. A pleasant-looking lady in her forties, she was draped in a red sari, with simple jewelry. (Her pictures usually depict her in a red or, occasionally, a white sari). As she descended from the car, local devotees fell at her feet in veneration. One prostrates before deities, teachers, and all elders in most Hindu communities. She came into the temple, spent a few minutes in quiet worship in front of the shrine dedicated to the goddess Durga, and eventually sat in a special chair right outside its door. Men and women of all castes and ages bowed before her as she prepared to give a talk and lead everyone in a worship ritual. It was a weekday and the crowd was limited—about fifty men and women, some of them of Euro-Americans, some of Indian origin, who settled down to hear her and worship the goddess Lalita (a beneficent form of the goddess Parvati) with a thousand names. She spoke in Telugu and her chief disciple, Swami, translated in English. Her talk was interspersed with a lot of singing, in which the audience joined occasionally. After the worship ritual, Ma Karunamayi (referred to as "Amma" or "Mother" by her disciples) gave fruits and raisins to those who had gathered there. She took the red *kumkum* powder that women put on their forehead, and put the marks on all who stood in line. She was touring the United States, and during her time in Atlanta met devotees and friends in at the Hindu Temple of Atlanta, which functioned as a community hall.

In the last several years—2000 to 2003—Ma Karunamayi has been touring Europe and through the summer criss-crossed the United States from Alaska to Atlanta. Her popularity has grown dramatically: in 1999, a few people were at hand in the Atlanta temple to greet her with reverence; on April 11, 2003, there were hundreds of devotees. The priests from the Hindu Temple of Atlanta received her with the full formal honors that one greets a deity, a member of the royal household, or a very revered member of society. Men and women held a jar brimming with water (*purna kumbham*), a sign of reverential welcome. A woman devotee held a huge cloth umbrella—again one used ordinarily for deities—over her head. Male priests recited the Vedas as she was escorted into the temple. During the evening program she spoke for more than an hour, in English, to several hundred people in the temple auditorium in the basement.

Ma Karunamayi's Life

Bhagavati Sri Vijayeswari was born on Vijaya Dashami ("the victorious tenth day"), considered to be one of the most auspicious days in the Hindu calendar. It is the last day of the nine-day festival of Navaratri which, in most parts of India, is celebrated in honor of the Goddess. Like most festivals, it marks the victory of good over evil; specifically, it celebrates the victory of the goddess Durga over the buffalo-demon, Mahisha. It is because she was born on the victorious tenth day of the festival that she was called Sri Vijayeswari or the goddess of victory.

As with other holy people in India, a number of miracle stories are associated with her life. It is said that when Annapoornamma, her mother, visited Ramana Maharshi (one of the saints who had appeared in front of Ma Jaya), he predicted that she would bear the *thai* (the Tamil word for "mother."). Eventually, she went with her husband to Mysore during the holy nine days of Navaratri or Dasara, the major festival which comes in September-October. Here, during the festival devoted to the Goddess, "Annapoornamma felt unusual illumination entering her body. She felt as if Sri Chamundeswari (the presiding deity of Sri Mahishamandala) had entered her body."[32]

Almost exactly a year later, on the last day of the same festival of Dasara, which ends with the Victorious Tenth day, Sri Vijayeswari Devi was born in Gudur, which is in the Nellore District of Andhra Pradesh. As is the case again in other hagiographies, we hear of holy men recognizing her as an embodiment of the divine. One Sri Bhavananda Saraswati Swami from an institution called Sri Vidyapeetham Kanva Bhoomi (which sounds like a monastic organization) wrote a testimonial in her biography. Apparently, after several years of meditation in the Himalayas, he had a vision (darshan) of the Goddess in her childlike form—the youthful Bala Tripurasundari ("the young beauty of the three worlds"). Many years later, he says, he came to the south, and came to the home of Annapoornamma during Dasara. Annapoornamma asked her daughter, the five-year-old Vijayeswari Devi to bring fruits to the visiting holy man. Sri Bhavananda says:

> Upon seeing this little girl, I became totally inert. Her figure resembled that of "Bala Tripurasundari" who had blessed me with Her *darshan* in my dream. This *darshan* was the result of the several years I had spent in quest of the Goddess. Her absolutely calm face and eyes appeared to be asking if I had recognized her . . . 'My hair stood on end. I stood up, and tears of joy flowed uninterruptedly from my eyes. . . . The bliss I enjoyed during this *darshan* cannot be explained in any words or language. . . . Great sages can easily attain salvation, but to get the *darshan* of the Mother is not easy. . . . I was astonished that the great Queen of the Universe, who is the cause of the *Aprameya Shakti* which creates this world, was appearing before me in the form of a young girl. . . . Then the girl, in a most surprising manner, placed Her hand on my head. My past and future lives

started moving before my eyes like a film on a screen. From the *mu-
ladhara* through *kundalini yoga*, I entered into divine ecstasy.[33]

There are many stories of how her father recognized that she was someone
special, and other incidents of miracles. Her father died when she was quite
young. Apparently, when she was about twenty-one (the date is given as June
9, 1980), Karunamayi Ma left home to go to the remote forest of Kanvaksendra.
The place is identified as Penchalakona in Rapore Mandala of Nellore District,
and is said to be in the vicinity of the Penusila Kshetram in Andhra Pradesh,
south India. She remained there for about fourteen years. According to one
biography, during this time her "only companions were the wild beasts and
birds who fetched her fruits and honey—Her only diet during that period."[34]
It is reported that she performed these "spiritual austerities on behalf of humanity."[35] The sojourn in the forest does not seem to have been uninterrupted;
the biography is filled with many stories of people meeting her in the ashram
nearby during this time period.

At the conclusion of her austerities (*tapas*), Sri Karunamayi founded the
Sri Mathru Devi Viswa Shanthi Ashram on the outskirts of the forest at Penusila. The Web sites dedicated to Karunamayi say that a beautiful temple dedicated to Bharat Mata (Mother India) is nearing completion there, and display
pictures of this temple. She also maintains an ashram, the Karunamayi Shanthi
Dhama, in the city of Bangalore and, according to the Web, more than a thousand people per month are fed at her ashrams. There are other institutions
that she is starting—an orphanage and a school for handicapped children and
those with special needs. Most recently, a forty-bed hospital for the indigent
tribes people in remote Penusila Kshetram is being built. The mission statement on the Internet gives us a good idea of her work:

The aim of Sri Karunamayi's mission is universal peace and spiritual upliftment of humanity. Her chief message to us is to achieve
higher levels of consciousness through the regular practice of meditation, and She advises a minimum of one to two hours daily practice. She regularly gives meditation retreats so as to refine the experience of the individual meditator and propel him or her along the
path to liberation. It is meditation, Amma says, which will yield genuine spiritual progress and Divine Knowledge. With this purpose in
mind, She provides initiation into the Maha Sarasvati Mantra, in-
scribing the mantra on the tongue of the devotee using a twig of
holy basil (tulsi) dipped in honey. The purpose of this loftiest of initiations is to render one's speech "as sacred as basil and as sweet as
honey," and to bestow upon the practitioner, in time, Supreme
Knowledge for the sake of individual as well as universal peace. The
Maha Sarasvati Mantra initiation is made available in India only to
students due to the large numbers of devotees who come for her
blessings. In the West, She has consented to initiate sincere adult
aspirants.[36]

Many of the pamphlets and books tell us about the importance of the Saraswati Mantra—this is called a *bija* or "seed" syllable; it is a kind of mantra whose syllables embody the divine Mother and that will transform the human being who meditates on it. The implication is that when this sacred syllable is written with honey and the sacred basil leaf on one's tongue by the holy Mother, a person gets a jump start into spiritual awareness. And this Divine Mother is none other than Karunamayi Ma, according to her followers.

Goddess as Guru

The books, pamphlets, and internet resources locate Karunamayi Ma as a "poorna avatar," a full incarnation of the Goddess (Devi), and in particular say that she is the incarnation of Sarasvati, goddess of knowledge and the performing arts in the Hindu tradition. Elsewhere, her brother and disciple Sri Vijayeswarananda introduces a book of her teachings by saying that she is the incarnation of the goddess Lalita (a form of Parvati). The book focuses on the meanings of the thousand names of the goddess Lalita (*Lalita Sahasranama*). The *Lalita Sahasranama* is a very popular devotional work in south India, and millions of women recite it regularly. Karunamayi Ma regularly gives discourses on it and explains the meaning of the names. In introducing one of the books that focus on this work, Sri Vijayeswarananda emphasizes that Karunamayi herself is an incarnation of Lalita: "Coming to the Lalita Sahasranama, who but Lalita Herself can explain its true meaning or significance? The present day generation is blessed, indeed, for they have the opportunity to see Lalita Devi in the *sakara* ["with form"] form of Sri Sri Sri Vijayeswari Devi. Secondly, they are able to hear Her melodious, mellifluous and soothing voice through Her illuminating discourses on spiritual subjects which have remained unintelligible for ages. . . . By amma's will, *Kali Yuga* is changing to *Krita Yuga*."[37] In yet other places, she is identified with the goddess Lakshmi. She is thus seen as a manifestation of all the main goddesses of the Hindu tradition.

Nowhere in the biographies or books that I read of her have I seen any mention of the caste or community that she was born into. From the viewpoint of devotion this is perfectly normal and acceptable; there are popular sayings all over India that one is not to inquire about the antecedents of holy people or streams. The saying implies that we should not let the apparent insignificance of the origins diminish their grandeur that we perceive when they are flowing full stream. Besides, in the context of identifying her as a goddess, this question does not seem to arise.

Karunamayi asks her devotees to learn the "language of God"; this is absolute silence. She says that absolute silence is not only physical but also mental. Her followers write:

> She desires that we become as "infant babies" in the arms of the
> Mother, content with what She gives, without thought, ever estab-
> lished in Supreme Consciousness. Amma has taken human birth

for the sole purpose of helping us achieve that highest of states. *She asks not that we abandon our path and accept Her as guru, but that we view Her as a loving Mother,* one who provides spiritual nourishment and education in human values. She is ever ready to guide each individual in his or her quest for spiritual illumination, and to lead the world towards Divine Love and Universal Peace.[38]

Here too we can hear the words of Ma Jaya, who has written eloquently about silence: "The silent place must be reached with the heart. It can't be found with the mind. The heart of the mother transforms all living beings."[39]

Karunamayi Ma is the guru and the goddess, the deity for her devotees, leading them into meditation and peace.

Teachings

Although the initiation into the Saraswati mantra and the emphasis on reciting the thousand names of Lalita are the special teachings of Karunamayi Ma, there are also teachings that are more generic in nature. Along with the regular practice of meditation, Karunamayi Ma advises control of the mind and asks one to keep anger and jealousy under control. She asks us to purify the heart and "abide in the Supreme State." According to her followers, "inner peace and selfless love are the qualities She values above all others. For Divine Mother to come and dwell in our heart, we must have Shanti (peace) and Shanti is the very essence of God."[40] Like many other teachers, she says that "human love is ephemeral, selfish and shortsighted in character." She contrasts this with Divine Love, which is eternal, selfless, and all-encompassing. It is this divine love that she asks us to have for other human beings, and to selflessly serve all. Karunamayi Ma says that promotion of meditation and service are the main teachings of her institution. She says that she would like everyone to meditate and follows it up by saying quite frequently that "service to humanity is service to God."[41] In this, her teachings certainly overlap with Ma Jaya's work and words.

Although most of Karunamayi's work has been centered in her native state of Andhra Pradesh and her teachings have been done there and in the United States, she is now opening up a new center in Bangalore. Here her devotees are building a "Peace Village" that seems to be a teaching institution as well. The areas of instruction and service are traditionally Indian in their scope, and this is a commentary on her priorities. There is an Ayurvedic center offering treatment and instruction, a yoga training center, and instruction in Sanskrit, recitation of scripture, advanced Sanskrit courses in Patanjali's *Yoga Sutras*, the *Bhagavad Gita*, and tantric texts. The performing arts, which are an integral part of the Hindu tradition, are also taught, along with workshops in *jyotisha* (astrology) and *vastu*, the Indian science of geomancy. The Internet describes the land that has been bought for this enterprise and says that it "has been chosen both for its serene beauty and its harmony with the laws of Vastu." The statement goes on to explain *vastu*; it is said to be "the science of building based on the subtle mechanics of direction and space to promote health, prosperity and happiness."[42] Karunamayi Ma's interest in *vastu* was evident even when she came to Atlanta in 1999; she commented upon the positioning of a new set of steps up a small hill, from the car park to the main entrance of the Hindu Temple. Although the temple faces east—an auspicious direction, the steps were to be from the south, the direction of discord, enmity, and death. Plans drawn by the traditional architect from India (who himself was well versed in *vastu*) were altered after one group of devotees who followed Karunamayi Ma's teachings prevailed—at least for a while—over those Hindus who were more skeptical of this art of geomancy.

Women Gurus: Themes in Tandem

Whereas many of the contemporary women gurus would have enjoyed only local popularity in the past, the advent of the Internet has made them into international celebrities. Even until the 1970s, very few women gurus were known—Sarada Devi, the wife of Ramakrishna Paramahamsa, Anandamayi Ma, and the Mother of Auroville were perhaps the most revered. The most popular today seems to be Ammachi. Other than these four, the best known women gurus who speak the Hindu idiom today are Ma Jaya, Karunamayi, Guruma, Shree Ma of Napa Valley, Ma Bhagavati, Shantimayi, Gurumayi Chidvilasananda (of Siddha Yoga), and Gangaji. Sivananda Radha (1911–1995) started the Yasodhara Ashram in British Columbia; Vimala Thakar, who is about seventy-four, was born a brahman, followed J. Krishnamurti, and has taught in about thirty-five countries. She now lives in Mount Abu in winter and in Dalhousie in the summer. Nirmala Devi was born as a Christian and is the founder of the Sahaja Marg movement. Mother Meera lives in Germany. Most of these women gurus teach meditation, the peace of silence, and service to humanity, and many have an interfaith inclination. Many of them (such as Sivananda Radha, Ma Jaya, and Gangaji) are Euro-Americans. In the context of this galaxy of gurus, we can begin to look at the two women who are the focus of this chapter.

We can start with a simple question: what kinds of devotees do Ma Jaya and Karunamayi Ma attract? Second, we can discuss an issue that jumps out at us when we consider their teachings; this is the question of their identity and how they relate to "Hinduism" and to other world religions. Finally, we can raise a question of divinity—how do they relate to the Goddess, and how do these "mothers" view the issue of gender?

Devotees of Ma Jaya and Karunamayi Ma

The quantitative question is not easy to answer; it is hard to say how many followers any woman guru has. There are many levels of devotion, ranging from those who follow these people everywhere as part of their entourage, to those loosely affiliated with the ashrams, to some who go listen to their talks when they are in the same town as the teachers. Judging by crude facts like the attendance at talks, frequency of tours, Web pages and chat rooms, size and financial investment in the charitable "service" organizations, it appears that Ammachi and Chidvilasananda (Gurumayi) are probably the most popular and well known of the living women gurus today. Although Ammachi is probably as well known—if not better known—than all other women gurus today and certainly many other male gurus, no woman guru is as famous as Sathya Sai Baba (b. 1926).

Most of Ma Jaya's followers are largely of European or African descent in America, though there are enclaves of followers in Africa as well—followers inspired by her work with AIDS patients. Ma Jaya travels regularly to San Francisco; recently she has also been giving darshans in Atlanta and Chicago. While in South Africa for the third Parliament of World Religions, she visited many shanty towns and later went to Uganda, where a child-care facility had been named in her honor.

Karunamayi Ma, on the other hand, has followers who are Hindus from India and the United States as well as Euro-American devotees. A few of her close followers are from Colombia, South America. Whereas Ammachi's appearances attract hundreds of devotees (sometimes thousands, especially in India), there were about sixty who came to participate in the worship ritual to the Goddess that she led at the Atlanta temple, on a weekday morning in May 1999. By 2003 the attendance had grown to a few hundreds, but there were larger numbers for the evening and weekend sermons and lectures. Karunamayi Ma's following is just beginning to grow—and in leaps and bounds—in the United States and Europe.

"Mother-Tongue"

On a normal festival day, about a thousand or more devotees come to the Hindu Temple of Atlanta. Very few from this crowd come to visit and hear gurus; despite the vision that this essay and this book presents, many Hindus do not opt to follow gurus. This may be particularly true with the devotees who frequent the Hindu Temple of Atlanta. There are about six or seven temples and meditational centers in the greater Atlanta area, each catering to Hindus from different parts of India, or Hindus from different religious communities. In general, more south Indians frequent the Hindu Temple of Atlanta and again, in general, they tend to be fairly orthoprax. Many of those who came to Karunamayi Ma's talks and ritual were from those who hailed from her area in India. Karunamayi Ma gives her talks in fluent Telugu; although she increasingly speaks English and also has a very good translator, she frequently speaks in her "mother tongue," her native language, and it is natural that people who speak that language are attracted to her. Ammachi, on the other hand, speaks very little; she embraces her followers physically. Some gurus, like Mother Meera, are said to maintain profound and mystic silences for lengthy periods of time, even with their followers, and they talk about experiences that are beyond words. A study of the ethnic and linguistic diversification of devotees and their correlation to the "mother-tongue" of these divine Mothers, along with the importance of silences and body language would be a separate and interesting investigation in itself.

"All Ways Are Mine": The Interfaith Worldview of Women Gurus

Ma Karunamayi and Ma Jaya are portrayed in this chapter as deriving their teaching from Hindu sources but being very eclectic in their teaching. Kali is predominant in Ma Jaya's worship, but she also worships other Hindu deities and it is important to note that her first vision was that of Christ.

We have discussed Ma Jaya's relationship to her guru and to her goddess, her service, and her river. One may ask "who is Ma Jaya?" in yet another way. We who are so used to categories and classifications are uneasy with those we cannot catalogue, those who protest a neat template of religious identities. Ma was raised Jewish, married a Catholic, and is predominantly Hindu in her practice, with sympathies for Tibetan Buddhism. Her teacher, Nityananda, and guru, Neem Karoli Baba, were both "Hindu" holy men; and yet her first full-fledged vision was that of Christ bearing a cross. In one place, she calls herself a "strange Hindu Jew who loves Christ."[43] The ashram where she lives is called "interfaith," and the pond is encircled by beautiful shrines dedicated to many religions of the world. There is a small Hindu temple, and there is a shrine to the Hindu deity Hanuman who is in a monkey form; there are Buddhist, Jewish, and Sikh shrines. The introduction to the ashram in the Web page emphasizes both the interfaith aspect and the special emphasis on Hindu deities and paths to the divine:

> Namaste and welcome to Kashi, a spiritual interfaith Ashram founded by Ma Jaya Sati Bhagavati. Ma teaches that all paths, followed with a pure heart, lead to the God within. At Kashi, both Eastern and Western traditions are embraced. Hinduism and Tibetan Buddhism are central to the spiritual practices woven throughout this teaching. Ma offers darshans at Kashi and throughout the country. Her teaching includes Kali Yoga, the practice of honoring and doing puja to Mother Kali; Kundalini Yoga, the practice of raising spiritual energy or shakti; pranayama and breath meditation; Karma Yoga or Seva (service); and Bhakti Yoga, devotion to the Mother Goddess that dwells within all of us. The shakti and silence that permeates this very sacred place is undeniable.[44]

Although the Internet message identifies the ashram as a place where Hinduism and Tibetan Buddhism are central to the practices, Ma Jaya's Jewish heritage is very important, and certainly the Hindu teachings seem central when one encounters her. She describes an evening when Rabbi Zalman Schacter celebrated Shabbat in her ashram. It apparently awoke her Jewish identity, but she also participates in rituals of other faiths. Speaking of that evening when her Jewish history was awakened, she says:

Something had been missing in my life, and that something was my heritage. I was a Jew, I am a Jew, and I will always be a Jew—a Jew who bows to the feet of my Christ; a Jew with a big red ribbon tattooed for life on my left hand, representing all the dead I have lost to AIDS; a Jew who is a Hindu and follows the monkey god of service, Hanuman; a Jew who loves the true tantric merge of man into God; a Jew who is a devotee of India's black mother Kali; a Jew who is the disciple of my guru Neem Karoli Baba; a Jew who worships the Buddha and tries to follow his life of compassion, love, and kindness; a Jew who listens to the ancient teachings of the Sikh gurus.[45]

When she first met Christ—according to her autobiography—he told her to teach that "all ways are mine." Eventually, she taught about the essence of Hanuman and Christ being the same to a group of Catholic priests. It is after this that she met her guru and felt the reunion with Christ.[46]

Ma Jaya's teachings are interfaith, and yet one may call her Hindu in many ways. Certainly, as she claims, she is Jewish, yet many significant markers of her life are Hindu. First, and perhaps the most important, marker of one's identity is the issue of names. Both she and her disciples have received names that are not just Hindu but religiously Hindu. By this, I mean that many Hindus have ritual names in which the term "das" or "dasa/dasi" ("servant") is added to their formal name, which may be that of a deity. Thus a woman called Haripriya may be called Haripriyadasi (the servant of the Beloved of Vishnu). Ma Jaya is the "victorious mother"; *jaya* is "victory." Sati is the name of Parvati, the Hindu goddess, and Bhagavati is the female form of Bhagavan or God. Ma Jaya's followers have names associated with Hindu epics and puranas. Anjani (the principal of the River School in the Kashi Ashram at Sebastian) is named after the mother of Hanuman. Krishnapriya, the "beloved of Krishna," and Yashoda, the beloved foster mother of Krishna who nurtures him, are very close to Ma Jaya. And there are others—Ganga Das, Durga Das, and so on. (Ma relates a funny incident when one of her dying disciples asks to be called "Häagen-Dazs" after the ice cream!) The place they live in is called Kashi after one of the holiest cities in the Hindu tradition; and the holy waters there are called Ganga. Many of the rituals are Hindu; the sacrificial fire burns and the smoke ascends to the sky accompanied by Sanskrit mantras. Ma Jaya wears the sacred marks of Shiva and the Goddess (three horizontal lines of ash and a red dot) on the forehead, though occasionally she wears Vaishnava signs. Above all, the forms of devotion are Hindu—the music in the hall where darshan was to take place included traditional Indian percussion instruments and Hindu devotional songs (*bhajans*). Names, sacred marks, rituals, music, predominant deities, and above all, a lineage of gurus, and experiences that are described with words that come from the Hindu tradition are all markers pointing to Hinduism as the primary source of their religious worldview.

Although neither Karunamayi nor Ma Jaya Sati Bhagavati fits into any orthodox lineage of teachers, Ma Jaya's autobiography, which speaks of a series

of visions and messages, marks her as being part of an eclectic teaching tradition seen in Neem Karoli Baba and Nityananda, and to some extent to Shridi
Sai Baba in earlier times.

Karunamayi Ma speaks constantly about the equality of religions. She does
not frequently evoke the names of Christ or Mary in her talks like Ma Jaya, but
is forthright about her view of other religions: "All religions should be honored.
They all teach truth, and they all seek to realize divinity. In following the teachings of their own religions, those followers should lead a very simple and very
peaceful life. Whatever has been said in their scriptures is what they must
practice in their daily lives. They must cultivate universal love and self-control.
This will make their lives peaceful and happy."[47] Mother Meera (b. 1960), who
married a German in 1982 and who lives in Thalehim, Germany, also emphasizes the oneness of religions, as does Ammachi. This eclectic strain seems to
pervade the teachings of many gurus, male and female, and is seen very clearly
in the messages of Sathya Sai Baba.

Goddesses and Gender

There is no ambiguity in the representation of Karunamayi Ma—she is identified as an incarnation of the Goddess—a generic Hindu goddess who is the
source of all power and who is presented as manifesting herself as Lakshmi,
Saraswati, and Durga. Some pictures depict her in a red sari that one associates
with Lakshmi or Durga, and in some she wears a white sari and holds the *vina*,
a lute-like musical instrument. This is probably because pictures of the goddess
Saraswati usually depict her as holding a *vina* and wearing a white sari. When
she came into the temple in Atlanta, Karunamayi Ma folded her hands in a
gesture of worship in front of the major deities, but lingered in front of the
icon of the very beneficent-looking Durga, and eventually sat in the special
chair reserved for her right outside that shrine. As far as I could see, she does
not speak about herself directly as the goddess, but in her talks where she
speaks of herself as the mother who knows everything about the child and
cares about it, and in using the same words to refer to herself and the Goddess
(Amma and Mother), there are strong implications that she is speaking from
an exalted position.

Ma Jaya, as we saw, worships Kali and all other deities. Nevertheless, the
importance of the Mother Goddess is very important in her teachings; she
frequently says that we should never, ever, forget the Mother. The Mother is
Mary, Durga, Lakshmi, Saraswati, and all other goddesses. For her all goddesses are ultimately the manifestation of the same power:

> I bow to the holy Mother in all of us—male, female, it does not mat-
> ter, for she possesses the ability to come into the heart and soul of
> every human being. . . . I bow simply to god, in the form of the fe-
> male aspect of Shakti . . . She manifests herself to the very poor in
> the form of hope for a brighter day. She manifests herself as Mother
> Mary, as St. Theresa, as Mother Uma, Usha, Parvati, Sita . . . She

manifests herself in all things, for all things are indeed she. As
Mary she gave her only son to the cross and had the strength to witness the death of god the son. As Durga she fought battles and con-
quered evil. As the woman in the kitchen she cooks for her children
everyday. . . . She is the manifestation of god in female form, for one
is used to running to the Mother. . . . She was the original God before goddesses. She was simply God. . . . She bathes her children in
the glory of the Ganga, the Jordan, of rivers all over the world. From
her womb flow oceans and oceans of compassion. . . . this Mother,
the great Mother of the universe, with so many thousands of names:
Artemis, Athena, Kali, Durga, Mary, Parvati, so many names, so
many disguises. . . . Can you not see? She is all that there ever was.
. . . She is you. She is me. She is God.[48]

As we can see, her words on the Goddess span a lot of territory. On the one
hand, she recognizes the divinity in every one of us and says that the Goddess
is in every one. She also recognizes that the Supreme Being can be manifested
in the female aspect—she does not say that the Supreme Being is seen *only* as
in the female mode. In fact, as we noted, she worships the Supreme in many
forms. Nevertheless, the manifestation as "the Mother" seems to be most important. In her autobiography, Ma Jaya says with urgency: "A thousand times
a thousand lifetimes are in store for those that search out the material world,
forgetting God. A thousand times a billion lifetimes are in store for those that
forget the Mother."[49]

We also see in the above passages that she recognizes that the supreme
Goddess manifests herself as Durga, Saraswati, and so on. Karunamayi's devotees, on the other hand, think that Durga, Saraswati, and so on manifest
themselves as one being, that is, as their teacher, Karunamayi Ma. Ma Jaya
does not limit herself to the goddesses of the Hindu pantheon—she lists Mary,
Artemis, Athena, and others. She also goes beyond the particular goddesses
and sees this divinity in all human beings. She sees the goddess in all forms
of maternal love, in simple acts like a mother cooking for her child. The final
point she makes is that the goddess is in the manifestation of God in female
form because "one is used to running to the Mother." The goddess then, is
essentialized as the feminine and as the mother, although we see in Ma Jaya's
writings that she worships Kali. Kali, to an outside beholder, is hardly maternal.
And yet it is not just Ma Jaya but also many other Bengali devotees from India
who have considered Kali as the Mother.[50] Ma Jaya sometimes uses the power
of the paradox to talk about the "Mother": she is the saint and the sinner.

Ma Karunamayi also speaks of the Mother Goddess being everywhere.
Explaining a particular prayer to the Goddess, she interprets it this way: "The
beautiful essence of this *sloka* [prayer] is that, Mother is everywhere! She is all!
So open up your third eye and see Amma everywhere. And in the seventh
mantra it says, 'Salutations to the Divine Mother in all beings in the form of
beauty' (as *kanti rupena*). Actually, 'kanti' means 'luminous,' not 'beauty.' "[51]
This of course is very interesting, because, although she is referring to the

Goddess as Mother and as Amma in this (and other talks), she frequently refers to herself also in the third person as Mother and as Amma. For instance, concluding a talk, she says, "Amma blesses you wholeheartedly on this *Guru Purnima* day, prays always for peace for everyone in this world and wishes that everyone should have a good day every day. . . . Amma is always meditating for your welfare and for peace in this world, Blessing you all, thus I bring this program to a conclusion."[52]

Karunamayi Ma thus uses words like "Mother" and "Amma" regularly to refer both to the Goddess and to herself. Although in some cases it may seem ambiguous, in some it is very clear that she is referring to herself as Amma. She ends her talks regularly by saying that "Amma gives you her blessings" or by urging her devotees to do something. For instance, speaking during her first visit to the United States in 1995, she said: "Finally, Amma is very pleased to meet you all in this country and She likes your love and affection towards spirituality. But still you have to study. . . . You have to study, study, and study!"[53] It is this role of motherhood that is central to her teachings. She continually speaks of herself as the Mother, and the spirit with which Ma Jaya says that "we run to the Mother" is present in Karunamayi's talks as well. Let us just consider two statements out of the hundreds on this issue from Karunamayi Ma's speeches:

> I have not come to you as a *Guru* or a God. I have come as your
> own mother. The initiation *mantra* given to you by your *Guru* [that
> is, herself] should be used during your meditation. I have come to
> see how fast you are progressing in your spiritual life. And I'm only
> interested in seeing this. When you come home from school, your
> parents look at your progress report in order to know how well you
> performed. Similarly I have come to see your progress. . . . Have you
> controlled your anger? Have you controlled your mind, your restless-
> ness, and the other bad qualities such as greed, jealousy and ego? If
> you have not controlled these qualities, I have come to you as a
> mother, asking you to conquer these bad traits.[54]

> Amma has spent nearly thirty to forty days in Philadelphia and has
> been saying all this before, giving you all these teachings. But when
> I return to India, there will be no one here to keep reminding you to
> do this or do that. So, as far as you have heard all these instructions
> from Amma, you must be able to practice them. . . . As a mother it
> is my responsibility to see that my children follow the right path.

She goes on to say that although we may not listen to ordinary human beings giving us advice, because of our egos, we should be able to listen to holy people. She adds: "When spiritual people such as Divine Mother descend, they have a lot of love and affection towards their children, which is why when they say something, we readily listen to them."[55]

In the final analysis, Ma Jaya is a person who, her followers think, is a human being who has ascended to a divine state of consciousness, whereas Karunamayi Ma's devotees would portray her as the embodiment of a goddess who has descended to earth. Ma Jaya's autobiography is called *How God Chose Me*—in other words she is seen as a human being whom God has chosen. From the viewpoint of the devotees, however, it is immaterial whether these gurus are women who ascended to divinity or divinities descended to earth—they are divine in their eyes.

With all this emphasis on "motherhood," one may ask how important the issue of gender is in the teachings of the two gurus we have met. Does their being women empower other women? This is difficult to answer. In 1999, when I asked Karunamayi Ma about issues pertaining to Hindu ideas of women and pollution (menstruation, for example, is considered polluting), she upheld the traditional teachings and said that during that time it would be better for a woman not to worship. It may be different with meditation, but there is not information available on that issue. Anandamayi Ma and others have had women leaders in their communities, and so it seems in Ma Jaya's ashram also. Ultimately, however, it is important to note that at least for Ma Jaya, the question of gender is *not* important for a guru. The last line in the following passage from her autobiography is important:

> I truly am the Guru to so many, but I could not accept that at first
> when my Baba tried to tell me. To me, Baba was the Guru, and that
> was all I could imagine. Billy, Bina, and a few others, no matter how
> I lied to them, their hearts told them the truth and little by little I
> had to acknowledge them as chelas. I kept confusing the others for
> as long as I could get away with it, telling them lies like "A woman
> can't be a Guru." (That's true, by the way, but it's also true that a
> man can't be a Guru, because a Guru is way beyond that kind of
> duality.)[56]

Seen from the viewpoints of striving for God and longing for liberation, the social and biological construction of gender seems to have little importance for these women. There is no other explanation of what Ma Jaya states here. Perhaps her view toward other religious traditions, humanity, and divine love gives us an understanding of a certain irrelevance that gender seems to have in her teachings. The last word that she (and Karunamayi Ma) leave us with is service; the service and love that, for them, is connected with motherhood:

> We come here not as Hindus. We gather as human beings, worship-
> ping once again the Mother Earth. . . . She has taken from me the
> burning ache for the moment, for I am a mother whose children are
> in this Ganga, whose children have turned to ash. I renew this vow
> that I will fight for the life of any child everywhere and every child
> anywhere. . . . We must not be idle in our prayers. . . . We must serve
> those in need. We must, we must, we must. . . . I am the mother of

the suffering children, and until there is no more suffering upon
this earth, I shall return and return and return, time after time
again, for I cannot rest until all are free.[57]

It is not just that the Mother promises to come again and again and can be
seen in the unfolding of diachronic events; if we hear the devotees of the many
female gurus, the action seems to be synchronic at this point of time. In the
words quoted in the beginning of this essay, "several incarnations of the Divine
Mother move among us, each with Her particular task of healing or protection,
or transformation." And this is a new chapter in the Hindu tradition.

NOTES

Mother Meera's home page, the source of the epigraph, is at http://mothermeera
.com/home2.html (accessed March 2001).

1. I had the opportunity to meet Ma Jaya Sati Bhagavati with Professors Kathleen
Erndl and Yudit Greenberg in October 1998 at Kashi Ashram, and later when she
visited Gainesville, Florida, in February 1999. I met Karunamayi Ma at the Hindu
Temple of Atlanta in May 1999 and again in April 2003. In August 1999, Sivaya
Subramaniya Swami graciously spent some time with me at his monastery in Kauai,
Hawaii. These teachers were extraordinarily generous with their time and hospitality.

2. Ma Sati Jaya Bhagawati, *How God Chose Me*, Preface, p. 1. The pages in Ma
Jaya's autobiography were not numbered. I have the disk version, and the page numbers as they appeared in my computer did not correspond with the numbers given in
the table of contents. I have therefore given the chapter number and page number as
it appears on my screen when citing the autobiography.

3. Ibid., ch. 2, pp. 14–16.

4. Ibid., ch. 1, p. 6.

5. Ibid., ch. 1, p. 5.

6. Ibid., ch. 2, p. 16.

7. Ibid., ch. 68, p. 516.

8. Ibid., ch. 70, p. 527.

9. Although Swami ordinarily means Master, Nityananda was not always known
by the title.

10. *How God Chose Me*, ch. 71, pp. 536–537.

11. Ibid., ch. 73, p. 549.

12. Ibid., ch. 78, p. 575.

13. Ibid., ch. 75, p. 558.

14. Hilda Charleton is portrayed in many Internet sites as being involved with
psychic phenomena (including seances with the dead), having visions of Indian deities, and so on. In the 1980s she became known to some south Indians connected
with the large Hindu Ganesha temple in Flushing, N.Y. In articles written by Mr. Ala-
gappan—one of the founding members of the temple—in some of the newsletters,
she is seen as a votary of a not particularly well known Hindu deity called Jyoti, said
to be a sister of Kartikeya or Murugan. In Ma's biography, however, she is portrayed
more as a psychic, involved with various spirits in different astral planes.

15. *How God Chose Me*, ch. 90, p. 645.

16. Ibid., ch. 76, p. 562.

17. Ibid., ch. 78, p. 556.

18. Ibid., ch. 90, pp. 651–652.
19. Ibid., ch. 90, p. 653.
20. Ibid., ch. 90, p. 654.
21. Ibid., ch. 90, p. 653.
22. Ibid., ch. 90, p. 648.
23. Kashi Ashram home page, http://www.kashi.org
24. Ma Jaya Sati Bhagavati, *She Who Rides the Lion*, p. 12.
25. Ibid., p. 15.
26. *How God Chose Me*, Preface, p. 1.
27. Ibid., ch. 43, p. 261.
28. Ibid., ch. 73, p. 547.
29. Ibid., ch. 73, p. 548.
30. Ibid., ch. 28, pp. 151–152.
31. Ibid., Preface, p. 2.
32. Murugan, *Sri Karunamayi: A Biography*, p. 10.
33. Ibid., pp. 90–91.
34. Karunamayi Sri Vijayeswari Devi, *Light on Sri Lalitha Saharanama*, p. vi.
35. Karunamayi's home page, http://www.karunamayi.org
36. Ibid.
37. Swami Vijayeswarananda, *Karunasagari: The Ocean of Compassion*, p. viii.
38. Karunamayi's home page, http://www.karunamayi.org; italics added.
39. Ma Jaya Sati Bhagavati, *She Who Rides the Lion*, p. 22.
40. Karunamayi's home page, http://www.karunamayi.org
41. Bhagavati Sri Vijsayeswari Devi, *Blessed Souls*, p. 149.
42. Karunamayi's home page, http://www.karunamayi.org
43. *How God Chose Me*, ch. 20, p. 113.
44. Kashi Ashram home page, http://www.kashi.org
45. *How God Chose Me*, ch. 25, p. 128.
46. Ibid., ch. 18, p. 87.
47. *Hinduism Today*, January 1997.
48. Ma Jaya Sati Bhagavati, *She Who Rides the Lion*, pp. 7–8.
49. *How God Chose Me*, ch. 99, p. 697.
50. See, for example, Rachel Fell McDermott, *Mother of My Heart, Daughter of My Dreams: Kali and Uma in the Devotional Poetry of Bengal* (New York: Oxford University Press, 2001).
51. Bhagavati Sri Sri Sri Vijayeswari Devi, *Blessed Souls*, pp. 222–223.
52. Ibid., p. 51.
53. Ibid., p. 183.
54. Ibid., p. 255.
55. Ibid., p. 63.
56. *How God Chose Me*, ch. 99, p. 697.
57. Ma Jaya Sati Bhagavati, *She Who Rides the Lion*, p. 21.

REFERENCES

Bhagavati Sri Sri Sri Vijayeswari Devi. *Blessed Souls: The Teachings of Karunamayi*. Volume One. New York: SMVA Trust, 1998.
Karunamayi Sri Sri Sri Vijayeswari Devi. *Divine Wisdom*. New York: SMVA Trust, 1999.
Karunamayi Sri Sri Sri Vijayeswari Devi. *Sacred Feet*. New York: SMVA Trust, 1999.

Karunamayi Sri Sri Sri Vijayeswari Devi. *Light on Sri Lalitha Saharanama*. New York: SMVA Trust, 1999.

Ma Jaya Sati Bhagavati. *She Who Rides the Lion Rides My Beating Heart*. Sebastian, Fla.: Jaya Communications, 1997.

Ma Jaya Sati Bhagavati. *How God Chose Me*. Unpublished Manuscript, 2001.

McDermott, Rachel Fell. *Mother of My Heart, Daughter of My Dreams: Kali and Uma in the Devotional Poetry of Bengal*. New York: Oxford University Press, 2001.

Murugan, *Sri Karunamayi: A Biography*. New York: SMVA Trust, 1999.

Sahasranama Sri Lalitha. Bangalore, India: Sri Mathrudevi Viswa Shanthi Ashram, 1997.

Vijayeswarananda Swami. *Karunasagari: The Ocean of Compassion*. Nellore: SMVA Trust, 1999.

Videos

Who Is Ma Jaya Sati, Bhagavati Kashi Foundation, Inc., 2000.

Internet sources

http://www.kashi.org
http:www.karunamayi.org

7

Shree Maa of Kamakkhya

Loriliai Biernacki

Parāparānām paramā tvameva parameśvarī
You are indeed beyond what is high and what is low, the supreme Goddess.

— *Devī Māhātmya*, 1.81b

Why on earth should we be on that impossible ahistorical quest
for purist positions?

— Gayatri Spivak, *The Postcolonial Critic*, p. 150.

The tantric individual in India has always conjured up an image of
multiple identity: a public Vaishnava and a private worshiper of the
Goddess; on the one hand upholding public hierarchies and on the
other bearing a secret iconoclasm, undermining society's rules. As
Karen Pechilis discusses in her introduction, the third wave of gurus
coming to America brought a number of women gurus. One of
these, a tantric saint and teacher, Shree Maa from Kamakkhya, Assam, arrived in California in 1984. Who is Shree Maa? We could say
that she is a non-resident Indian (NRI), as she lives in California
(though I do not think that she has American citizenship). We could
say that she is a postcolonial. We could say she is a woman, not a
brahman, not from a low caste. Her name helps us little, as it is no
name as such, simply a generic term of affection and respect, "revered mom." We could say she is a mystic. Some say she is a reincarnation of a mystic who died in 1920, Ramakrishna's wife, Sarada
Devi. In the midst of our attempts to name her, however, we create
an image of a person which then fits into the scheme of hierarchies
that validate and stabilize our world. As a woman or postcolonial,
she becomes for us a figure of the oppressed; as a mystic she be-

comes the inaccessible other, revered, and so on. What I want to address in this chapter is a particular feature in Shree Maa's life and actions, and in her style of organization, that moves to destabilize the world of social hierarchies that our naming of others entails, a feature that I will designate as a impulse toward "decentering."

In a landmark article, Stephen Katz focuses on what he sees as the underacknowledged conservative impulse of the mystic.[1] Perhaps in times of cultural fusions, as we have now, with populations leaving their homelands, with television and the Internet narrowing the world, the impulse toward conservatism becomes dislodged in some respects. In any case, I suggest that the decentering that I address in Shree Maa is in fact in many ways socially radical in that it unglues the conventional hierarchies that our world lives by—not very loudly, and not on a grand scale, but nevertheless.

Shree Maa does not conceive of herself as radically destabilizing conventional social hierarchies. Even though explicitly self-identified as tantric, the tantrism she subscribes to follows the generally right-handed model of Ramakrishna, the nineteenth-century mystic whom she sees as her guru.[2] Neither does Shree Maa explicitly celebrate the antinomianism stereotypically associated with tantrism. When we take a look at Shree Maa's organization in action, however, at stray incidents, at pervasive attitudes in her low-key style, we discover those things that give a flavor to the ubiquitous Hindu litmus test of the guru, which is that the guru's life as "text" speaks. In many cases the two "texts"—words and life—imperfectly translate into each other; indeed, the words and life blur as the life becomes a story told in words. Yet particularly with history's saints, we perhaps look more to their deeds than to their words as an index to gauge the phenomenon of an individual. We measure the person first by the life.

The model I propose for Shree Maa's organization in America is not one that she explicitly embraces or even articulates, nor is it one embraced by her followers. Specifically, I argue that her approach approximates an agenda of decentering, something we could perhaps associate with a postmodern, feminist theoretical stance, though Shree Maa has probably never heard of "postmodernism" or "feminism." Perhaps we could link this decentering to an essential impetus of tantra. The textual substantiation for such a claim lies beyond the scope of this paper, however, as does its corollary, that we might discover some sort of secret sharing between postmodernism, feminism, and tantra. In any case, the peculiar isolation chosen by Shree Maa is such that she does not read newspapers, much less keep a pulse on current critical theory. Perhaps one could assert that this makes the message of her life all the more compelling in that it is not intricately or self-consciously enmeshed in rhetoric but rather spontaneously enacts what we as theorists at best envisage. On the other hand, one might also suggest that it would simply lead to a muddle of intention. Whatever is the case, I suggest that she incorporates a style of decentering, of attention to margins and to relations similar to what we find in Chris Weedon's articulation of a postmodern feminist stance, or in Kathryn Adelson's valorization of a feminist razing of hierarchies, as in Joyce Trebilcot's or in Nancy Chodorow's notion that women operate on models of self that are more relational than those of men.[3] She embodies a way of being that successfully allows for an inclusivism, not a tolerance based on hierarchy but one based on what Rorty might call "solidarity." I should add however, that she would undoubtedly expand his category of "one of us" far beyond its conventional limits, and that in fact a prime modus operandi in her actions is precisely the illimitable expansion of this very category.[4]

Perhaps we could say she approaches what a fellow Bengali, a compatriot of a different ilk, Gayatri Spivak, calls "the condition of possibility of the positive." In her own inimitable "method" of "speaking" from the margins, Shree Maa's actions function to rewrite "the ethico-political in authoritarian fictions; call into question the complacent apathy of self-centralization; undermine the bigoted elitism (theoretical or practical) conversely possible in collective practice."[5]

I want to focus particularly on Shree Maa's style of organization. In this chapter I present first a brief account of her life and then an analysis of her organizational style, especially in America, and how it functions to decenter, to undo hierarchies.

History

Shree Maa was born in Assam, on some unknown date probably sometime in the 1940s. Although the hagiography surrounding her life is remarkably circumspect, perhaps in large measure due to the influence of the no-nonsense American swami who penned her biography, the vague outlines of the extraordinary nevertheless dogged the events surrounding her birth, albeit in vague inchoate silhouette.[6] Her birth was predicted before her mother was even pregnant by a mysterious wandering ascetic, a sadhu, who wished to initiate her into a mantra while she was still in the womb of her mother and again shortly after her birth. Although the official biography mostly excludes references to miracles in her childhood, Indian devotees of Shree Maa in conversation are thrilled to relate wonderful stories of her childhood *lila*, the wondrous play of miracles her childhood manifested. Many considered and consider her to be a reincarnation of Sarada Devi, Ramakrishna's wife, including some of the still-living relatives of Sarada Devi. Her biographer does emphasize her predilection for meditation and reciting Sanskrit scriptures, particularly the *Candi Patha*[7] and the *Bhagavad Gita*. Like Ramakrishna, whom she sees as her guru, her worship focuses especially on the dark goddess Kali, and like him, she would, both in India and America, often spontaneously go into profound incommunicative, unreachable states of meditation known as *samadhi*. Linda Johnsen describes a poignant and unruly scene in India in 1992 where Shree Maa evades a crowd of desperate devotees converging upon her by means of her entrance (read escape) into the unreachable solitude of *samadhi*.[8]

Like many saints before her, Shree Maa also had to contend with family disapproval. Perhaps this is a specifically hagiographic pattern.[9] In her case, her family attempted to coerce her into giving up her meditation, and, in keeping with her Bengali heritage, into eating white meat, such as chicken, goat, and fish. In response to these obstacles, in her early teens she tried to run away from home. She was, however, prevented by a seemingly unlikely figure—Jesus. She had packed her bags and left a note detailing the reason for her departure—her spiritual search. Then at the very moment of departure, on the door's threshold her eyes caught the glance of the portrait of Jesus above the door mantle. He spoke to her, saying, "I am with you always. You don't need to leave to find me." The intensity of the encounter sent her into profound meditation.[10] The family found her in this spot the next morning and implored her not to run away, making concessions to her spiritual inclinations. The next day in her meditation Ramakrishna explained to her that she needed to finish her education in order to be fit for her future spiritual vocation, the mission he had in mind for her.

Shree Maa's biography seamlessly weaves the central figure of Christianity into the text, as though this narrative were not about someone who actually spends much of her life singing the praises of the Hindu goddess Kali. Neither her biographer nor she finds it unusual that a young Hindu mystic who looks to Ramakrishna as her guru and the Hindu goddess Kali and the god Shiva as primary figures of worship should be guided on her spiritual goal by the Christian figure Jesus.[11] Integral to the view and message of this saint is an inclusiveness that oversteps the boundaries of organized religions, so for Shree Maa and her biographer, there is no sense of incongruity regarding the insertion of Christian elements in the scheme of a Hindu saint's spiritual journey.

After finishing her education, she finally did leave home to wander alone through the Himalaya Mountains, and especially northeast India, as well as Bhutan, Nepal, and Bengal, constantly performing *sadhana* (spiritual practice), or wrapped in meditation. During this period she became known as the Goddess of the Mountain for the thousands of villagers whose lives she touched, and the eternal Goddess of the River for the fisherman along the Brahmaputra River.

What is remarkable about her existence as a young woman in the 1960s and 1970s in India is how the presence of gender hardly comes into play in the events of her life. She spent her late teens and twenties wandering all alone through the Himalayan Mountains, spending months at a time subsisting on very little food. About five feet four inches tall—her biographer tells us—she weighed only sixty pounds during her wandering years.[12] Unmarried and without a house, she lived an exceptionally unusual life for most young Indian women her age, and a life entirely alien from anything most of us in the West might imagine. Her indifference to food may have functioned to some degree as a condition for her freedom. By transcending the tangible physical needs of the body, she moved also beyond its determining conditions such as gender.

If any pattern can be discerned in the story of her life, such pattern aligns itself with the traditions of many male saints like Ramana Maharshi, who left his home and family at the age of sixteen to wander and live as an ascetic on the mountain of Arunachala; or like Yogananda, who as a teen abandoned his family and home to follow the spiritual quest, though even he, unlike Shree Maa, took with him companions. Occasionally her biographer reminds us that she is a woman, and her fearlessness in her travels is all the more astonishing, even for the India of thirty years ago. However, in her approach and in the experiences she encountered, her gender seemed to play no role. It appears that for her, once she had entered the category of spiritual aspirant, the category of gender was implicitly erased.

For instance, the Bengali tradition of early marriage did not affect her, although both her mother and grandmother were married before age thirteen. Her uncles, in fact, protested her taking up the life of a wandering *sadhu* (ascetic) not so much because it meant she would not get married but because it meant she would not go on with her schooling, at which she was apparently quite gifted, though this is only modestly suggested in her biography.[13] By way of contrast, we can compare her life with her older Bengali contemporary, the famous Anandamayi Ma, who did marry. Anandamayi Ma was also known for wandering at will through India, but she was nearly always accompanied by someone, often male and frequently her husband.[14]

Just as Shree Maa rejects the normative and circumscribed expectations of her gender, she also evades the social proprieties of caste and status. In her life she seeks to live out, in a public way, the philosophical idea of nonduality, the unity of things, and specifically that notions of high and low belong purely to *maya*, the illusions of the mind. The result is that in Shree Maa's actions there is an undercurrent of social iconoclasm. In fact, she rejects caste and status to a much greater extent than her guru Ramakrishna did in his lifetime. Apart from a special period of time during his spiritual journey, Ramakrishna generally declined to take food not cooked by brahmans.[15] Similarly, Ananda-mayi Ma was generally fastidious in following caste rules. On the other hand, we find no such scruples with Shree Maa. Not only does she partake of food without regard for caste but she has also on occasion outrageously defied social strictures. For instance, her biography records an incident where an outcaste, a toilet sweeper, saw Shree Maa giving blessings in a crowd of a couple of hundred people, but hesitated to approach her for a blessing because of his caste status. Shree Maa instead walked up to him, saying, "open your mouth." When he did, she took out the piece of *paan* (betel nut wrapped in a leaf) that he was eating and placed it in her own mouth.[16] In India, food in another's mouth is considered highly impure, and no sane caste Hindu would ever dream of taking and eating it. With this Shree Maa publicly and dramatically expresses the idea that divinity resides in all, whether high or low.[17] When she sees the toilet sweeper, she looks beyond his caste. It is not that she does not notice it; if that were so, then this gesture of solidarity would be irrelevant, unnecessary. Instead her gesture actively redefines his essence. She presents a notion of Self as essence that eludes ascriptions of limited identity such as gender, caste, or status. And, here one is reminded again of Gayatri Spivak's statement, the call to rewrite "the ethico-political in authoritarian fictions; call into question the complacent apathy of self-centralization; undermine the big-oted elitism (theoretical or practical) conversely possible in collective prac-tice."[18]

With a gesture, Shree Maa defies thousands of years of elitism that irrev-ocably marginalizes and silences the outcaste toilet sweeper. Similarly an in-digent servant of one of Shree Maa's hosts in Calcutta wanted to have Shree Maa visit her house, but could not ask her because she felt her status and the accommodations were far too inferior. Again overturning notions of status, Shree Maa went to her house, and finding her not there, proceeded to cook dinner, clean her house, and perform a puja in her absence. Vocally and visibly she employs a nondual philosophical stance, that is, the idea of an essential unity underlying all beings, to reach out especially for the poor and the mar-ginalized.

In a related vein, she appeals to this same universality to minimize the conflicts that arise between different religions. Traveling in Bangladesh in the early 1980s, she was conducting a Hindu fire ritual with several dozen devo-tees. Late in the evening, several hundred Muslims, armed with sticks, arrived with the intention of breaking up the ceremony. With an aplomb mixed with fearlessness, she invited them to sit down and join the worship. Remarkably, undoubtedly due to something in her demeanor, they acquiesced, perplexed at first. Then as the ceremony continued, they became actively involved, partici-pating with the infectious joy that one also sees in the rituals that Shree Maa conducts today on her tours in the United States. At one point after the fire ritual was completed, she asked a Muslim youth present to bring her a glass of *pani* (water). He hesitated, out of a reluctance to violate caste restrictions. She insisted, drank it, and then turned to a Hindu Bengali youth, asking him to bring her a glass of *jal* (water). Drinking this as well, she asked a Westerner for a glass of water, which she drank. Then she proceeded to explain, "Whether you say it in Urdu, Bengali, Hindi, or English, we all drink the same thing! Why are you fighting with each other? . . . We are all the same. Just the names are different. Why do we not just respect each other?"[19]

Her guru, Ramakrishna, preached the same point in the 1880s, a hundred years earlier, employing a tantalizing variety of metaphors—that of the differ-ent stairs and ladders to reach the roof of the house; that of children calling their father "ba" and "pa" because they cannot pronounce the word for father, while the father knows what they are saying despite their ways of calling him; that of a watch, where everyone thinks his or her own timepiece has the correct time, among others.[20] In fact, one may say that the hallmark of Ramakrishna's message was his insistence upon the unity of the world's different faiths, which he too, demonstrated in dramatic fashion by means of his well-known "exper-iments" with the different world faiths and approaches in Hinduism. The prob-lems implicit in his assertion are not within the scope of this chapter; suffice it to say that this message of Shree Maa's is not an innovation.

What is remarkable about Shree Maa, however, is that in addition to the utilization of spiritual, philosophical insights to defuse tensions of religious communalism, as her predecessors did, she also employs them to critique her own community's self-conceptions, the invisible ways we humans as a group create hierarchies to valorize some members and marginalize others. I do not wish to suggest that her predecessors never did this, but rather to highlight the radical extent to which she carries this out.

In the religious communalist conflicts Shree Maa encountered in the early 1980s with Muslims, the immediate goal was the defusion of dissension and fighting. One advocates peace not merely for the sake of the enemy but also in an instinct of self-preservation. Our own lives and identities are prey to the violence of the conflict. However, Shree Maa's dramatic rejection of the toilet sweeper's caste impurity functions in a different register. Traditionally, intra-Hindu caste distinctions of high and low have not been fraught with the same threat of mutual violence.[21] The hierarchy is too firmly established for any disputation. As a prototypical example of the subaltern, the toilet sweeper chewing his *paan* has no voice. He cannot speak to Shree Maa. He must remain standing silent on the periphery of the crowd, wishing to make his way to the center, to make contact with Shree Maa, but unable to oppose the authority of his society's restrictions of caste. It is this lack of speech, of the toilet sweeper and the menial servant, that Shree Maa seeks to undo.

Vivekananda also often deplored the condition of the lower castes, attributing what he saw as their downtrodden state to the abuses of the hierarchies of the caste system. Even with his far-sighted benevolence, however, they remained for him always the "masses," a distant faceless metonymy, not the individual sweeper from whose mouth he could take *paan* and eat it himself.[22]

Shree Maa presents a capacity to speak to the downtrodden, the disempowered, without perpetuating the marginalization that "pity" or compassion of the excluded other often carries with it. She stands face to face with the sweeper and acknowledges his essential humanity, as she does through becoming the servant of the servant woman. In this way she speaks locally and publicly to the dispossessed other, seeing in them an essential divinity untainted by the particular political hierarchical conditions of gender and caste.

Her mystical conception of self, or perhaps we should say reconstruction of self, allows a communication that eludes what her fellow Bengali Gayatri Spivak, following Lacan and Derrida, calls "phallocentrism":

> [Phallocentrism consists of] the rationalist narratives of the knowing subject, full of a certain sort of benevolence towards others, wanting to welcome those others into his own understanding of the world, so that they too can be liberated and begin to inhabit a world that is the best of all possible worlds.
>
> In the process, what happens is that such a world is defined, and the norm remains the benevolent originator of rationalist philosophy so that there is a certain sort of understanding that the hero of this scenario, of this narrative, has been in fact Western man.[23]

What strikes us in Shree Maa's encounters with the marginalized is that rather than pulling them into her narrative, she moves toward them, and embraces the conditions of their worlds—*paan* and a slum apartment—which are not features of her own world, without passing an essentialist judgment upon their condition. One is reminded of Chodorow's notion that women respond to others in ways that are relational, or Gilligan's notion that a feminist ethics thinks more in terms of responsibilities of caring for others and of the consequences of actions on others and less in terms of the application of abstract rules of behavior.[24]

To put this all in perspective, I would like to stress that in fact her response is in line with a trend historically associated with bhakti movements in India, that is, a reaching out to the dispossessed as embodiment of divinity. One quick example would be the well-known account of how Namdev, seeing God in all beings, chases after the dog (the quintessential degraded "other" in the Indian context) who had just stolen his bread, so that he might butter it, to make it more tasty for the thief.[25]

Speaking of degraded "others," one may say that Shree Maa learned the lesson of the inherent divinity of everything very early in life. In one story that she likes to tell, Shree Maa recounts an incident of sweeping her house for her grandmother at age five. When finished, she threw the broom into a corner, whereupon Ramakrishna's voice chided her, telling her to give respect to all things, including something as pathetic as the broom that served her in her cleaning. Rorty's notion of "solidarity" is certainly operative here, although perhaps, in what we may anachronistically read as a postmodern extension of the limit, the limit itself is abolished. More accurate, however, would be to ascribe it to a tantric extension of consciousness to the whole of insensate, *jada, maya*—and a sense of agency ascribed to the broom. In fact what Ramakrishna says to her literally is, "That broom is your very good friend. Why do you treat it with such disrespect? If it weren't for his loving service, how would you clean your house?"[26] In this mundane application of nondualist philosophy, solidarity extends everywhere, and consequently ceases to be a solidarity of "our kind" against another kind. On a practical ethical level, if even brooms are entitled to respect, what to say of humans, whatever their caste?

Around 1980, Shree Maa met Swami Satyananda, an American who had journeyed to India in a spiritual quest in the heady, hippy, altruistic days of the late 1960s. He did not wind up along with the Beatles at the ashram of Maharishi Mahesh Yogi in Rishikesh, like many of his American contemporaries. Rather, for eighteen years or so he never left the country; he wandered through the Himalayas as a traditional ascetic, studied under a number of traditional gurus, and took vows of monkhood.

He and Shree Maa met in a somewhat mystical encounter. She sought him out after having received a message in her meditation to find him. She journeyed to where he was, greeted him, and left without speaking, but gave him a sweet. He also was later led to her, without knowing what he was looking for, by seeking out an obscure place, the name of which he heard in his meditation. In all of this, what is to be stressed is again her rejection of conventional hierarchies. In an Indian context, that her primary disciple would be a Westerner illustrates a social iconoclasm, a reconfiguration of ideas of the spiritual. Vivekananda had famously pronounced that India had spirituality to offer and the West had material progress. In accepting this American swami as her closest disciple, she revokes these categories.

Shree Maa came to America in 1984, under the aegis of Swami Satyananda Saraswati. Again, the decision to go to America was precipitated by a message in meditation from Ramakrishna, Shree Maa's guru. Once in America, the two traveled to various cities performing traditional Hindu pujas (worship ceremonies), fulfilling Ramakrishna's request to her in her meditation that she teach people to worship God and set up temples in individual people's homes. They established an ashram that relocated several times, including one location across from an oil refinery in Martinez, California, until they settled upon their present permanent location in Napa, California.

In America

The move to America forms a new chapter in Shree Maa's life. Watching Shree Maa's organization in action, one gets the sense that she is not keenly interested in creating a movement or leaving a mark on this country. Unlike, for instance, Maharishi Mahesh Yogi, who patronized stars like Mia Farrow and the Beatles in order to draw more interest in his movement of meditation, Shree Maa tends to shun publicity.[27] For instance, she consistently refuses to take out ads in popular magazines like *Yoga Journal* or *Hinduism Today*, which are especially geared toward a Hindu/yoga-interested American crowd, to publicize her tour or events in her ashram. Early in her stay in America, in 1985, she was tutored on the ways of the wise gurus in America by a certain well-wishing guru who had traveled the path before her. He bluntly advised her to run it like a business; "All the yoga teachers in the West put their businesses first," and he said that she would have to advertise or perish.[28] Shree Maa did not take his advice. Regarding the idea of advertising, she once said in conversation that "all that is only *maya*."[29] So when she and Swami Satyananda held their first *yajna* or fire ceremony in America at the Aurobindo Ashram in Los Angeles, they did not advertise it. In response to this naiveté, the manager of the ashram queried, "well who is going to come?" Shree Maa replied, "Mother Kali. Who else should come?"[30] In fact in 1994, when Linda Johnsen's popular book, *Daughters of the Goddess*, came out with Shree Maa on the cover, Shree Maa's ashram was deluged with visitors. Shree Maa's response in this was to shut down the ashram, allowing no visitors. About this decision she said, "so many people wanted to come and they just wanted to gossip; they didn't want to do *sadhana* (spiritual practice), so I closed the ashram. That's all." Although we may applaud this novel nonconsumerist representation (or nonrepresentation) of the exotic Asian "other," the mystic, in her case I do not think it appropriate to interpret it as a form of resistance (in the Foucauldian or the postcolonial sense) to a hegemonic and appropriating spiritually bereft and consumerist West. From her own perspective, the impetus is probably more original and more vague. Rather than a resistance against the center and hegemony, it represents a focus away from notions of centers and peripheries altogether, away from appropriations and the seductions of the imagined other, to her own vision of what a spiritual search or a spiritual life comprises—to a multiplicity of individual selves progressively expanding their visions of the Self through the ritual practice that Shree Maa teaches, the puja. Like much in a traditional Hindu approach, the path is often solitary, between the practitioner and the deity. What is special about Shree Maa is her capacity to make each of these individuals pursuing different paths—even to the extent of each individual sitting in the group reciting a different text, all simultaneously—into a viable interacting community.

What happens is this. In the large hall at the Devi Mandir that serves as temple, dining hall, and sleeping area for visitors, the northern end contains an elevated platform about thirty feet wide, upon which a variety of plaster deities reside. Several different people, including Shree Maa, sit at different places facing this altar, reciting and making various ritual offerings, never in unison. Besides this central shrine are numerous individual shrines next to it and along the adjacent walls. Devotees each take a seat at one among the various shrines and separately perform their own recitation of Sanskrit texts (or something else, English or vernacular) along with ritual offerings to whatever deity they choose. Upon entering, one finds a group of individuals each reciting a different text, each making separate offerings to different deities. With all this individual choice one might expect a chaotic cacophony, but the surprising effect is rather a melodic, pleasing drone. No voice becomes the central melody around which others must attune or harmonize or pitch themselves against. Instead, the effect of indistinct chanting remains, with occasionally one voice and occasionally another rising to a clear pitch of enunciation, only then to be submerged again in the general rhythm of chanting. This exemplifies the style of Shree Maa, her way of creating a community that does not function in accord with notions of central authorities and marginalized peripheries; hers is a decentralized mode of community that retains the individual autonomy of all participants. Without consciously attending to anything like a feminist agenda, Shree Maa nevertheless encourages the desideratum of Julia Kristeva, that "each one of us find her own individual language," as well as enacting Chris Weedon's articulation of the postmodern feminist agenda: one of "decentering of singularized notions of power."[31]

As a Guru

As we might expect, hierarchical configurations are notably absent in Shree Maa's organization. With the exception of Swami Satyananda, who was initiated as a sannyasi before he met Shree Maa, there are no monks and no hierarchical relations between the classes of householder and renunciate (a critical issue in the life of Ramakrishna).[32] There are no chains of command and no structure of different departments with their heads, so necessary to larger Hindu organizations in the United States. In fact, what strikes one most about Shree Maa's organizational style is its absence.

No doubt it helps to keep things small, and this appears to be a conscious choice on her part, specifically in her tendency to close her ashram for long periods when she starts to become popular, as she did, for instance, after her tour. This popularity carries with it a focus on her, and generates a type of cultish excitement that looks to her as center. Her consistent response is to nip such excitement in the bud, usually by closing her ashram or by being otherwise inaccessible.

Nor does she encourage traditional Hindu forms of respect toward the guru, such as touching the feet or bowing to the teacher. One sees these forms of tradition performed only occasionally by Indian immigrants and not at all or rarely by Western disciples. Nor is she served by disciples; rather, she often cooks for devotees and guests. In a somewhat Gandhian fashion, she often sews clothes for the devotees who come to her. Even when teaching disciples, both she and Swami Satyananda do not assume a spatially elevated or central position but rather sit on the floor randomly among the disciples.

Shree Maa does not call attention to this revolutionary overthrow of the Hindu time-honored hierarchy of the guru, who sits in the center on the *gaddi* (throne) and the disciple who sits below on the floor, supplicant toward the teacher. And in the midst of *sadhana*, spiritual practices, Shree Maa does not sit facing the disciples; such a spatial construction is itself a message suggesting that disciples look to the teacher in their spiritual endeavors. Rather she sits as one among many, facing her own image of Shiva. None look to her in the process of puja; all look to their own adopted or created images of God. What Katherine Pyne Adelson says regarding Jane, a women's feminist collective formed in the 1970s in Chicago with a view to giving women more choices, is not an inappropriate comparison here: "The Jane organization was built on nonauthoritarian, nonhierarchical principles," and "The question of equality which those in the Jane tradition raise is one which takes dominant-subordinate structures in the society as *creators* of inequality. Their solution to the problem of equality is the use of the perception and power of the subordinate to eliminate dominant-subordinate structures through the creation of new social forms which do not have that structure."[33]

Similarly, Shree Maa's organization functions on a rescripted model of the relationship between the guru and the devotee, one that seeks to undo the hierarchy of the relationship. One of her earliest American disciples writes, "This is something that also struck us right away about Maa and Swamiji. No generals and privates here! Both work alongside the rest of us."[34] She remains for her students the teacher and a role model, yet in her interactions with them, the authority of teacher arises more out of what Adelson calls "natural authority," where "a person, regardless of position, happens to have a great deal of knowledge, experience, or wisdom about a subject."[35] And in Shree Maa's own pronouncements she consistently reminds her disciples of the arbitrariness of her authority as teacher, and asserts their own divinity and that they also function as teachers for her.

As we might expect, Shree Maa is a far cry from the image of the lavishly wealthy guru, the imaginative synecdoche of the twenty Rolls Royces of Rajneesh. She lives in a small trailer with a few clothes, pots and pans, and little else. A number of disciples, Indian and American, have approached her with the suggestion of building a house for her, but she continues to decline. "Build your own home," she says. In India also she often meets with devotees who offer her land for an ashram. Shree Maa's response is, "Make yourself. When flower is blossoming, bee will come."[36]

Questions may be arising in the mind of the reader: first, if she is not keen on publicity, why is she allowing me to write this article about her? And second, why come as a guru to America if not to start some sort of movement, to spread some sort of message?

In response to the first, it is probably related to the fact that she knows that this article, as part of a scholarly publication, will not have a wide readership. In venturing to answer the second, I have nothing explicit from Shree Maa herself, but I believe the answer lies embedded in the very thesis of this chapter, in her unarticulated conception of a world that turns on a model of decentering, in breaking down what Joyce Trebilcot sees as the boundaries of dualisms. I would suggest that her model converges with what Weedon sees as poststructuralist feminist "decentering." And she uses what Gilligan sees as a primary element of women's morality, the attention to care of the other rather than to justice, as a means of teaching her devotees her own spiritual insights.[37]

Shree Maa came to America because she had a vision in meditation from her guru Ramakrishna, who told her to come. When she came to America she did much what she did in India—hours of reciting scriptures and meditation, giving advice and consoling those who came to her. But just as in India she did not set about to make a mission or an idea or a center to give followers something to hang on to, so in America when she speaks she does not speak in terms of meditation movements. She conceives of herself as one individual following her own small truth in the midst of other individuals, all with their own ways of finding truth and happiness. One often hears her saying to her devotees, "you and I are the same. You also do *sadhana* and find God. What is God? G-o-d—Go-On-Duty."

This decentering is not explicitly articulated and yet it is apparent in her ashram, where each person recites a different scriptural text, all at different pitches and different tempos, each pursuing his or her own ideal of perfection. There is no normative *sadhana*, or normative pattern. There is no exclusive "way," no center, and consequently no particular movement to missionize. Swami Satyananda has translated a large number of Sanskrit texts commonly recited in India, and many devotees choose one among these that appeals to them. Other devotees use other texts altogether (not necessarily from Sanskrit) and some do other types of spiritual practices. The lack of a normative pattern thus dislodges the question of the journey to America from its implicit framework, constructed within a history of Hindu missionizing in America (itself to large degree a reaction to an ideology implicit in Western Christian missionizing in India).[38] Why, in fact, would a Hindu guru come to America and speak with non-NRI Americans, if not to missionize? Bleakly, we grapple here with

an aporia; the question has already been framed in terms of a history privileging the Christian prerogative of missionizing. Vivekananda was also asked this
question many times, and his response was to keep the framework but displace
the actors. So in an interview with the *Sunday Times* of London in 1896 he
responded, "India was once a great missionary power. Hundreds of years before England was converted to Christianity, Buddha sent out his missionaries
to convert the world of Asia to his doctrine. The world of thought is being
converted. We are only at the beginning as yet."[39] Shree Maa's response is
different. In this difference, perhaps her response is superficially nonsensical,
eliding as it does the very terms of the question. However, in the anomaly she
presents she rewrites the script, earning and reclaiming her own voice, the
voice of a woman, not a high-caste Hindu, creating a space for a multiplicity
of voices, her own as well as those of "others."

This decentering—we may wish to call it the magical vanishing act of the
guru—tends to delocate her as center of authority. Much of what she does
makes her not powerful, not authoritative. And it is not merely that she evades
these in favor of some higher, more elevated or ethereal authority, which we,
in a species of romantic altruism, might envisage as the authority of a presence
transcending power based on self-assertion, that is, the last shall be first, the
meek shall inherit the kingdom. Rather she moves toward a loss of the model
of hierarchy all together. That is, in those areas where she has insight, if you
ask her she will give you advice. In areas where another may have insight she
will turn to them. In a move uncharacteristic of gurus in America, Shree Maa
often tells her disciples "go wherever you can go, go and learn and then you
come back and you can teach me."

After having lived in America for thirteen years in a local, mostly obscure
fashion, her presence here announced primarily through word of mouth, in
1997 Shree Maa made a shift. Again following the intuitions of her meditation
experiences of her guru Ramakrishna, she started an annual tour across the
United States.[40] When she makes a tour she accepts none of the extensive
hospitality usually proffered by zealous disciples who wish to treat their gurus
in a manner befitting their exalted status—most predictably symbolized in the
"vehicle" *vahana*, that is, in limousines and Rolls Royces and BMWs and occasionally, as in one instance with Maharishi Mahesh Yogi, in helicopters.[41]
Shree Maa prefers to travel in an RV, and sleeps and cooks and lives in this
space for the three months they spend in traveling.

Again, I should emphasize that this presentation of decentralization is not
stressed or remarked upon in the self-presentation of Shree Maa or Swami
Satyananda, except, however, in Shree Maa's frequent explicitly stated desire
of making every home into a temple and every person a priest, in itself a radical
voiding of the intrinsic hierarchy of the categories.[42] Nevertheless, for the most
part it stands as a difference not articulated in her own self-conception. And
yet this attitude is internalized, and it thoroughly pervades nearly every aspect
of life in her ashram. To give another example, in general when one sees *arati*,
the evening offering of lights performed in a temple in India, the priest or
pujari performs most of the ritual, offering the lamps and various items. He

is the performer and the rest of the crowd present are spectators. At most they participate by singing along; they do not actively participate by waving the flames themselves. In contrast, when the *arati* is performed in Shree Maa's temple and in the programs she gives when she tours the United States, every person present waves the flaming trays before the deities, if they wish. A democratic pandemonium reigns with nearly everyone singing and dancing, reminiscent perhaps of Chaitanya's Bengali tradition of public *kirtana* (public singing as worship). Each person participates because each individual is in direct relationship to the deity, each person is a priest. On a psychological level, it is fascinating to watch the reactions of individuals as they become public priest, become the center, for one moment. And then as the flaming tray is passed on, the moment of being center passes. The unarticulated and secret desire and fear of being the center is at once gratified and diffused. No person retains the center space, the space of offering the flames, and the momentariness of power undercuts the foundations of this power. After all, we may say that a key element in the very notion of power derives from its unattainability, from the boundaries that mark it off as not the common property of all, but as that which can be accessed only by the few. This strategy intuitively employed by Shree Maa rejects the discourse of the power of the priest at the center by democratizing and hence dissolving the very space of the center. In Indian temple festivities one often notes the subtle (and sometimes not so subtle) competition for honors in serving deity (and gurus). Shree Maa's strategy, however, preempts any sense of vying for honors in worship of god. The center becomes multiple and localized, and in a sense ceases to exist.

Even the style of artwork favored by the ashram evinces a postmodern decentralization. Scattered throughout, decorating the walls of the ashram are photo collages, fragmented clips of events lifted out of chronological and contextual framework to be pasted anew in a syncretized collage. In a humorously personalized context, Mark Taylor wryly asserts the postmodernity of the art of collage, with its extensive attention to surface.[43] Here the collage functions to dislocate implicit assumptions of center and periphery, authority and margin. One can see in the individual artworks no central figure performing worship on a single historic occasion, but again, a multiplicity of faces and voices all merged together, each discrete but none holding a place of preeminence. In these collages gods, gurus, and devotees all claim equally privileged space. And the overall artistic effect again undermines normative artistic hierarchies, displacing the center with a multiplicity of peripheries.

I focus on these apparently mundane aspects particularly because they reflect a deeper democratizing attitude that displaces normative conceptions of authority and the discreteness of categories that hierarchy engenders.

Puja

The type of spiritual practice Shree Maa teaches and herself performs both presents a contrast to that of a number of Hindu gurus who come to the

United States, and illustrates the razing of hierarchies on which I have been focusing.

The main *sadhana* (spiritual practice) that Shree Maa teaches is the practice of puja (ritualistic worship, particularly that of the right-handed tantric tradition). Most gurus when they teach in America to Westerners tend to ignore or avoid puja. There is of course a whole set of complex historical reasons for this tendency, which I will address briefly below. Puja usually involves the recognition of a deity with a specific form, such as the goddesses Kali or Lakshmi, two of the deities in Shree Maa's ashram. In the puja that Shree Maa teaches, one offers to the image of the goddess or god a number of different substances, such as flowers and incense and fruit and so on, all while reciting *mantras*, mystical verbal formulas.[44]

Almost all pujas predicate a certain degree of polytheism; at the very least one must first worship Ganesha, the remover of obstacles before continuing on with the worship of the puja's primary deity.[45] This is particularly true in the tantric mode that Shree Maa follows, in the wake of her guru Ramakrishna. One sees in her temple a whole array of plaster deities, daily recipients of worship, their eyes shining in what Freud might call an *unheimlich* sense. Most of the pujas performed by Swami Satyananda, for instance, involve the worship of several deities. Puja, then, particularly in its tantric variety, tends toward a variety relationships, not centered on a single authority but upon multiple voices, so if one wishes to worship the Mother, first one must worship and acknowledge Ganesha, and then there are the guardians of the door, and there also are the different directions with their protectors, all of which must be propitiated in the course of the puja. Thus is created a universe of multiplicity. This multiplicity diffuses hegemony. The multiple voices invariably move toward deprioritizing any single voice. This is suggestive of a postmodern view, as we see in Ato Quayson's definition: "postmodernism can be typified as a vigorously antisystemic mode of understanding, with pluralism, borders, and multiple perspectives being highlighted as a means of disrupting the centralizing impulse of any system"; the puja repopulates this religious relationship with a whole variety of "wholly others" preempting the possibilities for a jealous God.[46] And as our religious structures often mirror temporal arrangements of power, so here as well the temporal lacks a monolithic authority of the guru.

The multiple centers embodied in different deities are amply illustrated in the large altar at Shree Maa's temple. In a style somewhat counter to the classical Hindu temple in India, with a main shrine to a single deity and perhaps several smaller ancillary shrines, here we find some fifteen or more different plaster deities—Kali, Brahma, Shiva—each occupying its own space on the main altar; here is a multiplicity of discrete voices, all fifteen or more accorded a place at the center in the central shrine. And yet, like the experience of worship in the temple where the many voices of the participants separately sing their separate texts, with this altar as well, none of the *murtis* (consecrated statues) claims the privilege of center.

By now the reader must have recognized the mismatch between the historically Protestant and monotheistic soil of the United States and the polytheistic leanings of the tantric puja that Shree Maa promulgates.

What is striking about this stance is its contrast to that of most Hindu gurus who come to the West. The majority of Hindu guru groups in the United States do not emphasize puja; often they even actively avoid it, or else they reserve it for the later teachings for seasoned members. The Transcendental Meditation movement is a good illustration, though by no means the only one. In the more common presentation to Westerners, these groups offer a teaching presented in scientific terms. Notions of "religion" are eschewed in favor of "technique." Yoga is presented as a science and is in this respect free from the "biases" endemic to religious beliefs. As science, its effects can be objectively measured, if only we obtain the proper instruments for measurement. In addition to freedom from the biases of religion, the appeal to science serves also to establish an "objectivity" entailed in the scientific approach.

As Pechilis notes in her introduction, the many distinctions between the Hindu temple group and the guru self-help group in the United States need to be placed in historical context. Hinduism first arrived in America with Vivekananda's celebrated success at the Parliament of World Religions in 1893. With this he left a legacy that was to influence many of the gurus who came to the West in his wake. His view of his mission differed from that of his master Ramakrishna, in that he stressed the rational, the scientific, and saw Advaita Vedanta as in perfect attunement with notions of science. His popular *Raja Yoga* is devoted to explicating this congruence.[47] For Vivekananda, the appeal of Hinduism for the West lay in its capacity to include all other faiths. In particular, Advaita Vedanta represented the culmination of the religious impulse; in Vivekananda's theory, all people evolve religiously through three phases, exemplified in the three schools of Vedanta—dualism, dualism-in-nondualism, and ultimately pure nondualism, Advaita.[48] In one public lecture he states, "our claim is that the Vedanta only can be the universal religion, that it is already the existing universal religion in the world, because it teaches principles and not persons."[49] As a species of metafaith, with its focus on transcendence of particular deities, Vedanta embodied for Vivekananda a repudiation of polytheism (gainsaying the missionaries' charge leveled at the heathen Hindus). And in a single blow, this transcendence of the particular made it eminently alignable with what was currently the best of the West, or in any case, its predominant and exciting alternative to religious beliefs, that is, science. Vivekananda was also strongly influenced by his early association with the Brahmo Samaj, which inculcated a belief in the formless aspect of God, again easy to align with a generalizing, "objective" science.

Historically then, Vivekananda's Advaita Vedanta could transcend the messiness of the particular, could present itself as an objective science, and at the same time avoid upsetting the sensibilities of a Western populace with a predominantly Protestant background opposed to idolatry. He left a legacy that has set the tone for most of the gurus who succeeded him; the Hinduism they bring is a technique for altering consciousness, applicable to any religious belief system. With this, the particular forms worshiped in any given tradition become at once collapsable into a notion of the formless abstract *brahman* and not especially relevant.[50] In the process, the Hinduism of the Ramakrishna Mission had to diverge to some degree from the Hinduism Ramakrishna himself practiced.[51] This is most clearly reflected in the fact that the deity Ramakrishna daily worshiped, spoke with, danced with, and adored his entire life, Kali, is not present either as *murti* (consecrated image) or picture in the Ramakrishna Mission temple.[52]

For Ramakrishna himself, the tantric message of devotion to Kali held sway over the formless experience of Advaita Vedanta.[53] When the message of the Ramakrishna Mission came to America, however, it came in sanitized form. Excluding the messy idolatry of multiple deities, which were probably correctly deemed not palatable to the predominantly Protestant climate of turn-of-the-century America, the message of Ramakrishna was brought to America in Advaita Vedanta formlessness, not through the image of the wild, dark Kali, the Mother, that Ramakrishna communed with and adored his entire life, but rather as the transcendent attributeless *brahman*.[54]

So we should not be surprised to hear the Ramakrishna Mission abbot at Jayrambati saying to Shree Maa when she visited, probably sometime in the 1970s, "if Shree Ramakrishna were to come here, according to our rules we would not be able to give him a place to stay!"[55]

This consonance between the scientific rationality of a metareligious Vedanta and a Western world disenchanted with the apparently deleterious effects of opiate religion set the tone for much Hindu missionizing in the West through the twentieth century. At least in part, the success of this missionizing had to do precisely with the excision of multiple deities, with their multiple heads, and the exclusion of the seeming idolatry of offering food and lights, incense, and so on, to inert statues. For our purposes here, the historical irony of the exclusion of Ramakrishna's Kali from the Ramakrishna Mission temples becomes all the more striking when we focus our attention on Shree Maa's temple altar, where a ten-headed plaster Kali, stands with red tongues lolling. This new emissary of Ramakrishna brings his teachings in a completely new dress to the West a century after his demise.

For Shree Maa, the goddess Kali takes a prominent place on the temple altar, with her ten heads and dark skin, wearing a garland of skulls made with photographs of the devotees of the ashram. That which celebrates form and instantiates the particular in all its multiplicity takes precedence, eluding any hint or taint of an abstract transcendent view. In an essentially tantric maneuver, divinity becomes thoroughly embued in the mundane embodied dance of life. The main practice that Shree Maa teaches is puja, and the unity in her message is one that wends its way in and through the particular.

Just as this preference for the material and immanent over the abstract transcendent sets her apart from many Hindu gurus in the West, it aligns more with an attention to the specifics of a situation, which Carol Gilligan notes as a general female response to questions of judgment, as well as with the generally feminist tendency to focus on embodiment.[56]

It would not be correct, however, to see Shree Maa's teaching as simply a

celebration of multiplicity, a polytheism that stands as the counter to a hegemonic monotheism. On the contrary, just as Vivekananda does, she too teaches
Advaita (nondualism), not the Advaita of Vedanta but rather the Advaita of
tantra. Underlying the multiplicity of form is a unity, a divine consciousness
that has the capacity to embody itself in all the varieties of forms that can be
imagined. As her disciple Swami Satyananda puts it, "The truth is that we're
all incarnations of God, it's just that the saints know they are."[57]

Finally, one other effect of the decentering in which Shree Maa engages
is that it allows a space for including the "other," whether marginalized or
dominant, which does not lapse into what Diana Eck or Paul Hacker term
"inclusivism."[58] Eck describes inclusivism as the acceptance of many "communities, traditions, and truths, but our own way of seeing things is the culmination of the others, superior to the others, or at least wide enough to include
the others under our universal canopy and in our terms." This is superceded
by a pluralist model where "truth is not the exclusive or inclusive possession
of any one tradition or community. Therefore the diversity of communities,
traditions, understandings of the truth, and visions of God is not an obstacle
for us to overcome, but an opportunity for our energetic engagement and
dialogue with one another. It does not mean giving up our commitments;
rather it means opening up those commitments to the give-and-take of mutual
discovery, understanding, and indeed, transformation."[59]

It would probably not be unfair to suggest that Vivekananda's notion of
Vedanta fits the description of inclusivism. Shree Maa, on the other hand, may
to some extent represent a pluralist approach, yet viewed closely she resists
this configuration. Rather, she presents a model that regards the boundaries
of religious traditions as fluid or disregards them altogether. We saw earlier
how nonproblematically Jesus figured as a voice in her early teens, guiding her
not to run away from home. It was clearly the figure of Jesus and not that of
Kali who she felt spoke to her (not "our God listening" as Eck eloquently puts
it), and yet it becomes difficult to pin down just what "our God" would mean
to her in the first place.[60] Like the chameleon that Ramakrishna was so fond
of pointing to as a metaphor for God's shiftiness, Shree Maa's God is also
slippery.[61]

During her travels in India in the 1980s with her American swami, she
wandered through eastern India with a portable shrine featuring Krishna,
Durga, Jesus, and Mecca, conjoining Islam, Hinduism and Christianity, teaching a syncretist pluralism of tolerance. We may say in retrospect that her voice
was drowned in the din of escalating communalism, and perhaps her brand
of pluralism may have been considered suspect by those whom she wished to
reach, just as Gandhi's was. In any case, in fairness to her I think it important
to recognize that this multicultural inclusiveness is not deliberated, but exists
rather as a response to the presence of the others she encounters. In America,
many of her devotees are Christians. An equal or greater number are expatriate
Hindus, and many devotees identify themselves as neither or both. One of her
closest devotees is a self-avowed Buddhist. In her philosophical view, the path
is simply another name for the same water we all drink. As she often says, "we

can learn from many people."[62] So in America Jesus is not excluded from the plaster pantheon; he stands nestled between Saraswati and Lakshmi, the result of Shree Maa's own artistic efforts to celebrate Christmas one year. Similarly, once walking through a field in America, she heard the Goddess crying to her to dig her out of a muddy ditch. When she dug into the earth she discovered a Christian Madonna with child that now graces the temple altar, as well. Should we call this syncretism? pluralism? inclusivism? or a nonrecognition in the first place of what the rest of us conceive as difference? We meet this pluralism in her, perhaps as an afterword of decentering, and it pervades her ashram, in the music of hybrid jazzy rock-and-roll *bhajans*; in the food, a fusion of cultures—chili pepper lasagna; and again in the art of collage.

No doubt the climate of the 1990s made this religious fluidity, with its multiple deities and multiple faiths more acceptable than it could have possibly been a hundred years, or even thirty years before. As if coming full circle, from the early Hindu gurus like Vivekananda and Yogananda, who spoke to their foreign flocks in language constantly referential to Christianity (Yogananda consistently referred to his guru and other saints as Christlike sages),[63] through the turbulent 1960s and 1970s, when where the exotic other was valorized as the answer to Vietnam and other problems, up to the calmer multicultural 1990s, when Shree Maa can place Jesus alongside Lakshmi without the angst of delineating "ours" from "theirs" culturally. No doubt this is a superficial reading of a complex era, but this is a new form of religious awareness we see Shree Maa expressing. For Shree Maa, there is really only one spiritual path, and that is, with an openness, to give more than one takes.

Now we may ask, what are the implications of this reading of a Bengali mystic in America? I do not mean with this thesis simply to illustrate the time-worn adage that there's nothing new under the sun, all the while with a sideways glance at our own milieu's theoretical preoccupations. In an interview with Rashmi Bhatnagar and others, Gayatri Spivak was asked, "what are the possibilities for promoting indigenous [South Asian] theory?" She responded, "what is an indigenous theory?," and offered instead the prospect of negotiating with cultural imperialism through cultural syncretism.[64] Like her Bengali compatriot, Shree Maa enacts a strategy of cultural syncretism as she sidesteps notions of "our" culture and "theirs." At the same time, however, she manages to maintain the "continuity of native tradition," offering a feasible indigenous model for negotiating with and resisting dominant cultural forms in ways which merit greater exploration.[65]

NOTES

1. Katz, "The Conservative Character of Mysticism."

2. Right-handed refers to a mode of practicing the puja where illicit substances, such as liquor or meat, are not used.

3. Weedon, *Feminist Practice and Poststructuralist Theory*; Adelson, "Moral Revolution," in *Women and Values*, pp. 302–303; Trebilcot, "Conceiving Women," pp. 358f.; Chodorow, *The Reproduction of Mothering*.

4. Rorty, *Contingency, Irony and Solidarity*, p. 191, and pp. 189–198, passim. Like Rorty, she too sees the medium of telling stories as eminently suited for expanding our sense of compassion to a wider sphere of relations. Even her biography does not end with the story of her life, but rather includes a final section of her favorite stories.

5. Spivak, *The Spivak Reader*, p. 101.

6. See Satyananda, *Shree Maa: The Life of a Saint*.

7. This text is also known as the *Devī Māhātmya* and the *Durgā Saptaśatī*, and is a pan-India scripture recited especially during the fall Navaratri, the nine-day festival dedicated to the worship of the goddess Durga.

8. Johnsen, *Daughters of the Goddess*, p. 42.

9. For instance, see the biographies of Ramana Maharshi, Amritanandamayi Ma, and Satya Sai Baba.

10. Satyananda, *Shree Maa: The Life of a Saint*, p. 27. This capacity for sudden and profound slipping into *samadhi* was also a trait of Ramakrishna.

11. Ibid. Interestingly, her biographer, Swami Satyananda Saraswati, is of Jewish extraction.

12. Ibid., p. 38.

13. Ibid., p. 30.

14. See Mukherji, *From the Life of Sri Anandamayi Ma*, vol. 1. The connection between these two Bengali saints is more substantial. When Anandamayi Ma died in 1982, she appeared to Shree Maa in a vision, handed her a white lotus, and said, "now the responsibility is yours." Satyananda, *Shree Maa: The Life of a Saint*, p. 222.

15. Chetanananda, *Ramakrishna as We Saw Him*, p. 65. He was not inflexible in this rule, but broke it only with that cooked by those he deemed spiritually very pure, such as Naren-Vivekananda.

16. Satyananda, *Shree Maa: The Life of a Saint*, p. 68.

17. A somewhat related question is that of who eats with whom, a sensitive issue pervasive in Indian notions of caste, and one that leaves unspoken traces which are, for all their inarticulateness, rather loud. For the most part, Indian gurus who come to America retain the sensibility of the impermissability, the vulnerability, of eating with the other, the foreigner. Most Indian gurus dine solo, some occasionally dine with trusted devotees, often other Indians, usually in some semiprivacy. Just as the early anthropologists who studied India mapped out the different levels of status among castes through detailed charts delineating which castes could eat with which others, so I suspect similarly one might be able to map out hierarchies among gurus who visit or tour the United States by the degree to which they dine in the presence of disciples. I would suspect that the greater the claim to status, probably the lesser the amount of interdining; fledging gurus on their early tours to America probably tend to interdine more conspicuously. Then as they become established in America, interdining gradually decreases. Shree Maa, on the other hand, in keeping with her social iconclasm, tends to display very few qualms about dining publicly.

18. Spivak, *The Spivak Reader*, p. 101.

19. Satyananda, *Shree Maa: The Life of a Saint*, pp. 93–94.

20. Gupta, *Gospel of Ramakrishna*, p. 39. This particular incident appears to have been inspired by a request from a Muslim musician regarding the path to God.

21. At least not until recently. A striking counterexample was the recent case of a *dalit* (very low-caste) *bidi* seller who refused to sell to his upper-caste customers because of outstanding debt. In a fury they violently mutilated him, and this case was prosecuted.

22. For a couple of instances of Vivekananda's frequent tendency to see the lower castes as a monolithic group—which he often called the "masses of India" (with all its unconscious connotations of the helpless and the inferior), see *The Complete Works of Vivekananda* vol. 5, pp. 25–26, 96; vol. 7, pp. 146–147.

23. Spivak, *The Post-colonial Critic*, pp. 19–20.

24. Chodorow, *The Reproduction of Mothering*; Gilligan, "Concepts of the Self and of Morality."

25. Mahipati's *Bhaktavijaya*, p. 332.

26. Satyananda, *Shree Maa: The Life of a Saint*, p. 18.

27. See de Herrera, *Beyond Gurus*, pp. 206, 252–253.

28. Satyananda, *Shree Maa: The Life of a Saint*, p. 123.

29. All undocumented quotes come from conversations, interviews both with and without other persons present, and public talks that Shree Maa has given.

30. Satyananda, *Shree Maa: The Life of a Saint*, p. 121.

31. Kristeva, *The Portable Kristeva*, p. 372; Weedon, *Feminist Practice and Poststructuralist Theory*, p. 174.

32. See Gupta, *Gospel of Ramakrishna*, pp. 3–4, and Kripal, *Kālī's Child*, pp. 7–13.

33. Adelson, "Moral Revolution," in Pearsall, *Women and Values*, pp. 303, 306.

34. Satyananda, *Shree Maa: The Life of a Saint*, p. 155.

35. Adelson, "Moral Revolution," in Pearsall, *Women and Values*, p. 303.

36. Johnsen, *Daughters of the Goddess*, p. 38.

37. Trebilcot, "Conceiving Women," pp. 358–359; Weedon, *Feminist Practice and Poststructuralist Theory*, p. 174; Gilligan, *In a Different Voice*, and "Moral Orientation and Moral Development."

38. *The Complete Works of Vivekananda*, vol. 5, p. 124.

39. Ibid., p. 121. See also vol. 3, p. 223.

40. Swami Satyananda and an American disciple developed a Web site in the mid-1990s, and since 1996 one could detect a greater willingness on the part of Shree Maa to engage a larger group of Americans, though still in very tentative fashion; that is, after going on tour she still keeps her ashram unavailable to visitors. Her biography by Swami Satyananda was made available only in 1997, some thirteen years after she arrived in this country.

41. De Herrera, *Beyond Gurus*, p. 237.

42. Satyananda, *Shree Maa: The Life of a Saint*, pp. 155, 161, 202.

43. Taylor, *nots*, pp. 167–170, 190–191.

44. Most, though not all, mantras are in Sanskrit. Those used for puja often connect some particular aspect of the deity with the substance offered, and then the worshiper recites in Sanskrit, "I offer this fruit, etc." to the goddess.

45. The International Society for Krishna Consciousness (ISKCON) movement represents an exception to this general rule. Self-defined as essentially monotheistic, its members nevertheless adhere to puja as one of their primary practices. Without going into the subject here, I think this may be attributed to a certain conservative trend fundamental to this movement.

46. Quayson, "Postcolonialism and Postmodernism," p. 90.

47. Vivekananda, *Raja Yoga*.

48. *The Complete Works of Vivekananda* vol. 5, pp. 64–65, and elsewhere.

49. Ibid., vol. 3, p. 250.

50. Transcendental Meditation comes to mind here, of course, but also many other groups such as Self-Realization Fellowship, Maharajji, and kundalini yoga as taught under various teachers. ISKCON, on the other hand, as a species of a *dvaita*

bhakti tradition, presents a counter example to a large degree, appealing to the authority of the teacher and of scripture (*Bhagavad Gita*) as revelation.

51. Kripal, *Kālī's Child*, pp. 91–99. Also note that Ramakrishna, long after his experiments with Tota Puri (the Vedantic *sadhu* who befriended Ramakrishna and "taught" him the path of *jnana* yoga) were completed, still encouraged his disciples to go to the Kali Temple and bow to the image there, often against their own inclinations.

52. I have not seen all the Ramakrishna Mission temples, but the ones I have seen (San Francisco, Marin County, New York, Benares, Bangalore), do not have this image accessible.

53. Kripal, *Kālī's Child*, pp. 91–99.

54. Vivekananda was even occasionally leery of preaching that Ramakrishna was an avatar, often advising his fellow monks not to focus overly on him or his miracles. See *The Complete Works of Vivekananda*, vol. 7, p. 415; vol. 5, p. 41, 53.

55. Satyananda, *Shree Maa: The Life of a Saint*, p. 44.

56. Gilligan, *In a Different Voice*, and "Moral Orientation and Moral Development."

57. Johnsen, *Daughters of the Goddess*, p. 46.

58. Halbfass, *Philology and Confrontation*, pp. 244ff.

59. Eck, *Encountering God*, p. 168.

60. Ibid.

61. See the *Gospel of Ramakrishna*, p. 80, for one instance.

62. Satyananda, *Shree Maa: The Life of a Saint*, p. 170.

63. Yogananda, *Autobiography of a Yogi*; especially note his references to Yukteshwar, "that Christ-like sage." One finds this throughout the talks Vivekananda gave in the West. See, for one example, *The Complete Works of Vivekananda*, vol. 7, pp. 1ff.

64. Spivak, *The Postcolonial Critic*, p. 70.

65. Ibid., p. 150.

REFERENCES

Adelson, Kathryn Pyne. "Moral Revolution," in Sherman and Beck, eds., *The Prism of Sex*. Madison: University of Wisconsin, 1979. Reprinted pp. 291–308 in Marilyn Pearsall, ed. *Women and Values*. Belmont, Cal.: Wordsworth, 1986.

Bhagavad Gītā. Translated by Franklin Edgerton. Delhi: Motilal Banarsidass, 1994 [Cambridge: Harvard Oriental Series, 1944].

Chetananda, ed. *Ramakrishna as We Saw Him*. Calcutta: Advaita Ashrama, 1990.

Chodorow, Nancy. *The Reproduction of Mothering*. Berkeley: University of California Press, 1978.

Culler, Jonathan. *The Pursuit of Signs*. Ithaca: Cornell University Press, 1981.

de Herrera, Nancy Cooke. *Beyond Gurus: A Woman of Many Worlds*, Nevada City, Cal., Blue Dolphin, 1993.

de Lauretis, Teresa. *Alice Doesn't*. Bloomington: Indiana University Press, 1984.

Derrida, Jacques. *Limited Inc*. Evanston: Northwestern University Press, 1988.

Devī Māhātmya. English translation by Swami Jagadkhwarananda. Madras: Sri Ramakrishna Math, n.d.

Durgāsaptaśatī, Bhāsā tīkā. Ed. and commentary by Pt. Harishcandra Shastri and Nandakishor Paathak. Mathura: Śiksa Granthagar, 1992. Sanskrit with Hindi translation.

Eck, Diana. *Encountering God: A Spiritual Journey from Bozeman to Banaras.* Boston: Beacon, 1993.

Feder, E., M. Rawlinson, and E. Zakin. *Derrida and Feminism.* New York: Routledge, 1997.

Frye, Marilyn. *The Politics of Reality: Essays in Feminist Theory.* Trumansburg, N.Y.: Crossing Press, 1983.

Gilligan, Carol. "Concepts of the Self and of Morality." *Harvard Educational Review* 47 no. 4 (1977): 481–517.

_____. *In a Different Voice.* Cambridge, Mass.: Harvard University Press, 1982.

_____. "Moral Orientation and Moral Development." Pp. 19–33 in Eva Feder Kittay and Diana Meyers, eds. *Women and Moral Theory.* Totowa, N.J.: Rowman and Littlefield, 1987.

Gupta, Mahendranath. *Gospel of Ramakrishna.* Translated by Swami Nikhilananda. Mylapore, Madras: Sri Ramakrishna Math, 1964.

Halbfass, Wilhelm. *Philology and Confrontation: Paul Hacker on Traditional and Modern Vedanta.* Albany: State University of New York Press, 1995.

Hesse-Biber, Sharlene, Christina Gilmartin, and Robin Lydenberg. *Feminist Approaches to Theory and Methodology.* New York: Oxford University Press, 1999.

Hallstrom, Lisa. *Mother of Bliss.* New York: Oxford University Press, 1999.

Harding, Sandra, and Merrill Hintikka, eds. *Discovering Reality.* Boston: D. Reidel, 1983.

Hixon, Lex. *Great Swan.* Boston: Shambhala, 1992.

Isherwood, Christopher. *Ramakrishna and His Disciples.* New York: Simon and Schuster, 1965.

Johnsen, Linda. *Daughters of the Goddess.* St. Paul, Minn.: Yes Interational, 1994.

Katz, Steven. "The Conservative Character of Mysticism." Pp. 3–60 in Steven Katz, ed. *Mysticism and Religious Traditions.* New York: Oxford University Press, 1983.

Kittay, Eva, and Diana Meyers. *Women and Moral Theory.* Totowa, N.J.: Rowman and Littlefield, 1987.

Kripal, J., *Kālī's Child: the Mystical and the Erotic in the Life and Teaching of Ramakrishna.* Chicago: University of Chicago Press, 1995.

Kristeva, Julia. *The Portable Kristeva.* Edited by K. Oliver. New York: Columbia University Press, 1997.

_____. *Strangers to Ourselves.* Translated by Leon Roudiez. New York: Columbia University Press, 1991.

Mahipati. *Bhaktavijaya.* Translated and edited by Justin Abbot and N. R. Godbole in *Stories of Indian Saints.* Delhi: Motilal Banarsidass, 1982.

Mumukshananda Swami, ed. *Life of Sri Ramakrishna.* Calcutta: Advaita Ashrama, 1995.

Mother as Seen by Her Devotees, Varanasi: Shree Shree Anandamayee Sangha, 1967.

Mukerji, Bithika. *From the Life of Sri Anandamayi Ma.* Vol. 1. Varanasi: Shree Shree Anandamayee Sangha, 1970.

Pearsall, Marilyn, ed. *Women and Values: Readings in Recent Feminist Philosophy.* Belmont, Cal.: Wadsworth, 1986.

Quayson, Ato. "Postcolonialism and Postmodernism." Pp. 87–111 in Henry Schwarz and Sangeeta Ray, eds., *A Companion to Postcolonial Studies.* Malden, Mass.: Blackwell, 2000.

Rorty, Richard. *Contingency, Irony and Solidarity.* Cambridge: Cambridge University Press, 1989.

———. *Essays on Heidegger and Others*. Cambridge: Cambridge University Press, 1991.

———. *Truth and Progress*. Cambridge: Cambridge University Press, 1998.

Satprakashananda, Swami. *Swami Vivekananda's Contribution to the Present Age*. St. Louis: Vedanta Society of St. Louis, 1978.

Satyananda Saraswati, Swami. *Shree Maa: The Life of a Saint*. Napa, Cal.: Devi Mandir, 1997.

Schiffman, Richard. *Sri Ramakrishna*. New York: Paragon, 1989.

Sharma, Arvind, ed. *Neo-Hindu Views of Christianity*. Leiden: E. J. Brill, 1988.

———. *Ramakrishna and Vivekananda: New Perspectives*. New Delhi: Sterling, 1989.

Sivaramkrishna, M., and Sumita Roy. *Perspectives on Ramakrishna-Vivekananda Vedanta Tradition*. New Delhi: Sterling, 1991.

Smith, Jonathan Z. *Imagining Religion*. Chicago: University of Chicago Press, 1982.

Spivak, Gayatri Chakravarty. *The Post-colonial Critic*. Edited by Sarah Harasym. New York: Routledge, 1990.

———. *The Spivak Reader*. Edited by Donna Landry and Gerald Maclean. New York: Routledge, 1996.

Taylor, Mark. *nots*. Chicago: University of Chicago Press, 1993.

Trebilcot, Joyce. "Conceiving Women: Notes of the Logic of Feminism." In *Sinister Wisdom*, 11 (Fall, 1979). Reprinted pp. 358–364 in Marilyn Pearsall, ed. *Women and Values*. Belmont, Cal.: Wadsworth, 1986.

Vivekananda, Swami. *The Complete Works of Vivekananda*. Vols. 1–8. Mayavati, Advaita Ashrama, 1954.

Vivekananda, *Raja Yoga*. New York: Vedanta Press, [1899] 1973.

Weedon, Chris. *Feminist Practice and Poststructuralist Theory*. Oxford: Blackwell, 1997.

Willet, Cynthia, ed. *Theorizing Multiculturalism*. Oxford: Blackwell, 1998.

Yogananda, Paramhansa. *Autiobiography of a Yogi*. New York: Philosophical Library, 1946.

8

Ammachi, the Mother of Compassion

Selva J. Raj

My first visit to Mata Amritanandamayi's ashram in San Ramon, California, was on June 14, 1999. When I arrived at the ashram around 7 P.M, there was a long line of devotees gathered near the temple door. Standing in line were teenagers, small children, older men and women. Although some were first-time visitors like me, most seemed to be regular devotees of the temple. This was evident in their dress, their speech, and the ease with which they went about in the ashram and the temple. A notable feature of this predominantly Caucasian and non-Indian congregation was that many of them were dressed in the traditional Indian attire of saris, salwar kameez, and kurta. Some of them had name tags with Indian or Sanskritic names inscribed on them. A good number of devotees were also wearing rudraksha garlands and bracelets. Eyes closed in prayerful meditation, several hundred devotees were standing at the entrance of the temple, chanting the mantra "Om Amriteshwariye Namaha" (praise to the blissful one). I joined the devotees in this meditative chanting. Suddenly the chanting grew louder and more intense as a cream-colored Lexus sedan pulled in before the temple, and a tiny, dark-skinned Indian woman, clad in a simple white sari, emerged from it. Smiling radiantly at the visibly expectant and spiritually enthralled crowd, she walked briskly into the temple as devotees respectfully knelt, prostrated, or bowed their heads, and stood with folded hands on a brightly colored cloth in prayerful silence. The devotional mood at the temple was contagious. I found myself standing there with folded hands, awe-struck by the devotion, reverence, and ceremonial welcome accorded this tiny woman who evidently stood very tall in the minds of her devotees.

Upon entering the temple, Ammachi stood on a decorated floor mat whose four corners were dotted with roses. A female Indian disciple (*brah-macharini*) dressed in a white sari performed what is known as the *pada puja* (feet worship) rite to the "lotus feet of Her Holiness Sri Sri Mata Amritanan-damayi." She sprinkled a few drops of water on Ammachi's feet, gently wiped them away, applied sandal paste, and placed three rose flowers and petals on her feet as two saffron-robed Indian monks of the order—simply referred to as Swamijis by Ammachi's American devotees—recited the following San-skrtic slokas in praise of the guru and her feet: "I prostrate to the Universal Teacher, Who is Satchitananda (Pure Being-Knowledge-Absolute Bliss), Who is beyond all differences, Who is eternal, all-full, attributeless, formless and ever-centered in the Self; Whatever merit is acquired by one, through pilgrim-ages and from bathing in the Sacred Waters extending to the seven seas, cannot be equal to even one thousandth part of the merit derived from partaking the water with which the Guru's feet are washed."[1] Following the *pada-puja* rite, a female lay devotee offered *arati* (waving of a lamp) while another garlanded Ammachi, who responded to this honor by sprinkling a few rose petals on the devotees and blessing them. After this *pada-puja*, she walked briskly through the center aisle of the temple, touching and blessing devotees on either side of the aisle, and sat on an elevated platform.

Shortly thereafter a young Indian female renunciant delivered a brief spir-itual discourse on Ammachi's spiritual message. The discourse was filled with several anecdotes and testimonials of Ammachi's special spiritual power and unconditional love for all. This was followed by a ninety-minute ecstatic and soulful devotional singing (*bhajan*) led by Ammachi and her band of Indian musicians. At the conclusion of the devotional singing, temple lights were switched off to provide the proper setting for a ten-minute meditation; a senior male disciple, who led the congregation in the meditation, invited the devotees to surrender themselves at the feet of Ammachi, the divine Mother. After the ritual waving of the lamp (*arati*) in front of Ammachi that concluded the eve-ning devotional ritual, devotees approached Ammachi individually for a spiri-tual embrace. Ammachi hugs each one, uttering tender and loving words in the devotee's ear, and gives a Hershey kiss, a few petals of rose, and a packet of sacred ash. The spiritual embrace session, called Ammachi darshan, contin-ued for several hours into the wee hours of the next day. Around 3 A.M., Am-machi retreated to her quarters for a few hours of rest, only to return to the temple for the morning darshan session from 11 A.M. until 2.30 P.M. She was back again in the temple at 6.30 P.M for the evening darshan that continued, again, until the early hours of the following day.

Throughout her adult life, this tiny Indian holy woman has embraced, comforted, blessed, and healed with her gentle caresses thousands—some say millions—of devotees of all ages, races, colors, religions, and walks of life. Mata Amritanandamayi (Mother of Immortal Bliss)—affectionately called Amma or Ammachi (Mother)—is a forty-nine-year old woman of modest so-cioeconomic background from rural Kerala in south India. One of the most powerful figures of the third wave of gurus from India—the first two waves being associated with Swami Vivekananda in the late nineteenth century and

the male leaders of the Hare Krishna and Transcendental Meditation movements of the 1960s, respectively—Ammachi has emerged as one of the most
prominent female spiritual leaders of the later part of the twentieth century,
and commands a large following of devotees both in her native country and
abroad. Compared to Mother Teresa and revered as a great mystic and saint,
she is regarded by her devotees as the embodiment of the divine Mother. In
recognition of her contributions to the global community, Ammachi was invited to address the World Parliament of Religions in Chicago in 1993, at which
she was named "President of Hinduism."[2]

From its modest beginnings in the backwaters of the Indian state of Kerala,
the spiritual movement she has gently nurtured has matured into a dynamic
wordwide phenomenon with an impressive network of charitable institutions
in India and abroad as well as a growing number of transnational congregations in the West, including the United States. Today, the movement has thirteen educational institutions, including a medical college, eight institutions
devoted to social programs, and four medical centers including the high-tech
Amrita Institute of Medical Sciences (AIMS) in Cochin, India.[3] Her transnational congregations are found in the United States, Canada, Brazil, Mauritius,
Reunion Island, Spain, France, England, Finland, Italy, Netherlands, Sweden,
and Germany.[4] Ammachi's annual tours to the United States attract thousands
of devotees who endure physical and financial hardship to be in her compassionate presence and company in order to inhale her spiritual power. Based
on field research with two of her U.S. congregations (in San Ramon and Chicago), this chapter examines the spiritual career, charisma, appeal, and authority of Ammachi with particular reference to her "darshan discourse," where
tradition is at once defied, redefined, and transcended.

The Spiritual Career and Charisma of Ammachi

Ammachi's rise to spiritual fame since the early 1990s has occasioned several
hagiographical accounts of her spiritual career.[5] In his official biography entitled *Ammachi: A Biography of Mata Amritanandamayi*, Swami Amritswarupananda, one of Ammachi's senior disciples, traces the religious career of Ammachi, who rose from a humble and impoverished childhood of abuse and ill
treatment by her family to great heights of God-realization and spirituality.
Sudhamani, as she was known before her religious experience, was born on
September 27, 1953, into a poor, low-caste family in a rural fishing village in
Kerala, south India. A recent biographical account by Savitri Bess, one of Ammachi's Western devotees, speaks of the special circumstances surrounding
her birth. According to this account, before Ammachi was born, her parents
had unusual dreams that foreshadowed her special spiritual status and identity,
even though they failed to realize this fact for many years. Bess writes that
"Ammachi's mother, Damayanti, tells us that she had a dream of giving birth
to the Indian god Krishna the night before Ammachi was born. Ammachi's
father, Sughunandan, a devotee of Krishna, had a dream about Devi, the Uni-

versal Mother."[6] Despite some minor variations in detail, most hagiographic accounts of Ammachi's early life assert that she was a spiritually gifted child. Her official biographer claims that when she was barely six months old, she began speaking in her native tongue, and at the age of two began singing devotional songs to Sri Krishna. At the age of six, she is said to have composed devotional songs that were filled with longing for union with Sri Krishna.[7] According to the official biography, even at an early age Sudhamani exhibited certain mystical and suprahuman traits, including compassion for the destitute. In her late teens, she developed an intense devotion to and longing for Krishna. So intense was her devotion that she became oblivious to the surroundings. Sometimes she danced in spiritual ecstasy, and at other times she wept bitterly at the separation from her beloved Krishna. "Sometimes she would enter the bathroom for a shower" writes her biographer, "but would be discovered there hours later, oblivious to the surroundings." Sudhamani's parents and family members, who interpreted these spiritual excursions as symptoms of mental disorder or depression, subjected her to torture and harassment, and decided to get her married, which Ammachi resolutely rejected. As her family's ill treatment continued to worsen, Ammachi is reported to have contemplated, on one occasion, running away from home, and on another occasion, even killing herself "by jumping into the sea." It is reported that she eventually abandoned such thoughts. The hagiographic texts assert that the abuses and ill treatment Ammachi endured from her parents and relatives only convinced her of the "fleeting and selfish nature of worldly life."[8]

September 1975 marks a watershed moment in Sudhamani's spiritual career. One day, as she was returning home after grazing the cattle, she heard recitations from the *Srimad Bhagavatam*, a popular Hindu devotional text, emanating from a neighbor's house and went into spiritual rapture. She walked into the house and stood amid the devotees. It is said that her external appearance and mood changed dramatically, "transforming her features and movements into those of Sri Krishna himself!" At that moment she is said to have realized her identification with Krishna. Though she initially rejected others' demand for miracles as proof of her divine manifestation since, according to her, "Miracles are illusory. They are not the essence of spirituality," a month later she reportedly convinced her skeptics by changing water into milk. After this event, many other miracles, including healing a leper, were attributed to her. Later recalling her identity-experience with the god Krishna, Sudhamani said: "One day I strongly felt the urge to be absorbed in the Supreme Being. . . . Then I heard a voice from within saying, 'Thousands and thousands of people in the world are steeped in misery. I have much for you to do, you are one with Me. . . . I was able to know everything concerning everyone. . . . I was fully conscious that I, myself, was Krishna, not only during that particular moment of manifestation but at all other times as well."[9] For the next two years, Sudhamani manifested the Krishna *bhava* (the mood of Krishna).

A great shift in her spiritual career occurred when Sudhamani had an intense vision of the divine Mother in which she experienced oneness with her. She describes the experience: "One day at the end of the *sadhana*, I felt that a large canine tooth was coming out of my mouth. Simultaneously, I heard a terrific humming sound. I perceived the form of Devi with large canine teeth, a long protruding tongue, thick black curly hair, reddish bulging eyes, and dark blue in color. I thought, 'Quick! Escape! Devi is coming to kill me!' I was about to run away. Suddenly I realized that I myself am Devi." From that moment on, she embraced the Devi *bhava* (the mood of the divine Mother) that has become her spiritual trademark. According to her official biographer, in the months following the inner call to manifest the Devi *bhava*, Ammachi adopted the Devi *bhava* in addition to the Krishna *bhava*. The devotees, however, believed that "she had now merely become possessed by Devi as well as Krishna." Since then Ammachi has only been manifesting the Devi *bhava*. With the shift in divine mood also came a shift in Ammachi's personality. Her biographer writes: "Soon after the beginning of *Devi Bhava Darshan*, there occurred certain changes in Mother. During Her *Devi Sadhana*, She was generally aloof and uncommunicative. All the time She was devoted to prayer and meditation on the form of the Divine Mother. If Her parents or brother abused Her physically or verbally, She kept silent. Now She became more daring, even Her facial expression changed. Her nature became fearless and unyielding when it came to dealing with Her parents and brother."[10]

On Devi *bhava* nights, Ammachi is believed to reveal her identity as the divine Mother, according to her devotees, in certain visible physical changes in her person, most notable among these being the change in her facial hue; her face is believed to turn bluish. Ammachi's spiritual fame began to spread as her devotees told moving stories about her miraculous powers that include clairvoyance, bilocation, levitation, dramatic healing of various physical illnesses and psychological disorders, answering devotees' special needs, creating children for the childless, and absorbing or inhaling devotees' negative karma.[11] The following testimonial by a twenty-five-year-old woman named Trina from St. Louis attests to Amma's special grace and powers:

> After I graduated from University of Illinois in Chicago, I became a devotee of Satya Sai Baba and Ammachi. My devout Catholic mother who is a daily Mass-goer was not very happy with my interest in "guruism." I have been Amma's devotee for five years now and have made it a point to come for Amma darshan every year when she comes to Chicago. Even though I see Amma only once a year for a few days, I maintain contact with her daily. I pray to Amma daily and recite her 101 names every morning. I read Amma's teachings and meditate on them and stay connected to her. She answers my prayers even from afar. A particular incident in my life has convinced me of her presence and power. Recently I graduated in Art therapy and was looking for a job. I had applied to several places but received no positive replies. One morning I prayed to Amma and said, "Please give me a sign if you hear my prayer." Just as I finished saying the prayer, the telephone rang; it was a call from one of

the places I had applied. Though I did not get the job, my prayer for a sign was answered.[12]

Throughout these various spiritual phases, Sudhamani relied on direct realization of God without the mediation of a teacher or guru. "I never had a guru, nor was I ever initiated by anyone and given a particular mantra," says Ammachi. "The mantra I used to chant was 'Amma, Amma.' "[13] But this uninitiated mystic is revered by her disciples as the perfect spiritual master (*satguru*) who has the power to "directly induce God-realization."[14] A young man named Balu—now known as Swami Amritswarupananda—committed his life to following Amma's spiritual teachings in 1978 and became one of her first disciples. In 1979 two Westerners also joined him—Neal Rosner, an American Jew (now Swami Paramatmananda) and Gayatri, an Australian woman (now Amritaprana), who is Amma's devoted personal attendant and companion. A small thatched hut constructed near Ammachi's house served as the initial ashram.[15] Soon the inner circle of devotees grew as other young men and women joined the ashram. A formal ashram named Amritapuri was instituted in May 1981. Since then the number of male and female celibate aspirants (*brahmacharis* and *brahmacharinis*)—both foreign and native—has increased steadily. A recent announcement from the ashram declares that the Mata Amritanandamayi Math (hermitage) serves as home to "over a thousand full-time residents," who include, according to Swami Paramatmananda, fifteen fully initiated sannyasis and sannyasinis, dozens of aspirants, and a large number of short-term visitors in their twenties and thirties.[16] Although the movement has grown remarkably over the past two decades, Ammachi continues to function as the central administrative and spiritual authority. Despite her hectic and grueling daily schedule of spiritual activities, she is said to make all the important decisions concerning her ever-growing network of charitable and religious institutions.

Ammachi in the United States: Her Movement and Devotees

At the invitation of her American disciples, Ammachi first visited the United States in 1987. Her first visit to several major U.S. cities had a profound impact on scores of religious seekers who have embraced her as their personal guru. Since then her spiritual appeal in America has grown so immensely that her U.S. tour has become an annual feature. In 1989 she established her first U.S. ashram in San Ramon, California, on a hill donated by an American devotee. Known as Mata Amritanandamayi Center or simply MA Center, this ashram has grown into a full-fledged ashram housing several permanent and temporary male and female celibate aspirants. The aspirants follow a daily schedule of reciting the 101 names of Ammachi, the 101 names of the divine Mother, meditation, and selfless service (*seva*). Even while attached to the ashram, these aspirants pursue regular secular careers in the outside world. Swami Paramatmananda supervises the spiritual life at the ashram, which now serves as the U.S. headquarters for the Ammachi movement. Local chapters have been established in Seattle, Los Angeles, Dallas, Chicago, New York, Sante Fe, Boston, Washington D.C., and Rhode Island. Efforts are being made to institute local chapters in Ann Arbor, Hawaii, Indianapolis, and other major U.S. cities. During a three-day visit to Ann Arbor in November 1999, Ammachi instituted another Amma Center in the Midwest. In November 2002, she also conducted a retreat at the Holiday Inn in Detroit. Such retreats function as preludes to the establishment of local chapters. Her three-month annual tour to the West also includes stops in Japan, Brazil, Mauritius, Reunion Island, and numerous European cities.

Ammachi's U.S. devotees come from all walks of life, ages, religions, and races. I interviewed several with distinguished professional careers as industrialists, businessmen, university professors, social workers, university graduates, and medical professionals. As for ethnic composition, according to an estimate provided by a lay leader in Chicago, Caucasians constitute nearly 80 percent of her U.S. devotees. Immigrant Asian Indians, African Americans, and East Asians account for the rest. As for gender distribution, although Amma attracts a good number of male devotees, the vast majority are women who exercise prominent leadership roles and functions. They act as song leaders, receptionists, temple ushers, bookstore administrators, *satsang* leaders, preachers, interpreters, media representatives, darshan hosts, liturgical assistants, cashiers, and directors of food services.

Cultural reversal, manifest in devotees' dress, ornaments, speech, behavior, and performance, is a characteristic feature of Amma's U.S. congregations. When in Ammachi's presence, many of her Anglo-devotees wear white Indian clothing (since Ammachi generally wears white saris) such as salwar kameez, sari, and kurta, with an assortment of Indian accessories such as jewelry, beads, *tilak*, bracelets, and shawls. There seems to be a conscious effort among Anglo devotees to look and act Indian. Some have adopted Indian spiritual names. Such a deliberate shift in dress or behavioral code is conspicuously absent among their Indian counterparts. Whereas Indian men wear regular Western clothes, most Indian women wear brightly colored silk saris. The spontaneous comment by one of my students who accompanied me to Ammachi's *satsang* in Ann Arbor in November 1999 captures this dynamic of cultural role reversal. She remarked: "The Anglos seemed more Indian than the Indians and the Indians seemed more Anglo and less Indian." Another notable feature of Amma's U.S. devotees is their dual religious identity. While professing personal affection, faith, and loyalty to Ammachi's spiritual message, many maintain formal ties and affiliation with their traditional religions. Both in San Ramon and Chicago, I met several of Ammachi's devotees who claimed to be Christians in good standing in their respective denominations. This applies also to those devotees who maintain loyalty to two gurus. The case of Trina is instructive. She is a follower of both Sai Baba and Ammachi, who represent for her father and mother images of the Divine. "I don't have to give up either one since both are aspects of God."[17]

Ammachi attracts devotees from diverse religious, ethnic, and social groups who find her spiritual message and personal charisma uplifting and fresh. The vast majority of Ammachi's American devotees are converts from the Siddha Yoga and Transcendental Meditation (TM) movements popular in the United States during the second wave of gurus in the late sixties and early seventies. A great number of them came to Ammachi after Swami Muktananda's death in 1982. When I attended Ammachi's spiritual programs in Chicago in July 1999, I met a large number of former Siddha Yoga devotees from the Maharishi University in Iowa. Although many of these former members of the Siddha Yoga movement have switched their spiritual loyalty totally to Ammachi, some maintain dual loyalties and affiliation, retaining formal affiliation and membership with the movement as well as cultivating a personal spiritual loyalty to Ammachi. Besides former Siddha Yogis, there are other devotees who may be described as "avatar-tourists" in search of living saints. Still others are Christian feminists who see in Ammachi a validation for the feminization of the Divine. A colorful picture of Ammachi holding the child Jesus, on sale during Ammachi's darshan sites in the United States, reflects both Ammachi's appeal as well as her effort to appeal to her Western Christian audience in general and Christian feminists in particular. Immigrant Asian Indians who are disillusioned with what they perceive to be traditional, sectarian, ritualistic Hinduism and its scandalous, money-hungry male gurus of the seventies form a tiny minority of Ammachi's U.S. devotees.

Currently Ammachi's congregations in the United States are administered by lay volunteers and enthusiasts. Except for San Ramon and Santa Fe, where there are established ashrams under the spiritual leadership of an ordained monk or nun, most U.S. local chapters do not have a resident sannyasi or sannyasini to serve as a spiritual guide to devotees. Monthly *satsangs* (prayer/ meditation sessions), *bhajans*, and rituals are conducted by uninitiated and unordained lay local leaders in the living rooms of lay devotees. Ammachi souvenirs such as Ammachi pictures and dolls serve for these lay devotees as a medium of contact and as evocative symbols of Ammachi's physical and spiritual presence. Devotees testify that these souvenirs make Ammachi's presence in their midst concrete. One American devotees writes: "I always felt like I was feeding and dressing Mother whenever I did puja, and I felt blessed while doing this. Every time I took care of the altar, cleaning and tidying it up, I felt Mother's presence. . . . The puja articles were like a living entity, they were alive, and it was as though they were living, breathing parts of the Mother. Now I have the same feeling about the San Ramon, California, ashram. I can feel the whole place breathe as a unit, alive with Her."[18]

Embodied Guru, Embodied Goddess

Although by her own self-admission Ammachi was never initiated by a guru, she is revered by her devotees as a *satguru*, a true or perfect spiritual master. The *guru puja* offered to Ammachi each time she enters the temple confirms the devotees' estimation of her guru status. In her spiritual discourses and writings, she describes herself as a compassionate guru guiding her devotees to god-realization. She exhorts her disciples to cultivate attachment to the *satguru* since attachment to the *satguru* is both the means and end of spiritual quest. When asked whether attachment to the master's external form is necessary to realize the ultimate goal of god-realization, Ammachi responds:

> Children, first of all remember that attachment to the Master is an attachment to God. Your problem is that you try to differentiate between God and the true Master. Attachment to a true Master's physical form intensifies your longing to realize the Supreme. It is like living with God. He makes your spiritual journey much easier. Such a Master is both the means and the end. But at the same time there must be conscious effort to see the Master in all creation. . . . You cannot experience the state of God-consciousness through your mere senses or through the scriptures you have learned. To experience it, you need to develop a new eye, the inner, third eye. . . . The inner eye, or the eye of true knowledge, can only be opened by a real Master. . . . Being attached to the external form of a Satguru is like having a direct contact with the Supreme Truth.[19]

Ammachi's self-understanding as a *satguru* is reflected in the teaching roles she exercises in relation to both her celibate disciples and lay devotees. She offers regular spiritual discourses to her devotees. During her U.S. tour she offers formal spiritual discourses in her native Malayalam that is translated by a native interpreter, leads daily devotional singing, teaches meditation, and conducts regular retreats for her disciples. In addition, her teaching office includes cultivating personal and spiritual discipline in her celibate disciples to assist them in their path of self-realization. Amma's disciplining is said to be inspired by her real and transforming love for her disciples. About her teaching and disciplining role in relation to the spiritual formation of her disciples, she says: "I am like a gardener. The garden is full of colorful flowers. I was not asked to look after the beautiful flowers . . . but I have been asked to remove the insects and worms from pest-ridden flowers and plants. To remove the insects I may have to pinch the petals and leaves which is painful, but it is only to save the plants and flowers from destruction. In the same way, Mother will always work with the children's weaknesses. The process of elimination is painful but it is for your good. . . . Mother expects nothing except your spiritual progress."[20]

Along with her role and identity as a *satguru* is Ammachi's self-recognized and self-professed identity as the embodied goddess (*devi*). Ammachi's goddess identity is revealed in her weekly Devi *bhava* when she assumes the goddess mood or form. Ammachi declares that she assumes the Devi *bhava* only for the benefit and at the request of her devotees, and permits them to dedicate religious worship (puja) and meditation dedicated to her not only on the nights of Devi *bhava* but every evening. Thus Ammachi's dual and conflated roles and identities as guru and goddess seem to suggest a certain ambivalence in Ammachi's self-understanding and consciousness about her spiritual status and identity. A similar ambivalence and fluidity characterizes the devotees' perception of her identity and status. Although many of her devotees consider her the divine Mother, some seeing her as "the Great Mother Kali incarnate,"[21] others see her essentially as the perfect guru who inspires and facilitates their god-realization. Balachandran, an immigrant Indian lay leader of Ammachi's Chicago congregation, echoes the sentiments of a large number of devotees. He says: "Amma is the guru for my whole family. She is our *ishta guru* (chosen guru). I have had other male gurus in the past. But as a guru Amma stands unique. Whereas I had only an intellectual and rational relationship with other male gurus, I have a unique personal relationship with Amma. I experience an internal resonance with Amma, a heart-to-heart connection with Amma."[22] The ambivalence surrounding Ammachi's self-consciousness and the devotees' understanding of Ammachi is reminiscent of the theological debate over Christ's self-consciousness as the Son of God.

Embodied Ritual: Divine Hugs and Hershey Kisses

The spiritual hug, known to her followers as *darshan*, is the most intriguing and unique feature of Ammachi's interaction with devotees. Hundreds of devotees wait for several hours for a few seconds of personal darshan with Ammachi. Before going up for darshan, devotees receive "darshan tokens" from Amma's liturgical assistants who instruct them about proper darshan etiquette known as "darshan dharma," which includes specific instructions on how to embrace Amma during darshan. Devotees are also instructed to wipe their face with a tissue and/or remove facial make-up. After these instructions, devotees are individually ushered before Ammachi, who is seated on a colorfully decorated throne, flanked by a male sannyasi who translates devotees' special requests or questions and a female attendant. Ammachi receives the devotee into her bosom in loving spiritual embrace, applies sandal paste on the devotee's forehead, hugs, and kisses the devotee, frequently stroking the devotee's head, neck, chest, spine, or back and whispering the words "Amma, Amma" and "my darling son" or "my darling daughter." As the devotee rises to leave, Ammachi looks directly into the eyes and pulls him/her unto herself once more and lavishes another round of kisses. Then she places some *prasad* (blessed offerings) in the devotee's hands, including a packet of sacred ash, a rose petal, and a Hershey kiss. Visibly moved by the spiritual embrace and tactile love, devotees emerge tearful and speechless, from an apparently speechless yet powerful communication.

On an average, Ammachi gives spiritual hugs to over a thousand devotees a day. On the weekly Devi *bhava* nights, when Ammachi wears a bright sari and a silver crown to reveal the majestic glory and tender love of the divine Mother, the number of devotees receiving hugs is anywhere from 1,800 to 2,000. My darshan token number when I went for darshan on a devi *bhava* night at the MA Center was 1357. I was told that in India, Devi *bhava* nights attract over ten thousand darshan seekers. During Devi *bhava*, scores of devotees receive personal initiation and a mantra from Ammachi. Devotees assert that Ammachi imparts to her devotees mantras that resonate with their particular spiritual needs and religious identity. For example, she is known to impart "Christ mantras" to Christian devotees and Buddhist mantras to Buddhist devotees. In the final moments of a Devi *bhava* session, Ammachi also performs nuptial rites for a select number of couples, most of whom are Caucasian devotees dressed in traditional Indian wedding attire. The nuptial ceremony conducted by Ammachi is the only wedding ceremony for some couples, but for many it serves as a supplementary ritual to their civil or church ceremony.

During darshan, the atmosphere and ambience are intense, prayerful, relaxed, and festive at the same time. Devotional *bhajans* in Hindi and Malayalam led by a group of singers provides the spiritual and musical backdrop. As Ammachi receives into her lap the continuous stream of devotees, one by one, some sit in prayerful meditation as if inhaling the power and energy exuding from her person, some become spiritually intoxicated and dance in ecstasy, while others observe the darshan proceedings in a state of awe and wonderment. A few others saunter through the adjacent bookstore, browsing through various Amma souvenirs and India wares on sale. Throughout the darshan service, which lasts anywhere from six to seven hours, various groups of devotees take turns in leading the congregation in devotional singing. On Devi *bhava* nights, Caucasian children dressed in colorful Indian saris perform Indian classical dances. It is difficult to say whether her U.S. devotees fully comprehend the extent and significance of the assumptions and claims that undergird the Devi *bhava*, since during Devi *bhava* Ammachi is believed to reveal her "real" identity as the "divine Mother incarnate." Whereas some see it as a time when Amma wears a fine silk sari, jewelry, and a silver crown, others regard it, in the words of an American devotee, as "a spiritual disco night" for devotees.

Toward a Hermeneutic of Ammachi Darshan: Tradition Defied and Transcended

Evidently, *darshan* is the most intimate, direct, and personal mode of interaction between Ammachi and her devotees. Given that Ammachi does not deliver many formal spiritual discourses in the United States, as she has limited fluency in the English language, it also functions as her principal spiritual discourse to her American devotees. For her devotees, darshan is not merely a physical encounter between them and their spiritual master. Devotees tell moving stories about their direct, intuitive dialogue with Ammachi during darshan experience. When asked how they communicate with Ammachi, devotees repeatedly say: "We communicate in the language of the heart as a child communicates with its mother. We don't have to say anything to Amma as she knows all our thoughts even before we speak." In this ritual idiom, the message, the medium, and the messenger and her charisma are rolled into one. Apart from effecting a certain metacommunion between Amma and her devotees, darshan also provides a metadiscourse on the departures, innovations, and reforms Ammachi has subtly introduced into the Hindu ritual tradition. Ammachi's creative innovation of Hindu religious—more precisely ritual—praxis is best understood in light of traditional understanding of darshan.

Darshan literally means "seeing." Translated sometimes as the "auspicious sight" of the divine, in the popular Hindu devotional scheme, darshan is the auspicious seeing of the deity indwelling in an icon or image whereby the devotee seeks to establish contact with the deity. As Eck rightly observes, "in the Hindu ritual tradition it [*darshan*] refers especially to religious seeing, or the visual perception of the sacred."[23] The act of standing in the presence of the deity and beholding the image with one's own eyes, seeing the divine and being seen by the divine, is a central act of Hindu worship. Though it involves the body, darshan is primarily a mental, spiritual, and mystical contact. Direct bodily contact with the deity is both ritually inauspicious and forbidden for the average lay devotee. Even the priest whose ritual functions necessitate regular physical contact with the image, particularly when he performs his ritual duties of bathing, anointing, and dressing the deity, is governed by strict prescriptions and observances that are intended to offset the inherent dangers of such contact. But physicality, in direct contrast or defiance of Hindu ritual norms and prescriptions, is the hallmark of Ammachi darshans.

Given her status as the embodied divine Mother and the perfect spiritual master (*satguru*), darshan is no doubt the appropriate mode of interaction. But in form and function, the Ammachi darshan radically differs from the traditional pattern insofar as it entails close and intense bodily contact in the form of touching, hugging, and kissing. Beyond the ritual and religious contexts, touching and kissing a person of another gender, especially strangers, is a taboo in Hindu social relations—more so when it involves touching and kissing a religious teacher or guru. But Ammachi embraces, hugs, strokes, and kisses her devotees with total disregard to their gender, moral condition, and physical purity. Thus her darshan defies not only traditional Hindu norms concerning purity, pollution, and bodily contact between the devotee and the embodied divine but also societal norms and rules governing gender relations. Darshan is Ammachi's discourse on defiance. It is her way of defying and transcending traditional caste boundaries and the purity-impurity distinctions that undergird Hindu social and religious life. One wonders whether her low-caste status gives her the freedom and predisposition to transgress with relative ease the orthodox religious and social norms. Unschooled in Hindu ideas about ritual purity, devotional exercises, and caste considerations, many of her American devotees perceive darshan essentially as a novel psychospiritual experience. The vast majority seem oblivious of Ammachi's radical departure from and innovation of tradition. When these are explained, these devotees attribute Ammachi's defiance of tradition to her "metareligious" and "transcendental" identity as the "divine Mother incarnate."

Amma's flair for physical contact evokes a reciprocal response from her American devotees, who seek to prolong, memorialize, concretize, and perpetuate their darshan experience and physical contact with Amma with the help of an assortment of Amma souvenirs such as Amma's picture, beads, T-shirts, saris, bracelets, and dolls. These physical objects not only are believed to contain Amma's spiritual power and energy (shakti) but also function as effective mechanisms for staying connected to Ammachi. Most popular among these items are the Amma dolls that are believed to be charged with extra spiritual power, since they are reportedly made from the saris and petticoats worn by Ammachi. To her devotees, the dolls are emblems of her spiritual power and presence. Amma dolls and medals receive a prominent place in devotees's domestic spaces. Devotees carry Amma souvenirs in their cars and persons. These souvenirs serve as instruments for extending Amma's spiritual power and presence. The Amma dolls also represent the creative and innovative synthesis of Hindu image culture and American popular culture and market economy. The economic implications of this emphasis on physicality are no less significant, as these items generate sizeable revenue for the movement.

Although darshan constitutes the most dramatic and visible instance of defying and transcending tradition, subtler forms of this dynamic can also be discerned in other aspects of Ammachi's teachings and movement. Most notable among these innovations are the new temples she is establishing in India and the temple consecration that she performs. In April 1988, she consecrated the Brahmasthanam temple in Kodungallur in Kerala. Since then, she has consecrated twelve new temples in India.[24] Of particular note is the consecration of temples with Sri Chakra yantras and installing these by placing them on her lap for empowerment.[25] This consecration rite is another version of her use of intense physical contact that breaks every taboo, defying all norms of purity, pollution, and asceticism in Hindu culture by making full body contact the main form of transmission.

Another area where Ammachi's defiance and innovation of Hindu tradition is most significant is the empowerment of women's public ritual roles. Despite opposition from some Hindu scholars and pundits, recently Ammachi has been empowering her female renunciates (brahmacharinis) to study the sacred texts and installing them as temple priestesses authorized to perform puja in temples. In November 1997, she appointed women as priestesses (pujarinis) in her temples at Kaimanam and Kodungallur in Kerala. Devotees attribute Ammachi's daring innovation of the tradition to her firm belief in the equality of men and women in the religious realm. "In the eyes of God," says Ammachi, "men and women are equal. How can one possibly justify saying that a woman, who is the creator of man, is inferior to man?" Again, she is said to admonish her disciples that "it is not enough to just preach liberty to women. It has to be practiced and demonstrated."[26] Notwithstanding this empowerment of women's ritual roles, Ammachi's views on women seem to reveal a certain ambivalence, since they alternate between the orthodox negative appraisal of women and a clear rejection of the traditional devaluation of women. On one hand, women are portrayed as models of selfless service and given prominent roles and functions within her order. On the other hand, menstruating women are dissuaded from going for darshan with Ammachi. Darshan guidelines require women "to cover their shoulders and to wear dresses or skirts [and] not wear see-through dresses or tight dresses that reveal the shape of the body."[27] Perhaps this ambivalence illustrates the internal, essential dialectic between tradition and change that characterizes her message and movement. Another recent development initiated by Ammachi is the strong emphasis on the chanting and study of the tantra text *Lalitasahasranamam* with interactive CD, special *stotras* (hymns) composed to Amma as Lalita, and the direct claim that Amma *is* Lalitambika.[28]

The sites used for Ammachi's spiritual programs in the United States constitute another example of defiance and transcendence of tradition. During her United States tour, Ammachi rarely conducts her religious programs in the Hindu temples that have rapidly mushroomed across the country. Instead, they are held in secular or neutral spaces like public auditoriums, hotels, and nondenominational Christian churches. For example, during her numerous visits to Chicago over the past decade, only once did the local Hindu temple serve as venue for her programs. The Holiday Inn–Dearborn served as venue for Ammachi's spiritual retreat in Detroit between November 14 and 16, 2002. Ammachi also departs from and defies traditional monastic discipline regarding residence rules for monastics. During her U.S. tour, Ammachi usually chooses to reside in and receive hospitality from her lay devotees—ordinarily Keralite Indians—in their suburban houses instead of a traditional monastery or ashram. Although this might be due to the limited number of fully established ashrams in the American cities she visits, it reveals a subtle pattern of defiance and transcendence of tradition. These facts seem to suggest that Ammachi locates herself and her movement outside mainstream Hinduism while remaining deeply rooted in Hindu spiritual heritage and ritual tradition. Furthermore, although Ammachi was never formally initiated into monastic life, she has given initiation to scores of disciples in India and abroad. Moreover, although her monastics are technically affiliated with the Puri Math and its lineage, she has retained her distinct monastic tradition and jurisdiction. Finally, Ammachi, who is firmly grounded in the Hindu scriptural, ritual, and devotional traditions, transcends the confines of orthodox Hinduism to impart Christ mantras to her American devotees, some of whom regard her as the "female Christ."

Fidelity to tradition and defiance of tradition are the hallmarks of Ammchi's spiritual message and movement. Some might interpret her innovations as an effort to reestablish the pure Vedic tradition.[29] When seen in the total context of Ammachi's spiritual career and teachings, however, her various innovative measures and defiant steps seem to reemphasize and reiterate the simple message of love she has been preaching for over three decades. In her defiant rejection of some obsolete norms and practices as well as in the radical innovations she has sought to introduce into the Hindu religious and ritual tradition in which she is deeply rooted, Ammachi is calling her disciples and devotees to transcend the historical accidents and cultural constraints of a religious tradition and grasp its core truth and central message of god-realization through unconditional love to all. In her embodied self as guru and devi as well as in her embodied ritual of darshan, Ammachi concretizes and mediates this message of unconditional love.

NOTES

1. *Guru Gita*, vv. 157, 87, cited in Amritaswarupananda, *Awaken Children!* vol. 6, p. v.

2. http://www.hinduismtoday.com;/1997/6/1997-6-07.html

3. http://www.ammachi.org/charities/donations/html

4. http://www.ammachi.org/ashram-satsang/index.html

5. Amritswarupananda, *Ammachi*; Conway, *Women of Power and Grace*; Johnson, *Daughters of the Goddess*; Bess, *The Path of the Mother*; Cornell, *Amma*.

6. Bess, *The Path of the Mother*, p. 16. This version of Ammachi's birth, not found in other accounts, seems to belong more to the growing corpus of devotional biographies of Ammachi than to historical accounts.

7. Amritaswarupananda, *Ammachi*, p. 17.

8. Ibid., pp. 78, 71, 76, 77.

9. Ibid., pp. 85–87.

10. Ibid., pp. 143–145.

11. Conway, *Women of Power and Grace*, pp. 263–264.

12. Interview with Trina in Chicago on July 6, 1999.

13. Amritswarupananda, *Ammachi*, p. 114.

14. Conway, *Women of Power and Grace*, p. 258.

15. Ibid., p. 253.

16. Interview with Swami Paramatmananda, MA Center, San Ramon, Cal., June 22, 1999; http://www.ammachi.org/amma/growing-mission.html

17. Interview with Trina in Chicago on July 6, 1999.

18. Tina, "God Won't Put Away the Dishes," p. 128.

19. Amritswarupananda, *Awaken Children!*, vol. 7, pp. 231–234.

20. Amritswarupananda, *Ammachi*, p. 320

21. Bess, *The Path of the Mother*, p. 3.

22. Interview in Chicago, July 1, 1999.

23. Eck, *Darsan*, p. 3.

24. Cornell, *Amma*, pp. 132–136.

25. Central to goddess worship in the Sri Vidya school of south India, the Sri Chakra yantra is a symbol of the goddess Lalita Tripurasundari. It is a diagram consisting of nine large intersecting triangles in the center of which is a drop or *bindu*. These interlacing triangles are encircled by two sets of lotus petals, one of eight petals and one of sixteen, around which are three parallel lines forming four rectangular gateways. The four upward-facing triangles represent Shiva (the male principle) and the five downward facing triangles represent Shakti (the female principle). Their combination symbolizes the divine couple's union. The principal deity of the diagram, however, is Shakti, who is symbolized by the *bindu* (point) in the center. The Sri Vidya devotional tradition regards the whole diagram with its nine triangles, lotus, and four gateways as the goddess's mansion. I am grateful to Rachel Fell McDermott and Corinne Dempsey for providing valuable information to me on the Lalita cult. For more information see Douglas Renfrew Brooks, *The Secret of the Three Cities: An Introduction to Hindu Śakta Tantra* (Chicago: University of Chicago Press, 1990). Also see the Web: http://www.angelfire.com/ks/karnavati/souvenir/yantra.html and http://www.clas.ufl.edu/users/gthursby/tantra/tripura.htm

26. Cornell, *Amma*, pp. 137–139.

27. MA Center brochure, p. 14.

28. Along with the Sri Chakra yantra, the anthropomorphic goddess Lalita Tripurasundari (the red goddess) is a central figure in the Sri Vidya school of goddess worship in south India. Lalita is a benign goddess, who is a caring mother or devoted wife, queen of the universe, the supreme Shakti. She is described as seated on a lion's throne (sometimes on the lap of Shiva), with four hands holding a noose, an elephant goad, a bow, and arrows. She is dressed in red and adorned with numerous jewels. In the Lalita cult, the *Lalitasahasranamam* is one of the central hymns for Devi worshippers. See http://www.clas.ufl.edu/users/gthursby/tantra/tripura.htm

29. Cornell, *Amma*, p. 138.

REFERENCES

Amritaswarupananda, Swami. *Ammachi: A Biography of Mata Amritanandamayi*. San Ramon, Cal.: Mata Amritanandamayi Center, 1994.

_____. *Awaken Children!* Vol. 4. San Ramon, Cal.: Mata Amritanandamayi Center, 1993.

_____. *Awaken Children!* Vol. 6. San Ramon, Cal.: Mata Amritanandamayi Center, 1994.

_____. *Awaken Children!* Vol. 7. San Ramon, Cal.: Mata Amritanandamayi Center, 1995.

_____. *Awaken Children!* Vol. 9. San Ramon, Cal.: Mata Amritanandamayi Center, 1998.

Bess, Savitri L. *The Path of the Mother*. New York: Ballantine, 2000.

Conway, Timothy. *Women of Power and Grace*. Santa Barbara, Cal.: Wake Up Press, 1994.

Cornell, Judith. *Amma: Healing the Heart of the World*. New York: HarperCollins, 2001.

Eck, Diana. *Darśan: Seeing the Divine Image in India*. 2nd ed. Chambersburg, Pa.: Anima, 1981.

Gottler, Marty, ed. *Come Quickly, My Darling Children: Stories by Western Devotees of Mata Amritanandamayi*. Grass Valley, Cal: Sierra Vista, 1996.

Hallstrom, Lisa. *Mother of Bliss: Ānandamāyī Mā (1896–1982)*. New York: Oxford University Press, 1999.

Johnson, Linda. *Daughters of the Goddess: The Women Saints of India*. St. Paul, Minn.: Yes International, 1994.

MA Center. *An Introduction: Mata Amritanandamayi Devi*. Ashram brochure, 1999.

Tina (Hari Sudha). "God Won't Put away the Dishes." Pp. 123–134 in M. Gottler, ed., *Come Quickly, My Darling Children*. Grass Valley, Cal.: Sierra Vista, 1996.

9

Gurumayi, the Play of Shakti and Guru

Karen Pechilis

A diversity of divinity is strikingly apparent at the Siddha Yoga ashram in South Fallsburg, New York, through prominently placed images. Large, brightly colored paintings of the female Hindu saints Mirabai, Mahadeviyakka, and Lalleshwari, and the female Sufi saint Rabi'a, adorn one wall of the main dining hall, while the other walls display poster-sized photographs of the gurus of Siddha Yoga: Bhagawan Nityananda, Swami Muktananda, and Swami Chidvilasananda. Delicate paintings of Lakshmi, the goddess of wealth, grace the hallways, above tables holding pamphlets that solicit donations from devotees. On the pathway through the woods between the two main buildings of the ashram, one encounters larger-than-life-sized statues of Hanuman, the monkey god, and a meditating Shiva; Christian figures, including St. Francis of Assisi and Mary, stand silently in a circular clearing. A gigantic bronze Dancing Shiva greets visitors to the other main building of the ashram. Inside the building, there is a temple to Bhagawan Nityananda, a glassed gazebo-like structure surrounding a huge, golden image of the seated guru.

Throughout the ashram, amid these more formal tableaus, are brilliant color photographs of a young woman, often smiling gorgeously, though sometimes contemplative, and in all cases vibrant with life. She is the living guru for the here and now, Gurumayi (Swami Chidvilasananda), the current guru of the worldwide Siddha Yoga organization.

All of the images represent the intersection between the human and the divine, though they do so in distinctive ways. The images of the saints and the gurus serve as reminders of exemplars of spiritual achievement and stand as models and particular examples of that achievement in the context of the universalizing message of Swami

Chidvilasananda's predecessor, Swami Muktananda. Swami Muktananda's universalizing impulse is the reason that Siddha Yoga came to the United States and established its headquarters in South Fallsburg, New York. The theme of universalization looms large in the profile of Siddha Yoga, since as a worldwide organization it promotes the uplift of humanity through a collective "revolution" in spiritual consciousness, specifically through the bestowal of shakti: "With the decision in 1970 to launch his first world tour, Muktananda appears to have decided to make shaktipat [bestowal of shakti] the centerpiece of a worldwide movement of spiritual awakening, which later he was to call, quite forthrightly, the 'meditation revolution.' "[1]

Shakti is a metaphysical concept steeped in layers of Hindu tradition. For example, in the ancient Samkhya philosophy, shakti is understood to be a feminine energy that swirls the static male purusha to initiate creation. More popularly understood classical formulations are that shakti represents the divine power of the Goddess, and the moral power of women. Central to the Siddha Yoga teachings is the understanding that shakti is a universal power of which the guru is the preeminent worldly manifestation. The guru is the embodiment, the physical entity that both signifies and substantiates the abstraction. On this universal level, the three successive gurus of Siddha Yoga are indistinguishable in their nature as the embodiment of shakti and in their agency as transmitters of shakti to their devotees. Shakti constitutes the guru's leadership as well as the path of devotees' self-realization; the spiritual connection between the two is the bestowal of shakti, or *shaktipat*. "Shaktipat is thought to constitute a transmission [pat] of spiritual power [shakti] from the *sadguru* [true guru] to the initiate. When the essential, enlightened consciousness of the *sadguru* enters the disciple, shaktipat occurs, and it is thought to destroy the root or foundational impurity of spiritual ignorance."[2]

Devotees think of Gurumayi as this shakti "energy." One told me that the guru "seems to have sparks flying from her." Her formal titles also emphasize her existence in a state beyond ordinary reality, and thus as an appropriate conduit for shakti. The title Swami Chidvilasananda, bestowed by Swami Muktananda in April 1982 during ceremonies to initiate her as his successor, means "The Bliss of the Play of Pure Consciousness." She is also more familiarly known by the popular honorific title Gurumayi, "One Who Is Immersed in the Guru."[3] Her state beyond ordinary reality is described as bliss, pure consciousness, and immersion in the divine essence that permeates the world. Significantly, the guru is by definition able to share this experience with others. The experience of the divine within is accessible to humankind through the guru's bestowal of shakti. As the perfected embodiment of the divine essence, the guru leads others to the awareness of the divine within themselves.

Yet the particular is also significant, as is suggested by the multiplicity of images of forms of the divine, including the photographs, statues, and paintings described earlier. Saints, personified images of gods, and the gurus of the Siddha Yoga lineage are represented as constitutive of the path of spiritual awakening in the decor of the ashram and in the Siddha Yoga teachings. Most important is the physical being and personality of the current guru, for it is with this living form of shakti that devotees interact. The guru is both an ideal and one who responds directly and individually to devotees.

In contrast to other contemporary gurus, there is little mention of the avatar concept in Siddha Yoga teachings on the nature of the guru. Instead, the life stories of Swami Muktananda and Swami Chidvilasananda tend to emphasize the extended and intense spiritual practices (*sadhana*) each undertook after receiving guidance from his or her guru. In this manner, they perfected themselves and became eligible to become gurus. There is said to have been something special about each from the beginning—for example, Muktananda called Malti, who became Swami Chidvilasananda, a "blazing fire," as I discuss in more detail below—and they received guidance from their gurus, but there is a very prominent place given to spiritual practice in the tradition's account of their life stories, and it is here that the importance of the particular in the context of the universal can be seen. The gurus' emphasis on their own spiritual practice provides the foundation for their teaching that their followers engage in sadhana themselves. Thus, there are two connections between the guru and the devotee: the bestowal of *shaktipat* from the guru to the devotee, and the devotee's sadhana based on the model of the guru having him or herself performed sadhana. The Siddha Yoga ashrams, Intensive programs, workshops, retreats, and programs related to the yearly message are all dedicated to cultivating correct spiritual practices in the Siddha Yoga devotees.

As a particular embodiment of the guru, Gurumayi stands apart from her predecessors because she is female. To her devotees across the globe, and to interested persons who would point to her as an important example of a female religious leader, she is, in the words of one devotee, "very much a woman." In light of the demographics of devotional participants at the South Fallsburg ashram, one can assert that her womanhood is especially significant, since women form the majority group, especially Caucasian, educated, middle-class women.[4] In many ways, the guru seems an archetype of femininity. She is young and a great beauty, trim and elegant, dressed in flowing robes that she often complements with a matching hat. She is power in a refined and delicate package, embodying authoritative spiritual and administrative leadership.

The issue of gender illustrates the tension between the universal and the particular in the figure of the guru. In one view, gender is obsolete; the connection between and among beings through shakti creates an identity and thus a unity, obliterating dualistic conceptions of duality, such as gender. In another view, the feminine is universal, through the status of the guru as a perfected being, and through the traditional identification of the feminine with shakti, as a constitutive principle of creation (in Samkhya philosophy), as the power of universal rule (the Goddess), and as moral power (women). In still another view, the feminine is particular; the guru is a personality and a gendered embodiment, so that Gurumayi is perceived to be "very much a woman."

There is a radical discontinuity, however, between the "womanhood" of a female guru such as Gurumayi and the globally dominant patriarchal, heterosexual discourse that defines "womanhood." *The guru is not a sexual being.* The guru is an ascetic; she is usually not married, but if she is, then she is not married in the conventional sense, and she will not have children in her status as guru.[5] The female guru's persona as an ascetic contrasts with the worldly expectation—felt more or less intensely in a given culture, but a substratum of all cultures—that a woman will bear children. The guru can be viewed as a "third gender," as discussed by Judith Butler, citing Monique Wittig on lesbian identity:

> The second rather counter-intuitive claim that Wittig makes is the following: a lesbian is not a woman. A woman, she argues, only exists as a term that stabilizes and consolidates a binary and oppositional relation to a man; that relation, she argues, is heterosexuality. A lesbian, she claims, in refusing heterosexuality is no longer identified in terms of that oppositional relation. Indeed, a lesbian, she maintains, transcends the binary opposition between woman and man; a lesbian is neither a woman nor a man. But further, the lesbian has no sex; she is beyond the categories of sex. Through the lesbian refusal of those categories, the lesbian exposes (pronouns are a problem here) the contingent cultural constitution of those categories and the tacit yet abiding presumption of the heterosexual matrix. . . . Indeed, the lesbian appears to be a third gender, or, as I shall show, a category that radically problematizes both sex and gender as stable political categories of description.[6]

The female guru, who also refuses to be defined by a heterosexually determined binary and oppositional relation to a man, also refuses the "categories of sex." "Her" refusal challenges our conventional language of description, an ambiguity that is captured in the phrase, "a third gender."[7] The guru embodies the tension between woman and not-woman.

Moreover, the possibility of a "third gender" demonstrates the discontinuity between gender and ontology. According to Butler, gender is a performance, not an essence: "*gender* is not a noun, but neither is it a set of free-floating attributes, for we have seen that the substantive effect of gender is performatively produced and compelled by the regulatory practices of gender coherence. Hence, within the inherited discourse of the metaphysics of substance, gender proves to be performative—that is, constituting the identity it is purported to be. In this sense, gender is always a doing, though not a doing by a subject who might be said to preexist the deed."[8]

The female gurus' performance of a "third gender," however, "radically problematizes both sex and gender as stable political categories of description" in a different manner than the example of the lesbian. For the Hindu-based teachings of contemporary female gurus do point to an essence—shakti, or the divine within. This essence is not understood to be gendered, however. As a "third gender," female gurus perform the tension between this subtle, undifferentiated divine essence (universal) and the dualism of worldly convention, preeminently gender (particular), a dynamic that the female guru is in a unique position to enact. Female gurus simultaneously embody the universal and the particular in a way that male gurus cannot, since "male" is already associated with "universal." Through their performance of this tension, female gurus create spiritual paths that validate embodiment even as they undermine its ultimate significance. A prominent Hindu term for this rapprochement between the divine and the worldly is *lila* or play; the guru's performance is her *lila*.

Performance makes meaning. The female gurus' performance or *lila* will be distinctive to each, both in terms of the ways in which they perform gender, and in the role their performance of gender plays in their performance of leadership. Unlike all of the other twentieth-century gurus profiled in this book, Gurumayi does not have Ma (mother; divine Mother) in her titles.[9] Nor is she understood to be a goddess, as are Sita Devi (Lakshmi), Anandamayi Ma, Jayashri Ma (Adya Shakti Kali), Meera Ma (Adiparashakti), Ma Jaya Sati Bhagavati ("daughter of the black mother Kali"), Karunamayi Ma (Saraswati, Bala Tripurasundari, Lalita, Parvati, Lakshmi), and Ammachi (Devi). In her talks and discourses, Gurumayi does not especially privilege feminine images; discussion of women saints and women devotees as examples of spiritual adepts does regularly occur, but images of goddesses do not. In addition, Gurumayi is not associated with works directly related to the welfare of women specifically, as are Gauri Ma and Anandamayi Ma. She does, however, run socially helpful programs through SYDA, such as the Prasad Project and the Prison Project.[10]

Gurumayi performs gender through repetitive action; primarily, through her feminine appearance. In her live appearances and in official photographs that are sold to devotees for display and contemplation, the guru is a young beauty in robes that flow from the neckline to the wrists and ankles, and she is smiling warmly. In photographs, she is often depicted relating compassionately to animals, such as sitting with a deer or patting a parakeet. In her recent summer programs she has emphasized children, from saving front-row seats for them at her ashram appearances, to scheduling family retreats in the heart of the summer, to writing a children's book. Unlike other female gurus, however, Gurumayi does not seem to engage in physical contact with her devotees, as do Anandamayi Ma and Ammachi; nor in ministrations of the sick, as does Ma Jaya Sati Bhagavati, who houses AIDS patients at her ashram. Generally, Gurumayi does not play a "motherly" role, which accords with the lack of "Ma" in any of her titles. When I asked devotees to use another word besides "guru" to characterize what Gurumayi means to them, they most often responded with "teacher" or "guide"; a few said "goddess," and a few said "mother." Based on this evidence, I view Gurumayi's photographs and decisions on the focus of summer programs to be examples of her distinctive modes of teaching.

Gurumayi's style of appearance tends to be formal, as is appropriate for a revered teacher in the context of a very large organization. She is distinguished from other contemporary female gurus, notably Shree Ma and Meera Ma, who both eschew the development of grand ashrams, in that she is the leader of a worldwide spiritual organization, the SYDA Foundation, which promotes the Siddha Yoga teachings through ashrams, publications, and communications technology.[11] Gurumayi inherited a growing worldwide organization from her predecessor; the extent to which she has built it into a multimillion dollar entity is suggested by her recent appointments of a CEO and a COO of the SYDA Foundation from the business community. The increasing grandeur of Siddha Yoga highlights a key issue in Gurumayi's teaching: the balance between the appearance of the guru in their midst that is expected by devotees, and the absence of the guru as she travels to share her physical presence with her far-flung flock; and its analogue in terms of the spiritual path, the balance between the devotees' reliance on the guru's guidance, and the necessity of their independent motivation and practice toward achieving self-realization.

Groomed for Guruhood

Gurumayi's titles signify her connection to her guru, Swami Muktananda. Her formal name, Swami Chidvilasananda, echoes the title of Swami Muktananda's most famous and influential book, *Play of Consciousness*,[12] and her popular honorific name, Gurumayi, reinforces the continued sense of identity she has with him and his teachings. Further, her autobiographical accounts of her spiritual journey are entitled "Growing up with Baba" and *Ashes at My Guru's Feet*.[13] Thus, lineage is very important in Siddha Yoga: "The contemporary history of Siddha Yoga as a movement is essentially the story of three spiritual masters and their disciples."[14]

Although Siddha Yoga traces its origins to the medieval poet-saints of Maharashtra, the classical philosophers of Kashmiri Shaivism, and the numerous and diverse *siddhas* (perfected, in the sense of liberated, beings) in India and beyond, the first contemporary guru of its lineage was Bhagawan Nityananda (d. 1961), who settled in the village of Ganeshpuri, some ninety kilometers from Bombay, in 1936.[15] A mystic of few words and unconventional behavior, he was understood by villagers to have miraculous powers of helping and healing. Through the explication of Nityananda's disciple and successor, Siddha Yoga understands him to have been a siddha who spontaneously initiated the people around him. "Bhagawan Nityananda, as Swami Muktananda later said, had no need for such ceremonies [as one finds among conventional teachers]. Instead, he would usually give blessings through a piece of fruit or a casual look. Swami Muktananda often said that the uniqueness of his guru lay in this capacity to transmit spiritual knowledge and spiritual awakening spontaneously, without any apparent effort or even, necessarily, any conscious intent."[16] Notably, even people who were not in the presence of Bhagawan Nityananda when he was alive claim a spiritual connection to him. For example, Ma Jaya Sati Bhagavati had visions of Bhagawan Nityananda in 1973, in which he appeared to her in her bathroom, instructing her in Hindu scriptures, practices, and teachings, and requesting that she become celibate, in preparation for her to meet her true guru.[17]

In contrast, Swami Muktananda, Nityananda's successor, is remembered as a charismatic man of many words—he published some fifty pamphlets and books—and as a guru who was very accessible to his devotees, speaking personally to them and laughing with them. Biographies of Swami Muktananda generally divide his life into four periods.[18] The first period is the fifteen years from his birth in 1908 to his brief encounter with Nityananda and decision to depart from home. This was followed by a period of some twenty years of study, including his inititation as a monk of the Saraswati order, his pilgrimages across India, and his return to Maharashtra, where he began to attract devotees. The third period is characterized by his instruction from Nityananda; he experienced initiation from the guru on the day of India's independence, August 15, 1947, and then spent the next nine years away from the guru, effecting the spiritual realization that had been initiated (which is described in his *Play of Consciousness*).

The last period is characterized by Bhagawan Nityananda's designation of Muktananda as his successor, and Swami Muktananda's systematization and universalization of the Siddha Yoga path. In 1956, an event occurred that many devotees understand to have been Bhagawan Nityananda's public designation of Muktananda as his successor. The guru told his disciples to "install" Muktananda in a shrine they had built to honor the guru himself: "In a clear though symbolic fashion, Nityananda with this gesture was installing a living successor rather than offering the devotees a stone idol to worship after his passing."[19] More important than this public transmission of the guruship in the eyes of Siddha Yoga is the private transmission that took place while Bhagawan Nityananda was on his deathbed (his *mahasamadhi*, or entrance into an ultimate meditative state, occurred on August 8, 1961). At that time, the guru thrust his hand into Muktananda's mouth, and whispered secret teachings to him, of which Muktananda has said: "He said, 'The entire world will see you one day.' Some of the other things he told me are very secret. Such things are revealed only to the disciple on the final day."[20]

From the beginning of Swami Muktananda's guruship, Malti, who was to become Swami Chidvilasananda, was on the scene. She was the daughter of a Bombay restaurateur, who with his wife were devotees of Swami Muktananda in the 1950s. Malti Shetty, their oldest child, was born in 1955, and was first brought to the Ganeshpuri ashram was she was five years old. During her childhood, her parents brought her, her sister, and two brothers to the ashram on weekends.

Muktananda's style of weekend visits for devotees to dedicate themselves to spiritual practice was a departure from the traditional *gurukula* system, which may have been inspired by his formerly frequent peregrinations. *Gurukula* means "residence of the guru"; traditionally, it was required that a disciple—and certainly the successor to the guru—would live at the guru's house, to be in his presence at all times. In traditional Indian society, this was a male system, since it was deemed unsuitable in terms of propriety for a young woman to reside at a male guru's home. In India, Swami Muktananda's modification of the *gurukula* system permitted more devotees to practice spiritual discipline with a guru, and it permitted women to participate. This modification was also significant in terms of establishing Siddha Yoga centers around the world.

Notably, once she was old enough to pursue the path to self-realization in a mature fashion, Malti did undertake the traditional *gurukula* mode of study. After Swami Muktananda gave Malti formal *shaktipat* initiation at the age of fourteen, she began to live the traditional *gurukula* life: "Muktananda had pursued a solitary journey, often far from his guru's physical presence. Malti's destiny was to bring her into constant contact with her guru."[21]

In the Siddha Yoga tradition, Malti is understood to have possessed a combination of natural spiritual power, sincere dedication to working her way through an intense spiritual journey, and devotion to her guru.

Through her extraordinary natural power, she was set apart from others. For example, around the time of her initiation, Swami Muktananda singled her out from other disciples, by comparing her to a flame, which is a traditional symbol of the awakened shakti: " 'You know,' he said, 'that girl Malti is a blazing fire. One day she will light up the entire world.' "[22] Devotees view Swami Muktananda's statement as foreshadowing his selection of her to be his successor.

Through her performance of intense spiritual practices and through her reliance on the grace of her guru, Malti is understood to have been like others. For example, as her sprirtual journey progressed, she mastered the "physical *kriyās*, purificatory movements of the body that are characteristic of certain phases of inner development," and to have purified her experience of devotional love; yet these only served to make her long for the supreme state: "Now I began to realize that I would never be satisfied until I attained Baba's [Swami Muktananda's] own state. So I made one more request—I asked him for Self-realization. This time Baba said gently, 'It isn't time yet. When the right time comes, that will also happen.' "[23]

Siddha Yoga understands that Malti continued to progress toward the goal of self-realization—identified as "Baba's own state" and thus signifying the experience of unity—through her work as Swami Muktananda's translator. She was appointed to the position in 1975, during Swami Muktananda's second world tour, in Oakland, California. Her appointment occurred in the context of her guru's universalization and systematization of the Siddha Yoga path through his establishment of institutions in the United States, including the weekend Intensive program, through which *shaktipat* is transmitted en masse (first introduced in Aspen, Colorado, in 1974); the Oakland ashram (where devotees renovated the Hotel Stanford in 1975); the administrative body of Siddha Yoga in the West, SYDA (Siddha Yoga Dham—"abode of Siddha Yoga"—Associates); and a set of guidelines for those teaching courses on aspects of Siddha Yoga's theology.[24] In a real sense, Siddha Yoga as it is known today was established during the pivotal year of 1974–1975.

However, Malti's role as a translator of Swami Muktananda's public talks went beyond furthering the establishment of Siddha Yoga in the United States through translating her guru's Hindi-language discussions to English-speaking devotees. She experienced an "attunement" with her guru, a meeting of the minds, in which she was able to convey the essence of his teaching to his followers. According to devotees, this ability enhanced her own spiritual development: "Swami Muktananda always said that when a disciple's mind becomes inwardly united with the guru's, the disciple's inner state gradually becomes purified and uplifted by the guru's own elevated state of consciousness."[25] Malti was understood to be progressing toward "Baba's own state." In 1980, the guru decreed that she would deliver the public talks on Sunday nights; and in 1981, she was made executive vice-president of SYDA Foundation.

Purity is a major theme in Siddha Yoga's officially sanctioned representation of Malti's spiritual progress. She purified her body through physical *kriyas*, her heart through devotional love, and her inner state through intertwining her consciousness with her guru's. "Purity" in this religious sense means a mind and body devoted to guru and God; a complete realization of the divine power within; and a rejection of self-interest. The culmination of this path of purity was Malti's official initiation into the status of *sannyasa*, or ascetic mode, at the age of twenty-six, by her guru in April 1982, in Ganeshpuri, India. This was a necessary step to publicly recognize and affirm Malti's purity, and to raise her to the status of co-successor to Swami Muktananda, since the guru had named her brother, Nityananda, as his successor six months prior, and her brother had undergone initiation into *sannyasa* in 1980, in Los Angeles. Tradition understands her ceremony of renunciation to have indicated her unique status, especially insofar as Malti's head was shaved—in contrast to other women swamis in Siddha Yoga—and insofar as the guru took an active role in the proceedings, including the cutting of her hair.[26]

Shaving the head has cross-cultural resonances as a religiously meaningful ritual and symbol of shedding pride, and especially as an emblem of the deeper meaning of shedding the self, or ego. However, in terms of Siddha Yoga's own symbology, the setting apart of Malti—known as Swami Chidvilasananda after the ceremony—from other women renouncers (swamis) in the organization through the head shaving suggests a degree of masculinization of her *sannyasa* ceremony, which in turn supports the "third gender" status evoked through her ascetic status (purity; refusal of sex). Although the tradition does not interpret the action beyond an indication of Swami Chidvilasananda's status as "unique," it can be suggested that it was important that the sister's initiation mirror the brother's, since they were designated as co-successors to the guru, and the head shaving may have indicated that Malti had achieved a greater degree of purity and spiritual advancement than other women adepts in the organization. Although photos of Malti as the guru's translator show her with her long hair swept gracefully up in a bun (and often wearing reading glasses), photos of Swami Chidvilasananda over the past nearly two decades portray her with short-cropped hair (and no reading glasses), seemingly as an ongoing reminder of her initiation.

Within three years, the purity issue took on even greater significance as a defining feature of a Siddha Yoga guru. On May 3, 1982, Swami Nityananda and Swami Chidvilasananda took their final monastic vows, along with forty-three other candidates; on May 5 there was a ceremony to honor Swami Muktananda as the Siddha Yoga guru; and on May 8, the brother and sister were consecrated as his designated successors.[27] Sixteen days after Swami Muktananda passed into mahasamadhi on October 2, the two were officially installed on the Siddha Yoga throne (gaddi), or seat of the lineage, by brahman priests. They worked together for three years, until, in disputed circumstances, Swami Nityananda resigned his position and underwent a ceremony to remove his sannyasa vows in October 1985. In official Siddha Yoga statements made shortly after the event, and in comments Nityananda himself made to a journalist several years later, the issue was that he had broken his vow of celibacy.[28]

In the Siddha Yoga perspective, it is important to highlight Gurumayi's purity for several reasons: she is a pure person, her purity continues the tradition established by the gurus before her, and her purity is a constitutive credential for the spiritual leadership of the organization. In another view, it is possible to suggest that purity may have been an implicit credential for the first two gurus, but that it became explicit and greatly emphasized during the succession dispute and is now a primary lens through which to understand and represent Swami Chidvilasananda's spiritual journey.

Taking this latter view, it enhanced the guru's position that, although a "third gender" persona informed her initiation, she maintains a feminine persona in her appearance as guru. Traditional stories from India extol the powerful virtues of the chaste wife, chief among them her steadfastness and devotion to her husband, even if he is lacking in moral character. Stories of women saints appropriate these virtues and direct them to God, often creating discord with husbands or family members who expected their daughters to marry one day. In either case, the chastity of women—whether the woman is sexually and emotionally faithful to a husband or whether the woman eschews physical sex and is emotionally devoted to God—is represented in traditional Hindu stories, epics, and biographies as the source of their power. In some instances, the heroine can use this power to avenge wrongs done to her husband; in others, she can use it to shame her husband for his bad behavior; in still others, she can use it to hold fast to her spiritual aspirations in spite of social pressures.

Significantly, in contrast to many traditional stories of women saints and the biographies of most female gurus (though seemingly parallel to Jayashri Ma and Shree Ma), Swami Chidvilasananda's biography is unusual in that she is a young female Hindu spiritual leader whose biography does not represent marriage as having been an expectation for her; the issue does not appear even to have arisen. Rather than frame her purity by the presence or contested absence of a spouse, published sources emphasize her spiritual practices, culminating in her taking of the sannyasa vows. Thus, the biography of Swami Chidvilasananda merges the purity of women affirmed by traditional sources with the traditionally male-defined practice of sannyasa; the traditional discontinuity between the two models is alluded to in the anomaly of her shaved head. Her spiritual trajectory admits no doubts about the credentials of this female guru. Indeed, six months prior to her brother's reliquishment of his status as co-guru, at the time of the three-year anniversary of her initiation into *sannyasa* and anointment as the guru's successor, Gurumayi wrote the following reflection on her initiation: "Everything within and without/ Was bathed in white light./ No more questions, no more doubts,/ No more of those things which had gnawed at me."[29]

Being There: The South Fallsburg Ashram

In the United States, the South Fallsburg ashram, about ninety miles from Manhattan, has a special status as the world headquarters of the Siddha Yoga Dham Associates (SYDA) Foundation. The 550-acre ashram sits in Catskill country, a region famous from the 1930s into the 1960s as the "Borscht Belt," a recreation center for Jews from Manhattan. Swami Muktananda had apparently been attracted to the area by "the mountains, the weather, the sparse population and the proximity to New York City," not to mention the economic decline and resulting decrease in property prices in the mid-1970s. After using rented quarters in the area for several years in the mid-1970s, SYDA bought three of the best-known hotels within a seven-year period: the Gilbert Hotel in 1979, the Windsor in 1983, and the Brickman in 1986, transforming this large parcel of the Catskills into an ashram.[30]

The transformation of the Catskills is not simply to be explained by the displacement of one ethnic group, the Jews, by another, the Indians, which is a familiar model in urban and suburban areas. For one thing, the Jews are still there—most prominently, Hasidic Jews; for another, the majority of people associated with SYDA in the United States are not Indians but people of European descent. Rather, the transformation is one of ethos: from swimming pools and cabaret to spiritual campus.

The transformation had began a few years earlier than SYDA's purchase. "The Windsor had already made the leap from resort to retreat; it had been owned since 1976 by the Transcendental Meditation [TM] movement, which sold it to SYDA."[31] And it involves more than the development of Asian spiritual movements in the United States. When I visited the SYDA ashram twice in the summer of 1999, I noticed on the drive through the immediate area that there were numerous Jewish schools and camps for young people, advertised by signs in English and Hebrew; also, the riverside park near—but not in—the ashram was a recreation site for many Hasidic Jewish families. There is, then, a very traditional, spiritually devout population of Jews that visits the Catskills to educate their children in traditional values or to have a family vacation in this context. True, there is a residue of the club circuit in the area— Buddy Hackett was performing at one of the nearby hotels when I attended a spiritual seminar at the ashram that summer—but it is generally conceded that a new "Borscht Belt by the sea" has sprung up along Atlantic Beach, N.Y., in Nassau County.[32] The presence of Jewish schools and the SYDA ashram suggest that today, when people come to the Catskills to get away from it all, they actively seek to enhance their spirituality.

TM and then SYDA thus contributed to the spiritualization of the Catskills. In an important new book discussing the establishment of Asian traditions in the United States, *Asian Religions in America: A Documentary History*, Thomas Tweed and Stephen Prothero identify "mapping" as a key strategy. "*Mapping* refers to the ways that individuals and groups orient themselves in the natural landscape and social terrain, transforming both in the process."[33] In the case of Siddha Yoga, it is possible to see elements of the rapprochement between an Asian spiritual path and an American context at work.[34] Siddha Yoga's promotion of a "spiritual" rather than a "religious" path (similar to TM before it) is an example of this process, for Siddha Yoga successfully seeks to attract members of other religions, mindful of the exclusivity of membership the term "religion" signifies in the context of predominating monotheistic traditions. In addition, the organization's emphasis on spirituality rather than religion evokes the traditional Hindu theory of dharma as a way of life; yet it also appeals to the themes of personal quest and "ecstatic individualism" in American tradition (for example, Thoreau), or what Vasudha Narayanan calls the "self-help approach" to the religious quest.[35] In another example, the South Fallsburg ashram is in a relatively rural area, as would be a traditional retreat in India; yet promotional materials for SYDA make it clear that its over six hundred ashrams worldwide are strategically placed "near where people work and live"; hence its proximity to New York City.[36]

During Swami Muktananda's guruship, the South Fallsburg ashram was the place to be during the summer. "In the summer of 1979, Siddha Yoga students assembled from all over the world for what would become a yearly tradition: the summer retreat in South Fallsburg. These retreats became the setting for the international Siddha Yoga community to define itself, to take form. Several thousand people could experience living in an ashram, following a discipline, performing spiritual practices in a supportive environment."[37]

It was the custom for the guru to be in residence during the summer retreat, and to be accessible to the devotees. For example, Swami Muktananda offered "evening programs of lectures, question-and-answer sessions, and darshan [allowing people to view him for the purpose of honoring him]."[38] During the Intensives, which are two-day seminars he had designed for the transmission of *shaktipat*, Muktananda would deliver two lectures, answer questions, and lead chanting and mediation; during each meditation session, he would wander through the room "brushing every person present with his peacock feather wand, awakening the *kuṇḍalini* by touch."[39] One devotee remembers the energy of Muktananda's Intensives: "It was wild. The shakti was bouncing off the walls. People would be so wired by it that they would stay up talking, unable even to think about going to sleep." Other characterizations by devotees underscore the robustness of Muktananda's persona in their collective memory: his smile, his raucous laughter, his spontaneity, his mirth, and his bold gestures. In his teachings, Muktananda always emphasized that the guru need not be present in order for the transmission of *shaktipat*, an assertion that was supported by the following rationales: it is the intention of the guru, not the physical presence that is important; trained swamis can bestow *shaktipat* onto others on the authority of the guru; it is the self-realization of devotee that is most important; and that this transformation can occur spontaneously, through multiple modes, including being at the ashram, hearing a mantra, or seeing a photograph of the guru.[40] However, it is a recognizable pattern in Muktananda's activities that, to the extent possible given that he was transforming Siddha Yoga into an international organization, he sought to personalize the experience of *shaktipat* through his regular presence at the South Fallsburg ashram during the summer, as a center of his orbit of visits to ashrams around the world during his three tours.

For several years, Gurumayi embodied her guru's paradigm of personal interaction with devotees at the South Fallsburg ashram. Many devotees have provided testimonials that indicate that at the ashram, the guru "engaged directly with their weaknesses or negative tendencies" in order to help them spiritually progress to a more positive state.[41] Indeed, such testimonials still have a role in the Intensive programs. Longtime devotees also remember that Gurumayi used the peacock wand at Intensives. Increasingly, however, the guru sought to bring a different kind of order to the ashram. In 1994, the guru and the two Executive Management Councils of Shree Muktananda Ashram and Gurudev Siddha Peeth (in India) determined that:

> the ashrams were beginning to serve more as traditional *dharmaśā-lās* (temporary rest stations for a large number of pilgrims on a pilgrimage elsewhere) than as autonomous spiritual centers in which students not only performed seva [selfless service] but intensely practiced the contemplative aspects of sadhana [spiritual discipline]. Accordingly, in 1994, Swami Chidvilasananda began to shift the mood at the ashrams back to the more traditional *gurukula* model. Since then, ashram residents have been more like traditional Indian [students] who demonstrate their seriousness in pursuing their sadhana under the tutelage of the guru.[42]

The problem, carefully stated in this passage from within the tradition, was that the ashram became a stop for "pilgrims on a pilgrimage elsewhere." According to long-term devotees, people were coming to the ashram for superficial reasons, seemingly out of curiosity rather than spiritual discipline. Some of these devotees, who were there at the time, expressed to me that they felt people were overusing the Intensives, participating in as many as possible in a summer, without then undertaking the spiritual practices that are both initiated, and supported, by the Intensive.

Further, there was an official change in policy in 1996, when "it was announced that the practice known as the 'darshan line,' where students had the opportunity to spend an individual moment with Gurumayi, would no longer be a regular part of programs with her."[43] The tradition's account of that year indicates that there were still plenty of devotees experiencing personal interaction with the guru, although a number of the encounters were through dreams or visions. More recently, the tradition has sought to emphasize that even people who have not met the guru in person have experienced her shakti.[44]

This emphasis on the transmission of *shaktipat* and subsequent spiritual progress of devotees in the absence of the guru informed the activities at the South Fallsburg ashram a few years later. In the summer of 1999, Intensives and other programs were held at the Shree Muktananda Ashram in South Fallsburg while the guru was in residence at the Gurudev Siddha Peeth in Ganeshpuri, India. When I attended the Guru Purnima Intensive at the end of July that year, long-term devotees gave me the impression that they had never before participated in an Intensive at the Shree Muktananda Ashram in the absence of the guru, and that it was unusual for the guru not to be in residence there during the summer.[45] These same people were, however, sensitive to the fact that I was at the ashram for an Intensive, and they quickly affirmed that the Intensive in the absence of the guru would be an efficacious transmission of shakti through the guru's *shaktipat*, on the following grounds: First, the ashram is an especially concentrated zone of, and is permeated by, the guru's shakti and her intention (*sankalpa*) to bestow shakti; second, the swamis who would be leading the Intensive are authorized by the guru to bestow *shaktipat*; and third, the most important goal is realization of the inner self.

The reasons the devotees cited for the efficacy of the Intensive are recognizable as teachings from Muktananda; however, it may be considered an innovation on the part of Gurumayi to foreground these teachings by her absence. The modality of this change is emblematic of the dynamic tension between tradition and innovation involved in maintaining and enhancing a lineage. In a related example, another change that Gurumayi made was to rename the South Fallsburg ashram. Muktananda had called it the Shree Nityananda Ashram, in honor of his guru; after Muktananda's *samadhi*, Gurumayi renamed it the Shree Muktananda Ashram, in honor of her guru.[46] The innovation of changing the name of the ashram is contextualized by the tradition of honoring one's guru. Indeed, for the devotees, the ashram is an emblem of Gurumayi's generosity and humility. Time and again they told me that the ashram is "the guru's gift to and for us," which is also an affirmation of Gurumayi's purity of motive with respect to the wealth of the ashram.

The significance of the absence of the guru is also tied to the guru's own *lila*, or play. Long-term devotees and staff members told to me that the guru moves by her own lights, without necessarily giving anyone advance warning or explanation. The ashram, and for that matter books the guru has written, as well as photographs of the guru, are vehicles of shakti through the guru's intention (*sankalpa*).[47] According to devotees, however, there is a special charge of shakti that the guru bestows upon those in her presence; thus, the long-term devotees I spoke to at the Intensive passionately recounted their experiences in her presence, and encouraged me to try to take her darshan one day.

Throughout the early period of her guruship, Gurumayi interacted individually with devotees during Intensives, much like her guru, Muktananda. In the mid- and late 1990s, as evidenced by changes in policy and the guru's actions, especially concerning the South Fallsburg ashram, there was a period of transformation in the Siddha Yoga program. The curtailing of the guru's interaction with devotees and then the absence of the guru constituted a break with earlier styles of leadership enacted by Muktananda and Gurumayi herself.

Several nuances can be attributed to this change in policy and leadership style; what they have in common is an affirmation of the seriousness of the Siddha Yoga path and practices at the ashram. The guru and ashram trustees, as noted earlier, sought to limit access to the ashram, in order to attract spiritual seekers and to discourage curiosity seekers. In keeping with the teachings, the devotee can experience the guru's intention and shakti even though she is not in the presence of the guru; also, the absence of the guru highlights the fact that it is necessary for the devotee to maintain or intensify her own efforts towards self-realization. Sociologically, it is reasonable to speculate that in the first decade of Gurumayi's leadership there was entirely too much outside emphasis on her personhood as a young and beautiful woman, including media attention and celebrity, which was born from curiosity, interest in a woman spiritual leader, and the controversy over succession. The guru's decisions and behavior (her *lila*) sought to refocus the discussion on the spirituality of the path and the ashram.

Currently, the South Fallsburg ashram maintains a yearly schedule of devotional activities, with summer as the main "season" for programs and spiritual visitors. The guru appears at the South Fallsburg ashram on selected special occasions, such as her birthday celebration in June 2000; Guru Purnima in July 2001;[48] and January 1 (the yearly message presentation), 2002.

Being There through Technology

When Muktananda spoke of the guru's shakti as accessible to the devotee even in the absence of the guru through the guru's *sankalpa* (intention), there was a resonance between his assertion and his experience, since he had spent much of his discipleship apart from his guru. His performance of his own guruhood, however, was characterized by extraordinary accessibility; for example, Malti herself was nearly inseparable from him. Gurumayi's absence enacts her guru's teaching, but stands in contrast to her experience as his disciple. In this context, she has developed the use of technology to share her public appearances before a select group of devotees in a certain place at a certain time with all devotees, anywhere and at anytime.

The videotaping of teaching sessions was an approach pioneered by Muktananda: for example, his "Let Chanting Transform Your Life," "Wherever You Are You Attain the Self," and "I Am That" videotapes; notably, Malti appears on the tapes as his translator. Gurumayi, who is both fluent and graceful in English, has greatly developed this approach by videotaping a number of her talks; a regularly delivered talk in this genre is the yearly message. This is an innovation on Gurumayi's part, which she initiated in the years 1993–1994, and is now an established vehicle for her teachings.[49] Every January 1, the guru unveils a phrase for contemplation and delivers a talk on its meaning for assembled devotees. Examples include "Believe in Love" (2000), "Approach the

Present with Your Heart's Content: Make It a Blessed Event" (2001), and "Abide in Silence" (2002). As one of the teachers (swamis) at a South Fallsburg seminar noted: "The message is the frequency on which Gurumayi is broadcasting this year." The session at which the guru unveils the yearly message is videotaped and made available to devotees for purchase, so that devotees can experience the guru's presentation of the message, study the message in the context of a message course at the ashram, or study the message on their own at home.[50]

The yearly message has a special status as both the theme and the mode of practice for the year, and thus it provides a common focus for all devotees.[51] It is simultaneously a teaching, a mantra, and an image that relates directly to the devotees' practice. As Thomas Coburn has remarked, Gurumayi teaches through images.[52] According to Swami Durgananda, a persistent image in her teachings has been a "flame"; specifically, *yajna*, an ancient term for the fire used in sacrificial ritual, with the related meanings of intense yogic discipline, knowledge, and higher spiritual wisdom. Notably, fire is an image that Muktananda chose to characterize Malti's shakti, as noted earlier. In her reflections on the image of a flame, Gurumayi brings together both spiritual discipline and action in the world through a theory of unselfish action. "For several years, in the mid-1980s, she held courses in the ashram that explored the central theme of fire as a metaphor not only for yogic practice but for life itself. 'Life is an offering' and 'Let every action be an offering' are phrases that she often uses. . . . If one overall ethical teaching could be said to characterize her ministry, it is the teaching of unselfish action."[53]

The primary locus for the practice of unselfish action is the ashram, where it is institutionalized as *seva* or service. Even with the outreach of the guru's yearly message on videotape, the ashram remains a center; the guru always performs the message before devotees at an ashram, usually either in India or in California, although, notably, she unveiled the 2002 message at the South Fallsburg ashram. Further, in the daily program at the ashram, *seva* constitutes most of the activity, framed by sessions of chanting, meditation, and vegetarian meals. *Seva* includes serving in the food halls (cooking, serving, cleaning), cleaning the residence halls, performing work on the grounds, among many other activities. In her discourse on *seva*, the guru asserts that, as a distinctive performance by devotees, it transforms the ashram from a structure into a living spiritual center: "When you see the ashram, what do you truly perceive? Do you perceive it only with your physical eyes? Blessings have been cultivated here by hours and seasons and years of seva. All this seva has created a pond of nectar where seekers can quench their spiritual thirst. Seva creates a pond of nectar through which you experience the deeper purpose of life, the immortality of the Self."[54]

In addition to the ashram orientation, the yearly messages seek to widen the field of spiritual action, especially selfless service, to the outside world. The yearly messages tend to use more accessible language than the Sanskrit *yajna*, although they are also based on teachings from classical Hindu sources and their explication involves discussion of Sanskrit terms. In using more accessible language for the messages, such as enthusiasm and love, the guru focuses on the essential and good qualities of humankind, and their expression in daily life.

For example, the 1999 yearly message was "A golden mind, a golden life," which was based on teachings in the *Bhagavad Gita*. The *Bhagavad Gita* is the classical Sanskrit bhakti text promoting action in the world; in it, the protagonist, Arjuna, is instructed by Lord Krishna to perform his worldly duties with spiritual discipline. As a focus for contemplation, the yearly message encourages this approach. According to the seminar on the 1999 yearly message, led by Swami Purvananda and Swami Indirananda, the yearly message is an interactive mantra: "It is for everyone's darshan every day of the year; it is itself a deity or awakened being, from which to ask questions; it is a message installed inside the self; and it is a dear and trusted friend."

Gurumayi unveiled the 1999 message at the Santa Clara, California, center.[55] In an enactment of power, she sat on the *gaddi* (throne) on a stage before thousands of her devotees; in an enactment of humility, she sat under the gaze of a large photograph of Muktananda. In a visual and verbal statement of her special status and thus remove from her devotees, she sat apart from them and she alone spoke; in a visual and verbal statement of her intimacy with her devotees, she made eye contact, laughed with them, and spoke playfully at times. The guru's performance also involved engaging the video audience, since much of her eye contact was directed at the video camera—and thus into the eyes of the future viewer.

Leading up to its unveiling, she called the message "an initiation for the whole year," the power of which "will infuse your understanding and efforts with grace." Then, extending the audience's anticipation amid their knowing laughter, she playfully asked, "Do you recall having heard that the most precious gifts come in small packages?" After a pause, she revealed the message, "A golden mind, a golden life," which was received with enthusiastic applause.

Early in the talk, the guru suggested that she sought to blend the truth of self-realization with its application in daily life, or the harmonizing of knowledge and experience. A cornerstone in this effort is to turn the mind into a "golden mind": Just as "gold ore is valuable, but becomes more valuable in the hands of an expert" because it becomes refined, so, too, the "mind also needs to be purified in order to recover its own lustre." Citing Muktananda, Gurumayi called this process, "winning the grace of your own mind."

Toward this end, the focus of her talk was on five spiritual disciplines that should be practiced as "preparation for self-realization." She derived the five disciplines from a verse from the *Bhagavad Gita*, chapter 17, verse 16, which lists five "austerities (*tapas*) of mind": peace of mind, gentleness, silence, self-restraint, and purity of being, in the guru's terminology.[56] In developing this theme, the guru related each austerity to scripture, examples from daily life, and in relation to the message.

For example, in speaking of gentleness (*saumya*), the guru said that this is the "natural state" of the mind, but that in today's world one must consciously practice gentleness in order "to rid the mind of its tendency to bristle."

Like gold, which is a soft metal and is the least reactive among metals (it will not rust or tarnish when exposed to oxygen), so, too, the mind has both strength and elasticity. In order to develop strength of mind, one must practice discrimination (*vivek*) of that which is beneficial from that which is pleasurable. In support of her discussion, the guru recited another verse from the *Bhagavad Gita* that discussed the two approaches, concluding that beneficial actions free one from greed and have positive long-term results. In order to develop elasticity of mind, one must experience humility; for example, experiencing God within oneself during *shaktipat*. In closing her discussion of this particular mental discipline, the guru led the audience in a chant of the sacred syllable "Om" before turning to the next mental discipline.

The synergy of the yearly message in bringing together the multiple forces of guru and devotees, teachings and practice, ashram and wider world, and community and individual, is currently being amplified to an even greater extent by the technology of the global satellite broadcast. This technology, another innovation of Gurumayi's, has frequently been used for Intensives;[57] Its extension to the yearly message of 2002 is a milestone in the accessibility of the guru and the Siddha Yoga teachings, according to the official calendar:

> Each year, Gurumayi offers us a Siddha Yoga Message of timeless, universal teachings that speak to each one of us in our own lives. As Siddha Yoga students, when we experience, study and contemplate these teachings over time, we find that they can lead us to the source of our own inner wisdom. And when we come together as a global community to study these teachings, we find that there is even greater potential for us to move forward in our spiritual lives.
>
> I am delighted to let you know that this year we will all be able to do this through our first-ever year-long global curriculum focused on the Siddha Yoga Message for 2002: *Abide in Silence*. As you will see in this *Siddha Yoga Global Calendar of Events 2002*, there are many opportunities to participate together as a global sangham through regular broadcasts of Intensives and Siddha Yoga Message Courses for 2002. There are also opportunities to focus deeply on spiritual practices in the transforming retreat atmosphere at Shree Muktananda Ashram, Gurudev Siddha Peeth, or at the European Retreats in the Netherlands.[58]

This description by the chief teachings officer highlights a theme emphasized in this essay: the simultaneity of the universal and the particular as constitutive of the guru's nature and teachings. For example, shakti is both common to all and invested particularly in the guru; the guru's message is both timeless and appropriate to a given time; Siddha Yoga teachings are experienced in a community and individually. Through the global satellite, the guru is simultaneously in one place and in many places; the experience of her presence, intimacy, and interactive performance—"being there"—is expanded. The moment of a particular performance of shakti is universalized.

A Woman's Religious Leadership

To what extent is Gurumayi's leadership "feminine"? Catherine Wessinger suggests that, in contrast to many women religious leaders who come to their leadership primarily through charisma, Gurumayi has come to her leadership within an established institutional setting.[59] Pointing to this distinction, remarking on Siddha Yoga's use of masculine God-language (such as, Lord, Shiva), and betraying her own mistrust of submission to a guru, Wessinger concludes that the guru in Siddha Yoga is characterized by "patriarchal authority, even when it is being exercised by a woman," even though in her conclusion she states that women are attracted to Siddha Yoga because there is a deemphasis on the masculine nature of divinity, there are women in specialized religious positions (the swamis), and the tradition does not limit women's roles to wife and mother.[60]

There is also a problem with "fit" between Gurumayi and the analysis of female-dominated religions provided by Susan Starr Sered. Gurumayi is the leader of what could be considered a female-dominated religion (acknowledging that Siddha Yoga does not call itself a "religion"), since a woman is the leader, 20 percent of her teachers are women (the swamis), and most of the students are female.[61] Many of the characteristics Sered identifies for female leaders of female-dominated religions, however, including developing a leadership slowly, emphasizing healing, and inheriting leadership from mothers do not apply.[62]

My approach in this chapter has been to question the analysis of "feminine" ways of religious leadership through reference to positing a feminine "essence," drawing on Judith Butler's analysis of gender. "Feminine" is a performance of characteristics that are defined in patriarchal discourse as the opposite of "masculine" traits; if we do not acknowledge the role of patriarchal discourse in defining these traits, then we are ourselves uncritically reaffirming that discourse when we attempt to identify "feminine" ways of religious leadership.

In Siddha Yoga, Gurumayi has automomous power to shape the ongoing tradition as she sees fit, developing innovative strategies that relate to but build distinctively on received tradition. Her performance creates her personhood and her leadership. As we have seen, the guru acts in ways that the dominant patriarchal discourse would classify as "feminine"; further, she acts in ways that this discourse would classify as "masculine." The way that Gurumayi's performance serves to undermine this discourse is not by an oscillation between these two modes, however, but by her refusal to accept a definition of self that reifies these oppositions. A prominent theme in her refusal is the simultaneity of the universal and the particular in the guru's performance and in her teachings. She validates both body and spirit, especially in her teaching on *seva*; affirms a mutual relationship between guidance and independent practice; is present while absent; enacts honor through humility; and universalizes the individual self through shakti.

NOTES

I would like to thank the officers and scholars of the Muktabodha Indological Research Institute, including David Kempton, William Mahony, and Paul Muller-Ortega, for their kind reception at the South Fallsburg ashram and their sharing of ideas. This chapter contains my own formulations, however.

1. Muller-Ortega, "Shaktipat," p. 410.

2. Ibid., p. 409.

3. "The name came from an *abhanga*, a devotional song by the Maharashtrian poet-saint Tukadhyada which has the refrain 'Avadali Gurumayi.' In Marathi, *gurumāyi* means 'guru-mother,' although a closely related Sanskrit word, *gurumayi*, means 'one who is filled with the guru' "; Durgananda, "To See the World Full of Saints," p. 605, n. 247.

4. Personal observation at the ashram, supported by discussion with several long-term devotees (some with twenty years' experience). It was an interesting feature of my participant-observation fieldwork experience that I blended in with the dominant group. There was diversity among the devotees, including Caucasian men, African American men and women, Asian women and men, and Latino women and men. There was not as much diversity among socioeconomic classes; there were very wealthy devotees, but I did not see any lower-middle-class devotees.

5. I am careful in my wording here, because Anandamayi Ma was married while she was a guru, and Meera Ma is married. Also, Ma Jaya Sati Bhagavati was married and had children prior to becoming a guru.

6. Butler, *Gender Trouble*, pp. 143–44.

7. A. K. Ramanujan discussed bhakti saints as "a kind of third gender" because "the lines between male and female are crossed and recrossed so many times," in his "Talking to God in the Mother Tongue." Lisa Hallstrom discusses this meaning of the "third gender" in her article on Anandamayi Ma in this volume.

8. Butler, *Gender Trouble*, p. 33. See also her further remarks on "performativity" in *Bodies that Matter: On the Discursive Limits of "Sex"* (New York: Routledge, 1993), pp. 1–23, esp. pp. 2–3, 7–8, 12, 15.

9. However, Swami Durgananda understands the title Gurumayi to contain a reference to "mother" in the Marathi language. See note 3 above.

10. Under Gurumayi's leadership, Siddha Yoga runs programs that help people in need with medical, nutritional, and educational support (the Prasad Project), and people in prison (the Prison Project).

11. For an official discussion of the relationship between Siddha Yoga and the SYDA Foundation, see http://www.siddhayoga.org/community/syda/syda.html.

12. *Chitshakti Vilas* (Hindi, 1970); *Chitshakti Vilas* (English, unabridged, 1972); republished as *Play of Consciousness*, 1974, 1978. See Brooks, *Meditation Revolution*, Appendix 1, p. 571. On the power of the book: "many seekers over the years have actually received shaktipat while reading *Play of Consciousness*, as if the text itself were imbued with Muktananda's spiritual energy" (*Meditation Revolution*, p. 69).

13. Malti (Swami Chidvilasananda), "Growing up with Baba"; and *Ashes at My Guru's Feet*.

14. Durgananda, "To See the World Full of Saints," p. 3. The volume *Meditation Revolution* represents an officially sanctioned scholarly discussion of the history and theology of Siddha Yoga. Since my interest is in understanding and analyzing the ways in which Siddha Yoga represents itself, I draw on this volume in this section.

15. On the connection with Maharashtra poet-saints and philosophers of Kashmiri Shaivism, as well as a general discussion of the category of *siddha*, see Gold, "Guru's Body, Guru's Abode," esp. pp. 231–234. For a detailed discussion of the "classificatory category" of *siddha*, see Muller-Ortega, "The Siddha," esp. pp. 181–200.

16. Durgananda, "To See the World Full of Saints," p. 18. As with Swami Muktananda's discussion of Bhagawan Nityananda, the published accounts as well as devotees' oral reflections on the lives of all three of the gurus of Siddha Yoga are framed by piety and hagiography.

17. Discussed in Vasudha Narayanan's article in this volume. Narayanan quotes Ma as describing Nityananda as "naked except for a little loincloth, a fat man in a diaper . . ."

18. The identification of the four periods and discussion of them is drawn from Thursby, "Siddha Yoga: Swami Muktananda and the Seat of Power," pp. 3–5 on the Web site.

19. Durgananda, "To See the World Full of Saints," p. 42. See also Thursby, "Succession in the Siddha Yoga Movement," pp. 6–7 on the Web site.

20. From Swami Muktananda, *Where Are You Going? A Guide to the Spiritual Journey* (1981); cited in Durgananda, "To See the World Full of Saints," p. 48.

21. Durgananda, "To See the World Full of Saints," pp. 65–66.

22. Cited ibid., p. 65.

23. Chidvilasananda, "Growing up with Baba, Part II," p. 18. Cited in Durgananda, "To See the World Full of Saints," p. 67.

24. See Durgananda, "To See the World Full of Saints," pp. 92–98.

25. Ibid., p. 99.

26. Ibid., p. 118.

27. Thursby, "Siddha Yoga," p. 8 on the Web site.

28. In her essay, Swami Durgananda puts the emphasis on Nityananda's "lack of committment to his role as guru" ("To See the World Full of Saints," p. 131); she cites Gene Thursby's article to present the sexual nature of the issue: "Because [Nityananda] reportedly claimed that he was a victim of intimidation, [the ashram] had to make public that he had resigned due to the shame of having broken his monastic vows, thereby having made himself unfit to guide others. It also made him unfit to continue to serve as head of the Shree Gurudev Siddha Peeth, the home institution of the Siddha Yoga movement and a public trust in India, because lifelong celibacy was a requirement of the office" (Thursby, "Siddha Yoga," pp. 176–77; cited in Durgananda, "To See the World Full of Saints," p. 132).

Nityananda spoke to journalist Lis Harris in the winter of 1993–1994; Harris's article recieved mixed responses from devotees and former devotees; "Oh Guru, Guru, Guru," p. 102.

At the 1999 American Academy of Religion annual conference in Boston there was a panel session in which scholars—some of whom were former devotees—reviewed the volume *Meditation Revolution*. The session became emotional when some of the scholars criticized the volume for not providing a detailed discussion of events and allegations.

29. Chidvilasananda, *Ashes at My Guru's Feet*, pp. 30–32; cited in Swami Durgananda, "To See the World Full of Saints," p. 119.

30. Zuckoff, "Borscht Belt Meditates a New Existence," p. 15.

31. Ibid.

32. Wilgoren, "Sea, Sand and Seven-Card Stud."

33. Tweed and Prothero, *Asian Religions in America*, p. 5, drawing on publications by Tweed, Jonathan Z. Smith, and Charles H. Long. An additional resource for the study of yoga organizations in the United States (including Siddha Yoga) is Thursby, "Hindu Movements since Midcentury." On the role of gurus in the establishment of Hinduism in America, see Karen Pechilis Prentiss, "The Pattern of Hinduism and Hindu Temple Building in the U.S."

34. The Siddha Yoga Web site, http://www.siddhayoga.org/community/centers/index.html, lists Siddha Yoga meditation centers and ashrams in twenty-eight U.S. states, with the largest concentration in the Northeast.

35. Vasudha Narayanan presented information on self-help and Hinduism in America in a paper she gave as a keynote speaker at the American Academy of Religion's midwestern regional meeting in March 1998. See also her discussion in her website with the Harvard Pluralism Project Affiliates Web page.

36. Information from the SYDA Web site, http://www.syda.org.

37. Durgananda, "To See the World Full of Saints," p. 111.

38. Ibid.

39. Ibid., pp. 92–93.

40. See ibid., pp. 93, 98, and 141; see also Muktananda, "What Is an Intensive?" p. 12.

41. Durgananda, "To See the World Full of Saints," p. 129; see also pp. 128, 130.

42. Mahony, "The Ashram," p. 565.

43. Durgananda, "To see the World Full of Saints," p. 141.

44. Ibid., pp. 135–61, esp. pp. 141, 145, 147, 148, 151.

45. "The Guru Purnima Intensive: See the World through the Eye of the Heart" was held Saturday, July 31–Sunday, August 1, 1999. I also attended a course held just prior to the Intensive, "A Golden Mind, A Golden Life: Contemplating Gurumayi's 1999 Message Course" (Thursday, July 29–Friday, July 30), as well as a weekend-long introduction to Siddha Yoga program the month before, "The Welcome Weekend" (Saturday, June 12–Sunday, June 13).

46. Durgananda, "To See the World Full of Saints," p. 110; and Mahony, "The Ashram," p. 564.

47. Daniel Gold discusses the South Fallsburg ashram as a powerful "body" of the guru in his "Guru's Body, Guru's Abode."

48. I attended both of these sessions.

49. Information on when the guru began the yearly message is from the "A Golden Mind, A Golden Life" seminar, July 29–30, 1999.

50. Other modes for the outreach of Siddha Yoga include the established centers in twenty-nine countries, and the home-study course, *In Search of the Self*, developed by Ram Butler. Barbara De Angelis, the author of popular psychology books that focus on relationships and self-discovery in everyday life, applies the guru's teachings in her *Secrets about Life Every Woman Should Know*, esp. pp. ix, xiii, xxi–xxii, 17–19, 109–111.

51. Courses taught by Siddha Yoga teachers are also videotaped and used to create cohesion in the community: "The topics of 'elective courses'—which are taught by Siddha Yoga swamis, teachers, or visiting university professors—change each year. Some of these courses, however, are offered the following year as 'video courses' in other ashrams and centers," Brooks, *Meditation Revolution*, Appendix 3, p. 581.

52. Coburn, "Introduction," in Chidvilasananda, *Enthusiasm* p. xi. The book explores the yearly message for 1996, which was: "Be Filled with Enthusiasm, and Sing God's Glory."

53. Durgananda, "To See the World Full of Saints," p. 136.

54. Chidvilasananda, *Enthusiasm*, pp. 158–159.

55. My discussion is based on the videocassette by Swami Chidvilasananda, "The Message for 1999."

56. The guru noted that there are many possible translations of these terms. The Sanskrit passage is: *manaḥprasādaḥ saumyatvaṃ/ maunam ātmavinigrahaḥ/ bhāva-saṃśuddhir ity etat/ tapo mānasam ucyate*: "Mental serenity, kindness,/ silence, self-restraint,/ and purity of being/ is called mental penance," in Barbara Stoler Miller's translation, *The Bhagavad-Gita*, p. 139.

57. The global satellite technology has been used for Intensives since 1989; the guru "regularly gives shaktipat initiation via satellite television to students in as many as ninety Siddha Yoga centers worldwide"; Durgananda, "To See the World Full of Saints," pp. 150, 6, respectively.

58. Letter from Surabhi Dobson, Chief Teachings Officer, SYDA Foundation, at the top of the published calendar for 2002.

59. Wessinger, "Introduction," pp. 1–2; and "Woman Guru, Woman Roshi: The Legitimation of Female Religious Leadership in Hindu and Buddhist Groups in America," pp. 125–27, in Wessinger, *Women's Leadership in Marginal Religions*.

60. Wessenger, "Woman Guru, Woman Roshi," p. 129, 135, 140.

61. "Between 1977 and 1982, Muktananda performed four *sannyāsa* ceremonies. The first one was only for men. In 1978, 1980, and 1982, he also initiated women. By 1982, its peak, the total number of *sannyāsīs* in the organization was sixty-five, of whom fourteen were women"; Durgananda, "To See the World Full of Saints," p. 103. In a note, the author says that in 1996 there were five women swamis out of a total of 25 (p. 603). This means that both in 1982 and 1996, 20 percent of the swamis were women. My impression at all events I attended at the South Fallsburg ashram is that there are more female students than male; this was confirmed by long-term students.

62. Sered, *Priestess, Daughter, Sacred Sister*; many characteristics discussed in pp. 219–240. It is problematic that Sered deems "feminine" only those characteristics that have not been appropriated by men, and thus established as "masculine." As Catherine Wessinger notes: "The charismatic woman's experiences may be co-opted and contained by the structures of the patriarchal religion"; "Introduction" in *Women's Leadership in Marginal Religions*, p. 2.

REFERENCES

Brooks, Douglas Renfrew, et al. *Meditation Revolution: A History and Theology of the Siddha Yoga Lineage*. South Fallsburg, N.Y.: Agama, 1997.

Chidvilasananda, Swami. *Ashes at My Guru's Feet*. South Fallsburg, N.Y.: SYDA Foundation, 1990.

———. "Growing up with Baba," parts 1 and 2. *Siddha Path* (February and March 1982).

———. *Enthusiasm*. South Fallsburg, N.Y.: SYDA Foundation, 1997.

———. "The Message for 1999: A Golden Mind, a Golden Life. A Talk by Gurumayi Chidvilasananda." Videocassette. South Fallsburg, N.Y.: SYDA Foundation, 1999.

De Angeles, Barbara. *Secrets of Life Every Woman Should Know: Ten Principles for Total Emotional and Spiritual Fulfillment*. New York: Hyperion, 1999.

Durgananda, Swami. "To See the World Full of Saints: The History of Siddha Yoga as a Contemporary Movement." Pp. 3–161 in Douglas Renfrew Brooks et al., *Medi-*

tation Revolution: A History and Theology of the Siddha Yoga Lineage. South Fallsburg, N.Y.: Agama, 1997.

Gold, Daniel. "Guru's Body, Guru's Abode." Pp. 230–250, in Jane Marie Law, ed., *Religious Reflections on the Human Body.* Bloomington: Indiana University Press, 1995.

Harris, Lis. "Oh Guru, Guru, Guru." *New Yorker* 70 (November 14, 1994): 92–109.

Johnsen, Linda. *Daughters of the Goddess.* St. Paul, Minn.: Yes International, 1998.

Mahony, William K. "The Ashram." Pp. 521–568 in Douglas Renfrew Brooks et al., *Meditation Revolution: A History and Theology of the Siddha Yoga Lineage.* South Fallsburg, N.Y.: Agama, 1997.

Miller, Barbara Stoler, trans. *The Bhagavad-Gita: Krishna's Counsel in Time of War.* New York: Bantam Books, 1986.

Muktananda, Swami. "What Is an Intensive?" South Fallsburg, N.Y.: SYDA Foundation, [1976] 1995.

———. *Play of Consciousness: A Spiritual Autobiography.* South Fallsburg, N.Y.: SYDA Foundation [1974, 1978] 2000.

Muller-Ortega, Paul E. "The Siddha: Paradoxical Exemplar of Indian Spirituality." Pp. 165–221 in Douglas Renfrew Brooks et al., *Meditation Revolution: A History and Theology of the Siddha Yoga Lineage.* South Fallsburg, N.Y.: Agama, 1997.

———. "Shaktipat: The Initiatory Descent of Power." Pp. 407–444 in Douglas Renfrew Brooks et al., *Meditation Revolution: A History and Theology of the Siddha Yoga Lineage.* South Fallsburg, N.Y.: Agama, 1997.

Narayanan, Vasudha. "Profiling Hindu Temples in Georgia, Florida, and Michigan." Harvard University Pluralism Project Affiliates Web site: http://fas.harvard.edu/pluralsm/affiliates/narayanan.html.

Prentiss, Karen Pechilis. "The Pattern of Hinduism and Hindu Temple Building in the U.S." Harvard University Pluralism Project Affiliates Web page: http://fas.harvard.edu/~pluralsm/affiliates/pechilis-prentiss.html.

Ramanujan, A.K. "Talking to God in the Mother Tongue." *Manushi: Women Bhakti Poets* nos. 50, 51, 52 (January–June 1989): 9–14.

Sered, Susan Starr. *Priestess, Daughter, Sacred Sister: Religions Dominated by Women.* Oxford: Oxford University Press, 1994.

Thursby, Gene. "Hindu Movements since Midcentury: Yogis in the States." Available on the Internet: http://www.clas.ufl.edu/users/gthursby/pub/t2syd.htm.. The article was originally published in Timothy Miller, ed., *America's Alternative Religions* (Albany: State University of New York Press, 1995): 191–213.

———. "Siddha Yoga: Swami Muktananda and the Seat of Power." Available on the Internet: http://www.clas.ufl.edu/users/gthursby/pub/t1syd.htm. The article was originally published in Timothy Miller, ed., *When Prophets Die: The Postcharismic Fate of New Religious Movements* (Albany: State University of New York Press, 1991).

———. "Succession in the Siddha Yoga Movement." Available on the Internet: http://www.clas.ufl.edu/users/gthursby/pub/scsyd.htm. A version of the article was published in the *Proceedings of the Sixth International Symposium on Asian Studies* (Hong Kong: International Center for Asian Studies, Asian Research Service, 1985), vol. 4: 1397–1411.

Tweed, Thomas A., and Stephen Prothero. *Asian Religions in America: A Documentary History.* New York: Oxford University Press, 1999.

Wessinger, Catherine, ed., *Women's Leadership in Marginal Religions: Explorations Outside the Mainstream.* Urbana: University of Illinois Press, 1993.

Wilgoren, Jodi. "Sea, Sand and Seven-Card Stud: Guests Schmooze Days away at Aging Shore Enclave." *New York Times*, Sunday July 25, 1999, pp. 21–22.

Zuckoff, Michael. "Borscht Belt Meditates a New Existence: Hotels of the Catskills, Former Borscht Belt, Meditate a New Future." *Boston Globe*, 255 no. 137 (Saturday November 14, 1998): 1, 15.

Afterword

Kathleen M. Erndl

Observers have noted that there are many more Hindu female gurus than ever before in India, not to mention those in the West. That is not to say that there have been no holy women in the ancient Indian past. In the Valmiki *Ramayana*, for example, there is mention not only of male sage's wives such as Ahalya and Anasuya but also of independent female ascetics such as Sabari and Svayamprabha living alone and performing their spiritual disciplines in the forest. Likewise, there have always been extraordinary women who had powerful religious experiences and who were honored or considered to be saintly within the contexts of their family, neighborhood, or locality. A few of these women became widely known in the past, but most did not. Nowadays—and not suddenly today but at least from the time of the Hindu renaissance—social, economic, political, communication, and educational factors have opened up the possibility for the more public role of guru for women. This volume, *The Graceful Guru*, appears at a time when there is unprecedented interest in Hindu women gurus, both in religious and academic contexts.

The issues surrounding Hindu (or what one might call "Hindu-inspired") female gurus are numerous and complex, making generalizations difficult. The topic of female gurus in India is a difficult enough, but when gurus come to Europe or North America, the cross-cultural dimension adds further layers of complexity. This volume is a valuable contribution to the study of female gurus from at least two points of view. First, each essay stands alone as an engaging study of a specific female guru in her historical, cultural, and religious context. As so little has been written previously about many of these gurus beyond hagiographies or journalistic accounts, the contributions in this volume represent a significant advance in scholarship. Second, the fact that they are presented together in one volume encourages comparative insights from even the most casual reader. But there is nothing haphazard about this collection which, like the American Academy of Religion session with which it began, makes a significant advance toward a general theory of women's religious leadership by considering the phenomenon of the Hindu female guru. All of the authors implicitly or explicitly wrestle with the question of how gender matters, both for their individual subject and for female gurus in general. In particular, the issue concerning the relationship between charismatic and institutional leadership surfaces in several of the essays.

Charismatic religious leadership is that which stems from a direct relationship with the divine outside of institutional mainstream transmission of religious authority. Catherine Wessinger, in the introduction to her edited volume, *Women's Leadership in Marginal Religions*, poses the question of what kind of factors lead to this type of routine institutional transmission for women. She begins with four characteristics proposed by Mary Farrell Bednarowski in connection with nineteenth-century America: first, a perception of the divine that deemphasizes the masculine; second, a tempering or denial of the doctrine of the Fall; third, a denial of the need for traditional ordained clergy; and fourth, deemphasis of marriage and motherhood as the only proper roles for women.[1] To these Wessinger adds her own condition that the social expectation of women's equality must also be present in order for women to achieve continuous leadership roles in a religious movement. Bednarowski's and Wessinger's conclusions are a helpful starting point in trying to understand Hindu female gurus as religious leaders. One point that needs to be made, however, in relation to Hindu gurus is that although they are absolutely central (not marginal) to Hindu religious life, their authority *as gurus* is essentially dependent on their personal charisma. In order to be considered gurus, they must have disciples who recognize them as being divine or having extraordinary access to the divine. Without that, it does not matter how high they have risen in a spiritual or monastic institution, they will not be considered gurus. Hindu gurus are a noninstitutional institution. The essays in this volume recognize this paradox and thus, rather than privileging institutional over charismatic authority, seek to explore the relationship between the two.

This book contributes to a coherent theory of women's religious leadership. With it, we can start to build a comprehensive theoretical synthesis. When trying to compare or generalize about a large number of cases of similar phenomena, it is almost inevitable to start putting them into types or categories. It would be useful at this point to think about generating typologies as an intermediate stage between collection of material about specific cases and a grand coherent theory of women's religious leadership. To that end, I suggest here a few different typologies that are in no way exhaustive. Rather, they are a modest attempt to open up the discussion and suggest avenues for further study and comparison.

The first typology has to do with modes of succession or transmission of authority from guru to disciple, that is, how a disciple becomes a guru. In these essays, I found five different types of succession.

The first type is direct succession. This is succession from guru to disciple, what is in Sanskrit called a *parampara*, an unbroken lineage. This type comes closest to Wessinger's model of institutional leadership. This is the mode in which the guru names his/her successor before death, and in which the successor is recognized as the guru by the dominant core of the community. For example, Swami Chidvilasananda (Gurumayi), the subject of Karen Pechilis's essay, falls into this category. She was chosen by her guru Swami Muktananda and officially inaugurated as guru, and although there were some irregularities surrounding the co-guruship and subsequent removal of her brother, she is recognized as the successor of Swami Muktananda. Jayashri Ma, the subject of June McDaniel's essay, also appears to fall into this category, but it appears that a lineage will not continue beyond her.

The second type is sideways succession. In this type, a disciple becomes a guru of a lineage that is an offshoot of the primary lineage of her guru. An example of this type is Gauri Ma, discussed by Carol Anderson. Gauri Ma, having received transmission through Ramakrishna and also through his wife Sarada Devi, established a lineage and ashram specifically for women that is distinct from and largely unrecognized by the better-known Ramakrishna Mission.

The third type is ambiguous succession. In this type, a disciple has received training from a recognized guru and may function informally, though not officially, as a guru. An example is Sita Devi, the subject of Rebecca Manring's essay. As the wife of a Gaudiya Vaishvana guru, it is unclear whether Sita Devi was ever given authority to be a guru or not, and there is no clear direct lineage that comes down from her, although she is revered in the tradition.

The fourth type is spontaneous succession. In this type, the guru has no human guru. Rather, the guru's divinity is revealed to her, and subsequently to others, spontaneously. For example, Ammachi, the subject of Selva Raj's essay, has no guru, and is believed to be an avatar of the divine Mother by her devotees. However, she may well establish her own lineage. There are many other examples of guruless female gurus, but the most famous is Anandamayi Ma, the subject of Lisa Hallstrom's essay, also believed to be an avatar of the divine Mother by some, and as the unqualified *brahman* by others. Karunamayi Ma, discussed in Vasudha Narayanan's essay, falls into this category, as she has no human guru and is considered to be an avatar of the goddess Sarasvati. Meera Ma, the subject of Catherine Cornille's essay, may also fall into this category, though as the avatar or successor of Mother Mira (Mirra Alfassa) of the Sri Aurobindo Ashram, she may possibly fall into the fifth type discussed below.

The fifth type is posthumous visionary succession. In this type, the disciple is initiated and given transmission in a vision by his or her guru after the guru's death. This type is closely related to and may overlap with the fourth type, spontaneous succession, since the deceased guru may confirm the guru's already divine status. For example, Shree Maa of Kamakhya, the subject of

Loriliai Biernacki's essay, met Ramakrishna in a vision long after his death, and he became her guru. Some also believe her to be the incarnation of Sarada Devi, whom she also resembles physically. Ma Jaya Sati Bhagavati, discussed in Vasudha Narayanan's essay, first encountered in visions and had conversations with Jesus, Nityananda (guru of Muktananda), Ramana Maharshi, and Shirdi Sai Baba before meeting her own guru, Neem Karoli Baba, in her bathroom as a young Long Island housewife. Ma Jaya is also considered by her devotees to be a manifestation of the goddess Kali.

In addition to the mode of succession, there are many other types of categories one might explore that would shed light on the gendered nature of Hindu female gurus. One of these has to do with the guru's geographic and cultural location. How international is her movement? What degree of contact does it have in the West and to what extent has it become established there? To what extent is the guru an Indian visiting America, and to what extent is she an American with Indian antecedents? What are the cultural, religious, and ethnic backgrounds of her followers? These questions bears strongly on the issues of marginality and of gender norms and expectations. Sita Devi is the farthest removed from the West, since she lived in the sixteenth-century. But interestingly, an offshoot of her lineage is today one of the most well-established and visible Hindu-inspired movements in the West. The International Society for Krishna Consciousness (ISKCON) does not currently recognize women as gurus, but in response to a growing feminist voice within the movement now appoints women to its governing board and as temple presidents. More women within ISKCON are looking to the past for legitimation of women as gurus and look to such women as Sita Devi and Jahnavi Devi, a guru who had both male and female disciples, as role models. Gauri Ma, the nineteenth-century Bengali guru likewise never came to America, but her direct lineage descendent did and established an ashram in Michigan. Ammachi, one of the most famous women gurus today, lives in Kerala and comes to America only for visits, though she has started several ashrams and centers there. She does not speak English, so her contact with Western devotees is through interpreters. But, as Selva Raj points out, her practices diverge in some important ways from traditional practices. Her flouting of purity and pollution rules, though finding precedent in Indian bhakti and tantra, are surely reinforced in the American context.

Gurumayi and her SYDA are arguably more thoroughly part of the American scene than any of the other Indian-born gurus or movements discussed in this volume, as a new generation of American-born theologians codifies and elaborates the doctrines and practices of the movement. Shree Maa has settled permanently in California, where she has established the Devi Mandir. Her main disciple is an American, Swami Satyananda. The only guru discussed in this volume who comes from a non-Hindu, non-Indian background is Ma Jaya Sati Bhagavati, an American born into an Orthodox Jewish family, who teaches a practice of kundalini yoga connected with the goddess Kali. She has established an interfaith community called the Neem Karoli Baba Kashi Ashram in Sebastian, Florida. Though her followers are multicultural and multiracial, most are American-born. Her movement may represent the beginnings of a "homegrown" American form of Hinduism. Her movement is also the only one among those considered in this volume that is explicitly feminist, with the possible exception of that of Gauri Ma, whose mission was to educate women. Ma Jaya not only initiates both men and women as sannyasis but she has also done away with ritual restrictions during menstruation and is an activist for women's and gay and lesbian rights.

In conclusion, I simply mention two other among the many typologies worth exploring in relation to female gurus: the degree to which feminine images of the sacred are privileged, and the degree to which feminist values and practices are emphasized. In these essays, we find a range of emphasis on God as feminine, but I believe that all of the gurus and their movements here to a greater or lesser degree privilege the divine female. Even Gaudiya Vaishnavism (and its successor ISKCON), often stereotyped as extolling an exclusively male deity, places considerable emphasis on the feminine. The founder Caintanya is considered an avatar of both Krishna and his female consort, Radha, and in the well known mantra beginning "Hare Krishna," what is less well-known is that Hare is the vocative form of Harâ, a name of Radha. Other gurus and movements in this volume either explicitly emphasize goddesses such as Kali, Saraswati, or Adiparashakti or, as in the case of Gurumayi, a deity beyond gender who does not exclude the feminine. Though the presence of the divine feminine is not any guarantee that women will be recognized as leaders or will be equal within the movement, it does seem to help. The deciding factor is the degree to which the guru embraces feminist teachings and the degree to which she and her community engage in feminist practices, however those might be defined. Here, we return to Catherine Wessinger's important point that deemphasis of an exclusively masculine deity leads to women's leadership institutionally only when there is the social expectation of women's equality.

NOTE

1. *Women's Leadership in Marginal Religions: Explorations outside the Mainstream*, edited by Catherine Wessinger (Urbana: University of Illinois Press, 1993), pp. 1–19, citing Mary Farrell Bednarowski, "Outside the Mainstream: Religion and Women's Religious Leaders in Nineteenth-Century America," *Journal of the American Academy of Religion* 48 (June 1980): 207–231.

Appendix: Web Pages of Female Gurus, As of Spring 2004

Female Gurus Profiled in this Volume

Ammachi
    http://www.ammachi.org/ is the official Ammachi Web site. The guru's residence in India is the Amritapuri Ashram, Kollam, Kerala; the Web site for map and information is Amritapuri.org. In the United States, the main center is Mata Amritanandamayi (M.A.) Center in San Ramon, California. Mailing address: P.O. Box 613, San Ramon, California 94583-0613; physical address: 10200 Crow Canyon Road, Castro Valley, California 94552. See the Web site for information on *satsang* groups in twenty-three U.S. states, as well as European and other international venues.

Anandamayi Ma
    http://www.anandamayi.org/ is the official Web site, and provides biographical information, spiritual texts, and photos. The Shree Shree Ma Anandamayee International Centre is located at Daksh Mandir Road, P.O. Kankhal, Dist. Hardwar, 249408, Uttar Pradesh, India.

Gauri Ma
    This historical guru is mentioned in various articles posted on the Web; for example, there is a short biographical entry on her at http://www.vedanta-atlanta.org/stories/GauriMa.html

Gurumayi
    http://www.siddhayoga.org/main.html is the official Web site of Siddha Yoga Meditation. The guru's residence in India is the Guru-

dev Siddha Peeth in Ganeshpuri, Maharashtra. The mailing address for the
International Headquarters of the SYDA Foundation is SYDA Foundation, P.O.
Box 600, 371 Brickman Road, South Fallsburg, New York 12747–5313. See the
Web site for contact information on *satsang* groups in twenty-seven U.S. states,
as well as European and other international venues.

Jayashri Ma
   No Web site for this local guru.

Karunamayi
   http://www.karunamayi.org/ contains pictures, quotations, and information on world tours for the contemporary guru, Karunamayi, Bhagavati Sri
Vijayeswari, who maintains an ashram in Bangalore, India.

Ma Jaya Sati Bhagavati
   http://www.kashi.org/ is the official Web site for the guru. Her residence
is Neem Karoli Baba Kashi Ashram, 11155 Roseland Road, Sebastian, Florida.
The Web site includes contact lists of *satsangs* in New York, Los Angeles, and
Atlanta.

Mother Meera
   http://www.inthelight.co.nz/spirit/gurus/meera001.html,   http://www
.sannyasin.com/mothermeera.html, and http://www.geocities.com/ascended
master/MotherMeera.html are Web sites for the guru. Her residence is 10
kilometers southwest of the city of Limburg overlooking the River Lahn Valley
at the foot of the Schloss Schaumburg, Germany. Mailing addresses: Mother
Meera Schloß Schaumburg, 65558 Balduinstein, Germany; or Mother Meera,
Oberdorf 4a 65599, Dornburg-Thalheim, Germany. Reservations for darshan
must be scheduled in advance by phone.

Shree Maa
   http://www.shreemaa.org/shreema.htm is the official Web site for the
guru. Her residence is Devi Mandir, 5950 Highway 128, Napa, California
94558. The Web site provides information on her upcoming tours in the United
States and Europe, with contact phone numbers in each city.

Other Websites of Interest

General

http://www.geocities.com / Athens / Styx / 7153 / mother.html—an interesting
Web site listing diverse female gurus with links to official Web sites: includes
photos and links for Mother Meera, Anandamayi Ma, Ammachi, Karunamayi,
Guru Maa of Matrika Ashram, Nirmala Devi, Shree Maa, The Mother, Ma
Bhagavati, Shantimayi, Swami Chidvilasananda, Gangaji, Sivananda Radha,
Vimala Thakar, Sarada Devi, Durga Ma, and Srimad Rajarajeshwari.

http://www.indiayogi.com—click on Gurus, which brings one to the category of Indian Saints, Mystics, Philosophers and Gurus, in which there are entries, including photos and biographies, on Mira Alfassa and Ammachi (Mata Amritanandamayi).

http://www.om-guru.com—this Web site gives information on the category of "guru," as well as choosing a guru, and profiles thirteen gurus, of which two are women (Anandamayi Ma and Irina Tweedie, a British woman who lived and studied in northwest India with a Nakshmandia Sufi teacher).

Specific Gurus

http://www.chalandama.org/—home page of Chalanda Sai Ma Lakshmi Devi

http://come.to/amma—home page of a site dedicated to Sri Satya Sai Baba and Bhagavati Srimad Rajarajeshwari

http://www.gangaji.org/—home page of Gangaji

http://www.geocities.com/Tokyo/Bridge/1968/jk/brochure/sld001.htm; slideshow and biography of Bhagawati Srimad Rajarajeshwari

http://www.narayaniamma.org/—the Web site of the embodiment of the divine Mother as a man, Sri Narayani Amma, who resides at Malaikodi, near Vellore, Tamilnadu, India.

http://www.sahajayoga.org/—the offical Web site of Shri Mataji Nirmala Devi, who teaches self-realization through techniques of Sahaja Yoga meditation.

http://www.santosha.com—Web site providing information on the Yoga Anand Ashram, founded and directed by Gurani Anjali.

http://www.shantimayi.com—home page of Shantimayi

http://www.srisarada.org—home page of "Holy Mother's Cyber Tantu"

http://srv.org—official Web site of Sarada Ramakrishna Vivekananda associations of Oregon, San Francisco, Hawaii, and New England, providing photos, biography, and quotations of Sarada Devi, and the same for Sri Ramakrishna and Swami Vivekananda.

http://yasodhara.org/—home page of Swami Radha

Index